The Practice of Love

The
Practice
of
Love

Teresa de Lauretis

Lesbian
Sexuality
and
Perverse
Desire

Indiana University Press / Bloomington and Indianapolis

The paper used in this publication meets the minimum requirements of American National Standard for Information Sciences—Permanence of Paper for Printed Library Materials, ANSI Z39.48-1984.

™

Manufactured in the United States of America

Library of Congress Cataloging-in-Publication Data
De Lauretis, Teresa.
   The practice of love : lesbian sexuality and perverse desire / by Teresa de Lauretis.
      p.   cm.
   Filmography:
   Includes bibliographical references and index.
   ISBN 0-253-31681-2 (cloth : alk. paper). — ISBN 0-253-20878-5 (pbk. : alk. paper)
   1. Lesbianism—Psychological aspects. 2. Feminism. 3. Sexuality.
I. Title.
HQ75.5.D45   1994
155.3′4—dc20   93-44453

1 2 3 4 5 99 98 97 96 95 94

CONTENTS

Acknowledgments

This book has been some years in the making, has traveled and grown wiser with me in several countries, and owes much to many:
—first and foremost to Kirstie McClure and Jansje Roepman, much more than I can say. Then,
—to Valie Export for its title, which has haunted me since I saw her film *Die Praxis der Liebe;*
—to the friends who read parts of the manuscript at various stages, giving suggestions, criticisms, and encouragement: Tania Modleski, Sue-Ellen Case, Liana Borghi, Annette Foerster, Giovanna Grignaffini, Earl Jackson, Jr., Elizabeth Grosz, Nancy Stoller, Donna Haraway, and Carol Miller;
—to the students in my Spring 1992 History of Consciousness writing seminar for their comments on early drafts of chapter 5 and for the inspiration their own work has given me throughout the writing of this book: Julia Creet, Julia Erhart, Catrióna Rueda Esquibel, Yvonne Keller, Ekua Omosupe, Carla Scott, Vicky Smith, and Jeanne Vaughn;
—to all the participants of the seminar on "Psychoanalysis, Fantasy, and Lesbian Sexuality" I held as Visiting Professor at the University of Amsterdam in Spring 1990, organized by Dorelies Kraakman for the Homo- en Lesbische Studies program, where I presented the first, rough sketch of my project and received an enthusiastic response;
—to participants of subsequent seminars and colloquia where I presented this work at various stages of its progress: at the English Institute at Harvard (1990), the Critical Theory Institute at the University of California, Irvine (1990), the School for Criticism and Theory at Dartmouth (1991), the Humanities Institutes at the University of Michigan and SUNY, Stony Brook, the University of Utrecht in the Netherlands as Belle van Zuylen Visiting Professor of Women's Studies (1991), the University of North Carolina, Chapel

Hill (1992), the Centro di documentazione delle donne/University of Bologna and the independent cultural association L'Amandorla in Florence, Italy (1992), the Kulturwissenschaftliches Institut in Essen, Germany (1992), Syracuse University as Jeannette K. Watson Distinguished Visiting Professor in the Humanities (1993), and the Graduiertenkolleg "Theorie der Literatur" at the University of Konstanz, Germany (1993);

—to Esther Newton, Patricia White, Richard Dellamora, Geertje Mak, Rosi Braidotti, Anneke Smelik, Renate Lachmann, Sigrid Weigel, and others who have offered helpful comments on published versions of chapters 1, 3, and 5;

—to the Bibliotheek van de Nederlandse Vereniging voor Psychoanalyse (Dutch Psychoanalytic Association) in Amsterdam, as close to an ideal home library as one could wish for;

—to my colleagues in the Board of Studies in History of Consciousness at the University of California, Santa Cruz, for approving my request for leave from my teaching responsibilities in 1992–93; to Gary Lease, Dean of Humanities, for granting that leave and generously supporting my research in other ways as well; and to Billie Harris and Sheila Peuse, Administrative Assistants, for making my absence more productive and my heart yet fonder. Last but hardly least,

—to the National Endowment for the Humanities and the John Simon Guggenheim Memorial Foundation, without whose Fellowships in 1992–93 this book might never have been completed, and

—to Joan Catapano, Senior Sponsoring Editor at Indiana University Press, to whom I have entrusted it well before its completion.

*   *   *

I wish to dedicate this book to the memory of Lisa Summa, the youngest of my students, who wanted to get her Ph.D. in History of Consciousness before entering training to become a psychoanalyst.

A shorter version of chapter 1 was published in *Politics, Theory, and Contemporary Culture*, ed. Mark Poster (New York: Columbia University Press, 1992), pp. 111–30, and in *Discourses of Sexuality from Aristotle to AIDS*, ed. Domna Stanton (Ann Arbor: University of Michigan Press, 1992), pp. 216–34.

Different portions of chapter 3, in earlier versions, were published as "Film and the Visible," in *How Do I Look? Queer Film and Video*, ed. Bad Object-Choices (Seattle: Bay Press, 1991), pp. 223–76, and as "Il fantasma del cinema. Sulla funzione spettatoriale come rapporto di produzione fantasmatico-sociale," *Cinema & cinema* 18 (settembre/dicembre 1991): 3–18.

A very condensed and early version of chapter 5 appeared as "Perverse Desire: The Lure of the Mannish Lesbian," *Australian Feminist Studies* 13 (Autumn 1991): 15–26, and in Dutch translation as "De verwonding en het litteken· Narcisme, fetisjisme en lesbische fantasie," *Lover, literatuuroverzicht voor de vrouwenbeweging* 18.2 (June 1991): 72–79.

The following publishers have generously given permission to use quotations from copyrighted works:

From "The Weather-Cock Points South," by Amy Lowell, *Pictures of the Floating World, The Complete Poetical Works of Amy Lowell*. Copyright 1955 by Houghton Mifflin Co., renewed 1983 by Houghton Mifflin Co., Brinton P. Roberts, and G. D'Andelot Belin, Esquire. Reprinted by permission of Houghton Mifflin Co. All rights reserved.

From *Giving Up the Ghost: Teatro in Two Acts*, by Cherríe Moraga. Reprinted by permission of West End Press.

From "Transcendental Etude," by Adrienne Rich, from *The Dream of a Common Language: Poems 1974–1977*, by Adrienne Rich. Reprinted by permission of the author and W.W. Norton and Company, Inc. Copyright 1978 by W.W. Norton and Company, Inc.

From *Powers of Desire: The Politics of Sexuality*, ed. Ann Snitow, Christine Stansell, and Sharon Thompson. Copyright 1983 by Snitow, Stansell, and Thompson. Reprinted by permission of Monthly Review Foundation.

Introduction

"For the 'non-specialist,' sexuality is indeed the essential contribution of psychoanalysis to contemporary thought," wrote Jean Laplanche in 1970 (*Life and Death in Psychoanalysis* 27). A forthcoming essay by a young film scholar rejoins: "Homosexual subjects are governed by the psychic processes that affect 'everyone else'—there can be no argument but that homosexuality is indeed within psychoanalysis, each having contributed to the other's very invention" (White, "Governing Lesbian Desire"). I frame this introduction to my study of lesbian sexuality and perverse desire within two claims that, besides foregrounding the thematic and methodological concerns of this book, also delineate the historical and personal trajectory of my theoretical work—from the beginning of my critical engagement with structuralism, semiotics, and psychoanalysis around 1970, for which Laplanche's work has proved invaluable, to my current pedagogical activity in the doctoral program in History of Consciousness, of whose rewards the essay by Patricia White, a graduate of that program, is representative.

Between 1970 and now, in conjunction with earlier and contemporaneous social movements, feminism and poststructuralism have made way for the rise of minority discourse and gay and lesbian studies as fields of scholarly and theoretical research. Conceived from the vantage point of the latter, this book returns to Freudian psychoanalysis and semiotics, to the questions of representation, subjectivity, desire, and their relations to social signification and material reality that I broached in *Alice Doesn't* (1984) and *La sintassi del desiderio* (1976), but now refocused through what I call Freud's negative theory of sexuality—sexuality as perversion. For in his work from the *Three Essays on the Theory of Sexuality* (1905) to the unfinished, posthumously published papers of 1938, the notions of a normal sexuality, a normal psychosexual development, even a

normal sexual act derive from the detailed consideration of the aberrant, deviant, or perverse manifestations and components of the
sexual instinct or drive (*Trieb*). On the one hand, then, perversion
appears as the negative or nether side of sexuality, what so-called
sexual normality contains and overcomes. On the other hand, however, Freud's entire theory of the human psyche, in which the instincts, their objects, and their vicissitudes are overdetermined by
fantasies at once social and subjective, owes its foundations and development to his clinical study of the psychoneuroses; that is to say,
those cases in which the mental apparatus and instinctual drives
reveal themselves in their processes and mechanisms, which are
"normally" hidden or unremarkable otherwise. In this respect, the
"normal" is conceived only by approximation, is more a projection
than an actual state of being, while perversion and neurosis (the
repressed form of perversion) are the actual forms and contents of
sexuality.

Rereading Freud in this perspective, against the dominant interpretations that have extracted from his writings a model of positive,
"normal," heterosexual, and reproductive sexuality, I am looking for
a model of perverse desire that may account for the representation
of lesbianism in texts of fiction, film, poetry, and drama, as well as in
the interactions and conversations of many years of my own life.
What is the advantage of such a project to a lesbian theorist? Lesbian scholarship has not had much use for psychoanalysis. Developing in the political and intellectual context of feminism over the past
two decades, in the Eurowestern "First World," lesbian critical writing has typically rejected Freud as the enemy of women and consequently kept clear of neo-Freudian theories of sexuality. Certainly,
the feminist mistrust of psychoanalysis as both a male-controlled
clinical practice and a popularized social discourse on the natural
inferiority of women has excellent, and historically proven, practical reasons. Nevertheless, some feminists have persistently argued
that there are also very good theoretical reasons for reading and
rereading Freud himself. All the more so for lesbians, I suggest,
whose self-definition, self-representation, and personal and political
identity are not only grounded in the sphere of the sexual, but actually constituted in relation to a *sexual* difference from socially dominant, institutionalized, heterosexual forms.

This emphasis on the *sexual* is by no means intended (there should be no need to say it) to reduce lesbian subjectivity to a mere matter of sexual behavior or sexual acts, as if these could be isolated from all other aspects, qualities, affects, social determinations, and achievements that make up each human being as a complex individual and a unique contributor to her or his culture. Nor is it, therefore, intended to elide or diminish the symbolic and material effects of other cultural, and most significantly racial, differences in the constitution of the social subject; on the contrary, it underscores the central role that sexuality plays both in subjectivity, in the ways one understands and lives one's life, and in all sociosymbolic forms, especially the construction of "race" as well as gender.

What has psychoanalysis to offer a theory of lesbian sexuality? For one thing, in the perspective of Freud's theory of sexuality as perversion, lesbianism would no longer have to be explained by Freud's own concept of the masculinity complex. This amazingly enduring notion, which recasts homosexuality in the mold of a normative heterosexuality, has consistently precluded the conceptualization of a female sexuality autonomous from the male. Moreover, with regard to lesbianism, the masculinity complex has little or no explanatory power, for it fails to account for the non-masculine lesbian, that particular figure that since the nineteenth century has baffled sexologists and psychoanalysts, and that Havelock Ellis named "the womanly woman," the feminine invert. Secondly, if perversion is understood *with* Freud outside the moralistic, religious, or medical frames of reference, as a deviation of the sexual drive from the path leading to the reproductive object—that is to say, if homosexuality is merely another path taken by the drive in its cathexis or choice of object, rather than a pathology (although, like every other aspects of sexuality, it may involve pathogenic elements)—then Freud's theory contains or implies, if by negation and ambiguity, a notion of perverse desire, where perverse means not pathological but rather non-heterosexual or non-normatively heterosexual.

This book is an eccentric reading of Freud, through Laplanche and the Lacanian and feminist revisions, for the purpose of articulating a formal model of perverse desire. While my theoretical argument proceeds from the analysis of literary and filmic texts, and attends to the psychic and social modalities of lesbian sexuality, I would not exclude that perverse desire might be usefully considered in relation to male homosexuality or even to forms of sexuality that appear to be heterosexual but are not so in the normative or repro-ductive way. Having stated that my goal is the articulation of a for-mal model, I hasten to add that *formal* does not mean infinitely *generalizable* or valid for anyone at any time, in short, a theoretical model with *universal* pretensions. As the authors of one of my epi-graphs say of Freud's theories of desire, the only guarantee any the-ory can give about itself is to expose itself as a passionate fiction (Bersani and Dutoit). I shall endeavor to remind the reader, as dis-creetly as it can be done without offense to critical and stylistic con-ventions, that my theoretical speculations and my reading of the texts follow the yellow brick road of my own fantasies, the less-than-royal road of my personal or experiential history.

Thus, if I return to the authority of Freud, it is in part because his work is exemplary of the mode of theorizing that exposes itself as a passionate fiction and a self-analyzing practice; but it is also be-cause, although based on his own experience as a male-sexed and -gendered, racially marked, bourgeois subject in turn-of-the-century Vienna, his passionate fictions resonate in my life, for better or for worse, as they do in the lives of other women of my culture and generation. What I shall try to articulate is how the signification and a certain working of desire that can be read in Freud's theory of sexuality may be recast in relation to what *he* could not imagine but others can—a lesbian subjectivity. Therefore, I shall also look at other passionate fictions and scenarios of desire that, in represent-ing lesbian sexuality, not only resonate with my own but much more closely approximate them.

From the reading of psychoanalytic narratives and other fic-tional and critical texts, my argument will develop more in the form of a dialogue or dialogic meditation than as a straightforward expo-sition. Its progress will be interrupted by detours, deviations, and side arguments in the effort to address questions that each text brings up, requiring temporary shifts in focus and direction. But the concerns of the book remain consistently in sight. In Part I, after the "perverse" reading of Freud in chapter 1, chapter 2 retraces the early psychoanalytic discourse on female homosexuality through the case studies written by Freud himself ("A Case of Paranoia Running Counter to the Psycho-Analytic Theory of the Disease" [1915] and "Psychogenesis of a Case of Homosexuality in a Woman" [1920]),

J. H. W. van Ophuijsen (1924), Ernest Jones (1927), Jeanne Lampl–
de Groot (1928), and Helene Deutsch (1932). Whereas most of these
papers have not received much feminist attention, Freud's "Psychogenesis"—as a matter of fact, his only case history of a homosexual
woman—has been discussed by both heterosexual and lesbian feminists, as has the widely known case history of "Dora" ("Fragment of
an Analysis of a Case of Hysteria" [1905]), perhaps on a clue by Lacan, who read the two cases together in his 1964 seminar. Somewhat abruptly, therefore, in a chapter concerned with the classic
narrative of female homosexuality, I introduce some of the issues at
stake in the contemporary feminist discourse on lesbianism, which
will be discussed at length in chapter 4.

Part II introduces Laplanche and Pontalis's pivotal analysis of
the structuring role of fantasy in the constitution of the sexual subject. "An instinctual stimulus does not arise from the external world
but from within the organism itself," writes Freud (*SE* 14: 118); although the distinctive character of an instinct is its having origin in
the body, yet in mental life it can be known only by its representation or "psychical representative" (*SE* 14: 122). Such representations are the contents of fantasy, and the forms of fantasy, both
conscious and unconscious, elaborate them into images and narratives—from the unconscious fantasies underlying dreams and
symptoms to conscious daydreams, reveries, and erotic fantasies.
These are the scenarios (scripts or stage settings) of the subject's
desire. Initially shaped by the parental fantasies and subsequently
refashioned with new material drawn in from the outside world,
Laplanche and Pontalis argue, the contents and forms of fantasy
make up and structure the individual's psychic life. Thus fantasy,
not nature or biology, is at the origin of sexuality as a social, as well
as subjective, construction.

Of particular relevance are the original fantasies, which, like
myths, "provide a representation of, and a solution to, the major
enigmas which confront the child": the primal scene, Freud's *Urszene*, pictures the origin of the individual in parental coitus; seduction, the origin and upsurge of sexuality; and castration, the origin
of the difference between the sexes ("Fantasy and the Origins of Sexuality" 19). The fantasies of origin are cultural myths that have a
powerful hold in subjectivity. But they are not carriers of eternal
truths, for they are themselves historically structured, as well as

structuring of each subject's history: they lie "beyond the history of the subject but nevertheless in history" (18). In other words, even the original fantasies are passible of transformation along with historical change, and I will stress this dynamic character of fantasies and their capacity for transformation in relation to social practices and representations, or what I will call public fantasies.

Each of the three chapters in Part II examines one of the original fantasies as they are inscribed, recast, or redeployed in various textual practices. Chapter 3 is wholly concerned with cinema. It begins with a reading of *She Must Be Seeing Things* (McLaughlin, 1987), a film that portrays a lesbian relationship foregrounding at once the interdependence of sexuality and fantasy in it (the film literally recasts the primal scene in lesbian terms) and the problem of its representation, how to represent lesbian desire through cinematic codes imbued with heterosexual presumption. The chapter further explores the difficulties involved in the visual representation of lesbianism—how films may represent "lesbians" and yet fail to represent lesbianism as a specific form of sexuality—and discusses critical writings that obscure or minimize that problem by taking too much for granted, or not enough. Then it goes on to address the wider issue of the relations between fantasy and representation, or between private and public forms of fantasy, in the context of the feminist theory of spectatorship and the pornography debate.

The fantasy of seduction is central to the theory and clinical practice of psychoanalysis. In the latter, a fantasy of mutual seduction sustains the process of transference and countertransference that is essential to the therapeutic contract between analysand and analyst, and one of its conditions of possibility. In the theory, it provides a fantasmatic explanation for the upsurge of sexuality: the fantasy of seduction is how the subject initially represents to herself the apperception of the internal pressure of the drives, by *imagining* it (some say) as coming from the outside in the form of seduction by another, or by responding (others say) to the mother's and other adults' own fantasies as they handle or physically care for the child, be their stimulating gestures unintentional or deliberate (incestuous). Feminists have been as critical of this seduction theory as of the patriarchal prerogative written into the psychoanalytic contract. Yet the objections stand in contradiction with the interest increasingly shown by women and feminists in psychoanalysis as patients, interlocutors, analysts, or theorists, from the time of Freud to today (feminism and psychoanalysis are of approximately the same age). I will propose in chapter 4 that the seductiveness of psychoanalysis for women owes to its acknowledging woman, the hysteric, as subject of desire and to the power it grants women in the transferential contract—the power of seducing and being seduced as *sexed* and *desiring* subjects.

Similarly, I speculate, the seductiveness of lesbianism for feminism lies in the former's figuration of a female desiring subjectivity to which all women may accede by virtue of their "homosexual" relation to the mother. This accounts for the maternal imaginary of feminism, an idealized or fantasmatic construct in which the mother, Oedipal or pre-Oedipal, stands for what all women have in common as women, socially and sexually, including a tendency toward bisexuality, a fluid or oscillating pattern of identifications and object-choices. Without denying for a moment that the relation to the mother has a fundamental influence on all forms of female subjectivity, I will argue that woman-identification and desire or object-choice do not form a continuum, as some feminist revisions of Freud would have it. The seduction of the homosexual-maternal metaphor derives from the erotic charge of a desire for women which, unlike masculine desire, affirms and enhances the female-sexed subject and represents her possibility of access to a sexuality autonomous from the male. But in the great majority of feminist psychoanalytic writings (Rose, Doane, Silverman, Sprengnether, Gallop, Jacobus, etc.), such access is paradoxically secured by erasing the actual sexual difference between lesbians and heterosexual women. This prevents the understanding of lesbianism not only as a specific form of female sexuality but also as a sociosymbolic form; that is to say, a form of psychosocial subjectivity that entails a different production of reference and meaning.

Chapter 5 analyzes the fantasy of bodily dispossession in two texts that, in all ways except their militant defiance, stand at great distance from each other, Radclyffe Hall's classic novel of female inversion, *The Well of Loneliness* (1928), and Cherríe Moraga's Chicana feminist play *Giving Up the Ghost* (1984). While stressing the many differences between the two texts, I suggest that the fantasy scenarios they inscribe are similarly structured by an original fantasy of castration, and that such fantasy recurs in other lesbian self-representations. But a symptomatic reading of the texts, indebted to Bersani and Dutoit's perverse reading of Freud, instigates a reconsideration of the meaning of castration in relation to the female body and of the role of the paternal phallus in the signification of desire. I conclude that the castration complex rewrites in the symbolic as lack of a penis what is a primary narcissistic loss of body-image, a lack of being that threatens the imaginary matrix of the body-ego. On the disavowal of *this* lack depend what I call perverse desire and the formation of a fetishlike object or sign that both lures and signifies the subject's desire, at once displacing and resignifying the wished-for female body. My reading of *The Well of Loneliness* in light of Freud's account of fetishism diverges sharply from Hall's own views of sexuality (informed by Havelock Ellis) as it does from most contemporary feminist interpretations of the novel. And yet it is the reading of Moraga's *Giving Up the Ghost,* or rather, reading the two texts together, that enables a perverse reading of Hall (and of Freud). For it is only retroactively, from a moment in Western history when the symbolic is being altered by the production of the feminist, gay, and anti-racist discourse exemplified in Moraga's work, that it is possible to see the trace of a perverse desire in the ideologically conservative novel of Radclyffe Hall and to follow that trace through the ambiguities in Freud's work.

That I have tried to read Freud back into Moraga's text may seem both inappropriate and something of an appropriation: inappropriate, in view of the widely voiced feminist objection to psychoanalysis as a Eurocentric theory of the white, middle-class, Western, and modernist subject, and therefore inadequate to account for non-white, postcolonial, and postmodern oppositional subjectivities (a notable exception to this view is Pérez, "Sexuality and Discourse"). At the same time, it may seem an appropriation of the writings that inscribe those subjectivities to the end of rereading and rewriting, once again, the story of that white, middle-class, Western, and female subject. In reading Moraga with Hall and with Freud, however, I find that the subject of perverse desire is not a character of that story—her very perversion denies her citizenship in that "normal" world. She is part of another story not (yet) written, a subject overdetermined by fantasies that are, on the one hand, grounded in specific social histories but, on the other, open to the mobility of desire and to a multiplicity of discordant discourses, practices, and representations.

The ways in which subjectivity, fantasy, desire, and the drives themselves are oriented, structured, and restructured by psychic and social images, by technologies of the self as well as by the technology of sex (in Foucault's words), are the topic of Part III. Gathering together the threads of an argument advanced somewhat discontinuously in the previous chapters, chapter 6 elaborates a model of desire that goes beyond the Oedipus complex and in its own way resolves it. Meandering through recent works on female fetishism (Schor, Apter, Grosz) and its relation to various forms of sociosexual masquerade (Riviere, Lacan, Case), the argument circles back to the suggestion I drew from Freud's *Three Essays* and Deutsch's paper on female homosexuality in Part I—the notion of a sexuality of component instincts, which, unlike infantile polymorphous perversion, is inclusive of phallic and genital drives but, unlike "normal" sexuality, is not bound to a necessary phallic, genital, and heterosexual primacy. Reframed in the perspective of perverse desire, the picture of female homosexuality as a "return to the mother" appears to be rather an instinctual investment in the female body itself, whose loss or lack the fetish serves to disavow. This investment, I suggest, is both manifested and overdetermined by practices—practices of representation as well as specifically sexual practices—which inflect sexual identity or, as I prefer to say, sexual structuring.

Some women have "always" been lesbians. Others, like myself, have "become" one. As much a sociocultural construction as it is an effect of early childhood experiences, sexual identity is neither innate nor *simply* acquired, but dynamically (re)structured by forms of fantasy private and public, conscious and unconscious, which are culturally available and historically specific. The translation of public fantasy into private fantasy in sexuality, like the join of individual experience and social meanings in identity, I propose in chapter 7, rests on a process of mediation akin to what Peirce called habit, the term by which (in *Alice Doesn't*) I sought to identify the semiotic juncture of inner and outer worlds. In order to describe the process by which the social subject is produced as a sexual subject and a subjectivity, I consider sexuality as a particular instance of semiosis, the more general process joining subjectivity to social signification and material reality. Thus Peirce's notions of interpretant and habit-change may serve to articulate Freud's privatized view of the internal world of the psyche with Foucault's eminently social view of sexuality, by providing an account of the manner in which the implantation of sexuality as perversion actually occurs in one subject, one body-ego.

Finally, in titling this book *The Practice of Love,* I want to emphasize the material, embodied component of desire as a psychic activity whose effects on the subject constitute a sort of habit or knowledge of the body, what the body "knows" or, better, has come to know about its instinctual aims. In resignifying the demand for love, the sexual and social practices of lesbianism can effectively (re)orient the drives by providing a (new) somatic and representational ground for the work of fantasy.

PART ONE

Psychoanalysis and Lesbian Sexuality

My tactic has always been to take an apparently classic theme in Freudian psychoanalysis, and to call it into question, challenge it, and problematize it.
—Jean Laplanche (*New Foundations for Psychoanalysis* 1)

Chapter 1

Freud, Sexuality, and Perversion

Freud's theories of desire perform a certain violence against the very order on which their exposition depends. And perhaps the only guarantees we have of their "authenticity" are the agitations, and doctrinal uncertainties and mobility by which they are irremediably exposed as passionate fictions.
—Leo Bersani and Ulysse Dutoit (vii)

"One must remember that normal sexuality too depends upon a restriction in the choice of object," wrote Sigmund Freud in one of his lesser-known case histories. "In general, to undertake to convert a fully developed homosexual into a heterosexual does not offer much more prospect of success than the reverse, except that for good practical reasons the latter is never attempted" (*SE* 18: 151). The observation that the "practical reasons" of psychoanalysis as a social (clinical) practice were, as they still are, often at odds with its purer theoretical reason is hardly new or, consequently, very interesting. On the other hand, to read Freud's theories as *passionate fictions* is far more interesting a project, but one riskier and inevitably contested. This is especially so if such a reading project is carried out in the context of feminist theory, and all the more so in the effort to articulate a theory of lesbian sexuality.

Freudian psychoanalysis has been marked as the enemy of women more often than not throughout the history of Anglo-American feminism, undoubtedly for very good practical reasons. But, as some feminists have convincingly argued, there are also very good theoretical reasons for reading and rereading Freud. What has not yet been broached is how Freudian theories of sexuality relate to the passionate fictions of lesbian desire today, in the Eurowestern "First World," and it is this gigantic task that I have set myself in this book. I do not hope to *convince* the lesbian and feminist readers to whom the book is primarily, though not exclusively, addressed; nor do I intend to *prove* anything about lesbian sexuality or subjectivity. The only guarantees I can give of my work, paraphrasing the authors of my epigraph, are the subjective character of my speculations, the uncertainty of my footing in something as delusive as my own passion, and the bewildering mobility of my desire.

The question of what is "normal" sexuality—the term inexorably and almost imperceptibly sliding into "normative"—has been a focal point of feminist criticism since Kate Millett's tendentiously vulgar portrait of "Freud" in *Sexual Politics*. It then quickly spread across the spectrum of feminist critical positions ranging from what may be called the anti-Freudian "right" (e.g., Millett) to the neo-Freudian "left," for whom the value of psychoanalysis is its singular "insistence not upon the regularization or normalization of sexuality but upon the constant failure of sexual identity, its instability or even its impossibility," as Mary Ann Doane ("Commentary" 76) says à propos of the work of Jacqueline Rose. More accessible than Lacan, Freud has had his supporters as well as his detractors among feminists, although no one can apparently resist an occasional joke on penis envy, or his maladroit association of weaving with pubic hair, or the like. By the very fact that I have used the phrase "rereading Freud," I must be counted among the supporters, according to a certain logic. Be that as it must.

My intention, however, is not to praise Freud or to bury him, but literally to reread him. Yes, again. The incentive for this project came to me from writing an essay concerned with lesbian representation and (*pace* Rose and Doane) lesbian identity, in which I was trying to sort out one of the paradoxes that, to my mind, have both constrained and advanced the development of feminist thought in the past two decades. I called it the paradox of sexual (in)difference. Because that first attempt to articulate the discursive double bind in which my thinking lesbianism was caught is relevant to what I will be proposing here, I reproduce the first four paragraphs of that essay with only slight modifications below.

There is a sense in which lesbian identity could be assumed, spoken, and articulated conceptually as political through feminism—and, current debates to wit, *against* feminism; in particular through and against the feminist critique of the Western discourse on love and sexuality, and therefore, to begin with, the rereading of psychoanalysis as a theory of sexuality and sexual difference. If the first feminist emphasis on sexual difference as woman's difference from man has rightly come under attack for obscuring the effects of other differences in women's psychosocial oppression, nevertheless that emphasis on sexual difference did open up a critical space—a conceptual, representational, and erotic space—in which women could address themselves to women. And in the very act of assuming and speaking from the position of subject, a woman could concurrently recognize women as subjects *and* as objects of female desire.

It is in such a space, hard-won and daily threatened by social disapprobation, censure, and denial, a space of contradiction requiring constant reaffirmation and painful renegotiation, that the very notion of sexual difference could then be put into question, and its limitations be assessed, both *vis-à-vis* the claims of other, not strictly sexual, differences, and with regard to sexuality itself. It thus appears that "sexual difference" is the term of a conceptual paradox corresponding to what is in effect a real contradiction in women's lives: the term, at once, of a sexual *difference* (women are, or want, something different from men) and of a sexual *indifference* (women are, or want, the same as men). And it seems to me that the racist and class-biased practices legitimated in the notion of "separate but equal" reveal a very similar paradox in the liberal ideology of pluralism, where social difference is also, at the same time, social indifference.

The psychoanalytic discourse on female sexuality, wrote Luce Irigaray in 1975, outlining the terms of what here I call *sexual (in)difference*, tells "that *the feminine occurs only within models and laws devised by male subjects*. Which implies that there are not really two sexes, but only one. A single practice and representation of the sexual" (*This Sex* 86). Within the conceptual frame of that "sexual indifference" (the phrase first appeared in *Speculum* 28), female desire for the self-same, for an other female self, cannot be recognized. "That a woman might desire a woman 'like' herself, someone of the 'same' sex, that she might also have auto- and homo-sexual appetites, is simply incomprehensible" in the phallic regime of an asserted sexual difference between man and woman which is predicated on the contrary, on a complete indifference for the "other" sex, woman's. Consequently, Irigaray continues, Freud was at a loss with his homosexual female patients, and his analyses of them were really about male homosexuality. "The object choice of the homosexual woman is [understood to be] determined by a *masculine* desire and tropism" (*Speculum* 99)— that is, precisely, the turn of so-called sexual difference into "sexual indifference," a single practice and representation of the sexual.

> So there will be no female homosexuality, just a hommo-sexuality in which woman will be involved in the process of specularizing the phallus, begged to maintain the desire for the same that man has, and will ensure at the same time, elsewhere and in complementary and contradictory fashion, the perpetuation in the couple of the pole of "matter." (103)

> With the term *hommo-sexuality* [*hommo-sexualité*]—at times also written *hom(m)osexuality* [*hom(m)osexualité*]—Irigaray puns on the French word for man, *homme*, from the Latin *homo* (meaning "man"), and the Greek *homo* (meaning "same"). In taking up her distinction between the now common-usage word *homosexuality* and Irigaray's *hommo-sexuality* or *hom(m)osexuality*, I want to remark the conceptual distance between the former term, *homosexuality*, by which I mean lesbian (or gay) sexuality, and the diacritically marked *hommo-sexuality*, which is the term of sexual indifference, the term (in fact) of heterosexuality. I want to re-mark both the incommensurable distance between them and the conceptual ambiguity that is conveyed by the two almost identical acoustic images. ("Sexual Indifference and Lesbian Representation" 155–56)

The point of the terminological distinction, as I saw it at the time, on the basis of my analysis of several kinds of lesbian texts, was to suggest that there was no simple way of representing or even thinking lesbianism cleanly outside the discursive-conceptual categories of heterosexuality, with its foundation in a structural difference (masculine-feminine or male-female) that for all intents and purposes sustains a social indifference to women's subjectivities. Therefore, I concluded, our current efforts at lesbian self-representation would continue to be unwittingly caught in the paradox of sexual (in)difference unless we somehow managed to separate out the two drifts of the paradox and then rethink homosexuality and hommo-sexuality at once separately *and* together. I was thus escalating the paradox into an actual logical contradiction.

It seems to me now that my effort to understand one form of sexual (in)difference (heterosexual-homosexual) from the perspective of the other (male-female) as articulated by Irigaray, was not altogether unproductive—all analogical thinking has its usefulness initially—but was inherently limited. By showing that a paradox, or a seeming contradiction, hides what is in effect an actual contradiction, I did not yet displace the terms of the contradiction, although I may have clarified them for myself. Moreover, in borrowing Irigaray's notion of hommo-sexuality, I was dependent on a perspective that did not include the possibility of a difference between heterosexual and gay male sexualities. This further limited the conceptual horizon in which a non-heterosexual, non-hom(m)osexual, but homosexual-lesbian female sexuality might be thought.

I became more sharply aware of these limitations in reading Naomi Schor's "Dreaming Dissymmetry," a critique of what she calls "the *discourse of in-difference* or of *pure difference*" in the work of Barthes and Foucault (48). Schor forcefully argues that this French poststructuralist discourse on sexual difference "shades into sexual indifference" (49) in that, in discursivizing sex, it consistently desexualizes women even as it reclaims the feminine position for male sexuality or proposes a utopia of free-floating desire and sexual/gender indeterminacy (for a full discussion of the metaphor of the feminine in contemporary French philosophy, see Braidotti). Though not ostensively referred to Irigaray, Schor's term *in-difference* was very similar to my *(in)difference*, I thought, except that she did not address directly the issue of a heterosexual-homosexual difference in her—coincidentally?—chosen authors. (But could it be a coincidence, I wondered, that she was speaking of Barthes and Foucault?) While I did share Schor's concern with the returning marginalization of female sexuality in the philosophical, as well as the political, domain, I was struck by the ambiguity of the sexual *in-difference* she pointed to in Barthes and Foucault—an ambiguity that neither she nor they were willing to trace to a heterosexual-homosexual difference which, it seemed to me, loomed large in the background.

Thus Schor's essay helped me to see the limitations of my own concept of *(in)difference*, particularly with regard to the equation I made between it and Irigaray's *hommo-sexuality*. For the latter concept not only underscores the exclusion, the inconceivability, of lesbian sexuality (which is the point of her pun) but also forecloses the possibility to think of gay sexuality as another kind of male sexuality, one not homologous or easily assimilable to the "normal." Such foreclosure may or may not have been intended on Irigaray's part, but it is not on mine. Although I shall not concern myself with questions of male sexuality, I certainly could not preclude them, nor would I wish to, in my reading of what I call Freud's *negative theory* of the perversions. Indeed, the notion of *perverse desire* that I will be developing in a later chapter was in part suggested to me by an essay of Bersani and Dutoit's, and may have other implications beyond the ones I am able to pursue.

Freud's Negative Theory of the Perversions

If, in books such as this, one usually encounters the phrase *"normal" sexuality* with the first word between quotation marks, it is because their authors, whether they have read Freud or not, partake of a cultural and intellectual climate that follows from his work in the first decades of the century and has retained some versions of his "passionate fictions." For it was Freud who first put the quotation marks around the "normal" in matters sexual. He did it at a time of general agreement on the natural (i.e., procreative) function of the sexual instinct, which was also interchangeably called "genital instinct" (Davidson, "How to Do the History of Psychoanalysis" 47). And he did it by daring to pursue his exceptional insight—whether genius, vision, or fantasy—into what many see as a revolutionary theory of sexuality or, less romantically, if one attends to Foucault, by making explicit and giving systemic (and highly dramatic) form to certain strategies of power-knowledge and social regulation that had long been in operation in dominant European cultures and that constitute the modern "technology of sex"; namely, "a hysterization of women's bodies . . . a pedagogization of children's sex . . . a socialization of procreative behavior . . . and psychiatrization of perverse pleasure" (*History of Sexuality, I* 104–105).

These were indeed the four major themes of Freud's early work: the sexual instinct, revealed by the symptoms of hysteria and the neuroses at the join of the somatic and the mental; infantile sexuality; the Oedipus complex, with its attendant fantasies of parental seduction and the transformations of the sexual instinct at puberty; and the sexual aberrations—in short, the table of contents of the *Three Essays on the Theory of Sexuality* of 1905. While the concern with the normal in sexuality is clearly of paramount importance to Freud at this time (as evidenced by his closing the third essay with advice on the "Prevention of Inversion"), it is nonetheless the case that in this work the very notions of a normal psychosexual development, a normal sexual act, and thus normal sexuality are inseparable and indeed derive from the detailed consideration of the aberrant, deviant, or perverse manifestations and components of the sexual instinct or drive (*Trieb*).[1]

In his 1975 introductory essay to the Harper Torchbooks paperback edition of the *Three Essays*, Steven Marcus remarks on the peculiar form of this text, which, "in contrast to the grand expository sweep" of Freud's major writings, is made up of "small juxtaposed blocks of material . . . fragments that are both connected and easy to separate, manipulate, revise, or delete. They function as movable parts of a system" (xxi). And a systematic, coherent theory is just what Freud is proposing, Marcus argues, against Freud's own insistence that it is "out of the question" that the essays "could ever be extended into a complete 'theory of sexuality' " (Preface to the third edition of 1915 [*SE* 7: 130]). Marcus is right, of course, in his modern understanding of theory and in so reading, *après coup*, what Freud must have considered—even in 1915—a still-tentative, speculative foray into a conceptual space he was to inhabit and redefine incessantly throughout his life work. While I would rather stress the non-coherence, discontinuities, and ambiguities that lend Freud's theory of sexuality its enduring interest, I also find the *Three Essays* a necessary starting point for my reading.

In spite of the fact that the explosive material of the book is to be found in the second essay on infantile sexuality, Marcus observes, it is at the end of the first essay on the sexual aberrations that Freud, having first disaggregated the perversions and the sexual instinct into component parts, can then recompose them into the neuroses. And *that is* his theory, for after all, as he remarked, "the theory of the neuroses is psycho-analysis itself " (*SE* 16: 379).

> In a bewilderingly brief few pages on the neuroses he has recapitulated the entire structure of the earlier part of the essay, which was, one recalls, about actually perverse sexual behavior.

---

1. In concordance with the *Standard Edition*, I will mostly use the term *instinct* here, though not exclusively. On the English translation of *Trieb*, see the "General Preface" (*SE* 1: xxiv–xxvi), as well as the "Editor's Note" to "Instincts and Their Vicissitudes" (*SE* 14: 111–16).

> But the recapitulation is now on the level of the neurotic symptom,
> of unconscious mental life, of fantasies, ideas, and mental
> representations. It is, in other words, on the level of theory. . . . In
> the neuroses the language of sexuality begins to speak articulately,
> coherently, and theoretically. (Marcus xxxii)

If Marcus is right in characterizing sexuality as a language speaking
through the neuroses, and if "neuroses are, so to say, the negative of
perversions," as Freud himself put it (*SE* 7: 165), then his theory of
sexuality is based on both representations and practices of sex that
are, to a greater or lesser degree, "perverse." A few paragraphs later
he actually speaks of "positive and negative perversions" (*SE* 7: 167),
and three years later, recasting his sexual theory in sociological
terms, he reiterated that "the neuroses contain the same tendencies,
though in a state of 'repression,' as do *the positive perversions*" (*SE* 9:
191; emphasis added); so that indeed one has the impression that,
for Freud, "one does not become a pervert, but remains one" (Dollimore 172).

And we may recall, furthermore, that the whole of Freud's theory
of the human psyche, the sexual instincts and their vicissitudes,
owes its material foundations and developments to his clinical study
of the psychoneuroses; that is to say, those cases in which the mental apparatus and instinctual drives reveal themselves in their
processes and mechanisms, which are "normally" hidden or unremarkable otherwise. The normal, in all these respects, is conceiv-
able only by approximation, more in the order of a projection than
an actual state of being. If "an unbroken chain bridges the gap between the neuroses in all their manifestations and normality" (*SE* 7:
171), then the gap between pathology and non-pathology is bridged
at both ends: between neuroses and normality, on one side, and between normality and perversions, on the other. That bridge is the
sexual instinct in its various vicissitudes and transformations.

Freud's equivocation with regard to this issue—whether a normal sexual instinct, phylogenetically inherited, preexists its possible
deviations (in psychoneurotic individuals) or whether instinctual
life is but a set of transformations, some of which are then defined
as normal, i.e., non-pathogenic and socially desirable or admissible—is a source of continued but ultimately insoluble debate. For
example, here is one of the more liberal readings: "It is clear that

when Freud attempts to ascertain the point at which the sexual instinct emerges, this instinct (*Trieb*) appears almost as a perversion of instinct in the traditional sense (*Instinkt*)—a perversion in which the specific object and the organic purpose both vanish" (Laplanche and Pontalis, *The Language of Psycho-Analysis* 420). At this point, however, Laplanche and Pontalis are speaking specifically of infantile sexuality. In the section just preceding, on "Sexual Instinct," they present a more conservative—developmental and organic—view: "Psycho-analysis shows that the sexual instinct in man is closely bound up with the action of ideas or phantasies which serve to give it specific form. *Only at the end of a complex and hazardous evolution is it successfully organised under the primacy of genitality*, so taking on the apparently fixed and final aspect of instinct in the traditional sense" (417; emphasis added). When we turn to the section on "Perversion," however, we find an ambiguity that perfectly matches or replicates Freud's own.

First, Laplanche and Pontalis argue that "Freud's originality lies in the fact that he used the existence of perversion as a weapon with which to throw the traditional definition of sexuality into question" (307). They cite Freud extensively in support of this view and even speculate that "one could pursue this line of reasoning further still and define human sexuality itself as essentially 'perverse.' " "Which said [they add, incontestably], the fact remains that Freud and all psychoanalysts do talk of 'normal' sexuality" (308). In the effort to account for this, Laplanche and Pontalis then ask a series of rhetorical questions: "Are we to conclude that Freud returns [after posing the existence of stages of libidinal development culminating in the genital organization] to the normative conception of sexuality that he emphatically challenged at the outset of his *Three Essays on the Theory of Sexuality*—basing it now on genetic criteria?" Or, "Does he end up by categorizing as perversions exactly what has always been so categorized?" (308) These questions, and others like them, remain unanswered; for, if Freud's "explicit thesis" in the *Three Essays* is that it is "the establishment of the genital organization that institutes the norm," still Laplanche and Pontalis have to admit that "it is nonetheless reasonable" to doubt such a thesis: "Numerous perversions, such as fetishism, most forms of homosexuality and even incest when it is actually practised, presuppose an organisation dominated by the genital zone. This surely suggests that the norm should be sought elsewhere than in genital functioning itself" (308). But where, finally, the norm could be located, they do not say.

In his *Life and Death in Psychoanalysis,* first published in 1970, three years after *The Language of Psycho-Analysis* [*Vocabulaire de la Psychanalyse*], Laplanche devotes a chapter ("The Order of Life") to a reading of Freud's *Three Essays* through which he comes to a radical redefinition of sexuality: "sexuality, in its entirety, in the human infant, lies in *a movement which deflects the instinct, metaphorizes its aim, displaces and internalizes its object, and concentrates its source on what is ultimately a minimal zone, the erotogenic zone*" (23). In this context, he again takes up the relation of perversion to norm: "Perversion? The notion is commonly defined as a *deviation from instinct,* which presupposes a specific path and aim and implies the choice of a divergent path" (23). But the movement of Freud's exposition in the *Three Essays,* he adds,

> which is simultaneously the movement of a system of thought and, in the last analysis, the movement of the thing itself, is that the *exception*—i.e., the perversion—ends up by *taking the rule along with it.* The exception, which should presuppose the existence of a definite instinct, a preexistent sexual function, with its well-defined norms of accomplishment; that exception ends up by undermining and destroying the very notion of a biological norm. (23)[2]

For my purposes here, I will cite the concluding section of the first of the *Three Essays,* "The Sexual Aberrations," which comes shortly after the well-known analysis of neuroses and perversions as the respective negative and positive of each other. It is one example among many, in Freud's writings, of the ambiguities, inconsistencies, uncertainties, and—in his own word—ambivalence vis-à-vis

---

2. In a later work, Laplanche rephrases this argument by a literary reference (to Proust, more likely than to Milton): the theme of the *Three Essays,* he states, "could be summarized as 'instincts lost' and 'instincts regained' " (*New Foundations for Psychoanalysis* 29): "With its description of the sexual aberrations or perversions, which can be defined in terms of both object and goal, the text is an eloquent argument in favour of the view that drives and forms of behaviour are plastic, mobile and interchangeable. . . . The 'instincts regained' aspect of the *Three Essays* can be seen in its account of the transformations of puberty. . . . In a complex process of development, [the formerly mobile drives] are replaced by something which does, oddly enough, look like an instinctual level" (29–30). And he concludes: " 'Instincts regained' is, then, *simply the result of a complex and random process of evolution based upon reversals and identifications,* many of them bizarre" (30; emphasis added).

the topic at hand that have invited passionate interpretation and made his fictions eminently open texts.[3]

> The conclusion now presents itself to us that there is indeed something innate lying behind the perversions but that it is something innate in *everyone*, though as a disposition it may vary in its intensity and may be increased by the influences of actual life. What is in question are the innate constitutional roots of the sexual instinct. In one class of cases (the perversions) these roots may grow into the actual vehicles of sexual activity; in others [the psychoneuroses] they may be submitted to an insufficient suppression (repression) and thus be able in a roundabout way to attract a considerable proportion of sexual energy to themselves as symptoms; while in the most favourable cases, which lie between these two extremes, they may *by means of effective restriction and other kinds of modification* bring about what is known as normal sexual life. (*SE* 7: 171–72; second emphasis added)

Shortly before this conclusion, Freud had been summarizing his first formulation of the sexual instinct ("The concept of instinct is thus one of those lying on the frontier between the mental and the physical" [*SE* 7: 168]), a concept that would occupy much of his later work; and he had introduced the term *component instincts* thus: "perhaps the sexual instinct itself may be no simple thing, but put together from components which have come apart again in the perversions" (*SE* 7: 162). The words "have come apart again" refer proleptically to a period in the individual's psychic life that will be the topic of the next two essays in Freud's book, infantile sexuality and its transformations at puberty under the primacy of the genital organization of the sexual instincts; it is the period prior to the onset of mental forces, such as shame and disgust, which intervene to restrain the instinct "within the limits that are regarded as normal." The argument goes as follows.

In infantile sexual life the instinct was "predominantly auto-erotic [and] derived from a number of separate instincts and eroto-genic zones, which, independently of one another, have pursued a certain sort of pleasure as their sole sexual aim," whereas in puberty, with the appearance of "a new sexual aim," the sexual instinct be-

---

3. In this sense, for instance, Dollimore suggests an "intriguing connection between homosexuality, perversion, and deconstruction" (191), pointing to radical appropriations of psychoanalysis by writers such as Bersani, Hocquenghem, and Mieli.

comes "subordinated to the reproductive function; it becomes, so to say, altruistic" (*SE* 7: 207). Then the component instincts and erotogenic zones line up and combine to attain this new sexual aim which, Freud specifies, "in men consists in the discharge of the sexual products." But the earlier aim, the attainment of pleasure, is by no means displaced by this new aim, he adds, apparently speaking from experience: "on the contrary, the highest degree of pleasure is attached to this final act of the sexual process." For women, Freud admits, it may be otherwise; in fact, he has reason to suppose that "[the sexual development] of females actually enters upon a kind of involution" (*SE* 7: 207). But no more is said of women at this time except that, in them, "the intermediate steps" of the process leading from a sexuality of component instincts to one under the aegis of seminal discharge "are still in many ways obscure . . . an unsolved riddle" (*SE* 7: 208). And not by coincidence, perhaps, this same word *riddle* will be the leitmotiv of the psychoanalytic inquiry into female sexuality, from the case history of "Dora" (1905 [1900]) to the posthumous lecture on "Femininity" (1933).

There is a certain discrepancy of tone, a marked change in emphasis between the two consecutive pages that close the first essay and open the second. Let me attempt to point them out and suggest a possible explanation. If normal sexual life (or "what is known as normal sexual life," as Freud carefully notes in the long passage cited above) could be said to be *brought about*, to be achieved, even induced "by means of effective restriction and other kinds of modification" in the first essay on sexual aberrations—an area of research hardly new or controversial after several decades of work by sexologists such as Krafft-Ebing and Havelock Ellis, from which Freud admittedly drew most of his material at the time—here, on the other hand, in the second and third essays containing Freud's own, more radical and enormously controversial hypothesis of infantile sexuality and its transformations at puberty, "normal" sexual life is taken as the premise, rather than the end result, of sexual development and assumed to be coincident with adult, reproductive, lawful heterosexual intercourse.

In the last two essays, in other words, it is no longer a matter of bringing about the normal by effective restrictions, by channeling the component instincts and realigning the erogenous zones in the service of the one socially admissible form of sexual pleasure; there is instead the posing of an ideal norm, the normal, as the a priori, the essential kernel, the original potential and promise of sexual development, the seed that will come to maturation after puberty in "normal sexuality." It is as if heterosexuality were firmly in place from the beginning, in each newborn, as the promise and fulfillment of each component instinct. This is a far cry from the hypothesis of bisexuality offered to explain inversion and from other related statements in the first essay, such as the famous 1915 footnote addition that "from the point of view of psycho-analysis the exclusive sexual interest felt by men for women is also a problem that needs elucidating and is not a self-evident fact based upon an attraction that is ultimately of a chemical nature" (*SE* 7: 146).

To account for such discrepancy, it is not altogether unreasonable to think that, in setting forth his original theory of infantile sexuality, with its component instincts and polymorphous perversity, Freud felt that his reformulation of the sexual instinct must be theoretically restrained, rhetorically curbed, as it were, by the emphasis on an ideal normal development which would save the theory from itself partaking of the perversions that the first essay describes. I do not mean to suggest that this latter emphasis stems from expediency or is a merely rhetorical strategy on Freud's part. Such a suggestion, like the analogous claim advanced by Jeffrey Masson with regard to Freud's repudiation of the seduction theory (on which more will be said in Part II [chapter 4]), would amount to a failed reading, an inability to distinguish between hypocrisy and ambivalence. I think the two emphases more likely reflect a bona fide and structural ambivalence in Freud's thinking, due to the logic of the argument and its heuristic premise driving it in one direction, and to the drift of his ideological, emotional, and affective convictions pulling in a contrary direction. In support of this reading, which is not of much consequence in itself but will become so in the development of my argument, I will cite another and more extreme example of Freud's doctrinal inconsistency—the relation between instinct and object, painstakingly analyzed by Arnold Davidson in his reading of the *Three Essays*.

Freud's redefinition of the sexual instinct, Davidson argues in "How to Do the History of Psychoanalysis," was a revolutionary in(ter)vention in the medical discourses of his time, an overturning of the "highly structured, rule-governed, conceptual space" in which "psychiatric theories of sexuality had operated since about 1870" (53). And in a companion piece, "Closing Up the Corpses," he further argues that the emergency of psychiatry in the nineteenth century as a medical discipline autonomous from neurology and cerebral pathology coincided with the development of "a new style of reasoning," the formation of new concepts and "new kinds of diseases and disease categories" (295–96).[4] With the characterization of the sexual instinct as a sixth sense (*sens génital,* in the terminology first used by Moreau, who influenced Krafft-Ebing's *Psychopathia Sexualis* [1893], and then adopted by others, among whom Charcot), and with the introduction of the concept of perversion in 1842, reported by the *Oxford English Dictionary* as "one of the four modifications of function in disease," the sexual perversions "became a natural class of diseases" (307). Thus, for example, Carl Westphal's notion of the contrary sexual instinct (*Die conträre Sexualempfindung*) as a congenital perversion of the sexual instinct produced, in 1870, a new medicopsychological diagnostic category and a psychological, rather than anatomico-pathological, definition of homosexuality ("a woman is physically a woman and psychologically a man and, on the other hand, a man is physically a man and psychologically a woman"); this clinical conception of the perversion would remain operative in subsequent medical literature (309).[5]

While relying on these works, Freud accomplished his revolutionary in(ter)vention in the first of the *Three Essays* "by fundamentally altering the rules of combination for concepts such as sexual instinct, sexual object, sexual aim" (Davidson, "How to Do the His-

---

4. Useful and informative as this work by Davidson is, I must register my disagreement with his conclusion, which moves out of the field of medicine into broader cultural discourse: "All of our subsequent reasoning about perversion is afflicted by the historical origins of the concept. Moreover, we cannot think away the concept of perversion, even if we no longer claim to believe that there is any natural function of the sexual instinct. We are prisoners of the historical space of nineteenth-century psychiatry" (320). In my view, two decades of gay and lesbian reverse discourses and theorizing have brought about the development of another "new style of reasoning," another understanding of perversion, such that it is possible—as I am about to do here—to read the same text by Freud that Davidson reads, and find in it quite different implications and theoretical suggestions for the relation of sexuality and perversion.

5. But the *scientia sexualis* of the time relied on material that was not always clinical. Havelock Ellis's "Sexual Inversion in Women," a chapter of his influential *Studies in the Psychology of Sex* [1897], cites literary works, biographies, popular literature, criminal and cultural anthropologists, newspaper and travel accounts, a Catholic confessor, "a lady who cannot be called inverted" (216), and so on.

tory of Psychoanalysis" 62) and thus subverting the conceptual foundations of the notion of perversion and, in particular, its specific configuration in inversion. In order to show that inversion was a real, functional deviation of the sexual instinct, rather than merely a difference in its direction or object, "one had to conceive of the 'normal' object of the instinct as part of the very content of the instinct itself" (52). And indeed Davidson demonstrates that, in a "virtually *unargued unanimity*" (47), psychiatric theories of the time assumed that a specific object (i.e., members of the other sex) and a specific aim (i.e., reproductive genital intercourse) were integral or constituent parts of the sexual instinct. Freud, therefore, not only challenged the unanimously accepted view but "decisively replaced the concept of the sexual instinct with that of a sexual drive 'in the first instance independent of its object'" (54). Here is the crucial passage from the *Three Essays:*

> It has been brought to our notice that we have been in the habit of regarding the connection between the sexual instinct and the sexual object as more intimate than it in fact is. Experience of the cases that are considered abnormal has shown us that in them the sexual instinct and the sexual object are merely soldered together—a fact which we have been in danger of overlooking in consequence of the uniformity of the normal picture, where the object appears to form part and parcel of the instinct. We are thus warned to loosen the bond that exists in our thought between instinct and object. It seems probable that the sexual instinct is in the first instance independent of its object; nor is its origin likely to be due to its object's attractions. (*SE* 7: 147–48)[6]

Freud's originality, Davidson remarks, is not the introduction of a new word, *Trieb* in lieu of *Instinkt*, as other commentators have suggested, for the word *Trieb* was already used by his contemporaries, including Krafft-Ebing; the originality consists in the theoretical rearticulation that makes Freud's *Sexualtrieb* an altogether novel

---

6. Freud upheld this view in the much later metapsychological paper on "Instincts and Their Vicissitudes": "The object [*Objekt*] of an instinct is the thing in regard to which or through which the instinct is able to achieve its aim. It is what is most variable about an instinct and *is not originally connected with it, but becomes assigned to it only in consequence of being peculiarly fitted to make satisfaction possible*" (*SE* 14: 122; emphasis added).

concept. And one whose ultimate implications Freud himself seemed unable to grasp.

Inevitably, at this point, Davidson too is led to speculate on the reasons for Freud's inconsistent reintroduction, later in the book, of notions such as perversion and genital primacy which, on the very strength of his argument in the first essay, have been deprived of their conceptual ground and hence must now appear vacuous or nonsensical. For example, in a brilliant piece of textual exegesis, Davidson shows how Freud simply cannot mean what he says when he appears to disagree with other medical writers only to reiterate their very argument:

> [Freud's] claim that these writers are mistaken in asserting that an innate weakness of the sexual instinct is responsible for perversion, but that their assertions would make sense "if what is meant is a constitutional weakness of one particular factor in the sexual instinct, namely the genital zone," is astonishing, since this is, of course, exactly what they meant, and had to mean, given their conception of the sexual instinct. It is Freud who cannot mean to say that the absence of this particular factor, the primacy of the genital zone, is a condition of perversion. The last sentence of this paragraph reads, "For if the genital zone is weak, this combination, which is required to take place at puberty, is bound to fail, and the strongest of the other components of sexuality will continue its activity as a perversion." But the system of concepts Freud has been working with in the first essay requires a slightly different conclusion, one whose subtle modulation from Freud's actual conclusion must be emphasized. The appropriate formulation of the conclusion should read, "For if the genital zone is weak, this combination, which often takes place at puberty, will fail, and the strongest of the other components of sexuality will continue its activity." The differences between these two formulations represent what I have been calling Freud's attitude. (61)

Being perhaps of a cast of mind more philosophical than psychoanalytic, Davidson suggests that Freud's attitude or mental habits, formed in the conceptual-scientific mentality of his own time, "never quite caught up" with the new conceptual articulations he himself produced (63). This does not contradict, but rather complements, my own suggestion that one's most profound ideological and affective convictions may sometimes run counter to one's most brilliant critical or analytical insights. Nor, for that matter, does it contradict Freud's own view of the subject as divided between what it says and what it means, or what it knows and what it doesn't, even as, in the latter instance, it should know better.

Another critic, Jonathan Dollimore, remarks on Freud's enduring ambivalence toward sexual deviation, even in a sociological work such as "Civilized Sexual Morality and Modern Nervous Illness" (*SE* 9: 177–204), where "the teleological view of psychosexual development begins to look normative in much more than a descriptive sense" (188). Even there, however, Freud is "both speaking for and undermining the perspective of 'civilized' sexual morality." Thus, Dollimore argues,

> it is not necessary to insist that Freud was consciously writing a subversive text. He may have been; or his goal may have been a strategic ambiguity reflecting ambivalence. The important point is that, consciously or not, the dynamic he identifies within the subject, and within the social order, finds its way into his own text as a result of what he has "discovered" about perversion, its repression and sublimation. (*Sexual Dissidence* 190)

Or, as Elisabeth Young-Bruehl sees it, "Freud was forever fighting with himself, trying not to be a simple (or even an unsimple, Darwinian) teleologist, but being one all the same. His radicality . . . is his anti-teleology side; his conventionality rises when teleology wins back territory in him" (personal communication).[7]

But perhaps the best example of Freud's persistent ambiguity on the nature of homosexuality is encapsulated in his 1935 letter to the American mother of a young homosexual man, reported in Jones's biography. Freud was adamantly opposed to the view, predominant among his colleagues, that homosexuality was in and of itself pathological, and consequently also opposed the exclusion of homosexuals from analytic training. (He was almost alone in holding this position during his lifetime and is still so today, especially in the United States, as Henry Abelove points out in his scathing review of psychoanalytic moralism in America.) Nevertheless he did equivocate. "Homosexuality is assuredly no advantage," Freud wrote in English to the American mother, "but it is nothing to be ashamed of,

---

7. I am deeply grateful to Elisabeth Young-Bruehl for the many thoughtful comments she offered me as a reader of this book's manuscript.

no vice, no degradation, it cannot be classified as an illness, we consider it to be a variation of the sexual function produced by a certain arrest of sexual development" ("A Letter from Freud," quoted by Abelove 381). Not an illness, merely a variation; and yet a sign of arrested—incomplete, immature, or somewhat faulty—sexual development.

I have stressed the obtrusive presence of ambivalence, inconsistency, and structural ambiguity in the *Three Essays* to suggest that, if they do amount to a systematic, coherent theory (as Marcus asserts) or to a restructuring of our conceptual space whereby the sexual drive can be thought quite independent of its object (as Davidson argues), then Freud's theory of sexuality is not exactly the normative and normalizing synthesis of late Victorian views that many take it to be; nor is it a dramatic rendering of Foucault's technology of sex, but rather a conception of sexuality whose structural, constitutive ambiguity has *not yet* been fully taken up in its furthest implications. To this I will return, but for the moment I also want to suggest that Freud's theory of sexuality, as set forth in the early writings and never fundamentally altered in the later ones, is much closer epistemologically to his acknowledged "discoveries" or original conceptual formulations, such as the agency of the unconscious in the mind and his topographical and structural models of the psychic apparatus, than it is usually credited to be. In particular, I find a curious resemblance between his conception of sexuality in the *Three Essays* and the configuration of the psyche in his second model, with the triad of ego, id, and superego serving as a rough analogue for the exchanges among normality, perversion, and neurosis.

Before I go on to indulge in another bit of analogical thinking, fully aware that it may have limitations, I will offer one example of the kind of statement that has instigated my speculation: "From the point of view of instinctual control, of morality, it may be said of the id that it is totally non-moral, of the ego that it strives to be moral, and of the super-ego that it can be super-moral and then become as cruel as only the id can be" (*SE* 19: 54). The mind's threefold relation to morality, which evidently concerns Freud in *The Ego and the Id* (1923) as much as it did in the *Three Essays*, reproposes the three positions of the sexual instinct vis-à-vis morality in perversion, normal sexuality, and neurosis, respectively; it even redoubles the slippage of the last term into the first: the superego here rejoins the id as neurosis rejoined perversion in its negative form there. In this perspective, Freud's theory of sexuality could be seen as a system based on three interdependent agencies or modalities of the sexual, none of which has priority status with regard to causality or temporality, and one of which, the normal, would be defined by reference to the other two (as the ego is by reference to id and superego), rather than vice versa.

In *The Ego and the Id*, where Freud lays out his tripartite model of the mind, the following passage occurs:

> There are two paths by which the contents of the id can penetrate into the ego. The one is direct, the other leads by way of the ego ideal; which of these two paths they take may, for some mental activities, be of decisive importance: The ego develops from perceiving instincts to controlling them, from obeying instincts to inhibiting them. In this achievement a large share is taken by the ego ideal, which indeed is partly a reaction-formation against the instinctual processes of the id. Psychoanalysis is an instrument to enable the ego to achieve a progressive conquest of the id.
>
> From the other point of view, however, we see this same ego as a poor creature owing service to three masters and consequently menaced by three dangers: from the external world, from the libido of the id, and from the severity of the super-ego. Three kinds of anxiety correspond to these three dangers, since anxiety is the expression of a retreat from danger. As a frontier-creature, the ego tries to mediate between the world and the id, to make the id pliable to the world and, by means of its muscular activity, to make the world fall in with the wishes of the id. . . .
>
> But since the ego's work of sublimation results in a defusion of the instincts and a liberation of the aggressive instincts in the super-ego, its struggle against the libido exposes it to the danger of maltreatment and death. In suffering under the attacks of the super-ego or perhaps even succumbing to them, the ego is meeting with a fate like that of the protista which are destroyed by the products of decomposition that they themselves have created. From the economic point of view the morality that functions in the super-ego seems to be a similar product of decomposition. (*SE* 19: 55–57)

In contrast with the image of the ego as a poor creature in service to three masters, and with several other equally anthropomorphic similes that Freud uses to draw a picture of the ego (a man on horseback, a constitutional monarch, a politician, a submissive slave, a physician-analyst), the metaphor of the frontier creature and the comparison to the protista convey the sense of an instinctual energy, a material but non-human living substance, rather than a socialized or civilized person. Moreover, the figure of the ego as a frontier creature is reminiscent of the formulation of the sexual instinct as one "lying on the frontier between the mental and the physical" (*SE* 7: 168).

In reading this entire section on "The Ego's Dependent Relations," the frontier image seems by far the more precise in conveying Freud's concept of the ego as "a body-ego" (*SE* 19: 27), a physical site of negotiations between the pressures coming from the external world, on one side, and those coming from the internal world, from the id's instinctual and narcissistic drives, and from their representative, the superego, on the other. For the superego is derived from the child's Oedipal object-cathexes that have been de-eroticized and transformed into identifications: the superego derives from "the first object-cathexes of the id, from the Oedipus complex," Freud says, and thus "is always close to the id as its representative vis-à-vis the ego. It reaches deep down into the id and for that reason is farther from consciousness than the ego is" (*SE* 19: 48–49). In other words, the ego is not located between the id and the superego, but is the frontier between *them* and the external world. The dangerous and exciting domain of the real, comprising other people, social institutions, and so forth, on one side, and an equally treacherous domain, on the other—the internal world of instinctual drives, the libido with its vicissitudes, and the death drive—make that *frontier* creature, the ego, a site of incessant material negotiations between them.[8]

If my analogy with the triad of the *Three Essays* holds, then normal sexuality there would be in a position homologous to the position of the ego here. Normal sexuality would also be a frontier creature, or a frontier concept—not a particular sexual disposition or a mode of being of the sexual instinct itself, but rather the result of particular negotiations in the process of mediation in which the subject must constantly engage—the mediation between external

---

8. Put in somewhat different terms, the second Freudian topography "take[s] into consideration the 'unconscious aspects of the ego' or . . . a certain unconsciousness constitutive of the ego *itself* " (Borch-Jacobsen 8).

(social, parental, representational) pressures and the internal pressures of the sexual instinct (or the component instincts). And the latter's modalities would be perversion and neurosis, two sides of the same coin, each other's positive and negative faces, the twin modes of being of the sexual instinct. In this scenario, sexuality would not come in two varieties, "normal" and "perverse" (I omit "neurotic" since neurosis is but negative perversion, as Freud pretty much says in "Reasons for the Apparent Preponderance of Perverse Sexuality in the Psychoneuroses" [*SE* 7: 170–71]). Instead, one can imagine the sexual instinct as being made up of various component instincts—none of which would have a *necessary* priority since no originary relation binds the instinct(s) to a particular object (although certain object relations do become privileged in individual subjectivities as a result of each contingent and singular history)— and having two modalities, positive and negative perversion, depending on the presence and degree of repression (on the presence and specific mechanism of repression in perversion, see Sachs). Normal sexuality, then, would name a particular result of the process of negotiation with both the external and the internal worlds; it would designate the achievement, on the part of the subject, of the kind of sexual organization that a particular society and its institutions have decreed to be normal. And in this sense, indeed, *normal* becomes totally coextensive and synonymous with *normative*.

I may put it another way by retracing my steps so far. The theory of sexuality that emerged for me from the *Three Essays* on first reading it seemed to consist of two theories: one explicit and affirmative, a positive theory of normal sexuality, and the other implicit and negative, appearing as the underside or the clinical underground of the first. I thought of the latter as Freud's *negative theory* of the perversions. However, a closer reading of the text's conspicuous inconsistencies and self-contradictory assertions (most blatant in Davidson's analysis of the relation of the sexual instinct to its object[s]) has produced another picture. It now seems to me that what I have called Freud's negative theory of the perversions, that which neither he nor his followers could propose or count as a theory of sexuality, *that* is Freud's theory of sexuality. The positive theory of normal sexuality and normal sexual development that can be read, and has indeed been read almost unanimously, in the *Three Essays* now looks to me like the imposition of a historically determined social norm on a field of instinctual drives which, as Freud's entire work and the increasing fortunes of psychoanalysis go to prove, is not passible of much development but only of shifts, readjustments, and more or less successful negotiations with a real that is always waiting around the corner, at the frontier.

In using the terms *positive* and *negative* in reference to the two theories of sexuality that coexisted in my former reading of the *Three Essays*, I was playing with Freud's characterization of neuroses as the negative of perversions; it always struck me that, by phrasing it that way, Freud was in a sense qualifying the perversions as positive. And surely, in his case histories, the actual patients, those suffering or made dysfunctional from their symptoms, are the neurotics and the hysterics, not the perverts, most of whom would or did live as well as they could without the help of psychoanalysis—think of the protagonists of "Psychogenesis of a Case of Homosexuality in a Woman," "A Case of Paranoia Running Counter to the Psycho-Analytic Theory of the Disease," "Leonardo," and better still, the fetishists who, Freud writes, "are quite satisfied with [their fetish], or even praise the way in which it eases their erotic life" (*SE* 21: 152). With the phrase "Freud's negative theory of the perversions" I meant to ironize on this, by reversing his own definition of psychoanalysis as the theory of the neuroses, and troping on the high-contrast quality (as in a photographic negative) conferred to the perversions by the highlighting that is automatically set on the normal. (For an incisive discussion of the category of the normal as a statistical construction and its normalizing function vis-à-vis notions of the natural and the anomalous or deviant, see Jennifer Terry's reading of Foucault and Canguilhem's *The Normal and the Pathological* in relation to the stigmatization of homosexuals as "sex variants" in her "Siting Homosexuality" [60–73].)

Moreover, since I made the analogy between the theories of the *Three Essays* and the economic model of the psyche in *The Ego and the Id*, I must also remark on a further resonance between my terms and Freud's notion of a positive and a negative Oedipus complex in the latter work (*SE* 19: 31–34). There, as well as in the *Three Essays*, it is the case that the negative term, the "negative Oedipus complex," designates what is socially inadmissible (the girl's erotic attachment to the mother, the boy's to the father) and must therefore be transformed into identification, repressed, or sublimated, or all of the above. As for the positive term, the "positive Oedipus complex" (the girl's refocusing of her erotic cathexis from the mother onto the father, the boy's continued erotic, and now phallic, attachment to the mother) designates what Freud persists in calling the normal sexual development in the face of overwhelming evidence that such a development is rarer and less likely than it ought to be. In other words, in this case as well, at least for the girl, the positive or the "normal" is merely an approximation, a projection, and not a state of being. Once again the positivity of the normal is a function of social norm.

At this point, my earlier intimation that Freud's views on sexuality in the *Three Essays* have not yet been sufficiently considered, especially with regard to the further implications of its structural (if not structured) ambiguity, finds itself strengthened. And it finds support in Dollimore's discussion of "Freud's Theory of Sexual Perversion," a chapter of his recently published *Sexual Dissidence*. After tracing the discursive history of perversion from twentieth-century homosexual writers (Wilde, Gide) back through modern England to Augustine, he proposes that a "perverse dynamic" is at work in Freud's theory and writings as it is in earlier, religious, metaphysical, or non-sexual notions of perversion. In all of them, "the shattering effect of perversion arises from the fact that it is integral to just those things it threatens" (172). It is because of this constitutive paradox—which Freud reactivates at the theoretical level in his attempt to subvert traditional metaphysics—that "the challenge of the perverse remains inscribed irreducibly within psychoanalysis, as within metaphysics" (173).

Thus perversion, and homosexuality in particular, has a peculiarly paradoxical status in Freud: both central and yet disruptive; necessary and yet objectionable; a "deviation" from the norm and yet more compatible with positive social goals; degrading of human relationship and yet more pleasurable than "civilized" sexuality; regressive or involutionary and yet expressive of an original intensity of being. For, if it can be said that "the pervert expends unsocialized libido at the expense of the social order," yet "Freud several times makes the empirical observation that practising homosexuals may be especially civilized" (193). Homosexuality returns again and again throughout Freud's work, Dollimore remarks—speaking, of course, of male homosexuality—"and his preoccupation with it is symptomatic of just that which he would explain: its troubling centrality to, and disruption of, the normal." However, while Freud used them to disrupt traditional definitions of sexuality, homosexuality and perversion in general "remained as a principle of disruption within his own normative theories" (203). Dollimore's final, exquisitely ironic argument for the perverse dynamic that, he has shown, is "always already there" in any theory of perversion is the very myth that psychoanalysis appropriates to sanction and normalize heterosexuality, the Oedipus myth, which "has homosexuality inscribed at its centre" (204) as precisely, in the words of Marie Balmary, the hidden fault of the father (Laius).[9]

In many respects Dollimore's reading is consonant with mine (e.g.: "It is sexual perversion, not sexual 'normality,' which is the given in human nature" [176]); and in some ways I share his ambivalence toward Freud and cannot but sympathize with his effort to recover and retain the radical, critical, edge of psychoanalysis in the service of a materialist account of the dynamic of social struggle, while taking distance from some of its politically contested tenets ("I'm not persuaded by Freud's theory of the [Oedipus] complex" [195]). But as will become clearer later on, I am more persuaded by the latter than Dollimore is and remain unconvinced by his inchoate critique of the Oedipus, which is based mainly on Fletcher's schematic view of Oedipal law (in "Freud and His Uses") as a disjunction between desire and identification, and moves much too quickly to a huge claim such as "the Oedipus complex increasingly becomes a casualty of homosexuality" (198). Where Dollimore and I differ on the issue of sexuality and (as) perversion is in my reluctance and his propensity to romanticize perversion, notably in what he repeatedly calls "the insurrectionary nature of the perversions" (198).

As he sees it explored in the work of contemporary psychoanalytic critics, this inherently subversive or insurrectionary character of the perversions would present "a challenge not only to the Oedi-

---

9. In a chapter of her *A Lure of Knowledge* entitled "Freud Reads Lesbians," Judith Roof also remarks, à propos of the Dora case history, on what Dollimore calls the perverse dynamic. She quotes Freud: "The motive forces leading to the formation of hysterical symptoms draw their strength not only from repressed *normal* sexuality but also from unconscious perverse activities" (*SE* 7: 51). And she comments: "The paths of perversion are always already present. . . . Like his own text that acknowledges that he already knows what he subsequently forgets, perversions—lesbian sexuality—refer back to a place one has already been; they are always already there" (185). Unfortunately, Roof does not pursue the connection between perversion and lesbian sexuality further.

pal law, but to the entire Oedipal drama as a theory: perversion comes to challenge the integrity of the psychoanalytic project itself" (198). However, of the three critics he cites to buttress his claim (Chasseguet-Smirgel, Silverman, Bersani), the first two are no more challenging of the Oedipus structure than Freud himself was, although Silverman articulates more fully the complexities of the double (or complete) Oedipus complex, emphasizing its negative (same-sex) dimension and positing a convergence of identification and desire; as for Chasseguet-Smirgel, Dollimore himself calls her homophobic reading of Wilde "the nadir of psychoanalytic criticism" (199). Moreover, in these critics, he adds, the subversion operated by perversion is ultimately recontained within and by the psychoanalytic frame. Only in *The Freudian Body* are the perversions "shown to challenge the psychoanalytic project itself" (201), Dollimore states, in that "the marginality of sadomasochism would consist of nothing less than its isolating, even its making visible, the ontological grounds of the sexual" (Bersani, *The Freudian Body* 41). And this is indeed closer to my own project here; that is to say, the project of finding in the perversions—rather than in normative, reproductive, teleological, "normal" sex—a model of sexuality as it is subjectively lived through fantasy and desire. But Dollimore does not take up Bersani's point or develop it further. Thus, in the end, his assertion that "perversion proves the undoing of the theory which contains it" (197) remains an assertion, an unsubstantiated claim, or a wish; and Freud's theory is not undone but rather reconfirmed as a theory of perversion that, just as Dollimore suggests, is itself permeated by the perverse dynamic, the paradoxically perverse.

Which, indeed, raises the question of practice, of the clinical applications of psychoanalysis, its appropriation by medical and legal discourses, its uses in what Foucault has called the "multiple implantation of 'perversions'" (*History of Sexuality, I* 37)—in short, the political question. But that question, which for Dollimore is one of collapsing "the psychoanalytic project," of "discrediting not the theory *per se* but those historical developments within psychoanalysis wherein the Oedipus complex has been normatively deployed" (202), is not actually answered by a demonic, voluntaristic, or reverse reading of Freud which would undermine "the psychoanalytic project from within" (202). It seems to me that it is best answered, each time anew and always contingently, tactically (politically), by a

critical confrontation with those historically "diverse appropriations and developments" which, in fact, belie the very notion of *a*
single psychoanalytic project. Rereading Freud, therefore, is a theoretical enterprise, each rereading a passionate fiction, whose significance for social struggle and for psychoanalytic, political, or erotic
practice may be great or small or none at all, but in any case cannot
be assumed, let alone taken for granted.

It is with this in mind that I return to my reading of the *Three
Essays* to ask, What if one were to follow the path of the component
instincts left visible, if darkly, in the background of the picture?
What if one set out to pursue a theory of sexuality along the negative
trace of the perversions—let us say, fetishism? Such theory might
not, perhaps, account for the majority of people, but then the positive theory of sexuality does not either; and then again, the notion of
"the majority of people" is as troubled as the notion of "the normal"—it, too, is at best an approximation and at worst a projection.
At any rate, a theory of sexuality based on perversion, such as I have
suggested and will attempt to articulate further in the following
chapters, would be just as much of a fiction, and no less passionate
or even "true" for those who live it, than the theory of an elusive and
ever more troubled normal sexuality.

But now, since my project in this book is understanding sexual
structuring through fantasy and according to a model of desire that
may account for lesbian subjectivity, I must continue my reading of
Freud and other psychoanalytic texts on female homosexuality, although the venture, by his own testimony, does not offer much prospect of success.

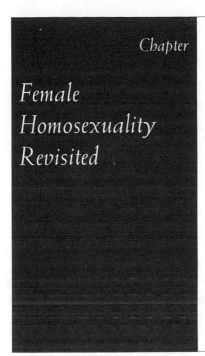

Chapter 2

Female
Homosexuality
Revisited

She sees herself in analysis with Miss
Anna Freud who is wearing men's
clothes.
—a patient's dream, reported by Helene
Deutsch ("On Female Homosexuality"
498)

In one of the rare attempts to look at lesbianism in a feminist and
psychoanalytic perspective, Diane Hamer suggests that the relevance
of psychoanalysis to lesbian life is demonstrable by the increasing
number of lesbians going into therapy, the general "antipsychoanal-
ysis consensus" notwithstanding. That this evidence may refer primarily or exclusively to white and probably middle-class women,
though Hamer omits to specify it, does not invalidate her point. For
lesbians are, of course, as socially diversified by racial, cultural, gen-
erational, and class identifications as we are subjectively by our singular psychical configurations and personal histories; but the fact (if
it is a fact) that some of us, within certain sociohistorical locations,
increasingly resort to psychotherapy is (or would be) sufficient to
raise the question of why, then, there is such mistrust or outright
dismissal of psychoanalytic theory on the part of women who, by
sheer arithmetic, must be located among those "some."

Hamer does not say, as one might, that most forms of "therapy"
today are hardly comparable to (psycho)analysis, that some are not

male-centered or dominated by male analysts, and again some are advertised by lesbian therapists. On the contrary, she believes that "the theoretical bases of many of our therapies will have been informed by psychoanalysis at some point" (134). So she admits to a contradiction, "a difficulty inherent in entering psychoanalytic discourse from a position of identification as a lesbian," that is, the danger that "our lesbianism will once again be read as 'the problem'" (135). Nonetheless, on the strength of the feminist readings of Freud and Lacan proposed by Juliet Mitchell and Jacqueline Rose—especially the latter's argument that feminism's affinity with psychoanalysis rests on its "recognition that there is a resistance to identity at the very heart of psychic life" (Rose, *Sexuality in the Field of Vision* 91)—Hamer sees in psychoanalysis the potential for understanding lesbianism "as a contingent identity constructed from individual biographical details rather than as something authentic, natural or pre-given—without pathologizing it" (135). I have already suggested, and will elaborate further later on, how Rose's notion of the unconscious as resistance to identity (specifically to feminine identity) may militate against the very notion, as well as the theorizing, of a lesbian subjectivity or sexual identity, and thus may be seen to undercut, rather than foster, Hamer's own project. But because that project is also in many ways consonant with the efforts of this book—although my goal is a theory of lesbian sexuality, not identity—I will consider it at some length.

The Masculinity Complex

Hamer goes further than Rose in stating that "sometimes, for some women," lesbianism may be "a psychic repudiation of the category 'woman'" (143) and proposing a direct correspondence between feminism as "a political movement based on a refusal to accept the social 'truth' of men's superiority over women" and lesbianism as "a psychic refusal of the 'truth' of women's castration." In this context, she remarks, "it is interesting to note that Freud referred to both his homosexual women patients as 'feminists'" (145). Even more interesting, to me, is to see a lesbian theorist decisively and explicitly reappropriate, in feminist perspective, one of psychoanalysis's most contended notions, the masculinity complex in women, which, Hamer emphasizes, *"can also result in manifest homosexual choice of object"* (Freud, "Female Sexuality" [1931], quoted by Hamer 140).[1] Once having taken this step—a giant step for our kind, in my estimation, one without which our theorizing may just keep on playing in the pre-Oedipal sandbox—Hamer has left behind years of debates on Freud's sexism and feminist outrage, and volumes on Freud's historical limitations and feminist exculpation (debates and volumes, I may add, to which I have myself contributed in some measure). She can then proceed to the obvious question: How does a lesbian feminist reappropriation of the masculinity complex distinguish itself from Freud's account? Unfortunately, Hamer's answer is rather confusing in that her attempt to redefine lesbian desire in Lacanian terms runs aground of the corollary to the masculinity complex, namely, the castration complex; the latter, she states, we must refuse.

> Classically, lesbians are thought to pretend possession of the phallus (they make a "virile identification" with it; Adams, 1989: 263) and are thus aligned, albeit fraudulently, on the side of masculinity. In this rather simplistic account lesbian desire becomes near impossible; desire cannot exist *between lesbians*, since they are both on the same side of desire, or, if a lesbian does experience desire, it is bound to be towards a feminine subject who could only desire her back as though she were a man.
>
> However, as I have suggested, lesbianism is less a claim to phallic possession (although it may be this too) than it is a refusal of the meanings attached to castration. As such it is a refusal of any easy or straightforward allocation of masculine and feminine positions around the phallus. Instead it suggests a much more fluid and flexible relationship to the positions around which desire is organized. (147)

Although a paragraph break separates the classic account of the masculinity complex from Hamer's revision, the same terminological/conceptual frame, drawn from the Lacanian revision of Freud, is applied to both accounts. For example, the idea that lesbians are "on the same side of desire" is not to be found in the classic account,

---

1. Freud had first mentioned the masculinity complex in "A Child Is Being Beaten" (1919), properly attributing the term's paternity to van Ophuijsen (whose paper I will discuss shortly), and referred to it again in "Some Psychical Consequences of the Anatomical Distinction between the Sexes" (1925), "Female Sexuality" (1931), "Femininity" (1933), and "Analysis Terminable and Interminable" (1937).

where the emphasis is rather on object-choice and/or identification with the father. While not absent in Freud, the notion of desire is much more specific and restrictive there than it is in current neo-Freudian use. As Laplanche and Pontalis state, "The Freudian conception of desire refers above all to unconscious wishes, bound to indestructible infantile signs," and these signs are what govern, through fantasy, "the search for the object in the real world." It is Lacan's revision that "has attempted to re-orientate Freud's doctrine around the notion of desire, and to replace this notion in the forefront of analytic theory" (*The Language of Psycho-Analysis* 482). Thus it is in the Lacanian reframing, with the phallus as "straightforward" allocator of masculine and feminine *positions* in desire, that one might, rightly or wrongly, think of the lesbian lovers as being "both on the same side of desire."

In the classic account, the meaning of castration that the girl refuses is the imperative of the positive Oedipus complex: you shall give up your phallic desire for your mother and turn toward the father, who will make a woman out of you (by confirming or giving formal recognition to your castration/femininity). This imperative does not leave open the possibility of "organizing desire" in a *fluid* or *flexible* relation to masculinity or femininity, as Hamer suggests of lesbianism; it may allow, at best, for an alternation or oscillation between female-object cathexis and male-object cathexis, that is to say, bisexuality (or hysteria). But, in this case, only one of the poles of the oscillation would count as a refusal of castration, while the other would signify its acceptance (femininity); in other words, only a female-object choice would classically define lesbianism, and that in turn would imply a masculine identification. So oscillation is not the answer, as Hamer would like to have it, assimilating "oscillation" to "fluidity" when she concludes: "Lesbians can be both masculine and feminine—simultaneously or at different moments—in relation to the desire of another. This fluidity and oscillation around the positions of masculinity and femininity signifies [*sic*] the splitting off of categories of gender from any biological determination" (149).

This conclusion is not convincing, for, whereas the constructedness of gender can be asserted without recourse to oscillation or fluidity of desire, the latter remains to be thought precisely in relation to castration, whose "meanings" or terms must therefore be rethought. The problem with Hamer's solution—the "refusal of the meanings attached to castration"—is that it begs the question. In the Lacanian framework, symbolic castration is both the condition of desire and what constitutes the paternal phallus as the "allocator" of positions in desire; castration and the phallus go hand in hand, as it were, one cannot stir without the other. Thus, for those who work with neo-Freudian psychoanalytic discourse, simply to reject the notion of castration or to refuse to rethink its terms is to find ourselves without symbolic means to signify desire, and hence without the means to theorize lesbian desire.

At the root of these problems lies, I think, Hamer's reliance on an essay by Parveen Adams, referred to in the long passage I cited, which, in a hasty and underinformed manner, offers some speculations on lesbian sadomasochism. This essay, it appears, is the key to Hamer's proposed revision of the classic masculinity complex in Lacanian terms, for she does not cite Lacan; and it must be, as well, the source of the notion of oscillation—a notion which fits Adams's argument but does not fit Hamer's equally well. Actually, Adams's argument in "Of Female Bondage," the essay that Hamer cites, is only tangentially about lesbian sadomasochism—which the author, moreover, sharply distinguishes from lesbianism—and more centrally about masochism in general, while the notion of oscillation is developed by Adams in another essay which Hamer does not cite, "Per Os(cillation)," a reading of *hysterical* identification in the "Dora" case history (see note 7 below). Although obviously disagreeing with Adams's pronouncement that a lesbian "who is not a pervert [i.e., who is not a sadomasochist] is fundamentally similar to the traditional heterosexual woman" ("Of Female Bondage" 263), and rightly skeptical of the privileging of heterosexuality in feminist psychoanalysis (139), Hamer nevertheless seems to accept Adams's agenda, which is ostensibly to "divorce" the question of sexuality from the question of gender.

The ensuing confusion, I believe, derives from Hamer's failure to clarify the possible stakes that heterosexual feminists may have in such an agenda and in looking at lesbianism in light of Lacan's sexual (in)difference instead of the classic masculinity complex which, as Freud reminds them, applies to heterosexual feminists as well as lesbians. A further source of confusion is Hamer's casual use of the term *disavowal* à propos of the masculinity complex ("the disavowal of the 'fact' of castration in the little girl's belief that she can indeed be a little man" [140]) and synonymously with the nontechnical *re-fusal* ("a refusal of the meanings attached to castration" [147]). Dis-avowal [*Verleugnung*], the psychic mechanism underlying fetishism, is not involved in (the classic account of) the masculinity complex or in its repudiation [*Verwerfung*] of femininity. Freud, as is well known, excluded the possibility of fetishism in women.

I will return to these questions in subsequent chapters to take up the challenge of rethinking lesbian desire in relation to the mean-ings of castration (chapters 5 and 6), and to consider the respective stakes that lesbians and heterosexual feminists may have in redefin-ing the relations of sexuality and gender (chapter 4). But now I want to pursue Hamer's suggestion and reexamine the notion of mascu-linity complex in the classic psychoanalytic texts on lesbianism—or rather, female homosexuality, as it is called there—Freud's two case histories of 1915 and 1920, Jones (1927), Lampl–de Groot (1928), and Deutsch (1932); and, to start with, the text in which the term was first introduced, "Contributions to the Masculinity Complex in Women" (1924) by J. H. W. van Ophuijsen. It was delivered as a paper before the Dutch Psycho-Analytical Society in 1917—and hence Freud's reference to it in his 1919 paper "A Child Is Being Beaten" (*SE* 17: 191); but the author had taken his cue from an ear-lier paper of Freud's, "Some Character-Types Met with in Psycho-Analytic Work" (1916):

> As we learn from our psycho-analytic work all women feel that
> they have been injured in their infancy, and that through no fault
> of their own *they have been slighted and robbed of a part of their
> body;* and the bitterness of many a daughter towards her mother
> has as its ultimate cause the reproach that the mother has brought
> her into the world as a woman instead of a man. (As quoted by
> van Ophuijsen [39])

(The *Standard Edition* gives a slightly different translation, nota-bly for the words I italicized above, which it renders as "having been undeservedly cut short of something and unfairly treated" [*SE* 14: 315]).

Remarking on the direct relevance of Freud's comment to five female patients suffering from obsessional neurosis, whose com-mon symptoms he proposes to label "masculinity complex," van Ophuijsen draws up a list of features pertaining to the complex:

"the wish to be a boy developed from the desire to be able to uri-
nate like a boy" (40); "a wish to take possession of a person, instead of devoting and subjecting themselves to him; or . . . the
feeling that they wish to penetrate someone else, instead of themselves being penetrated" (42); "the idea of being a male, an idea
based on identification with the father or the brother" (47–48);
"marked homosexual tendencies" (48, but also 41, 44, 47, and 49);
"envy of men for their possession of [a male organ]" and "an attitude to women which must be regarded as an over-compensation
for her embitterment against her mother for withholding it from
her" (49).

Two authorial comments are noteworthy in this otherwise familiar picture and deserve a brief digression. First, van Ophuijsen records that "three of the five patients informed me of their own
accord that they possessed 'Hottentot nymphae'" (41) but does not
relate this fact to his earlier statement that patient P. "sits down as
though she had to guard against crushing her genitals, as if they
were male organs" (40). Nor does he wonder, as Freud does about
Dora's sexual knowledge, where their knowledge of such a term as
"Hottentot nymphae" might have come from, or what meaning the
patients may attribute to it and, consequently, to their body-image.
Unlike Freud's, van Ophuijsen's patients are not given the opportunity to respond as antagonists in his scenario. Others, however, have
taken up the term and examined its history and implications for the
enduring association—in the straight, white, and psychoanalytic
mind—of sexual pathology with both lesbianism and the black female body.[2] In particular, the work of Carla Scott, starting from and
extending well beyond Sander Gilman's, is so compelling that I will
stretch my digression to give at least an idea of the rich potential
that such a line of critical inquiry holds.

---

2. In "A Perversion Not Commonly Noted" (1913), Margaret Otis, Ph.D., reported
on "love-making between the white and colored girls" in a reform institution for girls.
While romantic friendships and homosexual relationships of "the ordinary form"
took place "even in high-class boarding-schools" (113), she noted, the interracial
practices were more intensely sexual and ritualized, "some of them of so coarse a
nature that they cannot be written down" (116). As Kathryn Hinojosa Baker remarks
in her study of interracial and lesbian relations in reform schools, Otis was relatively
progressive and "able to look favorably upon female bonding even among delinquent
girls, but she seems much less comfortable with racial mixing than with lesbianism"
("Delinquent Desire" 53). Subsequent psychological works on delinquents similarly
"locate the 'problem' of homosexuality among non-white people" (62).

In "Black Bodies, White Bodies," Sander Gilman traces the formation of the dominant nineteenth-century Western stereotype of the black woman as representative of an excessive female sexuality (primitive, atavistic, degenerate, diseased, pathological) to the medical accounts of autopsies performed in France, Germany, and England on Hottentot women, beginning in 1815 with the autopsy of Saartje Baartman, known as "the Hottentot Venus" and previously exhibited as a public spectacle throughout Europe. The illustrated accounts of pathological abnormalities in female anatomy focused on protruding buttocks (steatopygia) and "the so-called Hottentot apron, a hypertrophy of the labia and nymphae caused by the manipulation of the genitalia and serving as a sign of beauty among certain tribes, including the Hottentots and Bushmen as well as tribes in Basutoland and Dahomey" (232). These medical accounts recast in "scientific" terms the descriptions of African women brought back by eighteenth-century travelers but maintained and recirculated their ideological, racist view of black women (and blacks in general) as not only culturally but *genetically* inferior, indeed antithetical, to whites. They also provided a paradigm, a negative standard, of female beauty and sociosexual health that was subsequently applied by positivist medicine in the criminalization of certain white females such as prostitutes and lesbians, to whom was also attributed an excess of "lasciviousness" caused by sexual disease or degeneration.

Carla Scott, a doctoral student in History of Consciousness at the University of California, Santa Cruz, extends Gilman's analysis in her reading of Audre Lorde's "biomythography." Scott argues that, although the "blackness" of the Hottentot Venus eventually disappeared from the paradigm of what constituted an "abnormal" female sexuality—an elision that further contributed to the invisibility of black women in all forms of Western representation—in fact, even today, the association of lesbianism with prostitution and with blackness continues to subtend societal fears of excessive or uncontrolled female sexuality. For this reason, in *Zami*, Audre's claiming of her black and lesbian difference "forces both her white and black lesbian friends to contend with her historical agency in the face of this larger racial/sexual history that would reinvent her as dead" ("The Hottentot Effect" 70). And for this reason Scott reads *Zami* and other black lesbian novels as sites of resistance to "the legacy of the Hottentot Venus" and as the creation of a new discursive space for theorizing black lesbian subjectivity.

The second comment of some interest in van Ophuijsen's paper is that he does not find in any of his cases "what is called a masculine disposition; nor indeed a masculine appearance and expression, a contempt for men, or a predilection for masculine activities" (41). In other words, the fantasy of masculinity would not be related to gender but only to sexuality, which leads van Ophuijsen to posit, in conclusion, an "intimate connection between the masculinity complex, infantile masturbation of the clitoris and urethral erotism" (49). Now I would gloss this by recalling that at the time he wrote "A Child Is Being Beaten," where he cited van Ophuijsen, Freud was analyzing his twenty-three-year-old daughter Anna, who was one of the cases on whom the paper was based, as can be established almost conclusively by reading Anna Freud's own "Beating Fantasies and Daydreams" (1922), in addition to her official biography by Elizabeth Young-Bruehl.[3] Having the opportunity to respond, as it were, to her father/ analyst and to present her side of the story, Anna Freud confirms his interpretation point by point, but significantly extends the description by comparing the instinctually compulsive beating fantasy with the consciously orchestrated daydreams that transcribed it so as to assuage masturbatory guilt; and finally with the sublimation of the fantasy into a written story addressed to others, which no longer provides its author with instinctual satisfaction or erotic pleasure (or, for that matter, the guilt accompanying masturbation) but gratifies her ego's ambitious and moral demands by transforming "an autistic into a social activity" (157).

The barely disguised psychoanalytic confession one can read in this paper is a portentous example of the formative effect that parental fantasies (of which more will be said in later chapters) can have on the subject's own fantasies, sexuality, subjectivity, and self-representation. But, more to the immediate point regarding van

---

3. To psychoanalyze one's daughter and include the material in a published case history may appear less than proper today, but in the 1920s and 1930s, "when the psychoanalytic community was very small, analyses that crossed family and friendship lines were common" (114), writes Young-Bruehl, giving an impressive list of examples to which yet others could be added, such as Anna Freud's analyses of Dorothy Burlingham's children, Sigmund Freud's of Dorothy Burlingham, Melanie Klein's analyses of Jones's wife and children, and of her own son Eric, from which she published her first work of child analysis (Nunziante Cesaro 108), and so on.

Ophuijsen, while Anna Freud makes no mention of the masculinity complex in her paper, both her biographer and her biography attest to an identification with her father, analyst, and teacher that at once informed and took precedence over her fifty-some-year-long relationship with Dorothy Burlingham Tiffany and her children. On the question of their rumored lesbianism, Young-Bruehl is adamant: "Anna Freud's life partnership was chaste . . . she did not, in the 1920s or afterward, have a sexual relationship, with Dorothy Burlingham or with anyone else. She remained a 'vestal'—to use the word Marie Bonaparte later chose to signal both Anna Freud's virginity and her role as the chief keeper of her father's person and his science, psychoanalysis" (*Anna Freud* 137–38). By her own account in "Beating Fantasies and Daydreams" (written, however, three years before she met Dorothy Burlingham), Anna Freud handled her not-so-successfully repressed Oedipal wish and the guilt associated with masturbatory fantasies by sublimating instinctual demands with the socially gainful, if masculine, activities of writer, training analyst, and heir to the Freudian institution. Thus her public life and work supported not only Freud's own lack of insight into lesbianism (in this way, too, she was his Antigone) but also the dismissive attitude toward lesbianism implicit in van Ophuijsen's statement and characteristic of psychoanalysis ever after: "A pronounced homosexual component makes no difference to this [rivalry with men in the intellectual and artistic spheres], as the resulting rivalry in sexual matters expresses itself only in symptoms and symptomatic acts" (41). From van Ophuijsen's analysis, which yields so little in the way of narrative pleasure, one must infer that, since these women do not *act* sexually like men, their masculinity complex presents no threat. As will be seen presently, however, when women do act sexually toward women, there is not only need to be concerned but also richer material for a story.

The Master's Narrative

"A beautiful and clever girl of eighteen, belonging to a family of good standing, had aroused displeasure and concern in her parents by the devoted adoration with which she pursued a certain 'society lady' who was about ten years older than herself." Thus begins, in the best fashion of the genre, the master's narrative of "The Psycho-genesis of a Case of Homosexuality in a Woman" (1920). Immedi-ately before this sentence, in the first paragraph of the case history, Freud makes his customary invocation to the muse of method: since female homosexuality has been heretofore neglected by psychoana-lytic theory as it has been by the law, then even "the narration of a single case, not too pronounced in type, in which it was possible to trace its origin and development in the mind with complete cer-tainty and almost without a gap may, therefore, have a certain claim to attention" (*SE* 18: 147). But the presumption of "complete cer-tainty" that opens what promises to be a full account ("almost with-out a gap") of the heroine's homosexual development is cast in serious doubt several pages later:

> This amount of information about her seems meagre enough, nor can I guarantee that it is complete. It may be that the history of her youth was much richer in experiences; I do not know. As I have already said, the analysis was broken off after a short time, and therefore yielded an anamnesis not much more reliable than the other anamneses of homosexuals, which there is good cause to question. Further, the girl had never been neurotic, and came to the analysis without even one hysterical symptom, so that opportunities for investigating the history of her childhood did not present themselves so readily as usual. (155)

This pattern of alternating assertion and disclaimer, certainty and doubt, presumption and condescension recurs in each of the four parts that make up the story and the analysis, each part containing elements of both: a diegetic section about the girl's history is preceded or followed by an exegetic or interpretive section, often augmented by considerations of a theoretical nature in the form of digressions on analytic technique and dream interpretation, as well as digressions on bisexuality and homosexuality itself. For example, part II opens with these words: "After this highly discursive introduction I am only able to present a very concise summary of the sexual history of the case under consideration. In childhood the girl had passed through the normal attitude characteristic of the feminine Oedipus complex . . . " (155); and the paragraph ends with the disclaimer about the unreliable anamnesis I cited just above. Part IV begins with the words, "I now come back, after this digression, to the consideration of my patient's case" (167). While the pattern may recall the actual movement of the analysis, with its slow progress, setbacks, and occasional breakthroughs, it also underscores the contrast between Freud's confidence in his doctrinal premises and the need to have recourse to them in moments of uncertainty, as if to find reassurance and interpretive strength against the difficulties caused by the patient's unreliability, her unforthcoming or negative transference, and his own problematic (unavowed) countertransference.

The latter difficulties are not new to Freud, since he encountered them in the analysis of "Dora" and recorded them in "Fragment of an Analysis of a Case of Hysteria" (*SE* 7: 1–122), published in 1905. There, as well as here, the stumbling block is the patient's resistance to an interpretation in which the father "played the principal part" both in the diegesis (the patient's father or his substitutes) and in the exegesis (Freud, the analyst, with his undisguised wish to be loved: "In reality she transferred to me the sweeping repudiation of men which had dominated her ever since the disappointment she had suffered from her father. . . . But I still believe that, beside the intention to mislead me, the dreams partly expressed the wish to win my favour" [164–65]). Once again the patient resists Freud's attribution of her problems to her resistance against the Oedipal imperative, and will not gratify him by assenting to what he can see only as "her keenest desire—namely, revenge" (160) against her father(s). Dora's "revenge" had been to break off the analysis, to give him a two-week notice as one would a paid employee, one socially inferior; and so does this girl, in effect, "by rendering futile all his endeavours and by clinging to the illness" (164)—so much so that he is forced to break off treatment himself and recommend *a woman doctor* as someone better equipped to continue the treatment.

However, whereas Dora apparently had problems, manifested by her various hysterical symptoms, this girl clearly does not.[4] So Freud now must explain why her homosexuality is a problem. It would be simple enough to repeat that it is a problem only for her parents,

---

4. Or rather, did not upon entering treatment, for in the course of the analysis she produces "a lying dream": "The intention to mislead me, just as she did her father, certainly emanated from the preconscious, and may indeed have been conscious; it could come to expression by entering into connection with the unconscious wishful impulse to please her father (or father-substitute), and in this way it created a lying dream. The two intentions, to betray and to please her father, originated in the same complex" (166).

who sought his advice because they were preoccupied with social conventions (although the father is more than just angry with her, as Freud perceptively notes: "there was something about his daughter's homosexuality that aroused the deepest bitterness in him" [149]). But Freud does not leave it at that. He has some stake in proving that it is a problem for the girl as well. For one might ask: so what if "she changed into a man and took her mother [substitute] in place of her father as the object of her love" (158)—what's wrong with that? What's wrong with a woman's masculinity complex provided she is not in the least neurotic and has no symptoms? Why is this not simply one outcome of that "universal bisexuality of human beings" (157), which Freud has just defined, a moment ago, with olympian serenity: "In all of us, throughout life, the libido *normally* oscillates between male and female objects" (158; emphasis added)? Pressed closely by such feminist arguments, however, his answer is adamant: no, the problem is that in her the libido did not oscillate, and "henceforth she *remained* homosexual out of defiance against her father" (159; emphasis added). Defiance and resistance, in other words, are the specific problems, and the symptoms, of female homosexuality, what makes it perverse and such that, unlike neurosis and hysteria, psychoanalysis is impotent to alter it.

From the start, it must be added in all fairness, Freud did caution us that this was not "the ideal situation for analysis." The girl was not ill, had no symptoms, no complaint of her condition, and no will to change: "She did not try to deceive me by saying that she felt any urgent need to be freed from her homosexuality. On the contrary, she said she could not conceive of any other way of being in love" (153). Thus his analytic task was of the most difficult, for it consisted not in resolving a neurotic conflict but in converting one variety of genital organization into the other. And "such an achievement," Freud pleads, if possible at all, is "never an easy matter. On the contrary I have found success possible only in specially favourable circumstances, and even then the success essentially consisted in making access to the opposite sex (which had hitherto been barred) possible to a person restricted to homosexuality, thus restoring his full bisexual functions" (151).

At this point in the text, the narrative has given way to a theoretical digression on the topic of homosexuality, where Freud discusses various cases in his experience, their causal factors, their prognoses, and their resolutions. If one has the definite impression that he is speaking of male patients here, it is less by dint of the masculine pronoun, or the familiarity one may have with his only other written case of (presumed) female homosexuality, "A Case of Paranoia" (1915), than because of Freud's dispassionate and almost benevolent tone, which is set early on by his equanimous admission of having a rather poor track record in successful treatments. It is as if these failures, these patients' "abnormalities," and their bisexual or homosexual genital organizations did not affect his professional self-esteem or make his analytic task particularly difficult, as does the case of the girl.

On the positive side, however, at least as far as the reader is concerned, the difficulties brought about by the latter make Freud work harder, both as analyst and as theorist. Somehow he is impelled by this case to come to terms with homosexuality, at least in its female form, to try to figure out how it fits into his overall theory, to explain why "full bisexuality" is not really an option, or a cure, when the patient is a woman, and just what kind of perversion it is. For all his troubles, he scores one victory and one defeat. The victory is diegetic and analytic: the enigma of the story is solved by the birth of a brother, when the girl was sixteen, and the dénouement provides the explanation for her homosexuality as a rejection of the Oedipal imperative compounded by revenge against the father. The enigma, as the narrative presents it, is: why did the girl become "a homosexual attracted to mature women, and remained so ever since" (156), when, in fact, her mother favored her sons, generally acted unkindly toward her, and vied with her for the father's love? Freud answers:

> The explanation is as follows. It was just when the girl was experiencing the revival of her infantile Oedipus complex at puberty that she suffered her great disappointment. She became keenly conscious of the wish to have a child, and a male one; that what she desired was her *father's* child and an image of *him*, her consciousness was not allowed to know. And what happened next? It was not *she* who bore the child, but her unconsciously hated rival, her mother. Furiously resentful and embittered, she turned away from her father and from men altogether. After this first great reverse she forswore her womanhood and sought another goal for her libido.
>
> In doing so she behaved just as many men do who after a first distressing experience turn their backs for ever upon the faithless female sex and become woman-haters. (157)

There are as many holes in this explanation as there are turns in the narrative: the girl is conscious of wanting a child but unconscious of wanting the father's child (his image); she is unconscious of hating the mother/rival yet consciously rejects her and, with her, both femininity and motherhood; she consciously hates and defies the father but unconsciously (still loves and) identifies with him; she consciously falls in love with a woman and becomes a woman-hater. Because the toggle-switch term *conscious/unconscious*—which Freud here uses in the common, rather than technical or systemic, sense— acts as a sort of joker in the exegetic game, the holes turn out to be, rather, loopholes, and make it as difficult to disprove or argue against each of the above propositions as it would be to prove them. However, it is clear that the whole house of cards rests on the founding stone of the positive Oedipus imperative (the wish for a child by the father), which is the first move of Freud's interpretive "journey" here as well as in the theory of female sexuality he will develop in later years, and the asymmetrical counterpart of the male's positive Oedipus complex—whence his conclusive parallel with men, here, leading to the last, paradoxical proposition: women who love women hate women. (Freud's notorious disregard for a girl's erotic attachment to the mother—what he would later call the negative Oedipus complex—was subsequently redressed and amended by women analysts such as Lampl–de Groot and Deutsch but, I will argue, not always with significant gain as regards changing the paradigm.)

On the strength of this interpretation, finally, it would seem that the girl's masculinity complex, already "strongly marked" since childhood, is reinforced and perverted by the "occasion" of the mother's late pregnancy, which pushes it over the brink and makes the girl "fall a victim to homosexuality" (168). Freud's hard-won interpretive victory, however, is a Pyrrhic victory in that it is accompanied by a defeat in the theoretical project of explaining homosexuality. For in part IV of the text, as he retraces forward the steps which the analysis had followed backwards, he must admit that "we no longer get the impression of an inevitable sequence of events which could not have been otherwise determined. We notice at once that there might have been another result" (167). This statement all but unravels the complicated exegetic skein: the causes of the girl's homosexuality, which the analytic narration reconstructed "with complete certainty and almost without a gap" into a seamless narrative, where every "external factor" could be accounted for, are now said to be by no means a necessary or sufficient condition of her homosexual disposition; a disposition that may or may not have been acquired but, at any rate, at least in part, "has to be ascribed to inborn constitution" (169). And if we search the text for signs of what that inborn constitution might be, we can find only that "strongly marked 'masculinity complex'" which the girl "had brought along with her from her childhood":

> A spirited girl, always ready for romping and fighting, she was not at all prepared to be second to her slightly older brother; after inspecting his genital organs [p. 155] she had developed a pronounced envy for the penis, and the thoughts derived from this envy still continued to fill her mind. She was in fact a feminist; she felt it to be unjust that girls should not enjoy the same freedom as boys, and rebelled against the lot of woman in general. (169)

Freud's concern with theorizing homosexuality beyond the context of this particular case—and hence what I have called his theoretical defeat—is evident in the digressions on the topic which appear in parts I and IV, where he makes reference to the sexological arguments he had addressed in the *Three Essays* fifteen years earlier, and which, by 1920, had already become known or popularized outside the domain of medical knowledge. Thus, in part I, Freud entertains the queries he expects of his non-specialistic readership: "Readers unversed in psycho-analysis will long have been awaiting an answer to two other questions. Did this homosexual girl show physical characteristics plainly belonging to the opposite sex [she did not], and did the case prove to be one of congenital or acquired (later-developed) homosexuality?" (153). He then offers the case history itself as his answer: "The second question, whether this was a case of congenital or acquired homosexuality, will be answered by the whole history of the patient's abnormality and its development. The study of this will show how far this question is a fruitless and inapposite one" (154).

Nonetheless, the fruitless question reappears in part IV, where Freud unabashedly contradicts himself by reproposing its terms as still viable instead of displacing or replacing them with something more apposite. He states that, if at first the analysis indicated that this might be "a case of late-acquired homosexuality," a fuller "consideration of the material impels us to conclude that it is rather a case of congenital homosexuality" (169). The subsequent cautionary remark, that "it would be best not to attach too much value to this way of stating the problem" (170), does not sufficiently undercut the previous statement to dispel the reader's sense of having just read a diagnosis of congenital homosexuality. In a similar way, in the *Three Essays*, he had reintroduced and continued to use as valid the notions of perversion and genital primacy which he had previously criticized and effectively shown to be theoretically untenable.

In "The Psychogenesis of a Case of Homosexuality in a Woman," the final appeal to an inborn constitution that might have affected what appeared to be an "acquired disposition (if it *was* really acquired)," as Freud perversely insinuates (169), leaves the reader with no clearer view of homosexuality—or, for that matter, bisexuality—than could be gleaned from the *Three Essays* and, if anything, with greater uncertainty.[5] It leaves Freud's position on homosexuality enmeshed in that same structural ambiguity or inconsistency that is so conspicuous in the *Three Essays*. Once again, the pivot on which the inconsistency turns is the imposition of a structuring narrative, or a structuring fantasy, onto the "material" of the case history. In other words, again the theory strains against the structure but is finally contained, as perhaps all theories must be, by a passionate fiction. In this case, the fiction is the fantasy of the "positive" Oedipus complex—the fantasy that a girl must desire the father and wish to bear a child in his image.

One Story in Two Versions

Other critics have noted the inconsistencies, reversals, or exegetic somersaults in Freud's account of female homosexuality in this case history, which in some respects resembles that of Dora published twenty years earlier, although here homosexuality, and not hysteria, is the explicit problem to be addressed.[6] But if both times

---

5. This is one more, sterling example in support of Dollimore's thesis that "the perverse dynamic" is operative in Freud's own narrative (see Dollimore 188 and my discussion of it in chapter 1).

6. The similarities, also noted by Merck and Roof, include the length of the analysis and its early termination, the patient's attempted suicide, her choice of an older female object, her resistance or failed transference, and Freud's unavowed countertransference.

Freud failed to cure or resolve the patients' problems, here he takes on directly the issue of female homosexuality, which he had relegated to the footnotes, almost an afterthought, in Dora's case (*SE* 7: 105 and 120); and if the unconscious "homosexual current of feeling" he surmised in Dora could be ignored in the analysis of hysteria, even as he remarked on the evidence of a "fairly strong homosexual predisposition" in neurotics (*SE* 7: 60), here he can no longer evade the issue. But what he then does is perform another disappearing act. For the unnamed girl of the "Psychogenesis," as Judith Roof cleverly puts it, "goes from being a daughter who loves her father to [a] girl who loves a woman to a son who loves her mother to a son who loves his father" (*A Lure of Knowledge* 211).

In her reading of the case history, Roof shows the various stations of Freud's interpretive journey, through which the discussion of female homosexuality is constantly brought back to male homosexuality and explained in terms of the latter: the daughter is (like) a son when she loves the mother; the daughter's love for the mother is (really) love for the father; the daughter's masculine identification with the father mimes a male homosexual attraction because "she becomes a man in order to love her father better" (204). Roof concludes that "Freud reads lesbians" either to find their repressed Oedipal wish for the father (to find them heterosexual) or "to make them the pretext for a more compelling consideration of male homosexuality—positions that can include and reflect Freud's own desire" (213). And she attributes Freud's evasion of "the lesbian possibility" for Dora to "his own potential homosexuality as the case follows the course of his dying friendship with Fliess" (182–83). It is quite possible that in speaking of Freud's "potential homosexuality" Roof overstates what might have been less dramatically a conscious homosexual wish toward Fliess; that is to say, a component of Freud's strong homosocial bonding with him during the time of the Dora analysis, which would subsequently wane for equally homosocial reasons, such as theoretical disagreement, as Jones suggests (*The Life and Work of Sigmund Freud* 204–208), or Freud's ethical and professional distrust of Fliess subsequent to the latter's malpractice in the Emma Eckstein operation (see Young-Bruehl 26). On the other hand, Roof's speculation might be validated by Freud's symptomatic fainting in Munich in 1912 and his remark, twelve years after the end of his relationship with Fliess, that "my relation to that man" was rooted in "some piece of unruly homosexual feeling" (Jones 207).

Either way, her point is well taken that Freud equates female homosexuality with both male homosexuality and female heterosexuality (Roof 183), and that both positions "include and reflect" his own desire. Or, as I would rephrase it: both positions, as they relate to the desiring subject/author of the text, are part of the fantasy which structures the narrative of "Psychogenesis" and the passionate fiction of Freud's theory. What makes this observation even more compelling is Roof's somber remark that "while we may see Freud as hopelessly patriarchal and sometimes obsolete, this same scenario replays itself in contemporary culture," reproducing "confusions and inconsistencies that tend to displace or erase the figure of the lesbian" (213). This, I will add, holds true for psychoanalysis in general and for feminist psychoanalytic theory in particular: Adams's "Of Female Bondage," cited above, is only one case in point. Indeed the assimilation or incorporation of lesbianism into female sexuality *tout court* occurs most conspicuously in contemporary feminist readings of Dora.

A paradigmatic figure of feminine resistance to patriarchy, Dora and her case history have been written about from many angles and critical concerns, but a recurrent theme is her alleged homosexuality. In the collection edited by Bernheimer and Kahane, for example, most of the essays mention or focus on Dora's "homosexuality" (Gearhart 114), her "homosexual desire for Frau K" (Moi 195), her "homosexual desires" (Ramas 164), her "preoedipal desire for the mother" (Kahane 28, referring to Ramas), her "beautiful, staggering, feminine homosexuality" (Cixous, quoted by Gallop 217), even her "lesbianism" (Gallop 217). Roof, too, following Gallop, unhesitantly refers to Dora's "lesbianism" and footnotes other essays in the collection (Rose, Gearhart, and Hertz) "that recognize the role of lesbian sexuality [*sic*] in the Dora case" (Roof 263). Thus it appears that what might be expected to be a rather complicated passage from one's bisexual or homosexual wishes or tendencies—in this case, Dora's—to actual homosexuality or—in this case, anachronistically—lesbianism, is made much easier in critical writing. One may well wonder why. For, if Freud gives the same interpretation in both cases, attributing to the girl as he did to Dora a wish for the father's penis and in effect telling two versions of the same story, yet the difference between the two characters (for such they are, constructed in Freud's narrative) is nonetheless quite evident.

One, the girl of the "Psychogenesis," asserts and acts upon her homosexual feelings, much to Freud's and her parents' displeasure; in the other, those feelings are merely inferred by the analyst/narrator and remain unconscious to Dora (whence, perhaps, the symptoms). To call Dora a lesbian, therefore, is to blur the distinction between fantasy consciously expressed and presumed unconscious fantasy, between homosexual object-choice and same-sex identification (this seems to be Lacan's reading of Dora's fascination with Frau K.), between homosexuality with or without masculinity complex and symptomatic or hysterical (bisexual) oscillation.[7] While an argument can be made for the latter with regard to Dora, this is clearly not pertinent to the girl of "Psychogenesis" who, Freud deplores, did not oscillate but "remained homosexual"—whatever her reasons. The question then arises: What and whose purposes does the blurring serve?

In pondering this question, I notice that the sliding of Dora's unconscious homosexual impulses into homosexuality or lesbianism seems to become easier still when the two case histories are read together; and their comparison, as Mandy Merck observes in her reading of "Psychogenesis," "has proved 'irresistable' to commenta-

---

7. In "Per Os(cillation)" Parveen Adams takes up a comment of Lacan's (also noted by Hertz 228) to reach her thesis that "hysterical identification is characterized . . . by oscillation" (9): when Freud says that Dora "pictured to herself a scene of sexual gratification *per os*" between her father and Frau K. (*SE* 7: 48), he uses the Latin term to mean fellatio, but by that expression Dora meant cunnilingus. Adams remarks that, depending on which meaning one takes, Dora's identification would be with her father (masculine) or with Frau K. (feminine); in one case she sucks, in the other she is sucked. But in view of the interchangeability of positions in fantasy discussed by Freud in "Instincts and Their Vicissitudes" (*SE* 14), Adams argues that Dora takes both the masculine and the feminine position, and further that "identification with one implies identification with the other" (17). From here onward, her argument becomes obscure to me, veering off toward a discussion of masochism, then to come back in conclusion to hysterical identification, which is now generalized as "the mechanism involved in the production of masculinity and femininity within the Oedipus complex." But since hysterical identification "involves the oscillation, not the fixing of positions" (28), Freud's theory of sexual difference does not work; only Lacan's theory of the phallus explains how humans take up relatively fixed, masculine or feminine, positions (around the phallus). While I admit to not following the move from Dora's hysterical identification to oscillation as a generalized model for identification and (bisexual) object-choice, I am willing to guess that Adams is simply taking for granted Lacan's notion of "the hysteric's desire" in his reading of Dora, which I will discuss a few pages below.

tors" (35). It seems to me that the reason for such lack of resistance is the possibility to read the story of the girl, with her conscious and explicit homosexuality, back into the story of Dora, and thus to find in its heroine a "homosexuality" that according to Freud was an unconscious homosexual wish.[8] The irresistible gain in reading Dora retroactively, as it were, is lucidly stated by Rose, who was possibly the first to do so. Halfway through her "Dora: Fragment of an Analysis," Rose devotes a single paragraph to "Psychogenesis"; embedded at the center of her reading of Dora, this paragraph is the first of the section following the subheading "In Fact She Was a Feminist." Because this statement has been very influential on subsequent feminist readings, and because the line I italicize represents a view of female sexuality now shared even by critics who disagree with Rose's Lacanian positions, I will quote the entire paragraph.

> The reference comes from Freud's case on the "Psychogenesis of Homosexuality in a Woman" [*sic*], and in one sense the step from the failure of the case of Dora to this case, which appeared in 1920, is irresistible—not, however, in order to classify Dora as homosexual in any simple sense, but precisely because in this case Freud was led to an *acknowledgment of the homosexual factor in all feminine sexuality,* an acknowledgment which was to lead to his revision of his theories of the Oedipus complex for the girl. For in this article he is in a way at his most radical, rejecting the concept of cure, insisting that the most psychoanalysis can do is restore the original bisexual disposition of the patient, defining homosexuality as nonneurotic. Yet, at the same time, his explanation of this last factor—the lack of neurosis ascribed to the fact that the object-choice was established not in infancy but after puberty—is then undermined by his being obliged to trace back the homosexual

---

8. Freud might have been wrong, of course, but the genre of the case history prevents us from having any other knowledge of the patient than what the text can produce. In this case, a small amount of additional information is given by Felix Deutsch, an analyst who saw Dora twice as a forty-two-year-old woman and, after her death some thirty years later, published a brief note about her life and continuing symptoms. But from this inexplicably vicious note—which calls Dora a "most repulsive" hysteric and seems to rejoice in her death from cancer of the colon as, at last, a real illness after the hysterical "trouble with her bowels" and so many other conversion symptoms (Felix Deutsch 43)—one learns that Dora hated her husband, reproached her son for his inattention, and loved only her brother; and nothing at all about any possible homosexuality. What is in Freud's case history is all there is on that score (cf. also the brief "Biographical Note" on Ida Bauer in Bernheimer and Kahane 33–35).

attraction to a moment prior to the oedipal instance, the early
attachment to the mother, in which case either the girl is neurotic
(which she clearly is not) or all women are neurotic (which indeed
they might be). ("Dora" 135–36; emphasis added)

The claims made here for this particular text ("Freud at his most
radical") seem somewhat exaggerated. In the first place, what led
Freud to revise his theories of the female Oedipus complex can
hardly be *an acknowledgment of the homosexual factor* in female sexuality since he had spoken of the subject's bisexual disposition as
early as the *Three Essays,* and the 1915 addition states that "all human beings are capable of making a homosexual object-choice and
have in fact made one in their unconscious" (*SE* 7: 145). Second, the
girl's pre-Oedipal attachment to the mother, which Freud later reformulated as the negative Oedipus complex, surely must be the cause,
instead of the consequence, of the *homosexual factor* in feminine
sexuality. Thus it is not Freud, but rather Rose, whom the analysis of
a case of homosexuality in one woman leads to the acknowledgment
of *the homosexual factor in all feminine sexuality.* Third, Freud never
defined homosexuality per se as neurotic (at worst he defined it as a
perversion, although perverts, too, can be neurotic [cf. Sachs]) and,
in this regard, was much more radical in the *Three Essays,* where he
excluded the hypothesis of innate inversion, than in "Psychogenesis," where he reintroduces a strong suggestion of congenital homosexuality. Moreover, to me as to Freud's patient—and I would wager
to most homosexual, lesbian, or gay readers of the case history—
Freud is hardly at his most radical when he attempts to "restore" a
bisexual disposition in a homosexual patient.

What can it be, then, that Rose finds so radical here? And how
does her generalizing from one woman to all women occur? The
concluding sentence of the paragraph quoted above provides a clue:
since the girl's homosexuality is traced back to the pre-Oedipal attachment to the mother, and since that attachment clearly must obtain for all women, then all women must somehow partake of
homosexuality. This seems to be the logic of the passage. And never
mind that not all women are homosexual; never mind that the particular case at hand is *not* illuminated by the universal female pre-
Oedipal attachment (all women might be neurotic, but this woman
clearly is not). Having found the possibility of claiming some kind of

homosexuality for all women, Rose then goes back to Dora and the question of femininity, which is, she concludes, the impossibility of feminine desire, "the impossibility of satisfaction" (144) or "the impossibility of subject *and* desire" (146). And never mind, again, that the girl's particular desire was evidently quite possible, if perhaps not satisfiable in the given situation.

I do not mean by this to imply that *all* female desire is possible, Dora being a good example of the contrary. And, to be sure, Rose's poignant plaint for "woman as object and subject of desire—the impossibility of either position" (146) resonates widely among women, feminist and not. There is good cause. But if that impossibility is grounded in the loss of the mother and in the consequent failure to assume one's feminine body and one's desire in relation to what Lacan calls "the virile object," then the impossibility of "subject *and* desire" cannot be ascribed to homosexuality, which is precisely the displacement of the paternal signifier and the circumvention of the law that would bar the female subject's access to the female body.

There is something of a paradox in locating homosexuality in the female child's pre-Oedipal relation to the mother, a relation which is by definition prephallic and pregenital, whereas the term *homosexual* takes its meaning within the understanding of sexual difference brought about by the Oedipus. The paradox, in Dora's case as in Rose's, stands on what seems to me a false equation between hysteria (as bisexual oscillation) and homosexuality, an equation that may be traced back to Lacan. For he, too, reads Dora. Moreover, as it happens, in his 1964 seminar, he also reads Dora and "Psychogenesis" (very briefly) together.

To his credit, Lacan does not read Dora as homosexual, although in discussing her alone he is ambiguous. "As is true for all women," he says of Dora, "the problem of her condition is fundamentally that of accepting herself as an object of desire for the man" ("Intervention on Transference" 99). Because of his countertransference, Freud failed to point out to her "the real value of the object that Frau K. is for Dora. That is, not an individual, but a mystery, a mystery of her femininity, by which I mean her bodily femininity" (97–98). As Lacan rereads her second dream, what Dora seeks through Frau K. is "to gain access to this recognition of her femininity" and "the assumption of her own body, failing which she remains open to the functional fragmentation (to refer to the theoretical contribution of the mirror stage) that constitutes conversion symptoms" (98). Had Freud not been detained by his "sympathy" for Herr K., he might have "directed Dora toward a recognition of what Frau K. was for her . . . thereby opening up the path to a recognition of the virile object" (99), and the treatment might have been successful. But, on the other hand, Lacan concludes, the function of transference is such that, despite "his insufficient appreciation of the homosexual tie binding Dora to Frau K." (100), Freud's persistent identification with Herr K. might—given time, or had the analysis continued— "have set off Dora in the favorable direction: that which would have led her to the object of her real interest" (102).

This oracular statement, which refuses to disambiguate what Dora's "real interest" might have been, is proffered in the context of Lacan's "Intervention on Transference" (written in 1951); and transference, not Dora's desire, is what is at issue for him there. Returning to Dora in 1964, this time invoked as the paradigmatic instance of the hysteric's desire and in reference to "the famous case of the female homosexual," he states unequivocally:

> Freud, on this occasion, failed to formulate correctly what was the object both of the hysteric's desire and of the female homosexual's desire. . . . Freud could not yet see—for lack of those structural reference-points that I hope to bring out for you—that the hysteric's desire—which is legible in the most obvious way in the case—is *to sustain the desire of the father*—and, in the case of Dora, *to sustain it by procuring.* [In the other case,] the female homosexual finds another solution, that is, to defy the desire of the father. [But that solution brings about her attempt at suicide, and hence:] Literally, she can no longer conceive, other than by destroying herself, of *the function she had, that of showing the father* how one is, oneself, an abstract, heroic, unique phallus, devoted to the service of a lady. (*Four Fundamental Concepts* 38– 39; emphasis added)

This passage makes it certainly easier to sympathize with Rose and her conception of the impossibility of subject and desire for woman, as Lacan would have her. It also helps to understand the *function* of female homosexuality in Lacan's world. To summarize: a female subject's homosexual interests—pursued by way of a masculine intermediary, with whom the subject must identify in order to be a subject (here is the masculine identification)—lead her (the subject) to gain recognition of her feminine body and to "assume" it (own it, or accept it) as an object of desire for the man; in this best-case scenario, one must infer, the subject will become safely hetero-sexual and have no symptoms. Alternatively, the homosexual inter-ests lead to a provocative but futile performance of masculinity intended to defy the desire of the father, and yet at the same time seek his recognition ("show" him) that the subject is herself a phal-lus, that is, the signifier of the father's desire. In this scenario, as well, the subject is sustaining—actually embodying—the desire of the father. In other words, since the homosexual woman's desire is the hysteric's desire, then for the girl of "Psychogenesis" and Dora it is again one story in two versions.[9]

Rose's reading of the story introduces the variant of the pre-Oedi-pal attachment to the mother, but its structural function remains the same one that a Frau K. could perform for a Dora in what I have called Lacan's best-case scenario. This variant, however, is a very important one. The idea that the daughter's relation to the mother is an absolutely central one, is virtually unquestioned in feminist psy-choanalytic studies in spite of the disregard, if not outright con-tempt, that both Freud and Lacan have shown for the maternal figure in relation to female sexuality; and the mother-daughter rela-tion has become a major stake in competing definitions of lesbian-ism and female sexuality or subjectivity. I will discuss its currency in contemporary feminist psychoanalytic studies in chapter 4. What I am about to explore here is the place of the mother in female homo-sexuality in conjunction, or in contrast, with the masculinity com-plex as presented in the texts of early Freudian psychoanalysis.

Now, to conclude this part of my argument: If a woman's desire can be only "the hysteric's desire," then the impossibility of her being both subject and desiring, "the impossibility of subject *and* desire" (Rose, "Dora" 146), is final and irrevocable. But that impossi-bility rests on the assumption—on Rose's theoretical assumption and on a woman's assumption—of the father's desire. "She was in fact a feminist," Freud thought of his homosexual patient who re-sisted that assumption; but we now know that feminism in fact is not enough. Though it may help transgress the law of the father,

---

9. On the structure of this story and its mythical and axiological status in Western cultures, I have written at length in "Desire in Narrative" (*Alice Doesn't*, chapter 5).

feminism does not counter or circumvent the desire of the father *if* the subject assumes it, whether fantasmatically or epistemologically; and that desire will coexist ambivalently with feminism for such a female subject, creating precisely the impossibility so keenly expressed by Rose.

Twists and Turns

Because the Oedipus complex and its correlative, the castration complex, are two of the structuring fantasies of psychoanalytic theory, it is not surprising that other analysts-theorists, especially the women who were Freud's immediate disciples, concerned themselves primarily with the manifestations, consequences, and interrelations of the two complexes in women. Nor is it surprising that it was their work that influenced the successive revisions of Freud's own views on female sexuality, for, as he realized, women patients were more forthcoming with women doctors and more willing to supply them with the necessary clinical evidence. Published in 1928, Jeanne Lampl–de Groot's "The Evolution of the Oedipus Complex in Women" had the advantage of drawing upon several other studies that elaborated on Freud's initial formulation of the complexes, including his own papers on "The Dissolution of the Oedipus Complex" (1924) and the now-infamous "Some Psychical Consequences of the Anatomical Distinction between the Sexes" (1925).

Lampl–de Groot's original contribution to the theory of sexuality is her emphasis on the female negative Oedipus complex, which Freud had outlined in *The Ego and the Id* (1923), but not in its specific configuration in women. More affirmatively than Freud, she postulates in the female child an active erotic attachment to the mother (negative Oedipus attitude) during the so-called phallic phase, which will be given up, together with onanism, as a result of the castration complex and the narcissistic wound that it entails. The wish for a child (which for her, unlike the wish for a penis, is a realizable wish) thus "acquires for the girl a similar narcissistic value" to that of the penis for the boy (337). *For this reason alone,* Lampl–de Groot argues, the girl adopts the positive Oedipus attitude and turns her love toward the father, seeking from him a narcissistic reimbursement, so to speak; if or when the request is not

met, the girl falls back on her previous and more spontaneous love
for the mother. Therefore, if the castration complex ushers in the
positive Oedipus complex, it is because it has succeeded in overcoming the earlier and more typically female negative Oedipus complex.

> In contradistinction to Freud, we are assuming that the castration-
> complex in female children is a secondary formation and that its
> precursor is the negative Oedipus situation. Further, that it is only
> from the latter that the castration-complex derives its great psychic
> significance, and it is probably this negative attitude which enables
> us to explain in greater detail many peculiarities subsequently met
> with in the mental life of women. (340–41)[10]

Among the latter she outlines three possible paths of development
alternative to "normal" femininity, which correspond somewhat to
Freud's schema, but not altogether. First: If the repression of the girl's
negative Oedipus attitude is not successful, or if it is, but her love for
the father is also subsequently disappointed, then she will either not
give up her "masculine attitude" or resume it after the failed attempt
to love the father passively. "In extreme cases," Lampl–de Groot remarks, this denial of castration (i.e., the masculinity complex) leads
to manifest homosexuality (338). Second: "The girl does not *entirely*
deny the fact of castration, but she seeks overcompensation for her
bodily inferiority on some plane other than the sexual (in her work,
her profession). But in so doing she represses sexual desire altogether, that is, remains sexually unmoved" (338; emphasis added).
Third: "A woman may form relationships with a man, and yet remain
nevertheless inwardly attached to the first object of her love, her
mother. She is obliged to be frigid in coitus because she does not
really desire the father or his substitute, but the mother" (339). This
latter psychic form, consisting of an apparently feminine sexual passivity but an actually masculine sexual aggressivity, Lampl–de Groot

---

10. In "Some Psychical Consequences of the Anatomical Distinction between the
Sexes" (1925), Freud wrote: "In girls the Oedipus complex is a secondary formation.
The operations of the castration complex precede it and prepare for it. As regards the
relation between the Oedipus and castration complexes there is a fundamental contrast between the two sexes. Whereas in boys the Oedipus complex is destroyed by
the castration complex, in girls it is made possible and led up to by the castration
complex. This contradiction is cleared up if we reflect that the castration complex
always operates in the sense implied in its subject-matter: it inhibits and limits masculinity and encourages femininity" (*SE* 19: 256).

suggests, would explain women's fantasies of prostitution, as well as actual homosexuality in (female) prostitutes.

Compared with Freud's more schematic model of the possible outcomes of the female Oedipal drama in "Femininity" (*SE* 22: 126), Lampl–de Groot offers a more detailed articulation, especially with regard to the masculinity complex.

Freud:

1. normal femininity (passive [positive] Oedipus attitude)
2. masculinity complex up to manifest homosexuality (perversion)
3. psychic illness (sexual inhibition or neurosis)

Lampl–de Groot:

1. normal femininity (with or without masochistic pleasure in the repeated submission to castration)
2. a. masculinity complex up to homosexuality
   b. masculinity complex, sublimated (without sexual desire)
   c. masculinity complex, disguised as femininity (but with [hetero]sexual frigidity)
3. Here, instead of outright psychic illness, are listed the two possible causes of any "disturbances in the woman's development to complete femininity" (339): either an unsuccessful repression of her phallic attachment to the mother (negative Oedipus), or a return to it after the disappointment of her passive attachment to the father (positive Oedipus).

What this third path leads to, however, is none other than the aethiology of the masculinity complex, which thus turns out to be *the* category comprehensive of all psychic disturbances in women. According to Lampl–de Groot, then, all "disturbances" in female psychic development are due to the negative Oedipus complex, whose overwhelming presence in her model of female sexuality thus appears to balance out Freud's emphasis on the positive Oedipus complex.

Moreover, the structuring narrative of the negative Oedipus complex would seem to supply a confirmation, at least in women, for the bisexuality Freud had initially postulated in the *Three Essays* and to which he often resorted subsequently, in the effort to account for homosexuality. But it is interesting to note that, in Lampl–de Groot's clinical evidence, such "bisexuality"—which Freud was later to allude to with the phrase "the enigma of women"—is in effect *an inhibition of sexuality:* "the patient constantly oscillated between a heterosexual and homosexual love. She had a tendency to regress to her first love-relation—with her mother—and at this stage tried to deny the fact of castration. To make up, however, she had to refrain from onanism and sexual gratification of any kind. She could not derive satisfaction from her husband . . . " (344–45).[11] This seldom-mentioned detail is particularly noteworthy with regard to the contemporary feminist studies I discuss above, which place so positive an emphasis on women's bisexuality or (hysterical) oscillation between masculine and feminine positions.

In conclusion, contrary to what one might have hoped or anticipated, Lampl–de Groot's richer articulation of female Oedipal relations does not lead to a new or better understanding of female homosexuality. For her as for Freud, female homosexuality is an "extreme" form of the masculinity complex based on the denial of castration and/or the regression to the infantile phallic phase. One further point of disagreement with him scores a minor victory against the father but adds little more than a twist to the well-known story:

> The phase of the negative Oedipus attitude, lying, as it does, so far back in the patient's mental history, cannot be reached until the analysis has made very considerable progress. Perhaps with a male analyst it may be very hard to bring this period to light at all. For it is difficult for a female patient to enter into rivalry with the father-analyst, so that possibly treatment under these conditions cannot get beyond the analysis of the positive Oedipus attitude. The homosexual tendency, which can hardly be missed in any analyses, may then merely give the impression of a later reaction to the disappointment experienced at the father's hands. In our cases,

---

11. A couple of years later Freud would write: "Regressions to the fixations of the pre-Oedipal phases very frequently occur; in the course of some women's lives there is a repeated alternation between periods in which masculinity or femininity gains the upper hand. Some portion of what we men call 'the enigma of women' may perhaps be derived from this expression of bisexuality in women's lives" ("Femininity," *SE* 22: 131).

however, it was clearly a regression to an earlier phase—one which may help us to understand better the enormous psychic significance that the lack of a penis has in the erotic life of women. (345)

Analytic Mothering

More suggestive for my purposes is a later paper by Helene Deutsch, based on the analysis of eleven cases, which allows for an explanation of female homosexuality not dependent upon the masculinity complex and only indirectly dependent on the castration complex. Like Lampl–de Groot, Deutsch postulates a "return to the mother" after the disappointment of the Oedipal wish for the father's child but, unlike her, articulates it as the regression to a pre-Oedipal phase of infantile sexuality "preceding the phallic organization" ("On Female Homosexuality" 501); that is to say, a phase in which libidinal attachments are defined by the component instincts, notably sadistic impulses and masochistic pleasure. The regression occurs during a phase that Deutsch characterizes as "a thrust into passivity" (*Passivitätsschub*); this takes place after the phallic phase and the establishment of the Oedipus complex (which, like Freud and unlike Lampl–de Groot, she considers only in its "positive" form, manifested in the wish for an anal baby by the father). After the disappointment of this Oedipal wish, the girl "returns" to the mother, seeking to recover the erotic pleasures and narcissistic satisfaction enjoyed during the pre-Oedipal relation. The latter, however, Deutsch does not construe simply as a blissful relation of fusion and undifferentiation, as feminist critics tend to do nowadays; on the contrary, she describes it as one marked by strong sadistic impulses, guilt feelings, fear, and intense masochistic excitement.

It is precisely the sadistic impulses toward the mother that, Deutsch speculates, during the phallic phase and under the blow of the castration complex, have provided the impetus for the girl's change of object and facilitated her transition to the (positive) Oedipus complex, with its attempt to exchange the wish for the penis with the wish for a baby, as well as the development of a passive masochistic attitude toward the father. Thereafter, while some of the aggressive impulses are also diverted toward the disappointing father (thus in some cases contributing to the masculinity complex), many remain attached to the mother, giving rise to a "bisexual oscillation between father and mother, which may eventuate in neurosis, heterosexuality or inversion"; but, whatever the outcome, the ambivalence usually results in "an obstinate narcissistic standstill . . . a standstill in the pendulum swing of libido" (505), and a severe emotional blocking of affect, which may be addressed successfully in analysis.

Much of the strength of Deutsch's argument resides in her narration of her patients' histories, especially two cases of overt and active homosexuality, which are atypical in psychoanalytic literature for two reasons: (a) one of them has practically no connection with the masculinity complex, and (b) both are said to have been resolved by analysis. What she means by resolution is, also atypically, not the renunciation of homosexuality or the recovery of "full bisexuality" (Freud's best-case scenario) but rather the disappearance of symptoms with the overcoming of the affective block or "narcissistic standstill," and the consequent ability for the patient to live out her homosexuality actively and in a manner that I would describe as authorized. Let's see how.

In the first case cited by Deutsch, the patient is a married woman, "blonde and feminine," and the mother of several children, who is suffering from depression, anxiety, and suicidal tendencies. "Although the patient was aware of her sexual inversion, she did not indulge in homosexual practices . . . even when she knew that the women [she fell in love with] had a perverse tendency like her own" (484). The analysis reveals that "the nucleus of her neurosis as well as of her perversion" (486; Deutsch uses Freud's words almost verbatim) was not the castration complex or penis envy, as Freud always axiomatically maintained. Indeed, penis envy "did not stand in the center of her personality, either characterologically or in her behavior towards men. She was not a woman with a 'masculinity complex,'" and what masculinity she had was "splendidly sublimated" in intellectual activity (489–90). Rather—and here Deutsch repeats herself, underscoring the allusion to Freud as she is about to disagree with him—"the nucleus of her neurosis as well as the nucleus of her perversion" (488) was the repressed sadistic impulses toward the mother (whose markedly sadistic behavior toward her daughter's infantile masturbation was disclosed by the childhood memories the patient produced during analysis). Hate and aggressive impulses toward the mother, and the attendant, reactive feelings of guilt "led to a transformation of the hate into a masochistic libidinal attitude" (489), which accounted for the patient's fear of actual homosexual relations lest she become "subjugated to the sexual partner"—a fear, in fact, of her masochistic attachment to the mother.

After about eight months of analysis, the narrative continues, "the father made his first real appearance as a topic of analytic material, and at the same time all of the impulses belonging to the oedipus complex were revived, starting with the chief, unremitting, reproach against the father that he had been too inactive to love his daughter" (490). At this point, believing in the gendered nature of the transference, Deutsch refers her patient to "an analyst of the fatherly type," just as (we recall) Freud had felt obliged to refer his "girl" to "a woman doctor"; but no transference with the male analyst occurred for this patient either. However, one year later, the analyst/narrator received confirmation that her work had been successful: her ex-patient "had become a vivid, radiant person. . . . At last she had found happiness in a particularly congenial and uninhibited sexual relationship with a woman" (490–91). The character of the relationship is described as a conscious acting out of "a mother-child situation, in which sometimes one, sometimes the other played the mother—a play with a double cast, so to speak," Deutsch remarks, where the contrast was not between male and female but between activity and passivity, and "the feeling of happiness lay in the possibility of being able to play *both* roles."[12]

> The result of her analysis was evident. Everything that had come
> to the surface so clearly in the analytic transference was now

---

12. In an expanded version of this text published in her book *The Psychology of Women* (1944), Deutsch wrote: "Women can play two roles (active, sadistic/passive, masochistic). The differences and similarity, nonidentity and yet identity, the quasidouble experience of oneself, the simultaneous liberation from one part of one's ego and its preservation and sexuality in the possession of the other, are among the attractions of the homosexual experience" (339). In an unpublished paper on the construction of the homosexual woman in psychoanalytic theory, written for a seminar I held in 1989, Magdalena Zschokke, a doctoral candidate in Literature at the University of California, Santa Cruz, cited this passage and commented: "I couldn't have said it better. Who wouldn't want that?" I am indebted to her paper for prevailing upon my skepticism and convincing me to consider seriously Deutsch's views on female homosexuality, in spite of what I still find quite unappealing in her tone of self-contented analytic mothering.

detached from the person of the analyst and transferred to other
women. The gratifications denied her in the analytic situation
could now be found in the relationship with the new objects. It
was evident that the overcoming of her hostility toward the analyst
had brought with it the overcoming of her anxiety and,
consequently, a positive libidinal relationship to women could
appear . . . only, of course, after the mother-substitute object had
paid off the infantile grievances by granting her sexual
satisfactions. The analytic treatment had not brought about the
further and more favorable solution of the mother attachment,
that is, a renunciation of her homosexuality and an inclination
towards men. (491)

The last, anticlimactic sentence in this passage reads as if it were
added on incidentally, perfunctorily. It has the effect of underscoring, for the reader, how words such as *perversion, perverse tendency,
inversion,* or *indulge,* which usually carry their weight of moral condemnation into the "scientific" discourse of psychoanalysis, here, in
the context of this case history, seem to lose their damning diagnostic power. The reason, I suggest, is not only the "happy ending" of
the patient's story but also the barely muted tone of narcissistic gratification produced in the analyst-theorist herself by a successful
analysis and (counter)transference.

Deutsch's theory of female homosexuality as a "return to the
mother" detoured and activated by the Oedipus complex is based on
the analytic scenario of this case. The patient's happy return is doubly mediated by the analyst (and the successful transference) and by
the "appearance" of the father in one with the revival of Oedipal
impulses. For if the woman analyst had facilitated the recovery of a
positive libidinal attitude toward the mother and other women, the
actual homosexual activity could be reached only by a detour
through the Oedipus complex and the reactivation of its genital and
phallic drives. As though in response to Lampl–de Groot, Deutsch
states that in her cases of female homosexuality "it was not a question of a simple fixation on the mother as the first love object, but
rather a complicated process of returning" (505). This process is
shown even more clearly in another case. This patient played out the
double role of child and mother with two distinct types of object-
choice—an older and authoritative woman, to whom she had a socially submissive and sexually passive relationship, and a younger,
childlike woman with whom she was active both as a nourishing

mother and in her "unsublimatedly homosexual" behavior (495). Whereas her homosexuality in relation to the first type of object-choice "as yet does not involve the oedipus situation," Deutsch comments, in the second type it "quite clearly makes use of new elements taken from the oedipus situation," in particular the wish for the (father's) child, which is now fulfilled by having a child in her sexual partner. Both pre-Oedipal and Oedipal wishes in relation to the parents appear to be satisfied in the "double cast" of this homosexual scenario.

One can certainly appreciate why Deutsch's account of the psychogenesis of female homosexuality has been ignored by lesbian critics or, when not ignored, then summarily dismissed. Merck, for example, citing this very text, writes: "While acknowledging the predominance of the 'phallic masculine form' of female homosexuality, [Deutsch] argued that this is often a cover for a joint infantilism reflecting a prephallic mother fixation, which displays itself in reciprocal mother-child role play" ("The Train of Thought" 41)—and that is all Merck says. I have myself responded with similar annoyance to Deutsch's insistence on the centrality of motherhood and the positive Oedipus attitude in women's psychosexual development. And yet, on further consideration, I think it very useful to reread this text critically, just as so many have, time and again, reread Freud's. This is not, of course, to find in Deutsch *the answer* to the question of lesbian sexuality or desire, but rather to consider what other questions may be effectively posed and addressed through her particular formulation.[13]

---

13. Because of its emphasis on mothering in women's affective and sexual life, Deutsch's work has not been ignored by Nancy Chodorow, who finds in it support for the idea that a woman's orientation toward the father and subsequently men as "primary *erotic* objects" coexists with her primary *emotional* attachment to the mother (*The Reproduction of Mothering* 167). As Shirley Nelson Garner points out, "Though coming from object-relations theory, she reaches a conclusion about sexual development that echoes that of Helene Deutsch, who, of course, follows in Freud's direction" (169). However, as Garner observes, Chodorow does not pursue the implications of her argument and fails to account for why women become heterosexual; she merely assumes an unexplained "heterosexual preference" (171). What Garner does not say is that Chodorow's inability to explain erotic object-choice follows precisely from her rejection of Freud's theory of the drives, from which also results her failure to grasp the meaning of lesbian object-choice as anything other than the continuation of "mother-daughter emotions and connections" (*The Reproduction of Mothering* 200). Deutsch, on the other hand, availing herself of Freud's theory of (especially) the component drives, succeeds in raising questions about female homosexuality that reach far beyond Freud's own, male-centered perspective.

As I proceed to do that, I want to remark a point she makes, which is of particular relevance to current feminist debates on the mother-daughter relation. Deutsch distinguishes homosexuality or "genuine inversion" from the "sublimated" or sexually inactive bond between women which is generally associated with the pre-Oedipal relation to the mother as recaptured in adult age—and which, I may reiterate, must then exclude, ignore, or repress the genital components of sexuality that become active and meaningful as such only with the awareness of the sexual difference brought about by the Oedipus.[14] She states it quite clearly: the "return to the mother" that is the basis of female homosexuality "needs the completion of still another process before it attains the character of a genuine inversion" (505). This other process, if I read her correctly, is the recognition, the validation, even the authorization of female sexual activity by what she calls a "consent to activity": "the sexual satisfaction of masturbation, which has been forbidden by the *mother,* must not only no longer be prohibited, but must be consented to by the *mother* by an active participation. The denial of the past must be made good by subsequent permissions, and indeed quite as much in reference to the original passive experience as to the subsequent active experience" (505–506; emphasis added).

It would seem beyond doubt that the term *mother,* twice used in the passage just quoted, refers to two distinct agents: the first time to the real mother (who prohibited masturbation) and the second time to the mother substitute (analyst or female lover). Nevertheless, the fact that Deutsch does not make the distinction here, as she does elsewhere in the case history, is a puzzling imprecision. It is as if the distinction has become less clear to the analyst-theorist in the process of reconstructing the patient's fantasy—a fantasy in which the analyst is directly implicated and productively involved, as her reader is constantly reminded. This might well be, then, the structuring fantasy of Deutsch's theory of female homosexuality as well as of the psychoanalyst's role—a fantasy of homosexual-maternal

---

14. As I already suggested and will come back to shortly, the importance of the (positive) Oedipus complex in women's psychosexual development is paramount in Deutsch's view, and precisely in that it breaks the pre-Oedipal bond with the mother. In this regard, she cites some "very special cases" in which "the oedipus complex had apparently played no role at all" and "whose whole neurosis had the character of general psychic infantilism" (509).

mediation, acted out in a scenario still patriarchal, where mother-hood still constitutes the "nucleus," Oedipal and pre-Oedipal, of a woman's sexual life.

Writing in the early 1930s, a time when female and male homo-sexual subcultures in Europe were as active and visible as ever be-fore, and as they would not be again until the 1970s and 1980s, Deutsch seems to make a virtue of a situation that, if not exactly necessary, is at any rate quite real. The undisguised presence of her voice and role as analyst in the narrative of the patients' histories conveys at once the sense of her participation as sympathetic and nurturing guide, and her benevolent distance and successful control of the analytic transference. One has the impression that, even though Deutsch would prefer her patients to become heterosexual as a result of her guidance, nevertheless she can be satisfied with a homosexual resolution, provided that it reconfirm the mother as the figure of women's primary attachment—which, not incidentally, es-tablishes the crucial role of women analysts in psychoanalysis. In this sense, although her analytic and theoretical persona, as it emerges from the case narration, is closer to Freud than is Lampl–de Groot's, Deutsch's victory against the father is actually greater.

Indeed, her narrative of female homosexuality is more interest-ing the more it deviates from Freud's master narrative and the more it approaches what I have called his negative theory of the perver-sions. Rephrased in the terms of my own argument, this paper by Deutsch suggests that

1. female homosexuality or "genuine inversion" is not dependent on the masculinity complex (the denial of castration and a necessary masculine identification), although the latter may be part of it;
2. it is a regressive pre-Oedipal (prephallic and pregenital) rela-tionship, but one that can be activated only retroactively by impulses belonging to the later Oedipal, phallic, and genital phases, including the wish for the father's child—which is to say the recognition of sexual difference;
3. its sexual character is defined primarily but not exclusively by the component instincts, that is to say, it includes genital drives but not genital primacy: sadistic, masochistic, and oral drives are prominent;

4. its condition of possibility is some sort of authorization, both discursive and in practice, by a woman analyst and/or by other women (in the practice of love);
5. the relation to the third term, the father, and hence to the structure of castration, is necessary but not itself the pivot or term of reference of the relationship;
6. homosexuality is a perversion of normal femininity, or a deviation from what is considered the optimal sexual orientation in women, but is not, in itself, a pathological or pathogenic condition.

It would appear from this (admittedly partial) recasting that Deutsch's views coincide with Freud's only on one point, the sixth. The remark she tosses off in closing, that "the cornerstone for later inversion" is laid "in the first infantile period" (510)—a peripheral remark leaning toward the supposition of the congenital nature of inversion—is also quite in concert with Freud's ambiguity on this issue. Conversely, the points of major divergence are the first and the fifth. Before pursuing further the implications of Deutsch's analysis, I want to look at a paper by Ernest Jones, which furnishes yet another scenario to the classic master fantasy of female homosexuality and its mainstay, the masculinity complex.

Zero Degree Theory

"The Early Development of Female Sexuality" (1927) opens on the promising note that "men analysts have been led to adopt an unduly phallo-centric view of the problems in question" (450); and Jones means "phallo-centric" literally. When he then adds that "the immediate stimulus to the investigation" was provided him by the "unusual experience" of simultaneously analyzing "five cases of manifest homosexuality in women," the reader is primed for a new take on the by now vexed question and, who knows, even for what today might be called a male-feminist take. But she is soon (you've guessed it) disappointed in her expectations. For she finds out that, under the guise of revising the Freudian narrative and giving women their due—namely, a feminine libido and sexual organ as central to their development as the penis is to the development of men, analysts and not—Jones uses the stimulus provided by his five homosexual patients the better to consolidate the centrality of "the phallo-centric view." Which is, put in a nutshell: All women equally have penis envy, but lesbians have it more. Ironically, while his project is mainly aimed at showing the divergence of his own views from Freud's, Jones not only reiterates the primacy of the masculinity complex in homosexual women, but literalizes it to the point of stating that it consists of "penis identification" (470): "They either [wish to] have an organ of the opposite sex or none at all; to have one of their own sex is out of the question" (467).

Jones's doctrinal quarrels with Freud, also presented as differences between the London school and the Vienna school respectively, concern mainly the role and definition of the phallic phase (see also Jones, "The Phallic Phase") and hinge on the former's unmitigatedly essentialist view that "femininity develops progressively from the promptings of an instinctual constitution," a view spelled out in Jones's 1935 paper "Early Female Sexuality" (273). Here is a characteristic passage:

> In London, on the contrary, as the result especially of the experience of Melanie Klein's early analyses, but also confirmed by our findings in adults, we hold quite a different view of this early stage. We consider that the girl's attitude is already more feminine than masculine, being typically receptive and acquisitive. She is concerned more with the inside of her body than the outside. Her mother she regards not as a man regards a woman, as a creature whose wishes to receive it is a pleasure to fulfil. She regards her rather as a person who has been successful in filling herself with just the things the child wants so badly. (265)

The passage may suffice to convey the tone of deferential homage to Melanie Klein and the distancing of Freud, down there in Vienna, in ominous 1935. (On the troubled relations between Freud and Jones, kept private for the sake of the common "cause," and on Freud's low opinion of Jones as an individual, as well as a psychoanalytic theorist, see Young-Bruehl, especially 166–81.) It also serves quite well to indicate to what extent Jones can literalize the psychoanalytic account of psychic processes: all one needs to keep in mind, in reading it, is that the "girl" in question is a zero-to-six-month-old child. "In the second half of the first year," he goes on, *"true feminine love* for [the father], together with the *desire for access to his sexual organ,* begins to conflict with his evident relationship to the mother" (266; emphasis added).

In the 1927 paper, Jones argues that "Freud's 'phallic phase' in girls is probably a secondary, defensive construction rather than a true developmental stage" (472); it derives from the girl's repression of her innate femininity, a repression due to her fear and hatred of her mother. He motivates it further by elaborating a distinction between castration and a term of his own coin, *aphanisis,* which alone applies to girls, he maintains: it is the fear of aphanisis (i.e., the fear of losing the capacity for sexual pleasure), and not the fear of castration, that produces penis envy and the phallic phase in girls. Jones's thesis is that the girl has "a primary natural wish for a penis," and he specifies that wish "not as a masculine striving in clitoris terms," but rather as "the normal feminine desire to incorporate a man's penis inside her body" ("Early Female Sexuality" 270). Later, however, "the continued disappointment at never being allowed to share the penis in coitus with the father, or thereby to obtain a baby . . . reactivates the girl's early wish to possess a penis of her own." Such "unendurable" privation is equal to the fear of aphanisis ("The Early Development of Female Sexuality" 465–66). Thus, the "heterosexual identification" with father or brother—also called "penis identification"—must be regarded as "a universal phenomenon among young girls," not only among future lesbians. For the latter, additional "inborn factors" must be computed, namely, "an unusual intensity of oral erotism and of sadism" (469). At this point, the reader is quite prepared for the predictable classification of "the two classes of [female] homosexuals" that follows: "Where the oral erotism is the more prominent of the two the individual will probably belong to the second group (interest in women) and where the sadism is the more prominent to the first group (interest in men)" (470).

In all honesty I must say that the two groups have already been described a few pages earlier in Jones's paper, but in the diegetic order of my exposition they must be presented now; and for the sake of clarity I will do so in Jones's own terms. The "interest-in-women" group, the first mentioned here, was actually his second: "(2) Those who have little or no interest in men, but whose libido centres on women. Analysis shows that this interest in women is a vicarious way of enjoying femininity; they merely employ other women to exhibit it for them" (467). These women have given up their feminine desire for the father and replaced it by identification with him, "but then lose further interest in him; their external object-relation to the other woman is very imperfect, for she merely represents their own femininity through identification, and their aim is vicariously to enjoy the gratification of this at *the hand of an unseen man* (the father incorporated in themselves)" (468).[15]

The other group Jones mentions, the "interest-in-men" group, consists of those who "retain their first love-object" (and here he means the father), but the object-relation "becomes replaced by identification, and the aim of the libido is to procure recognition of this identification by the former object" (468). Because this is rather confusing, I take the liberty of quoting a little more about this group: "(1) Those who retain their interest in men, but who set their hearts on being accepted by men as one of themselves. To this group belongs the familiar type of women who ceaselessly complain of the unfairness of women's lot and their unjust ill-treatment by men" (467). At pains to understand who belongs to which group, and what kind of identification prevails where, one's thoughts run back to Freud's well-wrought scenario with something like nostalgia: "Furiously resentful and embittered, she turned away from the father and from men altogether. After this first great reverse she forswore her womanhood and sought another goal for her libido" ("Psychogenesis," *SE* 18: 157).

What Jones has done, in effect, is to divide into two groups or "classes" what in Freud's sparer and more elegant formulation were

---

15. I highlight this image because it will reappear later on (in chapter 4) à propos of Lacan. I also note an interesting coincidence: in her discussion of two recent mainstream films about lesbians, *Lianna* (John Sayles, 1983) and *Desert Hearts* (Donna Deitch, 1985), Roof states that "both films solve the problem of imaging lesbian sexuality by providing a fetishistic hand that stands in for—is a metaphor of—what exactly cannot be seen in the scene. . . . The hand itself also functions as a fetish, providing something to see, disavowing the lack in the camera's mastery of the scene as its scopophilic gaze is partially blocked, standing in for the phallus literally absent between the women" (62–63). The function of "the fetish hand," Roof argues, is to allay the anxiety that may be caused in mainstream viewers by a sexuality without phallus: as a "substitute for the missing phallus," the hand "rephallicizes lesbian sexual activity [and thus] subordinates lesbian sexuality to masculinity, making it again the pretender, the imitation of the 'real' thing" (68). The references of Roof's discussion of cinematic fetishism are Mulvey and other film theorists, as well as Freud, but not Jones; and hence what I take as a coincidence in the return of this phallic hand in a rather distant sector (film) of the cultural imagination. In chapter 5 I will propose another way to think of the fetish in relation to the phallus and to lesbian sexuality.

correlative traits of a single character. But, to give Jones his due, his scenario surpasses Freud's in one element of composition and mise-en-scène, for he does not forget that sentimental drama requires three characters, as Freud also knew but often seemed to forget. The third character besides the father and the daughter is, of course, the mother, and in the scenario here under discussion that role is filled by the homosexual woman's love interest. For surely there must be some women who welcome the attentions of Jones's groups (1) and (2), and what about them, then? Where do they fit in? For Freud they remain distant figures in the wings, white-haired elderly ladies and *cocottes* of questionable reputation; for Jones they do not quite deserve a class of their own, but are at least given a footnote:

> For the sake of simplicity an interesting third form is omitted in the text, but should be mentioned. Some women obtain gratification of feminine desires provided two conditions are present: (1) that the penis is replaced by a surrogate such as the tongue or finger, and (2) that the partner using this organ is a woman instead of a man. Though clinically they may appear in the guise of complete inversion, such cases are evidently nearer to the normal than either of the two mentioned in the text. (467–68)

One is relieved at last to encounter a familiar character, popularized in the sexological fiction as "the feminine invert" and somewhat dignified in lesbian fiction by its prototype, the character Mary in Radclyffe Hall's *The Well of Loneliness* (1928).[16] That her near-normality earns her a role of unpaid extra in Jones's staging is one more instance of the unremitting phallocentricity of his perspective. As Jones concludes, "Identification with the father is thus common

---

16. Cf. Havelock Ellis's description of the "womanly" invert some thirty years earlier: "A class in which homosexuality, while fairly distinct, is only slightly marked, is formed by the women to whom the actively inverted woman is most attracted. These women differ, in the first place, from the normal, or average, woman in that they are not repelled or disgusted by lover-like advances from persons of their own sex. They are not usually attractive to the average man, though to this rule there are many exceptions. Their faces may be plain or ill-made, but not seldom they possess good figures: a point which is apt to carry more weight with the inverted woman than beauty of face. . . . One may, perhaps, say that they are the pick of the women whom the average man would pass by. No doubt, this is often the reason why they are open to homosexual advances, but I do not think it is the sole reason. So far as they may be said to constitute a class, they seem to possess a genuine, though not precisely sexual, preference for women over men, and it is this coldness, rather than lack of charm, which often renders men rather indifferent to them" (*Studies in the Psychology of Sex* 222).

to all forms of homosexuality" (468) to a greater or lesser degree—
the greater being embodied, one gathers, in the "woman who has
devoted herself to a penis-acquiring career (homosexually) having
at the same time fear, disgust and hatred of any real penis" ("The
Phallic Phase" 25). So much for his criticism of Freud and the pro-
feminine views of the London school. So much for Jones and his
profession of good faith: "I do not see a woman—in the way
feminists do—as *un homme manqué,* as a permanently disappointed
creature struggling to console herself with secondary substitutes
alien to her true nature. The ultimate question is whether a woman
is born or made" ("Early Female Sexuality" 273). The reader need
not puzzle long over the answer.

Off the Couch

It is, thus, with renewed interest that I approach again the implications of Deutsch's "On Female Homosexuality," whose finely articulated picture contains several suggestions I would like to pursue.
And I note incidentally that her emphasis on sadistic and aggressive
impulses toward the mother may owe something to Klein's work,
but the direction in which Deutsch's argument develops and her
avoidance of the essentialist premises embraced by Jones make for
another kind of Freudian revision. First, then, in contrast to Jones,
whose view of female sexuality is centered on the father even as he
would dismiss the structuring function of castration, Deutsch can
be read as saying that the castration complex is a necessary step in
the development of "genuine" homosexuality, but the role of the father there is less that of a love object than that of a symbolic agent of
castration. Commenting on the special emphasis that oral and sadistic drives have in the disposition to homosexuality, she credits
both Freud's *Three Essays* and Jones's 1927 paper with a similar insight, and then adds: "I can state, furthermore, with complete secu-
rity that not one of my cases failed to have a very strong reaction to
the castration complex; a complete oedipus complex with exceed-
ingly powerful aggressive reactions could be demonstrated in every
case. . . . The light or the shadow cast on the original relationship
by the father's presence has played an important and necessary part"
(508–509).

As I read her argument, it is the disappointment of the Oedipal wish for the father's child that brings home the awareness of sexual difference and boosts the phallic and genital drives; and in this sense the father, and the disappointment (castration) of which he is agent, are necessary. But the phallic and genital drives thus activated can then be redirected toward the female object, together with—rather than to the exclusion of—other component drives such as oral and anal drives, sadism, scopophilia, their respective opposites, and so on. While the phallic tendencies are "usually the most urgent," Deutsch writes, and "can indeed dominate the general picture" of female homosexuality, causing "the relationship of one female to another to assume a male character, whereby the absence of a penis is denied," they by no means make up the whole picture.

> It is then not very important whether the femininity of the object is to be emphasized, or whether both the subject and object are simultaneously affirming possession of a penis, so that the object may also take her turn in playing the masculine role. These are two sub-types of the same species. . . . The quantum of masochistic or sadistic component, that is to say, the preponderance of aggressive tendencies or of reactions of guilt, a more passive or a more active casting of the role—these are all merely details in the total problem of female homosexuality. I said that the phallic masculine form of homosexuality was the most outstanding one. But there are always many deeper currents hiding behind it. It is my impression, indeed, that this masculine form is sometimes brought into evidence for the very purpose of hiding the more infantile, but none the less predominating tendencies. The majority of the cases which I have analyzed were forced to an honest and extensive relinquishment of their masculine behavior by the strength of their pregenital urges. The mother-child relationship at pregenital levels, in the deeply entrenched fixation of the pre-phallic phases (whether consciously or unconsciously), dominated the perversion. The wish for activity belonging to the phallic phase is carried along in the regression, and reaches its most satisfactory fulfillment in the homosexual relationship. (506–507)

This is, I believe, the passage that Merck had in mind in her curt summary of Deutsch's theory. I quoted it extensively to show that, while Merck's reading is not wrong, it nonetheless misses a very important element in the story, that is, the symbolic function of the father. For the "phallic masculine form," reached through the detour of the positive Oedipus complex, is what enables the subject's active ("genuine") homosexuality. Without that detour, by Deutsch's own account, the infantile pre-Oedipal attachment would remain "prephallic," that is, sexually inactive in the adult subject. The father, then, functions as a third term between the subject and the mother, and his symbolic rather than objective status is corroborated by the symbolic equivalence that Deutsch repeatedly makes between the father and the father's child in the girl's Oedipal wish.

(Parenthetically, this function of the child as the third term is also suggested by Julia Kristeva ["Stabat Mater"], whose emphasis on motherhood as central to female sexuality is every bit as strong as Deutsch's. I will discuss some implications of Kristeva's notion of a "homosexual-maternal" aspect in the relationship between daughter and mother in chapter 4. But I will briefly anticipate here that, by Kristeva's account, *any* form of lesbianism harks back to a pre-Oedipal maternal bond which, lacking precisely the third term, is destined to end up in psychosis or worse [*Tales of Love* 81]. Her "homosexual-maternal" may be sexual in the sense of infantile sexuality but is not actively homosexual in the sense indicated by Deutsch, who clearly distinguishes between forms of "genuine" homosexuality—which she may call perversion or regression, while all along showing them to be neither pathological nor pathogenic—and other forms that are "infantile" and severely symptomatic. For instance, the already mentioned "cases in which the oedipus complex had apparently played no role at all" and in which "the libido had never known but *one* object—the mother . . . were very special cases, whose whole neurosis had the character of general psychic infantilism" [509]. In fact, Deutsch's account of *these* cases echoes Kristeva's diagnosis of psychosis, but Kristeva makes no such distinctions and pathologizes lesbianism altogether.)

In the Lacanian revision, the equivalence of father and father's child is subsumed in the phallus, which is in one the marker of sexual difference and the signifier of desire. It seems to me that the role of "the father's child" in the actively homosexual relationships described by Deutsch fulfills precisely this function of the phallus; and there is further evidence of the symbolic presence of the father (i.e., of the phallus) in two dreams of her second patient. In one, "she sees herself in analysis with Miss Anna Freud who is wearing men's clothes" (498), Deutsch reports, and in the other, a few days later, "I am sitting facing her instead of behind her (as I always do) and am holding a cigar in my hand. She thinks, 'The ashes are so long on the cigar that they will drop off any second' " (499). Deutsch interprets these obvious signifiers of masculinity (men's clothes, Miss Anna *Freud*, the cigar) quite literally, as the patient's wish to be analyzed by Freud—whose picture with a cigar in his hand stands on her analyst's desk—as well as a repressed "deep longing for the great man—the father." His reappearing in both dreams merged with the two women analysts, she believes, "testifies to the fact that the patient's turning to the woman corresponds also to a flight from the man," a flight that originated in "feelings of guilt toward the mother, fear of disappointment and rejection"; in spite of which, however, "her return to the mother had not made her relinquish her longing for the father" (500).

The language Deutsch uses here is somewhat equivocal, seeming to stress the father as love object (object-choice) rather than his symbolic function as marker of sexual difference and agent of castration, whereas the rest of the analysis consistently suggests the latter by reiterating the interchangeability of father and father's child. In responding to images that call on her quite personally and cast her in a scenario co-starring Freud and his daughter, it may well be that Deutsch has no choice but to read them as the quintessential family romance, with herself as the mother and Anna as the wayward daughter standing in for the patient's self. But it seems to me that the dream images themselves—*Miss* Anna Freud in masculine clothes and mother Deutsch with a cigar noteworthy for its impending downfall—do, in this case, speak louder than her words and configure the father (father Freud) not as love object but exactly as phallus. This phallus—incorporated in Anna Freud as the psychoanalytic version of the "mythic mannish lesbian" (I borrow Esther Newton's description of Radclyffe Hall's character Stephen Gordon) and in a phallic mother on the brink (of disavowal?)—is no longer attached to the paternal body, though its symbolic function is nevertheless necessary. What I mean by a phallus no longer attached to the father's body, and how I intend to account for lesbian desire by the notion of a non-paternal fantasy phallus (I will call it fetish), will become clearer in chapter 5. For the time being, I want to pursue a second suggestion I find in Deutsch, the notion of a "consent to activity."

Articulating her theory of female homosexuality as a return to the first object-cathexis (the mother), which is reactivated by the passage through the (positive) Oedipus complex with its phallic and genital drives, only temporarily invested in the father, Deutsch states: "First of all, the motives which once really induced the little girl to respond to the biological urge toward the father must be made retroactive." Accordingly, sexual gratification "must be consented to by the mother by an active participation" (505).[17] Having already discussed the ambiguity of the term *mother* in this context, I need not repeat the reasons why I take *mother* to mean mother substitute, i.e., the analyst and/or another woman who is the subject's current object-choice. Deutsch continues: "One might say that the interruption of the phallic activity is made up for by this consent to activity which had been impossible in the past" (506). It seems undeniable to me that the consent to activity that may be granted in the analytic situation of transference differs in kind from that which may be given by a woman lover; and perhaps either one is sufficient, though most likely both are necessary in cases of severe repression. But what I think can be inferred from the two kinds of consent is that while one is discursive and symbolic in nature, the other is of the order of physical, sexual practices. In other words, the consent to homosexual activity and gratification may be provided by a discourse that permits them, as well as by participation in the activity itself.

But what do permission, consent, and participation mean in matters that have been the target of repression? Deutsch is speaking from inside the analytic situation, where the mother's prohibition of masturbation, for example, may surface through childhood memories, screen memories, or dreams, and be then worked through jointly in the analysis, made accessible to the patient, and stabilized by secondary revision. In this clinical context, where physical acts or sexual behavior are by definition excluded, participation becomes synonymous with permission and consent; that is to say, it refers to the analyst's accepting or encouraging attitude and her manner of speaking, her discourse, about the activity. The further

---

17. In the specific instance, the sexual gratification is derived from masturbation, but other forms are not excluded, since Deutsch argues that "in the reactivation [of the mother-cathexis] *all* phases in which the mother played a role" are involved (505).

consent and encouragement given by a partner's physical participation in the sexual activity itself would then provide a knowledge of the body, so to speak, that I believe contributes just as directly, if not more so, to the effective reorganization of the drives; and this is why I think it may be just as necessary.

However, the notion of discursive consent has implications that far exceed the analytic situation, for it is the representational aspect of the drives, the realm of fantasy, that transforms what Deutsch calls "the biological urge" into sexuality and desire. Ironically enough, it is only this psychoanalytic notion of fantasy, developed by Laplanche and Pontalis in their reading of Freud, that allows us to theorize beyond a strictly psychoanalytic situation. Off the couch, so to speak, outside the analytic situation, then, the sadomasochistic impulses related to the mother's prohibition of masturbation may be recovered through fantasy in conjunction with public forms of representation, for example in film spectatorship, in reading lesbian s/m fiction, or in a lesbian bar. If, as Foucault has argued, sexuality is produced, rather than repressed, by the proliferation of discourses about it, then permission and consent, in the instance of lesbian sexuality, may mean no more than the public representation of certain activities and satisfactions *as sexual*. It may mean no more—and no less!—than the production of a discourse (in the widest possible sense of the term) in which sexual activities between women are given representation and signified as desire. Of course, it may be objected that female homosexuality has not lacked representation, including feminist representations. Indeed it has not. But what I attempt to demonstrate throughout this book is precisely that the major public discourses on lesbian sexuality available in this century are discourses of sexual indifference—of inversion, of masculinity complex, of lesbianism as pre-Oedipal fusion, psychosis, hysteria, bisexuality, or oscillation between masculinity and femininity—and they are all inadequate to the task.

In these terms, the "problem of female homosexuality" that can be inferred from Deutsch is a problem of representation—the unavailability, suppression, and proscription of discourses and other public forms of fantasy that inscribe particular scenarios of women's desire for women. The relation of sexuality to fantasy, which is a central theoretical premise of this book, will be addressed directly in Part II, where I will examine various scenarios of lesbian

desire in relation to what Laplanche and Pontalis call original fantasies. Finally, I will be suggesting that the public presence of a lesbian
discourse and self-representation—in various textual and performance modalities, verbal, visual, gestural, etc., including the representation of lesbian sexual practices—may serve as an authorizing
social force more widely effective than the privatized permission afforded by analytic mothering or the singular contribution by a partner in sexual practices. I will also draw on a third suggestion I
derived from rereading Deutsch and Freud's *Three Essays* (in chapter 1 above), in order to elaborate the notion of a perverse desire—a
sexuality of component instincts, which, unlike infantile polymorphous perversion, is inclusive of phallic and genital drives but, unlike "normal" sexuality, is not bound to a necessary phallic, genital,
and heterosexual primacy. It seems to me that such a scenario of
desire may happily supersede the fantasy of the masculinity complex by evicting from lesbian sexuality "the hand of an unseen man"
in one with the paternal phallus, and yet retaining the necessary
concept of sexual difference(s) and thus the agency of castration.

I have purposely delayed consideration of Freud's other bout
with female homosexuality in "A Case of Paranoia Running Counter
to the Psycho-Analytic Theory of the Disease" (1915) for two, mainly
self-serving, reasons. First, this case history—as even the customarily sober, scholarly, and factual editors of the *Standard Edition* are
impelled to introduce it—is "an object-lesson to practitioners on the
danger of basing a hasty opinion of a case on a superficial knowledge of the facts" (*SE* 14: 262). An application of his freshly formulated view of paranoia (the "theory that the delusion of persecution
invariably depends on homosexuality" [*SE* 14: 266]), this paper is
less an analysis than a peroration *pro domo sua* on the part of Freud,
who is seeking confirmation of his theory (the title only seems to
admit failure, the better to consolidate his success).[18] And confirm it
he will, regardless of the overwhelming odds against it: the case was
referred to him by a lawyer; the "patient" was even more reluctant
than Dora or the girl of "Psychogenesis," and Freud managed only
two meetings with her; her alleged homosexuality remains an

---

18. Freud developed his theory of paranoia in the analysis of Schreber, "Psychoanalytic Notes on an Autobiographical Account of a Case of Paranoia (Dementia
Paranoides)" (1911), *SE* 12: 1–82.

unsubstantiated inference of Freud's, based solely on the evidence of what he and the lawyer take as a delusion of persecution—a persecution, moreover, which the woman considers real and attributes to her male lover (thus contradicting the theory of its homosexual and delusional basis), while Freud attributes it to a white-haired elderly lady, an office supervisor and alleged mother figure (thus reconfirming his theory). In sum, not only is the woman's homosexuality merely presumed by Freud and nowhere admitted or suggested by the subject in question, but the case for homosexuality is even less convincingly argued here than in the feminist readings of Dora. It therefore contributes nothing to the understanding of female homosexuality as such, or to the role of the mother in it.

However—and here is my second reason—this text introduces the notion of primal fantasies (*Urphantasien*), which is indeed of the utmost relevance to my study of fantasy in lesbian sexual structuring and self-representation. It therefore provides a suitable transition from the discourse of the couch to that of literary, critical, and filmic texts, or from psychoanalysis to cultural analysis; from the first half of the century to the second and from female homosexuality to lesbian subjectivity; or from the theory of sexual (in)difference to a theory of lesbian desire developed through what I call the practice of love. As a graphic token of this transitional role performed by the notion of fantasy in this book, I will abandon the traditional psychoanalytic spelling *phantasy* in favor of the nontechnical and semantically plurivalent *fantasy*.[19] Any ambiguity or fuzziness that may derive from this choice will not have been unintentional. Finally, I end this first part of my project with Freud's words and a promise similar to the one contained therein.

> Among the store of unconscious phantasies of all neurotics, and probably of all human beings, there is one which is seldom absent

---

19. In the English version of Laplanche and Pontalis's *Vocabulaire de la psychanalyse* the preferred spelling is *phantasy*, with *fantasy* given in parentheses as an alternate spelling: "Phantasy (or Fantasy)" (no such choice was necessary in French and other romance languages in which the term is respectively *fantasme* and *fantasma* or *fantasia*). However, a note is added to the effect that the distinction proposed by Susan Isaacs between *fantasy* (for daydreams and other conscious forms) and *phantasy* (for primary or unconscious processes) should be rejected as leading to arbitrary interpretations of Freud's single term *Phantasie*, whose diverse connotations in common usage he purposely retained (*The Language of Psychoanalysis* 318).

and which can be disclosed by analysis: this is the phantasy of watching sexual intercourse between the parents. I call such phantasies—of the observation of sexual intercourse between the parents, of seduction, of castration, and others—"primal phantasies"; and I shall discuss in detail elsewhere their origin and their relation to individual experience. (*SE* 14: 269)[20]

---

20. As the editors of the *Standard Edition* note, "The subject of 'primal phantasies' is discussed at length in Lecture XXIII of Freud's *Introductory Lectures* (1916–17) [*SE* 16: 368–71] and in his case history of the 'Wolf Man' (1918b)" [*SE* 17: 59–60 and 97].

PART TWO

Original Fantasies, Scenarios of Desire

For its spectator the film unfolds in that simultaneously very close and definitively inaccessible "elsewhere" in which the child *sees* the amorous play of the parental couple, who are similarly ignorant of it and leave it alone, a pure onlooker whose participation is inconceivable. In this respect the cinematic signifier is not only "psychoanalytic"; it is more precisely Oedipal.
—Christian Metz (*The Imaginary Signifier* 64)

Narrative discourse, far from being a neutral medium for the representation of historical events and processes, is the very stuff of a mythical view of reality, a conceptual or pseudoconceptual "content" which, when used to represent real events, endows them with an illusory coherence and charges them with the kinds of meanings more characteristic of oneiric than of waking thought.
—Hayden White (*The Content of the Form* ix)

Nothing is stranger than this secret dismissal of the phallus in Freud's explanation of the fetishist's nearly mad reduction of differences to a permanent phallic presence. And this very dismissal encourages us to recognize the uselessness of the phallus as a term of comparison (as the term of comparison). The shock of "castration" can thus have the beneficent result of detaching desire from the phallus, and of promoting the discovery of new surfaces.
—Leo Bersani and Ulysse Dutoit (*The Forms of Violence* 72)

Chapter **3**

Recasting the Primal Scene: Film and Lesbian Representation

She goes to poetry or fiction looking for *her* way of being in the world, since she too has been putting words and images together; she is looking eagerly for guides, maps, possibilities; and over and over . . . she comes up against something that negates everything she is about: she meets the image of Woman in books written by men. She finds a terror and a dream, she finds a beautiful pale face, she finds la Belle Dame Sans Merci, she finds Juliet or Tess or Salomé, but precisely what she does not find is that absorbed creature, herself, who sits at a desk trying to put words together.
—Adrienne Rich (*On Lies, Secrets, and Silence* 39)

I. Sexuality and Fantasy

In 1964, rereading Freud in the context of the then-burgeoning structuralist thought, of which Lacan was the foremost representative in psychoanalytic discourse, Laplanche and Pontalis point out the continuous if ambiguous presence of the notion of fantasy in Freud's early writings up to and including his famous analysis of the beating fantasy, "A Child Is Being Beaten."[1] They note, as well, the ambiguous status of fantasy in psychoanalytic theory in general—an ambiguity due to the fact that the term *fantasy* was

---

1. Nineteen sixty-four was the year of Lacan's seminar on *The Four Fundamental Concepts of Psycho-Analysis*, originally published only in 1973. In it, Lacan also writes: "The phantasy is the support of desire; it is not the object that is the support of desire. The subject sustains himself as desiring in relation to an ever more complex signifying ensemble. This is apparent enough in the form of the scenario it assumes, in which the subject, more or less recognizable, is somewhere, split, divided, generally double, in his relation to the object, which usually does not show its true face either" (185).

semantically couched in a cultural opposition between illusion and reality which antedated psychoanalysis by centuries but which, like the opposition between mind and body, the psychoanalytic project was, in fact, engaged in undermining. (We need only think of Freud's redefinition of the instinct or drive [*Trieb*] in the *Three Essays:* "By an 'instinct' is provisionally to be understood the psychical representative of an endosomatic, continuously flowing source of stimulation, as contrasted with a 'stimulus,' which is set up by *single* excitations coming from *without*. The concept of instinct is thus one of those lying on the frontier between the mental and the physical" [*SE* 7: 168]; and then again in "Instincts and Their Vicissitudes": "an 'instinct' appears to us as a borderline concept between the mental and the physical, being both the mental representative of the stimuli emanating from within the organism and penetrating to the mind, and at the same time a measure of the demand made upon the energy of the latter in consequence of its connection with the body" [*SE* 14: 121–22]. And his radical reconceptualization of the sexual drive, in particular, has been discussed in chapter 1 above.)

By following up the development of Freud's thought through his various (re)formulations of concepts such as psychic reality, the seduction theory, and the primal scenes (*Urszenen*), Laplanche and Pontalis make a convincing case for the metapsychological status of fantasy and for its structural, constitutive role in subject processes. They reject the formal separation between conscious and unconscious fantasies—between daydreams, for instance, and memory traces or fantasies recovered in analysis—and instead see a "profound continuity between the various fantasy scenarios—the stage-setting of desire" in the history of the subject. They mention three primal fantasies—the primal scene, seduction, and castration—and call them original fantasies or fantasies of origins (*fantasmes originaires, fantasmes des origines*) because, "like myths, they claim to provide a representation of, and a solution to, the major enigmas which confront the child": the primal scene (Freud's *Urszene*) "pictures the origin of the individual" in the child's imaging of parental coitus; seduction, "the origin and upsurge of sexuality"; and "castration, the origin of the difference between the sexes" (19). But they also add—and this is an important emphasis against the structuralist postulate of universal structures—that if the primal or original fantasies can be understood as a structure in the subject's prehistory (what Freud called phylogenesis), it is in the sense of a "prestructure which is actualized and transmitted by the parental fantasies" (27). Thus the original fantasies lie "beyond the history of the subject but nevertheless in history—a kind of language and a symbolic sequence, but loaded with elements of imagination; a structure, but activated by contingent elements" (18). The fantasies of origin, in other words, are historically structured as well as structuring of the subject's history; that is to say, the constitutive role of fantasy in subjectivity is both structural and historically motivated, historically specific.

With a brilliant conceptual turn, Laplanche and Pontalis then link the fantasies of origin to the origin of fantasy (*origine du fantasme*). This, they argue, cannot be isolated from the origin of the drive itself, which in turn has its origin in autoeroticism; and they maintain that autoeroticism is not "a stage of libidinal development" but rather

> a mythical moment of disjunction between the pacification of need (*Befriedigung*) and the fulfilment of desire (*Wünscherfüllung*), between the two stages represented by real experience and its hallucinatory revival, between the object that satisfies [the real object, the milk] and the sign which describes both the object and its absence [the lost object, the breast]: a mythical moment at which hunger and sexuality meet in a common origin. (24–25)

This "mythical moment," they insist, stressing "its permanence and presence in all adult sexual behavior," is not to be understood in the object-directed sense, as "a first stage, enclosed within itself, from which the subject has to rejoin the world of objects." On the contrary, they argue on the side of Freud, "the drive *becomes* autoerotic, only after the loss of the object." So that, "if it can be said of auto-erotism that it is objectless, it is in no sense because it may appear before any object relationship," but rather because its origin is in that moment, "more abstract than definable in time, since it is always renewed," when sexuality, "disengaged from any natural object, moves into the field of fantasy *and by that very fact becomes sexuality*" (25, emphasis added).

In other words, it is through their representations in fantasy that the drives become properly sexual, in the psychoanalytic sense, and hence it is only through fantasy that desire is sustained. While any part, organ, activity, or function of the body can acquire erogenous value, "in every case the function serves only as support, the taking of food serving, for instance, as a model for fantasies of incorporation. Though modelled on the function, sexuality lies in its difference from the function" (26); not in the sucking of milk or in the function of feeding, but in the pleasure of sucking as such. For this reason, they suggest, the ideal image of autoeroticism is "lips that kiss themselves" (26). And they conclude:

> By locating the origin of fantasy in the auto-erotism, we have
> shown the connection between fantasy and desire. Fantasy,
> however, is not the object of desire, but its setting. In fantasy the
> subject does not pursue the object or its sign: he appears caught
> up himself in the sequence of images. He forms no representation
> of the desired object, but is himself represented as participating in
> the scene although, in the earliest forms of fantasy, he cannot be
> assigned any fixed place in it (hence the danger, in treatment, of
> interpretations which claim to do so). As a result, the subject,
> although always present in the fantasy, may be so in a
> desubjectivized form, that is to say, in the very syntax of the
> sequence in question. (26)

If this passage has appeared so germane to the process of film viewing and so pertinent in critical accounts of the spectator's relations to the film, it is in part because the figuration of the subject "caught up" in the sequence of images is an eminently cinematic trope; but the congruence between spectator and subject of fantasy, between film and fantasy, is no doubt one reason why (neo-)Freudian metapsychology has been so profoundly influential in the elaboration of the theory of spectatorship and of the cinematic apparatus in the 1970s.[2] I shall return to the subject of fantasy in the cinema and to the feminist theory of spectatorship later on in the chapter. But first I want to look at the reinscription of the original fantasies,

---

2. Cf., for instance, Heath's formulation of cinematic narrative space: "What moves in film, finally, is the spectator, immobile in front of the screen. Film is the regulation of that movement, the individual as subject held in a shifting and placing of desire, energy, contradiction, in a perpetual retotalization of the imaginary (the set scene of image and subject). This is the investment of film in narrativization; and crucially for a coherent space, the unity of place for vision" (*Questions of Cinema* 53). Besides Heath, see also de Lauretis and Heath (eds.); Metz, *The Imaginary Signifier;* Mulvey; Mayne; and Rosen (ed.), among others.

and in particular the recasting of the primal scene, in one film that specifically foregrounds the relations of spectatorship and the problem of representation with regard to lesbian sexuality.

I will attempt to articulate how a film's work with and against narrative codes and conventional forms of enunciation and address may produce modes of representing that effectively alter the standard frame of reference and visibility, the conditions of the visible, what *can* be seen and represented. At the origin of my own writing in this chapter is a subjective and self-reflexive question: How do I look?[3] This question implies several: How do I see—what are the modes, constraints, and possibilities of my seeing, the terms of vision for me? How am I seen—what are the ways in which I'm seen or can be seen, the conditions of my visibility? And more—how do I look *on,* as the film unrolls from reel to reel in the projector, as the images appear and the story unfolds up on the screen, as the fantasy scenario unveils and the soundtrack plays on in my head? For the question is, To see or not to see, to be seen (and how) or not to be seen (at all?): subjective vision and social visibility, being and passing, representation and spectatorship— the conditions of the visible, what can be *seen,* and eroticized, and on what *scene.*

"A Terror and a Dream" *(She Must Be Seeing Things)*

Sheila McLaughlin's *She Must Be Seeing Things* (1987) is an independent feature film about lesbian sexuality and its relations to fantasy, on the one hand, and to the problem of representation, on the other. Like the few other fiction films openly about lesbians that have been made in North America and Britain since the women's and gay liberation movements, this film portrays a lesbian relationship; but, unlike most of them, it is primarily concerned with sexuality and fantasy, even to the disregard of other fundamental aspects

---

3. *How Do I Look? Queer Film and Video* was the title of a conference organized in New York City by the Bad Object-Choices collective in 1989, for which an initial and partial version of this chapter was written. I am indebted to two of the organizers and members of the collective, Terri Cafaro and Douglas Crimp, for their comments on my conference paper and its revision for publication in the proceedings volume (see Bad Object-Choices, eds.), and for encouraging me to pursue my own passionate fiction through a theoretical fantasy that few others at the conference seemed willing or able to share.

of lesbian identity and subjectivity, such as race or class.[4] Unlike
them, moreover, it is informed by the critique of representation
produced by the work of avant-garde filmmakers as well as feminist
film critics and theorists. My purpose in discussing it will be not
only that of a textual reading, rewarding as that can be with a film so
rich and so brilliantly "cinematic," but I will also take the film as the
ground from which to pose questions of lesbian representation and
spectatorship.

At face value, the currency of its title is that "she" who must *be
seeing* things, who is imagining things that aren't "real." This could
be another "film about a woman who . . . ," to cite perhaps the fundamental text of feminist independent cinema (see Rainer 77–97);
or it could be yet another film of the genre ironized by Yvonne
Rainer—a film about a woman who, like Freud's hysteric who "suf-
fers from reminiscences" or like the paranoiac, at once produces
and is assailed by "things," images or hallucinations that are symptoms of her own mental world or psychic state rather than events in
the real world. However, such "things" are never simple, and this is a
different sort of film.

To begin with, *She Must Be Seeing Things* is about not one
woman but two, and one makes movies, the other doesn't. But
doesn't she? In a sense, they both do. Both make movies in their
minds, as they read novels or diaries and look at various pictures,
still photographs, snapshots, moving pictures—and then, from that
reading and seeing, Jo, the filmmaker, writes scripts, shoots, and
edits her rushes into films, while her jealous lover Agatha makes
pictures more like hallucinations, imagining Jo in sexual encounters
with men. Thus, whether imagined or imaged, both women "see
things," and hence the title really refers to both. Or, to anticipate a
point to be discussed further on, the two lovers in the film "inhabit
the subject position together," as Sue-Ellen Case suggests of the lesbian roles of butch and femme, who represent a coupled rather than
split subject and who, by playing "on the phallic economy rather

4. The two protagonists are a black latina lawyer, Agatha (played by Sheila Dabney), and a white independent filmmaker, Jo (played by Lois Weaver). Ethnic and
class or cultural differences between them are marked and often remarked upon in
the film, but primarily insofar as they inflect each woman's sexual fantasies and self-
image. For various criticisms of what has been taken as a disregard of racial difference on the part of both the film and my reading of it, I refer the reader to the discussion transcripts included in the conference volume (Bad Object-Choices 264–84).

than to it," succeed in "replacing the Lacanian slash with a lesbian bar" ("Towards a Butch-Femme Aesthetic" 56–57). Moreover, I propose that the word *Must* in McLaughlin's title is not descriptive but provocative, and does sustain another meaning: "she" *must* be seeing things, she cannot help seeing things the way she does. I shall come back to this as well, but now I want to pursue for a while this queer notion of a film about two women who . . .

If the most immediate reference of the title's "She"—as conveyed by the narrative and emphasized by the opening shot of Agatha looking off-space, screen-left, in extreme close-up—is undoubtedly Agatha, nevertheless Jo, too, is seeing things in or through her films. First, in directing the actress who plays Catalina (Kyle de Camp), telling her what she will see and how to look at it, and later in cutting the film (all of which we see her do, we see Jo seeing), she, the filmmaker within the film, constructs a *vision* of things—events, emotions, relationships, and possibilities. Take the scene in the editing room toward the end of the film, where Jo cuts the final sequence of her film, *Catalina*, the story of "a 17th-century woman who rebelled," as Jo tells Agatha.[5] The sequence, which we have previously seen being filmed in studio (with Jo directing the actress and the camera), has Catalina looking from behind a curtain at a woman and her male lover having intercourse; her eyes are riveted on the couple, expressing horror, fascination, and excitement. Suddenly an older man (presumably the woman's husband or father) enters the room with a knife and stabs the lover. Catalina rushes in, helps the woman disentangle herself from the two fighting men, and quickly leads her out of the room.

This sequence, which Jo projects for Agatha on the screen and watches along with her, is a rather trite, stock scene in a costume melodrama, a family romance with a twist, but has a pivotal narrative and representational function in McLaughlin's film, and calls for several considerations. First: Unlike the women in most of the movies we have seen, with very few exceptions and mainly in avant-garde or independent women's cinema, Catalina does not die or get

---

5. The source of Jo's film is Thomas De Quincey's *The Spanish Military Nun*, which we see her reading in bed. On the life of Catalina de Erauso, see Dekker and van de Pol and her own autobiography, cited there. See also the Spanish film *La monja alférez* (Javier Aguirre, 1987), scripted from De Quincey's novella and Catalina de Erauso's autobiography.

married (think of *Rebecca*, with the eponymous heroine always already dead and Mrs. Danvers going up in flames, or of *Jane Eyre's* quintessential female-narrative ending: "Reader, I married him").[6] Nor does Catalina end up surviving, even victorious, but alone, like Scarlett O'Hara in *Gone With the Wind* or Alex in the recent noir remake *Black Widow*. Instead, she escapes with the other woman, whom she does not hate, compete with, or prove herself "better" than, but whom she . . . desires? loves? is fascinated by? The question is left suspended, despite the film's conventional narrative ending. Second: Diegetically (in the world of the story and what happens in it), the Catalina sequence marks the end of the film-within-the-film as well as the resolution of the film *we* watch, for Agatha's suspicions are allayed after she sees Jo's film, and their relationship resumes. Thus both films end with two women leaving together and leaving men behind.

Third: What the film-within-the-film does diegetically, the film we watch does cinematically, by means of the apparatus of cinema and what film theory has defined as film language—framing, editing, sound-image mixing, and the deployment of the system of the look, the specific way narrative cinema has of mobilizing the looks of the camera, of the characters within the film, and of the viewer or spectator. That is to say, just as Jo and Agatha watch Jo's film and leave the cutting room together as lovers, so does McLaughlin's film construct for both spectator and filmmaker a new position of seeing in the movies, a new place of the look—the place of a woman who desires another woman, the place from where each one looks at the other with desire; and, more important still, a place from where I, spectator, *see* their look and their desire. In other words, the film positions its spectator in a place from where the equivalence of look and desire—which sustains spectatorial pleasure and the very power of cinema in constructing and orienting the viewer's identification—appears invested in two women, each of whom is both the subject and the object of that look/desire. Fourth: The Catalina se-

---

6. Among the exceptions that come to mind are Sally Potter's *Thriller* and *The Gold Diggers*, Chantal Akerman's *Je tu il elle*, Su Friedrich's *Damned If You Don't*, Ulrike Ottinger's *Madame X* and *Johanna d'Arc of Mongolia*, Lizzie Borden's *Born in Flames*, Monika Treut's *The Virgin Machine*, and Joy Chamberlain's *Nocturne*. That all these filmmakers are lesbians, or were at the time they made these films, is certainly a queer coincidence.

quence is the cinematic-narrative trope by which this particular investment of the look is accomplished. For, as I will show, this stock melodramatic sequence of the film-within-the-film functions as a representation of the primal scene recast in relation to the lesbian lovers and relayed through them to the spectator(s).

Finally, in reframing the Oedipal scenario through the convention of the film-within-the-film, and in rearticulating the function of voyeurism both diegetically and cinematically (in *Catalina*'s closing shots as well as several other scenes throughout *She Must Be Seeing Things*), McLaughlin foregrounds precisely the question of what *can* be seen, of the relations of seeing as imaging to seeing as imagining, the relations of spectatorship to fantasy, of subjectivity and desire to the imaginary—and in particular to the imaginary of cinema. Furthermore, by locating itself in the ambiguous space between seeing and not seeing, and in the play between conventions of seeing and conventions of cinema, her film takes up a different position of enunciation and addresses the spectator in what I will call a lesbian subject-position (reminding the reader that the function of address is conceptually independent from the empirical notion of audience or the actual composition of the audience).

She, the spectator who occupies or is addressed in that subject-position, is represented diegetically in Agatha sitting at the cutting table, watching Jo's film, and reacting with intense participation because the film does have something to do with her life. And she, the filmmaker who enunciates or sees/speaks from that subject-position, is represented in Jo who is also sitting there, watching the words and images she has put together into *a figure of her desire for Agatha.* For it is clear that Catalina represents what Jo finds attractive in Agatha—her rebelliousness to a repressive Catholic upbringing, her jealousy and anger at God's and men's claim of exclusive access to women, her lesbian difference, her pain and her defiance. (Throughout the film, all the scenes with Catalina are crosscut with shots of Agatha, visually establishing their equivalence in the fantasy scenario. Whether imagined by Jo or actually being shot on location, or finally edited by Jo in the cutting room, all the scenes of the film-within-the-film are intercut with shots of Agatha reading Jo's diary and looking at the pictures in it, or Agatha watching on the shooting stage, or Agatha watching the edited film.)

For the spectator of *She Must Be Seeing Things*, then, the scene where Agatha and Jo watch the film-within-the-film's final sequence models a way of seeing that is not new in its filmic grammar, strictly speaking, but is quite novel in its figural mediation of spectatorial identification and desire. In the film we are watching, the Catalina sequence functions as an enacted primal fantasy in relation to the lesbian lovers. For the girl Catalina, who is looking on the primal scene, enters the Oedipal stage as active agent, against all odds cinematic and otherwise, then actually exits it victorious, taking the mother with her in phallic defiance—no femininity for her! Except for the twist of the ending and the sex of the hero, some such fantasy recurs in many adventure films, but McLaughlin's recasting is no mere gender-reversal tale. Unlike the adventure genre film, calling for a direct spectatorial identification with the hero (and often straining our capacity for willing suspension of disbelief beyond the breaking point, as in *Back to the Future* [1985]), here the affective, deeply embedded, contextual meaning of Catalina's picture-story is overlaid and heavily inflected by its subjective, identificatory effects on the two more immediately involved spectators, Agatha and Jo, who mediate and complicate our own, purposefully distanced, spectatorial relation to it.

Consider, for comparison, the play-within-the-film sequence in Leontine Sagan's version of *Maedchen in Uniform* (1931), where the schoolgirl Manuela, crossdressing in the role of Schiller's Don Carlos, declares her (his) forbidden love for Elizabeth (the name of both the schoolteacher, Fräulein von Bernburg, and the Queen Mother in *Don Carlos*). As Ruby Rich observes in her detailed reading of the film, "despite the school's aura of eroticism," it is only when Manuela proclaims her love for Fräulein von Bernburg after the play, "in a coming out that is the opposite of Don Carlos' vow of silence," that the full sense of her trangression hits the audience both of and within the film (109–10). In other words, for its trangressive meaning to be seen and registered by the audience, Manuela must make explicit and publicly name what the Oedipal fantasy in the play-within-the-film only suggests. What I am proposing by this comparison of two rather similar uses of the play-within-the-film (or film-within-the-film) device is that their respective effects in spectatorship derive from the particular specification of the characters who mediate spectatorial identification and from their greater or lesser capacity to act as figures of spectatorial desire. The school play's audience in *Maedchen* is a general, if mostly female and sympathetic, audience, whereas Agatha and Jo in *She Must Be Seeing Things* are affectively involved, subjectively "caught up" in the Catalina sequence; and as we look at the sequence through them, we are also caught up in what appears to be a subjective fantasy scenario rather than a staged performance or an object of viewing. Their effectiveness in mediating spectatorial identification, as bearers of the look and subjects of desire, is much greater; they act as a two-way mirror admitting the spectator into their particular fantasy.[7]

For we first see the scene in its entirety at the end of *She Must Be Seeing Things*, when Jo projects it on the screen for Agatha and herself as its only spectators; and it is then, at the conclusion of both film(s), that the spectator fully realizes that *Catalina* represents Jo's fantasy as well as Agatha's. In the narrative and visual economy of *She Must Be Seeing Things*'s mirror construction (*mise-en-abîme*), Catalina's picaresque adventures, culminating in the enacted primal scene on the Oedipal stage, function as the recasting of an original fantasy in the sense specified by Laplanche and Pontalis—that of fantasy as scenario, setting, structuring scene, or mise-en-scène of desire. I am suggesting that this fantasy is shared by both Agatha and Jo, spectator and filmmaker, and that one and the same scenario sustains the lesbian lovers' respective and mutual desire.

> Fantasy . . . is not the object of desire, but its setting. In fantasy the subject does not pursue the object or its sign: [s]he appears caught up [her]self in the sequence of images. . . . [S]he forms no representation of the desired object, but is [her]self represented as participating in the scene although, in the earliest forms of fantasy, [s]he cannot be assigned any fixed place in it. . . . As a result, the subject, although always present in the fantasy, may be so in a desubjectivized form, that is to say, in the very syntax of the sequence in question. ("Fantasy and the Origins of Sexuality" 26)

Like the title of McLaughlin's film, the Catalina sequence seems to refer to Agatha alone, thematically and in its setting (the Spanish

---

7. A much more recent film that very effectively refigures the primal scene (with an all-female cast) through an ingenious version of the play-within-the-film device is Joy Chamberlain's *Nocturne*. On the particular modalities of its inscription of lesbian fantasy and use of cinematic codes, see Patricia White, "Governing Lesbian Desire."

locale, Catholicism, Catalina's crossdressing). In effect, like the film-within-the-film which reframes it, Catalina's primal fantasy is made up by Jo with absorbed, passionate involvement—so passionate that, ironically, she risks breaking up with her lover during the shooting of the film. If Laplanche and Pontalis are right, then, Jo is as much the subject of the Catalina fantasy, a subject present and participating, if in a "desubjectivized form," as they say, "in the very syntax of the sequence in question." And indeed what better figure of such participation than that of the filmmaker, "caught up [her]self in the sequence of images" (cf. the scenes of the shooting of *Catalina*, Jo's involvement with the actress, her nervous directorial concentration during rehearsals and the final shoot) and even more emphatically present in "the very syntax of the sequence in question" (the final cut in the editing room).[8] In sum, not only are Jo and Agatha both the subject of that fantasy, but they share it, and share it together. This is a film about two women who share a common fantasy, a lesbian fantasy of origins; and if "the origin of the subject [her]self" is located "in the field of fantasy," as Laplanche and Pontalis say (19), then this very fantasy, which they share, is part of what constitutes them as a lesbian subject. Not the least implication of which is that it takes two women, not one, to make a lesbian.

I would now like to pursue some implications of the last three sentences in relation to the film's spectator and to spectatorship and fantasy more generally. Shortly before the passage cited just above, Laplanche and Pontalis have been concerned to locate the origin of fantasy in autoeroticism. Autoeroticism, they contend, is not merely a phase of libidinal development prior to the formation of object relationships, but rather "a mythical moment," a structuring trope in the constitution of the subject: it takes place in the process by which the drive, after the loss of the object (the real object, the milk), turns inward into the field of fantasy and becomes autoerotic, hallucinating the lost object by a sign which stands for both the object and its absence (the breast). Autoeroticism originates, then, in that psychic turn where the need for the object becomes representation, where the drive "moves into the field of fantasy and by that very fact becomes sexuality" (25). That moment or turn, which will

---

8. On the function of montage in what may be called the syntax of film language (the *"grande syntagmatique"* of narrative cinema), see Metz, *Language and Cinema.*

thereafter recur again and again throughout the subject's life, is the psychic trope joining the subject and sexuality, together, to the field of fantasy. It is because fantasy and autoeroticism have a common origin in the loss of the object that Laplanche and Pontalis find an ideal image of autoeroticism in the " 'lips that kiss themselves.' Here, in this apparently self-centred enjoyment, as in the deepest fantasy, in this discourse no longer addressed to anyone, all distinction between subject and object has been lost" (26).

It is striking to re-find this image in a text dated 1964, that is, much prior to the other text that has made the image famous in feminist discourse, Irigaray's "When Our Lips Speak Together": "Kiss me. Two lips kissing two lips . . . " (*This Sex Which Is Not One* 210). In doubling the image, Irigaray would describe a specifically female eroticism, one that can take place only between two female bodies and that is autoerotic because of the bodies' similarity or sameness. Taken as a representation of lesbian love, this image has been criticized precisely for its blurring of differences between subject and object, and for confining lesbian relationships to the imaginary or to the pre-Oedipal, in either case coming short of the symbolic and of the possibility of articulating lesbian subjectivity and desire therein.[9] Without going into the merits or the criticisms of Irigaray's position at this time—a position, at any rate, never reiterated or further elaborated in her work—I will note that the association of women with the image and the imaginary is also strong in the feminist theory of spectatorship. There, such association is based on a notion of specularity as similarity or sameness of the female spectator to the female body on the screen.

"French theorists such as Irigaray, Cixous, Montrelay, and Kofman in a sometimes hyperbolic celebration of the only picture of feminine 'subjectivity' available from psychoanalysis . . . activate the tropes of proximity, overpresence or excessive closeness to the body," writes Mary Ann Doane. Although this may not be desirable as a feminist politics of representation, she argues, "nevertheless, it is the position allotted to the female 'subject' both by psychoanalytic scenarios and by the cinema" (*The Desire to Desire* 12). In Doane's

---

9. For a discussion of Irigaray's theory of sexual difference as "a theory of the *hetero-sexual* rather than the homo-sexual" that is feminist but not lesbian, see Grosz, "The Hetero and the Homo"; and for its relevance to the reading and reception of mainstream film, see Holmlund.

view, based on the classical Hollywood genre known as "the woman's film," the woman spectator cannot easily negotiate the distance from the image that is necessary for spectatorial desire; voyeurism and fetishism, the major forms in which such distance obtains in spectatorship, are not available to her; and as "the distance between subject and object, spectator and image, is collapsed," her spectatorial position is not that of a desiring subject but one of proximity to or identification with the image (13). Doane further suggests that this capture of the female spectator by the image is linked to the threat presented to the girl child by the maternal space according to Irigaray and Kristeva, that threat being "the collapse of any distinction whatsoever between subject and object" (83). Thus the proximity of the woman spectator to the image seems to be predicated on a sameness of her body, the female body on the screen, and the body of the mother—a sameness of all women insofar as they are body and image, or imaged as body; and this sameness is what gives female eroticism its autoerotic character and at the same time threatens the subject with the collapse of distinctions between subject and other (woman)—female child and mother, female spectator and image, or woman and monster (see Williams, "When the Woman Looks").

Laplanche and Pontalis's theory of fantasy allows for a more complex articulation of the relations of subject and other in sexuality and in cinematic specularization. Unlike Irigaray's, their image of the "lips that kiss themselves" is clearly referred to the subject's autoeroticism, and not to her or his relation to the object. It refers to the joint origin of subject and sexuality, or the origin of the sexual subject, in the field of fantasy after the loss of the (first) object.[10] The notions of

---

10. In his *Life and Death in Psychoanalysis*, published in French in 1970, Laplanche further elaborates on autoeroticism in relation to sexuality as a drive initially propped up on a non-sexual function, self-preservation, but actually consisting precisely in its displacement, metaphorization, or perversion of the vital function or self-preservation instinct (18–23). He suggests that the translation of Freud's *Anlehnung* with *anaclisis* or *anaclitic* (as contrasted to *narcissistic*, in the essay "On Narcissism") has contributed to the misunderstanding of sexuality as linked to the function of self-preservation: "The term *propping* has been understood in this tradition as a leaning on the *object*, and ultimately a *leaning on the mother*. It may thus be intuited how an elaborate theory of a relation with the mother has come to inflect a notion intended to account for sexuality in its emergence. In fact, if one examines that notion more closely, one sees that originally it by no means designates a leaning of the subject on the object (of child on mother). . . . The phenomenon Freud describes is a leaning *of the drive* . . . upon a non-sexual, vital function" (16).

women's maternal nostalgia, pre-Oedipal capture, and over-identification with the image may be indeed fostered by some psychoanalytic theorists and by classical cinema but, whether considered politically desirable or undesirable, they are themselves imaginary—and perhaps belonging more to a certain feminist imaginary than to the imaginary of cinema or psychoanalysis *tout court*. As Judith Mayne remarks, "It has become too easy an assumption in feminist theory [that] affirmations of female friendship and female communities entail of necessity an impossible and utopian return to the Lacanian imaginary, or a simple reversal of (male) oedipal priorities in favor of (female) pre-oedipal ones, or a romantic affirmation of the maternal as a refuge from the difficulties of the patriarchal, symbolic universe" (*The Woman at the Keyhole* 84).

In this original and richly detailed study of women's cinema as a reinvention of narrative and visual form, Mayne analyzes the figure of the screen as a site of ambivalence, a figure that "both resists and gives support to the representation of female agency and female desire" (51). The significance of this trope for a feminist practice of cinematic narration, she remarks in response to Doane, is that it makes it "possible to speak simultaneously of what the classical cinema represents and what it represses" (85). As the title of Mayne's book suggests, women—filmmakers, viewers, actresses, editors, etc.—are on both sides of the keyhole, that is to say, both sides of "the threshold that makes representation possible" (9) by both dividing *and* joining subject and object, spectator and image. In thus refuting the notion of women's capture by or overidentification with the image, Mayne argues that the screen is "a figure of permeability and division at the same time" (225), and hence perhaps the central trope of women's reinvention of cinematic narrative.

Just as Mayne's work marks an important shift in the feminist theory of spectatorship, Laplanche and Pontalis's notion of fantasy articulates a conceptual space in which to rethink female subjectivity in psychoanalytic theory. In the footnote that follows their image of the "lips that kiss themselves," Laplanche and Pontalis comment:

> Cf. also, in S. Freud, "Instincts and their vicissitudes" [1915], *SE*,
> vol. XIV, the analysis of the pairs of opposites, sadism-masochism,
> voyeurism-exhibitionism. Beneath the active or passive form of the
> phrase (seeing, being seen, for instance), we must assume a

reflexive form (seeing oneself) which, according to Freud, would be primordial. No doubt this primordial degree is to be found when the subject no longer places [her]self in one of the different terms of the fantasy. (34, note 64)

Highly suggestive with regard to the subjective processes involved in film spectatorship in general, this comment is especially relevant to the spectatorial subject-position constructed in the particular film I am discussing.

In the vicissitudes of the component instincts, with their oscillation between and co-presence of opposites, the subject is caught up in a doubling and a splitting, a reversible pattern of specularization *and* differentiation that presupposes at least two terms of the fantasy, two bodies, and in the present instance, two female bodies that are not simply the same but at once similar and different. Here the specularization involves both self and other, and both active and passive forms (seeing, being seen), producing the subject as both subject and object, autoerotically doubled and yet split from itself and invested in the fantasmatic pursuit of the other (and in this sense, as well, it takes two women, not one, to make a lesbian). The other, reflexive or primordial form of the instinct (seeing oneself)—if primordial is taken in the sense of a constitutive, originary narcissism-voyeurism of the bodily ego[11]— would seem to imply a different kind of specularization in which the subject would see herself reflected not in the terms of the fantasy (active and/or passive, subject and/or object) but in the very representation of desire, in the fantasy scenario itself. This reflexive, and perhaps more truly autoerotic, form of the drive may find a place in cinema in the position of the spectator as a subject seeing herself and yet not seeing herself, a subject not placed in either one of the terms of the fantasy but looking on, outside the fantasy scenario and nonetheless involved, present in it. To explore further the analogy between spectatorship and fantasy, it may be useful to summarize how Laplanche and Pontalis argue for a homology between different levels of fantasy, from daydreams and

---

11. "For the beginning of its activity the scopophilic instinct is auto-erotic: it has indeed an object, but that object is part of the subject's own body. . . . The only correct statement to make about the scopophilic instinct would be that all the stages of its development, its auto-erotic, preliminary stage as well as its final active or passive form, co-exist alongside one another" (Freud, *SE* 14: 130).

reveries to the delusional fears of paranoiacs and the unconscious fantasies of hysterics.

From the unconscious fantasy distorted and yet revealed under the dream-façade, to the form it takes as the secondary elaboration reworks it into a fantasy more acceptable to consciousness, Laplanche and Pontalis maintain, Freud "discovers the same relationship between the deepest unconscious fantasy and the daydream: the fantasy is present at both extremities of the process of dreaming" (20–21). In the daydream, or in Freud's "model fantasy," the reverie, "that form of novelette, both stereotyped and infinitely variable, which the subject composes and relates to [her]self in a waking state,"

> the scenario is basically in the first person, and the subject's place clear and invariable. . . . But the original fantasy, on the other hand, is characterized by the absence of subjectivization, and the subject is present in the scene: the child, for instance, is one character amongst many in the fantasy "a child is beaten." Freud insisted on this visualization of the subject on the same level as the other protagonists. (22)

Consider the positions of the subject in the various forms of the beating fantasy analyzed in Freud's paper "A Child Is Being Beaten": its final form, as given in the title, overrides and is a substitute for two earlier ones, namely, "My father is beating the child" and "I am being beaten by my father." The latter form represents a transition from the first, objective form ("My father is beating the child"), in which the subject is altogether absent or unseeing, to the third and final one, in which the subject appears as a spectator, looking on as "a child is being beaten." The transitional form ("I am being beaten by my father"), Freud states, remains unconscious, is never remembered by the subject, and must be postulated as a construction in analysis. This transitional, unconscious form, buried beneath the first, objective form and the final, voyeuristic form of the beating fantasy, would seem to correspond to the reflexive form of the scopophilic instinct, "seeing oneself," which Laplanche and Pontalis posit ("we must assume") beneath the active or passive form, and which also usually remains unconscious in the cinema spectator.

The analogy between the subject of fantasy and the subject in cinematic spectatorship may be extended further: the unconscious beating fantasy is both active and passive ("the form of this fantasy is sadistic; the satisfaction which is derived from it is masochistic" [*SE* 17: 191]), and the subject is directly present and participating in it in a fully subjectivized manner—and hence it remains unconscious. Similarly, the reflexive "seeing oneself" of the subject in cinematic spectatorship is both active and passive, as well as unconscious. If the three forms of the beating fantasy are different manifestations of the structural and imaginary "unity of the fantasy whole," as Laplanche and Pontalis remark (22), it is possible to argue that a similar "unity" could be produced as subject effect in spectatorship; that is to say, the film would address the spectator as subject of its fantasy in its different levels and forms, would provide at once the fantasy and the means of access to it, would make a place for the spectator as subject in its fantasy, by the solicitation of her "primordial" autoerotic and scopophilic instinct in its reflexive form. Hence Freud's insistence on the visualization of the subject in clinical practice acquires relevance for the practice of film viewing, as well as film theory: How do I look at the film? How do I appear in its fantasy? Am I looking on? Can I be seen? Do I see myself in it? Is this my fantasy? For if it is the case that all film viewing engages the spectator in the regime of the fantasmatic, and if the analogy theoretically postulated between film spectator and subject of fantasy is (as I believe) a critically useful one, yet it does not follow that every film or every film's fantasy is capable of engaging every spectator. As I will be arguing later in the chapter, spectatorial admission into the film's scenario of desire is complex, overdetermined, and not always possible.

Returning now to McLaughlin's film: the significance of its reframing the Catalina fantasy as a film-within-the-film—a fantasy within what is already a fantasmatic regime in spectatorship—and of presenting it to the spectator mediated by the two framing characters of Jo and Agatha within the larger narrative frame of *She Must Be Seeing Things*, is that the latter film embeds the primal scene, "the deepest fantasy" (which, by the way, occurs very late in both films, as it does in clinical anamnesis), within a situation of adult lesbian sexuality where the symbolic, as well as the imaginary, is conspicuously present and foregrounded (what could be more symbolic or socially marked—technologically, semiotically, and ideologically—than the apparatus of film production?). Here autoeroticism, which Laplanche and Pontalis locate at the origin of the sexual subject, is represented in the girl Catalina, spectator of the primal scene and participant in it in the fantasmatic regime of the film-within-the-film. But because that primal fantasy is also the fantasy of the two spectators of the framing film, autoeroticism coexists with post-Oedipal homosexual object-choice in the two spectators who, by this very co-existence, may be identified as lesbians.

It is because of such reframing, mediation, and symbolic inscription of fantasy in lesbian terms that the film's mirror construction effects its particular specularization, working through the code of the film-within-the-film. In acting as the relay of spectatorial desire, Agatha and Jo provide a *visualization* of the subject of fantasy and the figure, *mise-en-abîme*, of the very processes of spectatorship; namely, imaginary identification with the image(s) (of the primal fantasy), symbolic production of reference and meaning in the narrative construction (the selective [re]arrangement of the images into a secondarized, narrativized scenario), and affective participation *at a distance.* As if to counteract the notion of women's proximity to the image by tampering with and recoding the genre of the woman's film on which that notion is based, McLaughlin has two women (again, not one but two) signify the spatial and representational distance of the spectators from the screen and of the voyeur from the scene looked on, as well as the psychotemporal distance of the subject from that "other scene," the original fantasy.

In other words, the two spectators of the film-within-the-film activate precisely the figure of the screen proposed by Mayne, with its permeability and division; they enact for the spectator of *She Must Be Seeing Things* the function of the "threshold" between viewing and fantasy, spectator and image, seeing and being seen; and, being two clearly distinct and almost antithetical spectators, though each in her way involved in the filmic fantasy, they also make visible the non-coincidence of the subject with any one term of that fantasy, eliciting the spectator's reflexive look (seeing herself) in the scenario, and thus making possible at once representation and self-representation. Finally, then, by addressing the spectator in the place of the desubjectivized subject looking on the fantasy it represents— once again, a fantasy self-reflexively marked as a primal fantasy, recast and reframed symbolically as a lesbian fantasy—McLaughlin's film does not merely portray a lesbian fantasy (as other recent films have done) but effectively constructs a scenario of lesbian *spectato-rial* desire and enables the visualization—it would be appropriate to say the invention—of a *lesbian* subject of viewing.

Since McLaughlin's film is centrally concerned with fantasy and subjectivity in relation to vision, it is not surprising that the other primal fantasies are traceable in it as well. The origin of the seduc-tion and castration fantasies is also located in the film-within-the-film, as the young orphan (pre-Oedipal) Catalina and her girlfriend in the convent are discovered sleeping in the same bed, immediately separated, and threatened by a nun with God's punishment for an "evil" of which they have no knowledge. Enter the symbolic as deus ex machina, the prohibition at once producing loss, fantasy, and de-sire—and the perversion is implanted in the subject, as Foucault might have said. Subsequently and throughout the film, these fanta-sies are re-presented reframed as cinematic images and thus in the terms of the heterosexual symbolic, but at the same time recoded with specific reference to contemporary lesbian subculture, its prac-tices and discourses concerning the vicissitudes of the sexual in-stincts, especially sadomasochism, voyeurism, and exhibitionism.

The seduction and castration fantasies are recurrently figured from the very beginning of the film in Agatha's conscious fantasies or daydreams of Jo's sexual encounters with men; in her sadistic fantasies of Jo machine-gunned in the street (reminiscent of Valie Export's *Invisible Adversaries* as well as the ending of *Bonnie and Clyde*) or strangled with the telephone cord (as in *Dial M for Mur-der*); and in her hallucinations (unconscious fantasies). Most force-ful is one scene in which, from her office window, Agatha sees Jo walking down the street below, flirting with a man, and kissing him. The film presents this scene, constructed as a series of quickly alter-nating shot/reverse shots and jump cuts, specifically as a hallucina-tion: for the woman walking in the street, in the first reverse shot and jump cut, is clearly recognizable to the spectator as Jo (i.e., Lois Weaver), but suddenly, after the second cut to the reverse shot from Agatha, she is revealed to be not Jo but an unknown woman who *looks like* her. If Agatha's jealousy is consistently imaged in relation to men—whereas, to this viewer, the jeweler (played by Peggy Shaw) or Agatha's friend Julia (played by Elizabeth Cunningham) would seem much more likely causes for jealousy—it is not only because the film explicitly engages with the standard (heterosexual) codes of visual representation but also because it acknowledges the presence of the castration fantasy in jealousy itself, whatever the immediate cause of jealousy may be. (Speaking of her lover, Julia says: "With Kate, I know she's gay. She's been with women. I don't get jealous of men." Agatha replies: "So what? You get jealous of women.")

In the scene in the porno shop, where Agatha goes to confront the phallus in its humbler manifestation and commodity form, the dildo, the three fantasies come together and are in one de-romanticized and de-naturalized in the ironic figure of the "sex toys," the dildo and the rubber doll. The irony is underscored by the disgusted look of the saleswoman at the greedy male customer who demands to buy the window display doll (the others being sold out), and by the unctuous, supercilious attitude of the salesman assisting Agatha in the selection of a "realistic" dildo: gender asymmetry in men's and women's access to a sexuality defined by sexual commodities is made explicit in this exchange, and is one of the points of the irony. However, if Agatha leaves the store without buying into the commodified heterosexual fantasy, nevertheless the primal fantasies rearticulated by the film in relation to a lesbian subject still rigorously include and have to come to terms with heterosexuality.

The dominance of the heterosexual institution in the symbolic order of Western cultures need not be demonstrated here; its ubiquitous presence in practices of daily life as well as in the media, language, art, science, literature, etc., informs the very structures of thought and knowledge that Monique Wittig has called "the straight mind," with pointed reference to Lévi-Strauss's *The Savage Mind*. "When thought by the straight mind, homosexuality is nothing but heterosexuality," she writes (*The Straight Mind* 28), because the social contract and symbolic exchange which establish culture and society itself are founded on the presupposition or, as I prefer to say, the presumption of heterosexuality (see de Lauretis, "The Female Body and Heterosexual Presumption," and also Pajaczkowska). What McLaughlin's film takes on is the imaginary of heterosexuality. In working through the codes of narrative cinema, she both explores and makes visible how that imaginary also informs or over-determines lesbian fantasy and subjectivity.[12] Thus the film re-

12. McLaughlin's foregrounding of the heterosexual imaginary, so pervasively implied and conveyed by most cinematic and other forms of representation, and her

presents at once the dominance of heterosexuality and the struggle against it, not coincidentally represented as a struggle with codes of visual representation, including the appropriation of masculine gender signifiers (Catalina's uniform, Agatha's male drag) and the camp reappropriation of feminine gender signifiers (Jo's baby doll performance).

When Agatha puts on a man's suit to signify her desire in socially visible form, to wear the countenance of seduction, effectively to come out publicly and *visibly to herself* (as suggested by the scene in front of the mirror);[13] or when Jo performs her desire for Agatha in the boa striptease act, clearly marked as a seduction scene, and a fully cinematic fantasy (with hints of Marlene Dietrich, Rita Hayworth, and Marilyn Monroe rolled into one, and Amina's aria from Bellini's *La sonnambula* on the soundtrack); then the film is referring their personal story back to a whole subcultural history past and present, lesbian and gay, of sexual and gender transgression, reverse discourse, (re)appropriations and resignifications of sexuality through public forms of fantasy that both acknowledge and deny the dominance of heterosexuality. Male drag is an old and venerable trope of lesbian subculture and self-representation; used sparingly by Hollywood cinema, it has been almost continuously reactivated by successive generations since Radclyffe Hall's notorious book trial in 1928. With spectacular femininity, it has been the other way around: first appropriated from Hollywood cinema by the gay subculture, it has entered the lesbian subculture more recently, and then not without resistance, even as the notion of femininity as masquerade has acquired currency in feminist film theory.

The camp reappropriation of heterosexual images of sexual roles—the fact that these are standard positions, as it were, in which desire is represented and defined, indeed prescribed, in a culture predicated on heterosexual difference—is foregrounded in the film

---

analysis of its effects in lesbian subjectivity have earned her film a controversial reception (see Brownworth). On the aesthetic and political project of the film as intervention in a lesbian and feminist discourse where women's desire and fantasy are often undercoded or prescriptively cleansed of any reference to heterosexuality, see Alison Butler's interview with the filmmaker.

13. The homology between this scene and the mirror scene in Radclyffe Hall's *The Well of Loneliness*, which I consider central to an understanding of lesbian perverse desire, may be pure coincidence or fully intentional on the filmmaker's part. I will return to it in chapter 5, in my discussion of the castration fantasy.

by the amateur quality of the performance, its being acted, marked as a performance (both the scene of Agatha's crossdressing and Jo's femme masquerade open with Agatha and Jo coming out from behind a curtain in their respective apartments), and distanced by parody (the hole in the stocking) or by lack of fit (Agatha in a man's suit). So that we see the face behind the mask, the mask doesn't quite fit, and the masquerade is never quite successful; or rather, it is successful *as* a masquerade—not an embodiment. For Agatha is clearly not a man, even as she "preferred identifying" with her father to falling in love with him, as the film's pop psychology would have it. And Jo is not the female star in her full-drag impersonation of femininity but is in fact the filmmaker, the director, whose desire (for Agatha) is inscribed and figured, not to say sublimated, in her work. Which, when you think about it, is a very "masculine" position, as is her near-total absorption in her work.

In other words, it is *the active, conscious, and even flaunted assumption* of masculine and feminine gender positions as expressions of desire, signifiers of seduction, and the performance and reversal of sexual roles as a means of taking up and signaling the position of desiring subject, that reframe these scenes—much as the film-within-the-film does—as a lesbian fantasy. Unlike the primal scene ("the deepest fantasy"), however, the seduction and castration fantasies are not embedded *en abîme* within the film-within-the-film but constructed as cinematic spectacles whose obvious iconographic references to cinema, movie stars, and popular Hollywood scenarios reframe the fantasies in an ironic, camp self-reflexivity. Here, then, the recasting of fantasy, narratively mediated by the diegetic characters, is effected through the very codes and tropes of Hollywood cinema and camp aesthetic, by the figures of masquerade and crossdressing with their long-term presence in Western history and their specific subcultural articulations (see Dekker and van de Pol, Garber, and Newton among others).

II. Lesbianism and the Theory of Spectatorship

The figures of masquerade, transvestism, and crossdressing have been recurrent tropes of feminist discourse in the eighties, and in the theorization of female spectatorship in particular (for example,

Mulvey, "Afterthoughts on 'Visual Pleasure and Narrative Cinema' Inspired by King Vidor's *Duel in the Sun* [1946]," in *Visual and Other Pleasures* 29–38; Mary Ann Doane, "Film and the Masquerade: Theorising the Female Spectator," in *Femmes Fatales* 17–32; Elaine Showalter, "Critical Cross-Dressing: Male Feminists and the Woman of the Year"; Sandra Gilbert, "Costumes of the Mind: Transvestism as Metaphor in Modernist Literature"; and Jane Gaines, "The Queen Christina Tie-Ups"). In her essay "Towards a Butch-Femme Aesthetic," Sue-Ellen Case takes up the issue of masquerade in the context of performance theory and lesbian camp aesthetic. Discussing the Split Britches' production of *Beauty and the Beast,* where Peggy Shaw as the butch, "who represents by her clothing the desire for other women, becomes the beast—the marked taboo against lesbianism dressed up in the clothes of that desire," and Lois Weaver as the femme plays Beauty, "the desired one and the one who aims her desirability at the butch," Case writes:

> This symbolism becomes explicit when Shaw and Weaver interrupt the Beauty/Beast narrative to deliver a duologue about the history of their own personal butch-femme roles. Weaver uses the trope of having wished she was Katherine Hepburn and casting another woman as Spencer Tracy, while Shaw relates that she thought she was James Dean. The identification with movie idols is part of the camp assimilation of dominant culture. It serves multiple purposes. One, they do not identify these butch-femme roles with "real" people, or literal images of gender, but with fictionalized ones, thus underscoring the masquerade. Two, the history of their desire, or their search for a sexual partner becomes a series of masks, or identities that stand for sexual attraction in the culture, thus distancing them from the "play" of seduction as it is outlined by social mores. Three, the association with movies makes narrative fiction part of the strategy as well as characters. (67–68)

The purpose of Case's essay is to articulate a feminist subject-position "outside the ideology of sexual difference and thus the social institution of heterosexuality" (56); and such position, she maintains, can be only that of "the butch-femme subject" (63). Her thesis requires, on the one hand, bringing "the lesbian subject out of the closet of feminist history" (57), which she does by retracing the steps of the interaction between feminism and lesbianism in North America to the early seventies and the project of the Daughters of

Bilitis, whose outcome was the alliance between lesbians and heterosexual feminists—an alliance that resulted in the elision of the
material reality of the crossdressing or passing woman and the appropriation of her strategies, safely metaphorized into discursive
tropes, by a heterosexual feminist discourse primarily concerned
with femininity and the female subject/body in relation to "sexual
difference," and hence to masculinity and to men. On the other
hand, Case's own project entails reactivating the discourse of camp,
the style and mise-en-scène of butch-femme roles—roles which "are
played in signs themselves and not in ontologies" (70).

The recuperation of camp to the side of a lesbian aesthetic and a
lesbian-and-feminist politics requires, first off, a distancing of the
latter from the discourse of a generalized "postmodernism." For, as
Case remarks, "camp style, gay-identified dressing, and the articulation of the social realities of homosexuality have also become part of
the straight, postmodern canon." She cites Herbert Blau's quip "Be-
coming-homosexual is part of the paraphilia of the postmodern"
("Disseminating Sodom" 233–34, cited by Case 61) in order to
launch her critique of contemporary theory's appropriation of gay
and especially lesbian discourses, an appropriation which again
goes hand in hand with the elision of their social and material
realities.[14] Case's recapitulation of the vicissitudes of the figure of

---

14. On the function of camp as a means to propose "female homosexuality as an
aesthetic and not only a sexual choice," see Sabine Hake's interesting reading of
Ulrike Ottinger's film *Madame X.* Hake, however, unlike Case, seems unconcerned
with distancing the postmodern taste for camp from the material and social realities
of homosexuality, or with making any distinction between lesbian, gay, and "homosexual" (the only term she uses) consciousness, sensibility, or sexualities: "The retro
mode characteristic of camp presupposes an alienated consciousness and an aesthetic appreciation that are essential both to the homosexual and the postmodern
sensibility. Camp functions as an aesthetic position on sexual difference by exposing
all categories of meaning production to a play with the pervasive/perverse levels of
many sexualities" (97). How important it is to distinguish between a lesbian and a gay
camp aesthetic, a distinction that devolves from the sexual and gender asymmetry
between "homosexual" subjectivities as they are constituted both discursively and
materially at this moment in history in North America, is evident if one reads Case's
essay with Leo Bersani's "Is the Rectum a Grave?" Bersani sees homosexual camp not
as irony or erotic but as parody, "largely a parody of women," and parody, he states,
"is an erotic turn-off, and all gay men know this. . . . The gay male parody of a certain
femininity [is also] a way of giving vent to the hostility toward women that probably
afflicts every male": it "speaks the truth of that femininity as mindless, asexual, and
hysterically bitchy, thereby provoking, it would seem to me, a violently antimimetic
reaction in any female spectator" (208). I owe this observation to my friends of the
Lesbian and Gay Faculty Research Group at the University of California, Santa Cruz.

masquerade, first proposed by the Kleinian lay analyst Joan Riviere in her analysis of a heterosexual woman patient, begins with a brief and, itself, campy synopsis of Riviere's paper.[15] "Thus began the theory that all womanliness is a masquerade worn by women to disguise the fact that they have taken their father's penis in their intellectual stride, so to speak. Rather than remaining the well-adjusted castrated woman, these intellectuals have taken the penis for their own and protect it with the mask of the castrated, or womanhood" (64). Then she goes on to take issue with Mary Ann Doane's concept of masquerade as the term of a possible subject-position for female spectators.

In order to make the argument fully intelligible, I will briefly summarize Doane's thesis, which is as follows: Psychoanalytic and film theory, as well as dominant cinema, negate the female gaze, or rather inscribe it as overidentified with the image, and hence unseeing, empty of desire (she acutely points to the figure of the woman with glasses, a recurrent motif of classical Hollywood cinema, counterposed to the figure of the man with binoculars).

> The pervasiveness, in theories of the feminine, of descriptions of such a claustrophobic closeness [to the image], a deficiency in relation to structures of seeing and the visible, [results in] a tendency to view the female spectator as the site of an oscillation between a feminine position and a masculine position, invoking the metaphor of the transvestite. Given the structures of cinematic narrative, the woman who identifies with a female character must adopt a passive or masochistic position, while identification with the active hero necessarily entails an acceptance of what Laura Mulvey refers to as a certain "masculinization" of spectatorship. (*Femmes Fatales* 24; the internal reference is to Mulvey 29–38)

By transvestism both Doane and Mulvey mean a metaphoric transfer of female to male point of view in the spectator: "The transvestite adopts the sexuality of the other—the woman becomes a

---

15. On the fortunes of masquerade as *the* figure of femininity in Lacanian psychoanalytic theory and in cinema, see Heath, "Joan Riviere and the Masquerade." A different reading of Riviere's paper is given by Fletcher, "Versions of Masquerade," which also provides a comprehensive examination of masquerade and its extensions in (1) the conceptualization of Lacanian femininity and sexual difference, and (2) the translation of Freud's theory of fetishism into a generalized logic of representation. I will return to this in chapter 6.

man in order to attain the necessary distance from the image" (25). This slipping into male clothes is both easy for women, Doane thinks, and culturally accepted; seen as a manifestation of women's sexual mobility or bisexuality, it may be recontained within the terms of current definitions of woman—her being body (as Cixous declared), close to the image, or outside the symbolic.[16] The masquerade, on the contrary, with its hyperbolic, excessive demonstration that femininity is a cultural construct, effectively resists those terms and "is not as recuperable as transvestitism precisely because it constitutes an acknowledgement that it is femininity itself which is constructed as mask" (25). As a metaphor of spectatorship, then, in the process of viewing, the masquerade holds femininity at a distance, produces "a certain distance between oneself and one's image" (26), a distance that Doane believes is "necessary for an adequate reading of the image" (31).

Case criticizes Doane on two counts. First, she objects that the masquerade of femininity as a position of spectatorship, whereby the (heterosexual) female viewer can "appropriate the gaze for [her] own pleasure," is still a passive, conventionally feminine position as compared with the femme who "performs her masquerade as the *subject* of representation" (66; emphasis added). Here Case's own frame of reference, which is *theatrical* representation and performance—and hence the specific subject effects and positions in spectatorship produced in theatrical (as contrasted with filmic) representation—is most likely responsible for her erroneous assumption that film spectatorship is a *passive* or *object*-like mode of subjectivity, as opposed to the *active* mode of stage performance. As I have suggested earlier with regard to cinema as fantasmatic production, film spectatorship can be just as active and constitutive for the subject as a more public or *visible* "activity" (once again, the question of visibility, what *can be seen?*). In fact, Doane herself makes clear that what she is trying to articulate, against Hollywood and other representations of women as incapable of vision, is a posi-

---

16. On the problematic notions of women's sexual mobility, oscillation, bisexuality, or what Rose calls "the homosexual factor in all feminine sexuality" deriving from the pre-Oedipal relation to the mother, see my discussion in chapter 2. Here Doane seems to accept these notions and at the same time resist their implication, most lucidly stated by Rose as "the impossibility [for women] of subject *and* desire" ("Dora" 146).

tion of (heterosexual) female spectatorship that is not only actively looking but also distanced from the image, not captured by its specularity, and so capable of seeing and desiring. Unfortunately, as she herself admits, her effort is not successful—in part, it seems to me, because she is ultimately committed to the theory of women's narcissistic capture by the image.[17] And indeed, Doane's notion of masquerade as a metaphor for the process of female spectatorship does not deny that narcissistic capture: for the female spectator's *distance* from the image of woman would derive from her *identification* with the image of masquerade (performed on-screen by Marlene Dietrich in drag, Rita Hayworth's femme fatale in *Gilda*, and so on). Thus, in the end, Case is not altogether wrong in questioning the novelty of masquerade as a subject-position in spectatorship.

On the second count of her critique, however, Case is not mistaken. The femme, she argues, "delivers a performance of the feminine masquerade rather than, as Doane suggests, continuing in Riviere's reactive formation of masquerading compensatorily before the male-gaze-inscribed-dominant-cinema-screen" (66). Between the femme, who foregrounds her masquerade of femininity by playing to a butch, and the butch, who foregrounds her own masquerade of the phallus to the femme, "the fictions of penis and castration become ironized and 'camped up.' . . . In other words, these penis-related posturings were always acknowledged [in lesbian bar culture] as roles, not biological birthrights" (64–65). In my own words, the problem with trying to claim masquerade as a "non-recuperable" position of agency for the female subject is precisely its compensatory nature of reaction-formation, that is to say, of defense mechanism against the male's requirement that women acquiesce and accept what he defines as femininity and lay no claim to masculine prerogative. As such, masquerade is not only inscribed within a

17. In the same issue of the journal *Discourse* where Case's essay appeared, perhaps coincidentally, Doane's own afterthoughts were published as well. " 'Film and the Masquerade,' " writes Doane, is an "attempt (which fails in many respects) to tear the concept of masquerade out of its conventional context. Generally, masquerade is employed not to illuminate the agency usually associated with spectatorship, but to designate a mode of being for the other. . . . Masquerade would hence appear to be the very antithesis of spectatorship/subjectivity" ("Masquerade Reconsidered: Further Thoughts on the Female Spectator," originally in *Discourse* 11 [1988 89]: 42, reprinted in *Femmes Fatales* 33).

male-defined and male-dominant heterosexual order but more inexorably, in the current struggle for women's "equal access" to pleasure in heterosexuality, the masquerade of femininity is bound to
reproduce that order by addressing itself—its work, its effects, its
plea—to heterosexual men.[18] This "daughter's seduction" (the phrase
is Jane Gallop's) is most certainly recuperable in contemporary
Western culture, and in fact recuperated even within the academic
institution.

What is not, on the other hand, is the female—butch, femme,
bad girl or good girl—who does not address her masquerade to men.
That this possibility has not been seen or even contemplated in feminist theorizations of masquerade is the point made by Case and
elaborated in another context by Patricia White. In the course of her
reading of Ottinger's *Madame X*, White also discusses Doane's notions of masquerade and transvestism, retracing the latter to Mulvey, who put it thus: "as desire is given cultural materiality in a text,
for women (from childhood onwards) trans-sex identification is a
habit that very easily becomes *second nature*. However, this Nature
does not sit easily and shifts restlessly in its borrowed transvestite
clothes" (*Visual and Other Pleasures* 33). But "why must *transvestite*
clothes be 'borrowed'?" asks White, pointing out the absurdity of the
statement that for the transvestite "clothes make the man" (94). She
thus renders explicit two implicit assumptions of this feminist theory of spectatorship: (a) that women are uncomfortable in masculine clothes because of their real sex (the first nature) and/or their
feminine desire, and (b) that women can and do crossdress, meta-
phorically and otherwise, *with impunity* by virtue of their alleged
"sexual mobility." Such assumptions are all the more insidious in
the frame of reference and visibility of contemporary theory alluded
to by Case, in which lesbians and gay men who crossdress and/or
masquerade *must be seen* as simply and safely acting out "the paraphilia of the postmodern," like everyone else.

In the terms of my reading of McLaughlin's film, the butch-
femme role-playing is exciting not because it represents heterosex-

---

18. As Irigaray puts it in *Ce Sexe qui n'en est pas un*, "the masquerade . . . is what
women do . . . in order to participate in man's desire, but at the cost of giving up
theirs." Or as another woman laments, "When women give up the masquerade, what
do they find in bed? Women analysts, how do they cause erections?" (cited in Heath,
"Joan Riviere and the Masquerade" 54–55).

ual desire, but because it doesn't; that is to say, in mimicking it, it shows the uncanny distance, like an effect of ghosting, between desire (heterosexually represented as it is) and the representation; and because the representation doesn't fit the actors who perform it, it only points to their investment in a fantasy—a fantasy that can never fully represent them or their desire, for the latter remains in excess of its setting, the fantasy that grounds it, and that continues to ground it even as it is deconstructed and destabilized by the mise-en-scène of lesbian camp. It is in that space between the fantasy scenario and the self-critical, ironic lesbian gaze—a space the film constructs evidently and purposefully—that I am addressed as a spectator of *She Must Be Seeing Things,* and that a subject-position is figured out and made available to me, spectator, in terms of a sexual difference that is not a difference between woman and man, between female and male sexuality, but a difference between heterosexual and lesbian sexuality. So I do not identify with either woman or role, for the film works as a fantasy for me as well, offering not the object but the setting of my desire. What I do identify with is the symbolic space of excess and contradiction that the role, the lack of fit, the disjuncture, the difference between characters and roles make apparent in each of them, and the scenario or imaginary space in which that difference configures a lesbian subject-position.

The distinction I'm trying to make between, on the one hand, the representation of desire heterosexually conceived, even as it is attributed to a woman for another, and, on the other hand, the effort to represent a homosexual-lesbian desire is a subtle and difficult one. The controversial reception of McLaughlin's film is evidence of that difficulty, which not only is due to the diverse meanings that have accrued to those two words *lesbian* and *desire,* but even more derives from the complexity of representation itself, the weight of its culturally established codes and expressive forms, and the overdetermination of its effects, the ways it engages the viewer's subjective processes, both conscious and unconscious. So I will backtrack a moment from this film to the historical and cultural ground from which it so singularly emerges.

In all the culturally dominant forms of representation that surround us, from television to museum art, from the most banal love story to the most sublime one can think of, desire is predicated on sexual difference as gender, the difference of woman from man or femininity from masculinity, with all that those terms entail—and not as a difference between heterosexual and homosexual, or straight and gay sexuality. This is the sense in which I read Mc-Laughlin's interview statement that heterosexuality "defines and in a sense creates our sexuality" (Alison Butler 20–21)—where heterosexuality stands for the *institution* of heterosexuality, and not mere heterosexual behavior, the event of sexual intercourse between a woman and a man, which may or may not occur. But even for those whose sexual behavior or whose desire has never been hetero-directed, heterosexuality is "inescapable," though not determining. For, if sexuality is represented as gendered, as the direct result of the existence of two sexes in nature—on which basis culture has constructed gender, and onto which in turn civilization has attached meanings, affects, and values, such as love, social relations, and the continuation of the human species—then it follows that sexuality is finally inescapable for every single human being, as is gender; no one can be without them, because they are part and parcel of being human. Thus sexuality is not only *defined* but actually *enforced* as heterosexuality, even in its homosexual form.

Moreover, as feminist theory has argued for well over two decades, sexuality in the dominant forms of Western culture is defined from the frame of reference of "man," the white man, who has enforced his claim to be the subject of knowing, and woman—all women—his object: object of both his knowledge and his desire. Heterosexuality, therefore, is doubly enforced on women, as it were: enforced as hetero-sexuality, in the sense that women can and must feel sexually in relation to men, and enforced as hetero-sexuality in the sense that sexual desire belongs to the other, originates in him. In this standard frame, amazingly simplistic and yet authoritative, and reaffirmed again and again, alas even in feminist theory, whatever women may feel toward other women cannot be sexual desire, unless it be a "masculinization," a usurpation or an imitation of man's desire.[19]

---

19. For example, describing the female spectator's relation to the image ("She must look, as if she were a man with the phallic power of the gaze, at a woman who would attract that gaze, in order to be that woman"), Doane relies on Kristeva's authority to suggest an analogy with this most conventional view of female homosexuality: " 'I am looking, as a man would, for a woman'; or else, 'I submit myself, as if I were a man who thought he was a woman, to a woman who thinks she is a man' " (*The Desire to Desire* 157, citing Kristeva, *About Chinese Women* 29). While it is not

This, then, is what makes the Barbara Stanwyck character the villain in *Walk on the Wild Side* (Edward Dmytryk, 1950), and what the protagonist of Sergio Toledo's *Vera* (1987) has so well internalized that she is convinced she is a man because she desires a woman: one may not be born a woman or a man, but one can desire only as a man. And this is, of course, the classic representation of the mannish lesbian since Stephen Gordon in Radclyffe Hall's *The Well of Loneliness*, a novel continuously and widely read since its obscenity trial in 1928 and the focus of debate among lesbian feminists even recently. In fact, McLaughlin's film refers to that representation explicitly in the interchange between Agatha and Jo on the bed, after the striptease scene, where Jo taunts Agatha about phallic desire. Agatha admits to feeling it "maybe—sometimes" but also adds with clear conviction, "But I don't want to be a man." Shortly after, the scene in the porno shop further explores and ironizes this contradictory relation of Agatha's "masculine" identification to the representation of phallic desire signified by the gingerly held, ironically "realistic" dildo.

By calling up this iconographic and cultural history, in conjunction with current lesbian practices of both reappropriation and resignification of what is and is not our history, *She Must Be Seeing Things* asks what in feminist film culture is clearly a rhetorical question: What are the things Agatha imagines seeing and those Jo "sees" in her film, if not those very images, "a terror and a dream" (as Adrienne Rich so sharply put it), that our cultural imaginary and the whole history of cinema have constructed as the visible, what can be seen, *and eroticized?* Namely, the female body displayed as spectacle for the male gaze "to take it in," to enter or possess it, or as fetish object of his secret identification; the woman as mystery to be pursued, investigated, found guilty or redeemed by man; and above all, what can be seen and eroticized—though it is not actually imaged or represented on the screen, but only figured, implied, in the look—is

---

clear why female homosexuality needs to be invoked in the heterosexual context of *Caught,* the film Doane is discussing (a woman's "desire to be desired"), or what purpose it serves in her theory of (heterosexual) female spectatorship, the point I want to stress is the banality of that "image" of the lesbian-who-would-be-man—an amazingly conventional image for a feminist theorist and a contemporary psychoanalyst to commit to print, and one whose arrogance can be explained only by the homophobic threat it must present to the minds of the writers. But I shall return to this image again (and regretfully again) in the next chapters.

the gaze itself, the phallic power of the gaze invested in the male look as figure and signifier of desire. Feminist film criticism and theory have documented this history of representation extensively. Now, the originality of McLaughlin's film, in my opinion, consists precisely in its foregrounding of that frame of reference, making *it* visible, and at the same time shifting it, moving it aside, as it were, enough to let us see through the gap, the contradiction; enough to create a space for questioning not only what *they* see but also what *we* see in the film; enough to let us see ourselves seeing, and with what eyes.[20] The importance and the novelty of the film's question, What are the "things" she must be seeing? consist in that, insofar as the film addresses the spectator in a lesbian subject-position, the question is addressed to lesbians. Thus it is no longer a rhetorical question in the sense that the answer is already known or can be taken for granted, but is reactivated as a rhetorical question in the sense (elaborated by Paul de Man) that it can turn around, suspend, subvert, the expected answer.

This is not the case in films or other visual practices that set out to represent "lesbians" without attempting to shift the standard frame of reference, without reworking the conventions of seeing and the established modes and complex effects of representation. I am not convinced, for instance, by Jill Dolan's assertion that the reappropriation of pornographic imagery by lesbian magazines such as *On Our Backs* offers "liberative fantasies" and "representations of one kind of sexuality based in lesbian desire" (171). I am not at all convinced by her argument because its very premise, lesbian desire, is merely assumed to be, and taken for granted as, a property or a quality of individuals predefined as lesbians; whereas it is precisely that "lesbian desire" which constitutes the kind of subjectivity and sexuality we experience as lesbian and want to claim as lesbians; and which therefore we need to theorize, articulate, and find ways of representing, not only in its difference from heterosexual norms, its ab-normality, but also and more importantly in its own

---

20. My argument here runs somewhat parallel to Marilyn Frye's essay "To Be and Be Seen" in *The Politics of Reality*, but I am less certain than she is that the simple visibility of lesbians is a sufficient condition for the representation or the formation of lesbian subjectivity. My argument for McLaughlin's film as a text that foregrounds the complexity and difficulty of lesbian visibility is also, in this sense, in dialogue with Frye.

constitutive processes, its specific modalities and conditions of existence. Simply casting two women in a standard pornographic scenario or in the standard frame of the romance, and repackaging them as a commodity purportedly produced for lesbians, does not seem to me sufficient to disrupt, subvert, or resist the straight representational and social norms by which "homosexuality is nothing but heterosexuality"—nor *a fortiori* sufficient to shed light on the specific difference that constitutes a lesbian subjectivity.

In Donna Deitch's *Desert Hearts* (1985), for instance, heterosexuality as sexual behavior remains off-screen and is diegetically cast off in a quick Reno divorce, but heterosexuality as institution is still actively present in the spectatorial expectations set up by the genre, the Western romance, with its seamless narrative space, conventional casting and characterization, and by commercial distribution techniques, which make this love story between women in every other respect the same as any other.[21] If I single out this film for its failure to engage with the problem of representation—which is never a problem just of the film, but of the whole cinematic apparatus as a social technology and of the much larger field of audio-visual representation beyond that—it is because *Desert Hearts* (though necessarily an independent and courageously self-financed film) makes no attempt to pass itself off as anything but a mass-audience, commercially viable entertainment product, and nonetheless declares itself a lesbian's film. As such, for better or for worse, it bears a social responsibility, a burden of accountability, greater than those of other commercial products (*Black Widow*, *Personal Best*, or Wertmueller's despicable *Sotto sotto*) which unabashedly exploit the currently fashionable discourse on lesbianism to the end of an effective delegitimation of the lesbian—

---

21. Consider, for example, the woman (who will remain nameless in the film) whom Vivian sees in Kay's bed when she first goes to Kay's house, and who then reappears briefly only once, in the car scene, to be treated by Kay as the "slut" vs. the love interest (here Vivian) of the classical Western: her narrative characterization as the stock character "whore" is completed by her makeup, looks, pose, speech, etc. *Desert Hearts* does not distance this image and role or reframe them in a lesbian camp tradition or in the lesbian history of the forties and fifties, as it might have done, but only invokes a general fifties mood typical of many films of the eighties. The film remains squarely within Hollywood conventions, including the casting of two self- and media-identified heterosexual actresses. On the inscription of films about lesbians within iconographic and generic conventions, see Merck, " 'Lianna' and the Lesbians of Art Cinema."

and perhaps even the feminist—politics of sexual difference. And in this sense Deitch's film is much more honorable, in my eyes, than other independent films apparently benign, "sensitive," or pro-lesbian, such as John Sayles's *Lianna* or Patricia Rozema's *I've Heard the Mermaids Singing*, which more subtly appropriate the issue of lesbian difference for art-entertainment purposes, and resolve it much too simply, and all too safely, in a banal notion of sexual preference. (I have written of this at greater length in "Guerrilla in the Midst.") There, as well, representation seems to pose no problem.

And yet, problems there are aplenty. Not only problems manifested by the massive reaction to homosexuality and gay politics surfacing in the frightful misrepresentations and repressive strategies of the Right in the context of the AIDS crisis, but also problems in the representation of lesbianism within feminist theory itself. To many feminist critics and theorists, lesbian subjectivity is a subset, a variation, or a component of female subjectivity; few would agree with Wittig that "lesbians are not women" (32). A case in point is Eve Sedgwick's work on the representation of homosexual desire, which concerns itself exclusively with men because, as she sees it, lesbianism is not about desire. In contrast to "the *radically discontinuous* relation of male homosocial and homosexual bonds," she writes, "the *relatively continuous* relation of female homosocial and homosexual bonds . . . links lesbianism with the other forms of women's attention to women: the bond of mother and daughter, for instance, the bond of sister and sister, women's friendship, 'networking,' and the active struggles of feminism" (*Between Men: English Literature and Male Homosocial Desire* 2; emphasis added).

Conspicuously, the word *desire* is absent from this itemized list of what Sedgwick can only bring herself to call "women's attention to women." Yet, in the subtitle and throughout the book, she repeatedly uses the word *desire* rather than *love* precisely, she stresses, in order "to mark the erotic emphasis." One cannot but conclude that if desire—with the erotic emphasis—exists between women, it is of no great consequence; it is no source of conflict or contradiction, no bond as strong as that of mother and daughter, as significant as friendship, or as important as women's political struggles. This, she adds, "seems at this moment to make an obvious kind of sense." And it certainly must make sense to those straight feminists for whom heterosexual female desire is apparently so impervious to theorization that they have turned to theorizing either men's stakes in feminism or male subjectivity itself, both gay and straight. As Blakey Vermeule observes, "Eve Sedgwick's school of criticism is by now a well known intervention into canons of literature . . . to enable gay-affirmative investigations," but in her self-canonizing account of lesbian sexuality "there is essentially no difference between lesbian acts and vaguely female practices": the smooth continuity she envisions from homosocial to homosexual female relations "is impervious to such corrosive compounds as sex, desire, difference, lust, or political oppression" ("Is There a Sedgwick School for Girls?" 54–55). What is more disturbing, and more to my immediate point here, is that the sweeping of lesbian sexuality and desire under the rug of sisterhood, female friendship, and the now popular theme of the mother-daughter bond, has become canonical in feminist criticism to the point where it vitiates the analytical efforts of even those critics—lesbian critics such as Vermeule—who are wise to it (see note 23). In all three parts of the rug, what is in question is not desire, but identification.

"Intra-feminine Fascinations"—From Eve to Madonna

By way of demonstration, I now turn to one of the few essays in film theory that attempt to engage the question of desire between women, which trips precisely on that rug, on the confusion of desire with identification. I hope that the importance of McLaughlin's recasting of the question of lesbian desire so that it cannot be confused with simple narcissistic identification will come out into sharper focus, and that so will the consequence of my theoretical distinction between a representation of lesbianism that is heterosexually conceived and one that is not. Jackie Stacey's article "Desperately Seeking Difference" offers a reading of two films, the classic *All about Eve* (starring Bette Davis and Anne Baxter) and the independent *Desperately Seeking Susan* (starring Madonna and Rosanna Arquette). While these are not "lesbian films," she claims, they offer women spectators particular pleasures connected with "women's active desire and the sexual aims of women in the audience in relationship to the female protagonist on the screen" (49).

In spite of her doubtful choice of films, Stacey's project runs parallel to mine. She is looking for a way to articulate "the specifically homosexual pleasures of female spectatorship" (48) against a model of spectatorship developed from the theory of sexual difference with its "psychoanalytic binarism" of masculine-feminine and active-passive positions. The effect of these "oppressive dichotomies," she observes, also citing Doane's reading of *Caught* and her unfortunate reference to Kristeva, is that they "necessarily masculinise female homosexuality" (52). And then she argues that the two films she is analyzing "offer particular pleasures to the women in the audience which cannot simply be reduced to a masculine heterosexual equivalent" (53); and that "the fascinations which structure both narratives" are not only those of identification with an ideal image of woman but also those of differences between the women characters "which are not merely reducible to sexual difference" and yet produce desire in the spectator.

The problem is, however, that in rejecting the theory of female spectatorship in which desire and identification are conflated, Stacey also rejects its psychoanalytic framework; that is to say, she overlooks the possibility of using psychoanalysis precisely to distinguish between desire and identification, and is thus left without any theoretical ground for the distinction in her reading of the films. Because the notion of desire remains unspecified and based on undefined "differences" or "forms of otherness between women" (61 and 53), her reading of the films only articulates various forms of identification between women. This may be in part a result of the films themselves, which are indeed about identification and not desire, in my view: in both cases one woman—the younger or more "childlike" of each pair—wishes to be *like*, to become or literally to impersonate the other, either in order to take her place in the world, to become a famous star like her, and to replace her as the object of desire of both her husband and the audience (*All about Eve*), or in order to acquire her image as a woman liberated, free, and "saturated with sexuality" (as Stacey says of the Susan played by Madonna in *Desperately Seeking Susan*). In short, both are terminal cases of identification, the first with an Oedipal mother/rival image, the second with a feminine ego-ideal.

In psychoanalytic terms, this "childlike" wish is a kind of identification that is at once ego-directed, narcissistic, and *desexualized*, devoid of sexual aim. It is either, if we attend to Freud, "a direct and immediate identification [with a parental figure, the ego-ideal] and takes place earlier than any object-cathexis" (*SE* 19: 31), or an object-identification, "an object-cathexis [that has been given up, introjected, and] has been replaced by an identification" (*SE* 19: 28). In the latter case, Freud specifies, "the transformation of object-libido into narcissistic libido which thus takes place obviously implies an abandonment of sexual aims, a desexualization—a kind of sublimation, therefore" (*SE* 19: 30). The distinction between object-libido and narcissistic or ego-libido is crucial here, for one is sexual and has to do with desire, wanting to have (the object), the other is desexualized and has to do with narcissistic identification, wanting to be or to be like or seeing oneself as (the object).

The issue, however, is complicated by the fact that narcissism operates in several ways in psychic life: Freud speaks of a primary narcissism, original in all humans ("an allocation of the libido such as deserved to be described as narcissism might be present far more extensively, and . . . might claim a place in the regular course of human sexual development" [*SE* 14: 73]), and a secondary narcissism, acquired during development ("the narcissism which arises through the drawing in of object-cathexes" [*SE* 14: 75]). The latter is what constitutes the narcissistic or ego-libido and, if not predominant over object-cathexes, determines a narcissistic object-choice—as, Freud suggests, in "perverts and homosexuals" (*SE* 14: 88). If, however, it is predominant—as in "narcissistic women," whose need does not "lie in the direction of loving, but of being loved" and who love only themselves "with an intensity comparable to that of the man's love for them"—then the narcissistic or ego-libido stands in the way of a "complete object-love" or "is unfavourable to the development of a true *object-love*" (*SE* 14: 88–89).[22] The introduction of the term *object-love* [*Objektliebe*], which appears in this section of the essay interchangeably with *object-choice* [*Objektwahl*], makes it possible for Freud to salvage the woman from total self-absorption in her own narcissism by allowing that she may develop an object-love (he could hardly call it object-choice) for her child, as an externalized part of her self or a retrieval of her own long-abandoned "boyish nature" (*SE*

---

22. I have slightly altered the *SE* translation of this phrase, substituting the italicized word *object-love* for its *object-choice*, because the German reads: "der Gestaltung einer ordentlichen . . . Objektliebe ungünstig ist" (Freud, "Zur Einführung des Narzissmus" 55).

14: 90). But Freud is typically ambiguous in the theory of narcissism. Particularly with regard to (heterosexual) women, he does not say when or how the narcissistic object-choice of "the purest and truest" female type (*SE* 14: 88) trespasses into the "self-sufficiency" of secondary narcissism with its inaptitude for object-love. Thus one is left to wonder: if the narcissistic choice of object is made with ego-directed, and hence passive, aims (the need for "being loved" rather than "loving"), does it still count as object-choice or object-libido, or is it rather ego-libido? The addition of the term *object-love* only muddles the matter further.

(The contradictory character of Freud's essay "On Narcissism" in relation to his distinction between sexual instincts [object-orienta-tion] and ego instincts [narcissism] is the focus of Borch-Jacobsen's deconstructive reading. He contends that, in "dissolv[ing] object ori-entation in general in narcissism" [101] and vice versa, Freud actu-ally appropriates Jung's idea of a non-sexual or desexualized ego while denying that he is doing so. In this "classical schema of mi-metic rivalry" [69] vis-à-vis Jung [analogous to his earlier relation-ship with Fliess], Freud ends up in a flagrant contradiction involving "two different theories both of libido and of object orientation" [104], such that the essay "On Narcissism" is "unreadable" [125]: all object-choice is narcissistic, all narcissism is objectal, Borch-Jacob-sen concludes. Thus his deconstructive exercise neither clarifies nor improves on Freud, and leaves this reader with the less than novel idea that the ego, Freud's own in particular, is narcissistic and that desire, at once mimetic and narcissistic, is a kind of *"rivalrous homosociality"* [78] between men.)

Perhaps, then, one may take the *via regia* mapped out by Freud himself and look for an answer in one's personal and experiential history: it seems to me fairly incontrovertible, since I have known them both, that the ego-libido or narcissistic disposition is not to be confused with the object-choice component of *sexual* desire toward an other that characterizes adult (post-Oedipal) lesbian sexuality, whether that object-choice be of the anaclitic type or of the narcis-sistic type, which latter, says Freud (with his characteristic incapac-ity to envision lesbians), is most evident in homosexual men, though by no means exclusive to them.

Indeed, both film narratives bear out my point, and Stacey her-self confirms it: "Roberta's desire to become more like her ideal—a more pleasingly coordinated, complete and attractive feminine im-age—is offered narrative fulfilment" (61); and as for *All about Eve*, Stacey concludes her analysis with these words: "The reflected im-age, infinitely multiplied in the triptych of the glass, creates a spec-tacle of stardom that is the film's final shot, suggesting a perpetual regeneration of intra-feminine fascinations through the pleasure of looking" (57). In sum, the "feminine desire" Stacey pursues, as Eve is transformed into Madonna in the eighties, is still a form of identi-fication with the image of woman, if a powerful and attractive wom-anhood, a feminine role model or ego-ideal, and a quintessentially heterosexual one; it is not desire between women but indeed "intra-feminine," self-directed, narcissistic "fascinations." And so if the ar-ticle does suggest some of the reasons why "the specifically homo-sexual pleasures of female spectatorship have been ignored" (48), it does so quite unintentionally and precisely by an equivocation of the very terms of its argument—not only the term *desire* but also the term *homosexual*, which very much as Sedgwick sees it, when it comes to women (including the women characters in these films, or more recent ones such as *Thelma and Louise*), really means homosocial, i.e., woman-identified female bonding.

In plainer words, in these representations, desire between women is not sexual. This is obviously a widely recurrent problem in feminist theory, and I will address it again at greater length in the next chapter. Here it may serve to elucidate what I mean by a repre-sentation of lesbianism that is heterosexually conceived—and in ef-fect heterosexist. Far from suggesting another kind of sexuality for women and between women, it implies that sex, "real sex," happens only with men: between women and men or between men. However, the passionate response of lesbian spectators and critics such as Sta-cey, Vermeule, and Traub to these representations does not only speak to the need to theorize and produce an adequate representa-tion of lesbian sexuality, but also suggests that *both* woman-identifi-cation *and* desire (*both* autoerotic and narcissistic drives, *and* female object-choice or object-love) may be simultaneously present in it.[23] Which is why fantasies of Oedipal rivalry, as well as

---

23. Vermeule's critique of "Eve Sedgwick, the 'queen' of gay studies" (57)—a cri-tique that is self-admittedly "as adoring as it is aggressive" (70)—is in fact the pre-text for Vermeule's own attempt to produce a lesbian reading of the film *All about Eve*. For Traub, see note 24.

identification, with the mother remain powerful magnets in lesbian spectatorship. But the relation of identification and desire in lesbian subjectivity is still altogether unexamined; it cannot be blithely taken for granted but must be articulated theoretically. One of the aims of this book is to begin its articulation. As I have suggested in my elaboration of Deutsch's paper on female homosexuality (in chapter 2), if lesbianism does involve what she calls "a return to the mother," that is no simple nostalgia for pre-Oedipal bliss and mother love but a complicated passage (in developmental terms) through Oedipal—phallic and genital—drives and such instinctual vicissitudes as sadomasochism, exhibitionism, voyeurism, and especially, I will be arguing later, fetishism.

More important still (and this in psychosocial terms), it is a passage through forms of "discursive consent," fantasy, and representation. The pleasures afforded the lesbian spectator by Oedipal rivalry in *All about Eve* or *Desperately Seeking Susan,* for instance (but also by, say, the figure of the matriarch or older-woman villain of television soap operas discussed by Tania Modleski in *Loving with a Vengeance*), may be those of a sadomasochistic maternal fantasy *made safe* by the films' heterosexual narrative logic: the daughter becomes like the mother, Eve becomes Eve, the first and only woman (here one plus one makes one, not two), the threat and the guilt are assuaged even before they can be avowed. Similarly, the famous kiss scene in *Black Widow*, which has acquired cult status among lesbian filmgoers in spite of the film's blatantly heterosexist narrative and characterization, may offer a moment of "discursive consent" *because* the threat of its sadomasochistic fantasy is immediately thereafter recontained by the standard (heterosexual) frame of the narrative and the "lawful" punishment of the mother at the hand of the daughter-detective.[24] These may be also lesbian, as well as

---

24. Or perhaps not. In her incisive reading of *Black Widow* as an instance of "the paradox of 'lesbian' representation within a heterosexist field of reference" (318), Valerie Traub argues to some extent along these lines, although she, too, like Stacey, unfortunately ends up assimilating desire and identification (322–23). While its narrative structure works to affirm the Law of the Father and the maintenance of heterosexual hegemony, she writes, the film "invites, even produces, 'lesbian' pleasures" (308) in its viewers by offering "moments of textual excess—moments not required by the logic of the plot, but instead functioning to upset the coherency of the narrative," such as the kiss exchanged between the two women protagonists. Thus lesbian spectatorial pleasure is not denied, is indeed incited by the film, but is also "subtly controlled and disciplined under the male heterosexual gaze" (319). Traub has reason to

heterosexual, female pleasures. But the incentive or incitement to fantasy that such representations yield is finally at the cost of a representation of lesbian sexuality in its instinctual, fantasmatic, and social complexity. Thus, their consent to a safe and lawful fantasy, in replacing what Deutsch calls the consent to activity, ultimately deauthorizes or forecloses actual lesbianism.

It is in contrast to these films that I go back one last time to *She Must Be Seeing Things*, to re-emphasize the significance of its taking the question of lesbian desire seriously and trying to work through the difficulty of representing it against this barrage of representations, discourses, and theories that negate it, from Freud to Hollywood to contemporary feminist theory. In contrast to the lawful narrative genres of the love story, the romance, or the fairytale-detective story adopted by *Lianna, Desert Hearts*, or *I've Heard the Mermaids Singing*, McLaughlin's film locates itself historically and politically in the contemporary North American lesbian community with its conflicting discourses and (why not say it) its instinctual vicissitudes, posing the question of desire within the context of actual practices of *both lesbianism and cinema*. It at once addresses and questions spectatorial desire by disallowing a univocal spectatorial identification with any one character or role or object-choice, and foregrounding instead the relations of desire to fantasy and its mobility within the fantasy scenario. It does not simply incite to fantasy but shows its risks and its disruptive force in subjectivity, constructing a representation of lesbian desire that gives "consent to activity," but not facile and not unqualified. Finally, in reclaiming the cinematic function of voyeurism and rearticulating it in lesbian terms (as Martha Gever has observed), this film does allow an account of not only the "specifically homosexual pleasures of female

---

believe that insofar as "the film is seen to gesture toward 'lesbian' desire, it invokes more anxiety than pleasure in even the 'liberal' heterosexual viewer" (321). I have suggested that such anxiety may also accompany the pleasures of lesbian viewers, and see signs of that anxiety not only in the self-doubting or cautionary quotations marks within which Traub encases the word *lesbian* throughout the essay, but also in her statement that, if the kiss would be narratively incomprehensible without some prior indication of the women's mutual desire, nevertheless that scene "is also the moment when the film most forcefully *dis*articulates 'lesbian' desire: neither sensual nor friendly, the kiss in its brutality comes close to the iconography of rape, a taking of possession, an assertion of both knowledge and power" (319–20). Or, in the terms of my argument, the *Black Widow* fantasy is not safe at all—that is, if one wants to see lesbian desire as only "sensual or friendly," and immune from the risks of aggressiveness, possession, knowledge, and power.

spectatorship" but also why they have been ignored, mistaken, or misplaced in feminist film theory.

To conclude, I will look again at a short scene in the film which condenses many of the issues I have been discussing—the scene where Agatha, from her office window, sees Jo kissing a man in the street below. What marks Agatha's "seeing" as a hallucination is the profilmic substitution of another woman for Lois Weaver, whom the viewer recognizes as Jo. The other woman, unknown to perhaps most spectators but not to all, is played by Sheila McLaughlin herself, who thus makes a very interesting cameo appearance, inscribing herself in a particular role in the film written and directed by her. This directorial choice supports my reading that Agatha is not the only desiring subject of the film—the subject of the Catalina fantasy, the voyeur, the "she" who must be seeing things, the crossdressing woman, the *culturally visible* representation of lesbian desire. McLaughlin's appearance in the place of Jo/Lois Weaver, that is to say, in the place of the object of Agatha's desire, is a performative personal statement, the masquerade of a femme "who aims her desirability at the butch," as Case would put it. By the very fact that McLaughlin is the filmmaker, and that she is also, therefore, in the place of Jo, the diegetic filmmaker, whose film gives visual, symbolic form to her desire for Agatha in Catalina, McLaughlin's appearance in this scene sustains my reading that she, too, is the desiring subject of the Catalina fantasy, the voyeur and exhibitionist, the "she" who "must be seeing things," and the desiring subject of her film as a whole. The scene does represent, finally, the lesbian subject as a double one, as Case suggests, and renders performative my earlier statement that it takes two women, not one, to make a lesbian. But it also shows that other *visible* representations of lesbian subjectivity and desire are already there for all to see, if only we know how to look.

III. On the Subject of Fantasy: Representation and Spectatorship

In the first part of this chapter I have argued for the relevance to cinematic representation and spectatorship of Laplanche and Pontalis's notion of fantasy as narrative scenario and mise-en-scène, or structuring scene of desire. In the second section I have discussed some problems in the feminist theory of spectatorship with regard to the foreclosure of lesbianism or its homologation to female sexuality under the umbrella of woman-identification and through the figure of masquerade. Here I would like to consider other readings of Laplanche and Pontalis's work that bear on recent developments in the theory of spectatorship and on the relation of fantasy to representation.

"Fantasy and the Origins of Sexuality" was first published as "Fantasme originaire, fantasmes des origines, origine du fantasme" in *Les Temps Modernes* in 1964 and translated into English in the *International Journal of Psycho-Analysis* in 1968. But its impact on film, performance, and visual studies has been especially noticeable since its republication in a 1986 collection edited by Victor Burgin, Cora Kaplan, and James Donald, which also reprinted Joan Riviere's "Womanliness as a Masquerade" (1929) and included new essays about or influenced by the two earlier psychoanalytic texts. Indeed, both notions of fantasy as constitutive of sexuality and femininity as masquerade have been increasingly taken up in cultural studies as metaphoric sites or figures for the articulation of the psychical and the social, as the editors auspicated (*Formations of Fantasy* 3). In film studies, however, Laplanche and Pontalis's psychoanalytic theory of fantasy was first elaborated and extended with regard to film spectatorship by Elizabeth Cowie in 1984, while the (Lacanian) notion of masquerade was introduced by Claire Johnston in 1975 (as John Fletcher notes in "Versions of Masquerade" [48]). Of the fortunes of masquerade in film and feminist theory I have written earlier in this chapter. Now I would like to take a closer look at Cowie's influential essay "Fantasia," which has significantly inflected the current views of fantasy in film spectatorship. My purpose in discussing it is twofold: to articulate further the relations of fantasy to representation and its effects in spectatorship, and to resist a move afoot in film criticism to metaphorize lesbianism and altogether evacuate sexual difference(s) from the spectator.

Fantasy and the fantastic have long been familiar words to filmgoers and critics in reference to certain films, certain film genres or styles of filmmaking, certain traditions within the history of cinema, such as the one traced back to Méliès and contrasted to the equally old tradition of realism. And then the idea of fantasy as illusion (and in contrast to reality, in the very opposition that Freud set about to dissolve) has often served to characterize the phenomenon of cinema in its entirety, whether seen as a production of ideology or as entertainment, commodity, popular culture, or art. When cinema is equated with fantasy (cinema as the dream machine), fantasy may mean utopian promise or artificial escape, or both at once, in contradistinction to "real life," the real of socioeconomic relations and political struggle, the daily business of living, and so forth. When fantasy is predicated of the spectator-subject in contemporary film-critical discourse, it usually means a private, subjective, conscious or unconscious, process and a socially inconsequential event—something that takes place behind closed doors, inside one's head, in the dark of the movie theater, or between consenting adults. (For a sample of current critical trends, see Donald, ed., *Fantasy and the Cinema.*)

My title for this section is a double trope, a phrase by which I mean, first, to turn the meaning of fantasy as a topic or theme (and as opposed to "reality") into that of a psychic process; a process that, with Laplanche and Pontalis, I believe is directly involved in the constitution of the sexual subject—Freud's bodily ego—in its identity, divisions, and multiplicity of agencies. Second, the trope wants to perform a further semiotic turn from the private, psychoanalytic notion of the subject, with her or his individual psyche, unique personal history, and subjectivity (as the subject of a psychoanalysis is imagined to be), to the notion of social subject: one whose subjectivity and psychic configuration are effectively shaped, formed, and reformed, but also disrupted and even shattered, by social technologies, representations, and practices inside and outside the cinema, which overdetermine that unique personal history. I place my subject of fantasy in this very turn, this sliding back and forth from the subjective dimension to the social, because this is the sense in which the psychoanalytic notion of fantasy seems to me most useful to a theory of spectatorship or visual representation. In other words, the psychoanalytic subject of fantasy and the spectator-subject in the cinema are not identical entities or coterminous theoretical objects. If the former is a site of articulation of the psychic and the social *in* subjectivity, I would define the latter more specifically as a site of articulation *of* individual subjectivity with social subjecthood, of fantasy with representation, or of private with public fantasies.

That cinema produces public forms of fantasy, in the specific sense elaborated by Laplanche and Pontalis, was first proposed by

Elizabeth Cowie in a rich essay that extended their theory to the public realm via the connection of creative writing to daydreaming suggested by Freud. "Fantasia" speculates on the parallelism between the forms and processes of private fantasy in the psychoanalytic subject and the *"public* forms of fantasy" (73) that are made available by a dominant apparatus of representation such as Hollywood cinema. "By far the most common form of public circulation of fantasy is what Freud described as 'creative writing' of which film can also claim to be a part" (83), Cowie states, listing as further examples psychoanalytic case studies, feminist articles in the sex issue of *Heresies* (1981), and women's fantasies collected in anthologies such as *My Secret Garden,* as well as men's fantasies appearing in magazines such as *Men Only* or *Penthouse* (in this respect, see also Theweleit). Indeed the cinema, she argues, with its highly developed generic and formal conventions—visual, narrative, acoustic, thematic, etc.—is a major apparatus for the production of popular scenarios or public forms of fantasy, and thus the structuring of spectatorial desire through representation.[25]

However, Cowie continues, if Freud "open[ed] up the study of fantasy in public forms of representation," he also saw "the author [the writer or teller of a story or joke], as origin of the fantasy" (85). Thus the question she must address is, "If fantasies *are* 'personal' in this way, how can they work for a general public, for a mass audience?" (85). Or, how can the film's "author's" fantasy become, or work as, the film's spectator's fantasy? Her answer seems to be, first, that what makes a film work as a fantasy for an audience is less the contingent content of its story than its formal construction as a film. Because of the culturally established opposition between fantasy and reality, and hence the "vehement demand that we should be able to tell the difference between reality and fantasy even in fiction" (85), she writes, "the fiction will fail as ready-made fantasy . . . if it is felt to be too 'far-fetched' "; and the criteria for its acceptance "depend on the conventions of realism, of verisimilitude," that are implemented in the representation of the fiction. Moreover, the author

---

25. I quite agree with her, of course, though I would also argue the same of all other cultural and subcultural representational practices—not only avant-garde and independent cinema, theater, performance, and various forms of "writing," but also less formal or formalized representational practices such as clothing or hair styles, gay and lesbian subcultural practices, and so on.

must rework her or his fantasy "for public consumption" by means of "a further secondary revision," that is, through the employ of narrative and aesthetic conventions (85–86).

> Conventions are thus the means by which the structuring of desire is represented in public forms, inasmuch as, following the arguments of Laplanche and Pontalis earlier, fantasy *is the mise-en-scène* of desire. What is necessary for any public forms of fantasy, for their collective consumption, is not universal objects of desire, but a setting of desiring in which we can find our place(s). And these places will devolve, as in the original fantasies, on positions of desire: active or passive, feminine or masculine, mother or son, father or daughter. . . . Two sets of questions arise, however: first, if fantasy is the *mise-en-scène* of desire, whose desire is figured in the film, who is the subject for and of the scenario? No longer just, if ever, the so-called "author." But how does the spectator come into place as desiring subject of the film? Secondly, what is the relation of the contingent, everyday material drawn from real life, ie from the *social,* to the primal or original fantasies? (87)

In writing the word *"author"* between inverted commas, Cowie rightly marks it as a questionable notion and one especially problematic in reference to commercial film (whose complex socio-technological context of production, by the way, makes the analogy with "creative writing" less useful than it might seem). But she does not put the word *audience* between quotation marks or otherwise distinguish between the (sociological) notion of "general public" or "mass audience" and the film-theoretical notion of spectator. The distinction is important, I would argue, because the passage of the film's fantasy from "author" to spectators is not a passage from origin to destination or from production to reception, as the notions of audience, general public, and "collective consumption" would suggest, but rather a passage or a transference, if I may say so, from origin to origin, from subject to subject. In this transference the spectator becomes the desiring subject of the film's fantasy; that is, the film becomes the mise-en-scène of the spectator's desire. This, Cowie suggests, occurs through (a) the film's application of representational conventions and (b) subjective spectatorial identification with the film's scenario of desire and the various positions figured in it, which are, like those of the original fantasies, Oedipal positions.

But what grounds the spectator's fantasmatic identification, it seems to me, is more the latter positions and less the cinematic narrative conventions, which may be applied more or less successfully in any given film. If both Pasolini's *Edipo Re* and *Back to the Future* can work for some spectators as fantasy scenarios (and evidently both do), identification must have less to do with the aesthetic or narrative quality of the representation, or the particular employ of conventions of realism or verisimilitude, than with *the contents of the fantasy* they inscribe. For the contents and the structure of the original fantasies may perhaps be distinguished theoretically or for analytical purposes, but they are inseparable in their effects in spectatorship: those "positions of desire: active or passive, feminine or masculine, mother or son, father or daughter" in which I may find my place(s) in the film's fantasy are precisely *the content of the original fantasy as a structure of subjectivity.*[26] Thus, in Cowie's argument as I understand it, it is the "universality" of the original fantasies as *structures and contents* of subjectivity that activates the movement of fantasy and identification in the spectators, even as narrative conventions shape the contingent materials of the story. But then, how do we account for a film's failure to engage or "place" a spectator, or some spectators, in its fantasy (a possibility "Fantasia" does not consider)?

While the structure of fantasy may be "universal" (a term even more questionable than "author"), what is absolutely not so is the

---

26. The best explanation I know of the Oedipus complex as both a structure and a content of subjectivity is Shoshana Felman's in "Beyond Oedipus" (in *Jacques Lacan and the Adventure of Insight*). Although she asserts that "for Lacan, the Oedipus complex is not a signified but a signifier, not a meaning but a structure . . . not an answer but *the structure of a question*" (103), her reading of Lacan's reading of Melanie Klein's analysis of the four-year-old "little Dick" makes it perfectly clear that what the analyst gives the child ("Dick—little train, Daddy—big train, Dick is going into mummy"—whereupon the boy produces his first word: "station") is not only a linguistic structure but precisely the structure, as Felman herself then puts it, "in which meaning—sexual meaning—can later be articulated and inscribed" (114). Yet, for reasons I fail to understand, Felman continues to equivocate on the terms *meaning* and *structure*. A few pages later, she states: "The interpretive gift [that the analyst gives the patient] is not so much a gift of truth, of understanding or of meaning: it is, essentially, a gift of language" (119)—as if the performative insertion or interpellation of a child into the Oedipal patriarchal symbolic were not a question of meaning. Hayden White has most effectively expressed the relation of meaning to structure (in historical representation) by the phrase "the content of the form": "narrative, far from being merely a form of discourse that can be filled with different contents, real or imaginary as the case may be, already possesses a content prior to any given actualization of it in speech or writing" (*The Content of the Form* xi).

contingent material of each film, of each representation, with its marked historicity and ideological structuration; and that, too, may engage *or prevent* spectatorial identification (as mine is prevented in *Back to the Future* but fully engaged in *Edipo Re*). So that the question of spectatorial desire and identification in any particular film must rest less on cinematic conventions or form as such than on the spectator's subjectivity and what I have called subjecthood; that is to say, not only her or his psychic and fantasmatic configuration, the places or positions that she or he may be able to assume in the structure of desire, but also the ways in which she or he is located in social relations of sexuality, race, class, gender, etc., the places she or he may be able to assume as subject in the social. And these latter could be in contradiction, as well as in unison, with her or his psychic and fantasmatic configuration. I believe that these complex subject processes have more weight in a spectator's acceptance of a film as "ready-made fantasy" than do verisimilitude or aesthetic-narrative conventions.

Thus the distinction Cowie implies between contingent material ("real life," "the social") and "universal" structures (the original fantasies) in the film's narration seems to me misplaced. For, on the one hand, the original fantasies are themselves part of "the social." Transmitted as they are by parental (philogenetic or culturally hegemonic) fantasies, they constitute a psychic structure that, like language, lies "beyond the history of the subject but nevertheless in history . . . a structure, but activated by contingent elements" ("Fantasy and the Origins of Sexuality" 18);[27] and to suggest otherwise is to fall back in the opposition universal-contingent of the structuralism-historicism debate which Laplanche and Pontalis effectively sidestep. On the other hand, however, that distinction and the conflict or contradiction it often entails between fantasy and

---

27. Again Laplanche: "We should accustom ourselves to the idea that the meanings implicit in the slightest parental gesture bear the parents' fantasies; for it is, in fact, too often forgotten when we speak of the mother-child relation or of the parent-child relation that the parents themselves had their own parents; they have their 'complexes,' wishes marked by historicity, so that to reconstruct the child's oedipal complex as a triangular situation, while forgetting that at two vertices of the triangle each adult protagonist is himself the bearer of a small triangle and even of a whole series of interlocking triangles, is to neglect an essential aspect of the situation. In the final analysis the complete oedipal structure is *present from the beginning*, both 'in itself' (in the objectivity of the familial configuration) but above all 'in the other,' outside the child" (*Life and Death in Psychoanalysis* 45).

representation or between the psychic and the social, remain an important issue for film and cultural theory. What I am saying is that these conflicts or contradictions are best located not in the film but in the spectator(s).

What this means for the theory of spectatorship is that only subjective readings can be given, however many other spectators may share them, and thus share in the fantasy that each reading subtends; and that no one spectator's reading of, or identification in, a film can be generalized as a property of the film (its fantasy)[28] or merely an effect of *its* narration. In other words, I am saying that, when it comes to engaging the spectator's fantasy and identification, a film's effects are neither structural (if structural is equated with universal) nor totally structured by the film (by its fantasy, narration, or form); rather, they are contingent on the spectator's subjectivity and subjecthood (which are themselves, to some extent, already structured but also open to restructuration). The success of a critical analysis or reading of a film, therefore, consists in showing how those contingent effects are structured for and by one particular spectator (that is, for that spectator by the film and by that spectator in the film) in her/his interpretation or critical reconstruction (secondarization) of the film as fantasy. This, I suggest, is also the case with "Fantasia." When Cowie proceeds to analyze two Hollywood films of the forties, arguing that in both cases the subject of the film's fantasy, of the film as fantasy, is not only the main character(s) but the spectator as well, her reading is quite subjective, in spite of her attributing the fantasy to the film and generalizing it to all spectators.

What Homosexuality? (Two Readings of *Now, Voyager*)

In the concluding passages of her analysis of *Now, Voyager,* Cowie writes:

> The scenario, the *mise-en-scène* of desire thus emerges for us not just in the story, but rather in its narrating: that series of

---

28. Unless so marked specifically in the film, as I argued of *She Must Be Seeing Things* in the first section of this chapter, and consequently with the particular effects that such an intentional inscription of fantasy may then have on spectatorial identification and desire.

images bound into the narrative structures, in the devices, delays, coincidences etc that make up the narration of the story. The pleasure then not in *what* wishes Charlotte obtains but *how*. A how which refers to a positioning, ultimately of the spectator rather than Charlotte, in relation to desire; an oscillation between mother and child. (92)

> In a sense, Dr Jacquith, Jerry, are both substitutes for the phallic mother, and they are finally unnecessary once the conditions are set for Charlotte herself to be the phallic mother. . . . Charlotte is both mother and daughter, Mrs. Vale and Tina. This is not Charlotte's fantasy, but the "film's" fantasy. It is an effect of its narration (of its *énonciation*). If we identify simply with Charlotte's desires, that series of social and erotic successes, then the final object, the child Tina, will be unsatisfactory. But *if* our identification is with the playing out of a desiring, in relation to the opposition (phallic) mother and child, the ending is very much more satisfying, I would suggest. A series of "day-dream" fantasies enfold an Oedipal, original fantasy. The subject of this fantasy is then the spectator; inasmuch as we have been captured by the film's narration, its *énonciation*, we are the only place in which all the terms of the fantasy come to rest. (90–91; second emphasis added)

I emphasize that *if*, which is just the question I raised earlier: Does this fantasy work for me, spectator? Am I the subject of *this* fantasy? Cowie acknowledges this question and answers it subjectively and conditionally, but at the same time generalizes her reading to all spectators:

> Such a reading implies a homosexual desire played across the film, and if this is the case (and my reading is not too far-fetched), it is also a way of understanding the pleasure for the *masculine* spectator, since the film figures the eviction of the father and the re-instatement of the now "good" phallic mother. By suggesting this I am assuming that the place of the spectator is not one of simple identification with Charlotte Vale. (90–91)

If both the author of the statement and the emphatically *masculine* spectator (by which I assume that Cowie means a *male* spectator, otherwise her argument would not make sense) can find their places in the film—in the specified positions of mother, daughter, and phallic mother, or in their so-called "homosexual" relations (which retroactively become "pre-Oedipal" after the "eviction" of the father)—then, the statement strongly implies, this film's fantasy works for everyone, women and men, straight and gay. Yet for me the question lingers: Can he (that male spectator), or I, or everyone, identify "with the playing out of [that particular] desiring"? Obviously, these are empirically unanswerable questions (though I will shortly report the reading of at least one other empirical, and male, spectator), but they are theoretically necessary nonetheless.

I, for one, cannot find my place in the fantasy of "homosexual desire" that Cowie reads in the film. What is meant, I ask myself, by "homosexual desire" in speaking of a daughter's pre-Oedipal relation to the mother? Isn't the term *homosexual* vastly ambiguous in this context? And just as ambiguous—and strangely so, for a writer as lucid and precise as Cowie—is the designation *masculine* for a spectator who, in the logic of the argument, we must take to be a man, but whose desire, inscribed in a scenario of paternal eviction and fetishistic-maternal desire, perhaps unwittingly suggests a "masculine woman." In this regard, it may not be coincidental that her analysis of *Now, Voyager* ends with a reference to masquerade: if the re-figuration of Charlotte's "body as beautiful, desirable, places her desire there as subordinate to masculine desire," Cowie argues, nevertheless the narrative works to represent her "femininity as the masquerade." The implication of that *desirable* (read: to men) cannot be lost on a lesbian reader, who will then recall that Riviere's notion of womanliness as masquerade was developed in her analysis of a heterosexual woman with a strong and anxiety-producing masculinity complex, as Freud(ians) called it. Could this be, I wonder, the "*masculine* spectator" (the "masculine woman" spectator) whose pleasure is produced by the masquerade of *Now, Voyager?* Undoubtedly, my own reading (or projection) of a fantasy scenario into Cowie's text may also be rather far-fetched, but the point I want to make is that her viewing Charlotte's femininity as masquerade, while convergent with a narcissistic fantasy of phallic motherhood, casts a further burden of doubt and ambiguity on the alleged "homosexual desire" that Cowie sees played out across the film. *What homosexuality* can be fantasized, I ask, in a woman's masquerade of femininity which is addressed to men, or in a surrogate motherhood that reconstructs for the subject the fantasy of a phallic mother?

As if in answer to these questions, by one of those coincidences not infrequent in academic life, a conversation with Stanley Cavell alerted me to his reading of *Now, Voyager* (published in 1990) which, although unaware of "Fantasia," could well be taken as its companion piece. Cavell's reading is both a testimonial to the pleasure *Now, Voyager* may afford a "masculine spectator" and the confirmation that a sophisticated, nuanced, and compelling response to the film can come only from a particular spectatorial position, one sustained by a very personal set of identifications and a subjective, fantasmatic engagement in the film's scenario. Moreover, while it supports Cowie's assumption "that the place of the spectator is not one of simple identification with Charlotte Vale" (90), in that the male critic's identification with Charlotte Vale is not at all simple, as I shall suggest, Cavell's reading at the same time refutes that assumption, in that its spectatorial identification is most emphatically *with* Charlotte Vale and/as Bette Davis. As he puts it, "I find that to say how I take the films I must from time to time speak for their central women. I feel that I am amplifying their voices, listening to them, becoming them" (232).

Cavell's "Ugly Duckling, Funny Butterfly" bears witness to a male spectator's passionate identification with "Bette Davis and her memorable ways of walking and looking and of delivering lines" (218)— Bette Davis and/as Charlotte Vale, the actress and her character, the woman and her powers:

> a certain hysteria, or hysterical energy, about her character on film. It taps a genius for that expressiveness in which Freud and Breuer, in their *Studies on Hysteria*, first encountered the reality of the unconscious, the reality of the human mind as what is unconscious to itself, and encountered first in the suffering of women. It is Bette Davis's command and deployment of this capacity for somatic compliance, for the theatricalization of desire and of its refiguration or retracking that, so it seems to me, made her one of the most *impersonated* of Hollywood stars. (227; emphasis added)

As for Charlotte Vale, to Cavell she is a figure of transcendence, of metamorphosis and ironic transfiguration, rather than of sacrifice, reaching a "level of spiritual existence" so beyond the "second-rate sadness" of Jerry's world that by the end of the film he "no longer knows where to find her" (230), and "his last protestation of passion for her has become quite beside the point, no longer welcome"

(232). With the famous closing line "Oh, Jerry, don't let's ask for the moon. We have the stars," spoken from her place of attained transcendence of his conventional world, she is tactfully and "gallantly providing the man, quite outclassed, outlived, with a fiction that they together are sacrificing themselves to stern and clear moral dictates." But for herself, there is no sacrifice, no renunciation, for she is giving up only something that she no longer wants, and perhaps never did want. "In her metamorphosis she is and is not what she is; in his incapacity for change, for motion, he is not what he is not. . . . So one may take the subject of the genre of the unknown woman as the irony of human identity as such" (234).

It is this subject, or the fantasy of this subject with its ironic, unfixed, mobile identity, that appears to draw the critic's spectatorial identification (Cavell cites Whitman's lines from which the film's title is taken and his metaphor of the open road for the overcoming of fixity and conventionality); it is the "feminine voice that the male philosopher is refusing to let out" and to acknowledge in himself (283) that Bette Davis/Charlotte Vale re-presents for Cavell through the film's narrative and her womanly body. The spectatorial identification with a femininity defined as emotional (hysterical) expressiveness gives way to a rewriting of the feminine in philosophical terms as the "human" capacity for spiritual transcendence. In thus degendering the feminine, the critic appropriates the woman's voice, her pathos, for the male philosopher, at once confirming and denying, as Tania Modleski observes, women's "dispossession in relation to language and discourse" (*Feminism without Women* 10).

But what of the phallic mother and "homosexual desire"? Here, Cavell's reading is amazingly consonant with Cowie's, not only in locating Camille/Charlotte's defiant strength in "her identification with her mother's power" (21) but in further suggesting that her appropriation of Tina, Jerry's child, for her own is sustained by the Oedipal fantasy of receiving a child from the (phallic) mother: "If Charlotte undergoes a fantasmic 'delivery' then she can have produced a deferred understanding of her fatness as (fantasied) pregnancy. Since . . . her fatness is her mother's doing ('My mother doesn't approve of dieting') then something her mother had put into her has now come out of her" (243). And of Charlotte's identification with Tina as her own younger self, Cavell writes, "I assume that both men and women are capable of tracking desire in a fantasy of parthenogenesis" (244). Which spells out, in more clearly gendered terms, Cowie's "if our identification is with the playing out of a desiring, in relation to the opposition (phallic) mother and child, the ending is very much more satisfying" (92).

How gender does make a difference in spectatorial identification and desire becomes apparent when Cavell—again, with amazing consonance—is led to speculate further on what he calls "Charlotte's homosexual possibility" (282). This he infers from several clues in the film (e.g., "Bette Davis's invitation to camp," Charlotte's self-avowed "idiosyncrasy" and her refusal to marry Livingston, the slip of paper with Whitman's title "The Untold Want" that Dr. Jaquith hands Charlotte at the termination of her treatment with the words "If old Walt didn't have you in mind when he wrote this, he had hundreds of others like you" [282]); but he infers it, as well, from his own spectatorial intuition that Charlotte "has transcended this man's realm" and "is contemplating, perhaps refusing, a homosexual possibility, hence perhaps for that reason all future erotic possibility" (279). Now, it would be difficult to remind Dr. Jaquith that "old Walt" did not have anyone *like* Charlotte in mind as he was almost certainly thinking of male-desiring men when he wrote the poem. But I will respond to Cavell that Bette Davis's invitation to camp and to impersonation may clue the spectator to a *male* rather than a *female* homosexual possibility; and that male homosexuality does not usually require the sacrifice of one's erotic possibilities as the price for ironic transcendence, a price that Charlotte has to pay, contrary to Cavell's thesis and yet by his own reading. For if it is the case that Charlotte no longer wants "a man of my own, a house of my own, a child of my own" (279), and thus is not making the banal sacrifice—the renunciation—that is commonly attributed to her, nevertheless, the refusal of "all future erotic possibility" that Cavell sees in her "homosexual possibility" would be an even greater sacrifice, and one whose effects of transcendence would liken it to the sacrifice—the execution—of a Joan of Arc.

Again, the intimation of a female sexuality that entails a denial of all present and future erotic possibilities (at present with men, in the diegetic context of the film, and in the future perhaps also with women, in the spectator's fantasy scenario) appears to be predicated on a sexually inactive or even (oxymoronically) nonsexual female homosexuality bound to the pre-Oedipal relation to the (phallic) mother, in Cowie's terms, or, in Cavell's, to the specific feature of melodrama that is "the woman's search for the mother" (279). However, as I will try to show, these seemingly parallel readings ultimately subtend different, gender-related fantasies, although the parallelism between the terms *homosexual desire* in Cowie's essay and *homosexual possibility* in Cavell's appears to be sustained by their common reference to masquerade.

Expanding the contours of "homosexual possibility" and its effects on the relationship between Charlotte and Jerry by a detour through the crossdressing personae of Marlene Dietrich and Greta Garbo, Cavell writes: "Their male dress would accordingly declare that they have, among others, the same tastes in bodies that the male they will choose has, and they wish his gratification as well as, so to speak, their own, as if their own bodies are an instance of what they desire" (281). This can be taken as a perceptive rendering of the effects of feminine narcissism and of the masquerade of woman-as-phallus on the men to whom it is addressed; but its not-so-hidden implication is that if Garbo and Dietrich in drag appear to desire women's bodies (their own and other women's), the men they attract must be men who really want men but will make do with women provided that they at least look like men.[29]

Indeed, when he subsequently recasts the *Now, Voyager* scenario with Jerry as "a feminine object" for Charlotte (the film itself does feminize him, he insists), Cavell wonders whether their relation would be constituted as homosexual or heterosexual. His answer is all the more remarkable for being virtually the only instance in the essay where Cavell assumes the point of view of Jerry, whom he otherwise treats rather unsympathetically: "It *needn't be* that she is . . . a masculine object for him. Here, rather, her morbidity must

---

29. In its two classic definitions, Riviere's and Lacan's, the masquerade of femininity is addressed to men. Here is Lacan's: "Paradoxical as this formulation may seem, I am saying that it is in order to be the phallus, that is to say, the signifier of the desire of the Other, that a woman will reject an essential part of femininity, namely, all her attributes in the masquerade. It is for that which she is not that she wishes to be desired as well as loved" ("The Signification of the Phallus," *Écrits* 289–90). Of instances of masquerade addressed to women, such as the butch and the femme performances in a lesbian subcultural context, which obviously have quite different valences, I have said something earlier in the chapter. In the two instances here in question—the feminine masquerade of Bette Davis in *Now, Voyager* (Cowie) and the crossdress masquerades of Dietrich and Garbo (Cavell)—the arguments of the two critics assume, respectively, a male address and a male point of view. I will return to masquerade, in relation to fetishism, in chapter 6.

come into question, that is . . . he takes her as homosexual" (282; emphasis added). This at first surprising reading (they can't get it on, so someone must be homosexual; but if someone has to be homosexual, it cannot be he, so it must be she) finds its logic, I suggest, in the idea that Charlotte's "wish for a passionate existence" gives her "a male direction" or valence; in other words, makes her a masculine woman (and thus a safe anchoring point for male spectatorial identification). This idea will then justify the appropriation of her feminine voice and hysterical expressiveness, together with that masculine "compulsion to desire," for the ironic identity of the philosopher—not the masculine philosopher who refuses his "woman's voice," but rather the skeptical, Nietzschean philosopher who, like the Spencer Tracy character in *Adam's Rib* (the example is Cavell's), can shed real tears, just like a woman, and hence partake of that double, mobile, ironic subjectivity that marks "human identity as such" in the persona of Charlotte Vale.

I might put it this way: the "homosexual" possibility in Charlotte literalizes Dante's figure of the "screen woman," *la donna dello schermo*. It is the possibility for a male spectator to identify with a desiring figure that combines the distinctive features of both genders, but that identification is the projection onto Charlotte of a male and not a female homosexual "possibility," akin to the "masculinization" Mulvey attributes to the female spectator in relation to the image of woman on the screen.[30] Like her "compulsion to desire," then, Charlotte's transcendence of the conventional man's world is, paradoxically, a male achievement. As to the woman Charlotte, such as she is, all "erotic possibility" is axiomatically denied her or, perhaps better, expropriated from her, and she stands as yet another figure of what Rose calls "the impossibility [for woman] of subject *and* desire." For Cowie, on the other hand, "Charlotte is 'phallic' for the narrative in being bound to pre-Oedipal relations, rather than because of any male, 'phallic' imaging of her" (93), and the spectator's desire is positioned in the "oscillation

30. Another male spectator has suggested that possible reasons for male homosexual identification with the Davis persona and with Charlotte Vale in particular include "the ability to be expressive during the repressive 1940s and 1950s, sense of style, sexual self-assuredness, and (somewhat tragically or ironically) the fact that women like Charlotte don't get the man *either*" (Earl Jackson, Jr., in a personal communication). I am indebted to Jackson for his acute comments on an earlier version of this chapter.

between mother and child." Which seems to outline a fantasy of woman's desire as a desire to be the virgin mother. In both readings, then, Charlotte's identification with the phallic mother results in her desexualization—her refusal of "all future erotic possibility" (Cavell) and her regression to a pre-Oedipal fantasmatic (Cowie). This is consonant with Freud's view (discussed in the previous section of this chapter) that "the transformation of object-libido into narcissistic libido" through parental identification (that is, a former object-cathexis that has been given up and introjected to become an identification) "implies an abandonment of sexual aims, a desexualization—a kind of sublimation, therefore" (*SE* 19: 30).[31]

Returning to my earlier question, *What homosexuality* can be fantasized in Charlotte's transcendence (Cavell) or in her phallic motherhood (Cowie), the answer I have found in these two texts is either a fantasy of male homosexuality (rejected in actuality but achieved fantasmatically through identification or impersonation) or a fantasy of phallic femininity whose sexual threat to both men and women must be neutered by desexualization (pre-Oedipal motherhood) or make-believe (the masquerade). In neither case is there any "possibility" of *female* homosexuality as such or of actual "homosexual desire," but both readings more than suggest what I will later call the seductions of lesbianism. (Here, in anticipation of my own argument, I refer the reader to Mayne's original work on Dorothy Arzner which, among other things, impressively documents how the "mannish" image of Arzner has been widely circulated and reproduced in books of feminist film theory and criticism, even as they "resolutely bracketed any discussion of lesbianism" ["Lesbian Looks" 110].)

The reading styles of the two essays differ, as do their implications for the theory of spectatorship. In spite of its universalizing claim that Charlotte represents "the irony of human identity as such," Cavell's reading of *Now, Voyager* is marked as a singular, I would say even personal, response to a film most critics have interpreted otherwise. One may or may not share it, depending on one's own subject-position, but one has a clear sense of the subject-position from which this reading, this spectatorial desiring, proceeds. Cowie's essay, after the

---

31. The inhibition of sexual aims and/or sexual gratification is also Lampl–de Groot's assessment of the female negative Oedipus complex, which I discuss in chapter 2 ("Twists and Turns").

brief parenthesis in which her personal location as spectator and desiring subject is acknowledged ("if . . . my reading is not too far-
fetched"), goes on as if her particular desiring were fully generalizable, universally available. While Cavell's universalist interpretation
of Charlotte is based on his explicit identification with the heroine, as
well as the generic structure of the woman's film, for Cowie it is the
universality of the fantasy inscribed in the film's narrative that captures the spectator—any and all spectators—in its play of subject-
positions. "In each film," she concludes, "the subject-positions shift
across the boundary of sexual difference but do so always in terms of
sexual difference. Thus while subject-positions are variable the terms
of sexual difference are fixed." Or, put another way, "while the terms
of sexual difference are fixed, the places of characters and spectators
in relation to those terms are not" (102). This, to my mind, is a very
equivocal conclusion, whose potential effects on feminist film criticism are much more consequential than Cavell's.

Escape from Sexual Difference, or, Return to Sexual Indifference

The conceptual sliding of "Fantasia" between spectator and film,
spectator and audience, or fantasy and representation, actually invites reductive applications and ultimately undercuts the theoretical
step forward that can be made in the theory of spectatorship by
rearticulating (not simply transposing or applying) the psychoanalytic concept of fantasy to the processes of spectatorial
identification.[32] I will say more explicitly what concerns me.
"Fantasia" is usually cited to buttress the view, now popular among
some feminist critics, that every spectator can identify with any
character and any or all relational positions in a film's narrative.
This view has been promoted as an "escape" from the "impasse" of a
feminist film criticism bound to "the binarism of sexual difference"

---

32. I use the term *application* here in the sense of word-processing format, as my
Macintosh manual defines it: "an application is a software program that helps you
perform your work," like Microsoft Word, for instance, or WordPerfect. When the
application is punched in, we have something like this: "The desire represented in the
time travel story, of both witnessing one's own conception and being one's own
mother and father, is similar to the primal scene fantasy, in which one can be both
observer or one of the participants. (The possibility of getting pregnant and giving
birth to oneself is echoed in *Back to the Future*'s TV ad: 'The first kid to get into
trouble before he was ever born.')" (Penley 202). The kid alluded to here is the male
protagonist.

(Greig 185). Thus Cowie's carefully argued theoretical proposal is translated into the optimistically silly notion of an unbounded mobility of identities for the spectator-subject; that is to say, any spectator would be able to assume and shift between a variety of identificatory positions, would be able to pick and choose any or all of the subject-positions inscribed in the film regardless of gender or sexual difference, to say nothing of other kinds of difference. Moreover, the spectator is collapsed into the psychoanalytic subject of fantasy, and spectatorial identification equated with unconscious identification. One critic, for example, states:

> Recent film theory has taken up Freud's description of fantasy to give a more complete account of how identification works in film. An important emphasis has been placed on the subject's ability to assume, successively, all the available positions in the fantasmatic scenario. Extending this idea to film has shown that spectatorial identification is more complex than has hitherto been understood because it shifts constantly in the course of the film's narrative, while crossing the lines of biological sex; in other words, unconscious identification with the characters or the scenario is not necessarily dependent upon gender. (Penley 202)[33]

While the first two sentences of the passage ostensibly refer to the psychoanalytic subject, the word *successively* belies the movement of film watching. Conversely, in the last two sentences, ostensibly referred to the film spectator, identification with the characters or the scenario is said to be unconscious. The underlying theory of fantasy attributed to Freud in the passage is the one articulated by Laplanche and Pontalis, but in fact the essay does not cite or refer to them or even Freud's "A Child Is Being Beaten," and its single reference to Freud is one sentence from the *Introductory Lectures on Psychoanalysis*. It is quite evident, in any case, that the passage relies on Cowie's essay, although merely footnoting it with two others as "recent film theory" [211, n. 8]). Of course, Cowie cannot be held responsible for the banalization of her argument by other critics. Nonetheless, the structured ambiguity of "Fantasia" does leave ample room for such an effect; and its equivocation of "fixed" and "variable" terms may be held accountable for the eventual eviction of all

---

33. For various other criticisms of this position see Copjec (241), Mellencamp (235), and Doane ("Responses" 145). In support, see Donald 137–38 and Greig 185.

sexual differences, and in particular of lesbian-homosexual difference, not only from the film but from the spectator as well. There is
an unwelcome irony in the thought that, if the pre-feminist discourse on film ignored the cinematic production of spectatorial positions in sexual difference, this post-feminist discourse on fantasy,
which began as a critique of Mulvey's alleged eviction of the female
spectator from the movie theater, gives the spectator unlimited powers and pleasures by rendering actual sexual differences, as well as
gender and "biological sex," altogether irrelevant.

Obviously much is lost in the simple equation of the psychoanalytic subject of fantasy with the film spectator (as subject of the
film's fantasy), and in the assimilation of all forms of fantasy and
visual representation to unconscious (original) fantasy. In the first
place, while film almost certainly engages the spectator's fantasy,
spectatorship does not consist of purely unconscious processes, and
the processes of secondarization and conscious or preconscious
identification can hardly be discounted. Even as they insist on their
homology, Laplanche and Pontalis distinguish between conscious
and unconscious forms of fantasy. In the daydream and the reverie,
"the scenario is basically in the first person, and the subject's place
clear and invariable. The organization is stabilized by the secondary
process, weighed by the ego: the subject, it is said, lives out his reverie. But the original fantasy, on the other hand, is characterized by
the absence of subjectivization, and the subject is present in the
scene" (22). If it is rare to see a film that fits our own individual
reverie so closely as to mark our spectatorial subject place clearly
and utterly compellingly, surely it must be equally rare for a spectator, going to the movies on a Saturday night, to respond to the
images on the screen with nothing but the raw materials of her or
his primary processes. (Were that the case, the entertainment industry could hardly prosper as it does, or else the psychoanalytic/thera-
peutic profession would not.) And hence, I suggested, Freud's
insistence on the visualization of the subject in clinical practice acquires relevance for the practice of film viewing, as well as the theory: How do I look at the film? How do I appear in its fantasy? Am I
looking on? Can I be seen? Do I see myself in it? Is this my fantasy?

In the second place, by merging spectatorship into the psychoanalytic subject of fantasy, not only are two distinct theoretical concepts
of subject collapsed into one, but so also is the differential location of

those two subjects in the relations of production of fantasy; that is to say, their different locations in the analytic situation and in the movie theater, respectively. In this manner, the question of who produces the fantasy, of whose fantasy the film represents, and the distinction between representation and fantasy are preempted or mystified, leaving the theory of spectatorship with a re-found universal subject unmarked by sexual, gender, racial, or other differences, and free to move in and out of subject-positions at its leisure. For it is one thing to say that I am the subject always and everywhere present in my own fantasies, which sustain my desire, but quite another to say that a film, any film, addresses me constructing my desire as the subject of its fantasy, whatever *it* may be. This is not to appeal to a controlling intentionality on the part of the film or the filmmakers, nor to deny that heterogeneous and unforeseeable effects may be produced in spectatorship by the multiple agencies at work in the spectator's subjectivity as well as in the making of the film (the particular contributions of actors, screenwriter, editor, sound editor, camera, etc.). But it is to reaffirm two fundamental premises of film theory, which appear to have been lost in the escape from "binarisms"; namely, the historical situatedness of the spectator and the formal and technosocial specificity of cinematic representation.

Earlier on, in my reading of *She Must Be Seeing Things,* I suggested that McLaughlin uses the film-within-the-film device to recast the primal fantasy in relation to lesbian subjectivity and spectatorship. By rearticulating fantasy, masquerade, and voyeurism in lesbian terms, I argued, the film constructs a lesbian subject as the subject of its fantasy. It does not merely represent a fantasy but marks it as such, recasting and reframing it, working through it, to address the spectator in a lesbian subject-position. Thus, by particular enunciative strategies and by its intervention in the cinematic codes, the film constructs particular paths of spectatorial access to the fantasy it re-presents, inscribing a particular subject-position in its very mode of enunciation and address. This is not to say, however, that such a position is automatically accessible to all viewers, or even to all lesbian viewers, because the film's fantasy (the fantasy self-reflexively foregrounded by the film) may very well *not* be their own. The lack of attention this film has received in heterosexual feminist circles and its divided and controversial reception among lesbians certainly suggest that the latter is the case.

Some Special Effects of Fantasy

Another instance of controversial representation that bears a close relation to fantasy is pornography. In order to articulate further the distinction between the psychoanalytic subject and the social subject, between subjectivity and subjecthood, between fantasy and representation, and between private and public forms of fantasy, I will refer to another essay that invokes Laplanche and Pontalis to argue in behalf of pornography as fantasy. Judith Butler's "The Force of Fantasy" is a critique of the "discursive alliance" of anti-pornography feminists with the New Right in their respective efforts, the former to secure legal measures against the pornography industry, and the latter to push through the passage by the United States Congress of a bill prohibiting federal funding of artwork deemed "indecent" or "obscene." Both groups, Butler maintains, share a common theory of fantasy, or rather, a "set of untheorized presumptions" about fantasy: they rely "upon a representational realism that conflates the signified of fantasy with its (impossible) referent and construes 'depiction' as an injurious act" (105–106), and thus see fantasy (pornography) as "the causal link between representation and action" (112). Arguing, on her part, for pornography as fantasy, but with another understanding of fantasy and its effects, Butler quotes the famous passage in Laplanche and Pontalis that I quoted at the beginning of this chapter:

> Fantasy is not the object of desire, but its setting. In fantasy the subject does not pursue the object or its sign; one appears oneself caught up in the sequence of images. One forms no representation of the desired object, but is oneself represented as participating in the scene although, in the earliest forms of fantasy, one cannot be assigned any fixed place in it (hence the danger, in treatment [and in politics] of interpretations which claim to do so). As a result, the subject, although always present in the fantasy, may be so in a desubjectivized form, that is to say, in the very syntax of the sequence in question. (Butler, "The Force of Fantasy" 109–10)[34]

She then remarks:

---

34. The somewhat different wording of the passage would suggest that the translation has been altered by Butler, although the reference given is *"Formations [of Fantasy]* 26–27" (incorrectly, as it is only 26) without further comment.

There is, then, strictly speaking, no subject who has a fantasy, but only fantasy as the scene of the subject's fragmentation and dissimulation; fantasy enacts a splitting or fragmentation or, perhaps better put, a multiplication or proliferation of identifications that puts the very locatability of identity into question. In other words, although we might wish to think, even fantasize, that there is an "I" who has or cultivates its fantasy with some measure of mastery and possession, that "I" is always undone by precisely that which it claims to master. (110)

The reading would be quite plausible if Laplanche and Pontalis had written only the passage Butler quotes. However, distinguishing this (unconscious) form of fantasy from the conscious reverie or daydream, they also wrote that in the latter forms of fantasy "the scenario is basically in the first person, and the subject's place clear and invariable. The organization is stabilized by the secondary process, weighed by the ego: the subject, it is said, lives out his reverie" (22). Laplanche further writes:

After all, "life has to be lived" and a human being can supplement a love of life that is occasionally deficient only by a love of the ego or of the ideal agencies which are, in turn, derived from it, but also—if the essence of the ego function is indeed *binding*, before being adaptation—because a minimum of intervention by that function is indispensable for even an unconscious fantasy to *take form*. (*Life and Death in Psychoanalysis* 125–26)[35]

On the strength of this theory of fantasy, therefore, there is *also* a subject who fantasizes herself in the scene and whose *fantasy* (precisely) is one of mastery, even as that fantasy may be in contradiction with her own unconscious fantasy. And indeed what else if not such contradiction would bring about the splitting of the subject or the undoing of the ego's self-possession? In Freud's analysis of "A Child Is Being Beaten," the unconscious ("transitional") form of the fantasy ("I am being beaten by my father") is an interpretation or a reconstruction in analysis, and is never remembered by the subject;

---

35. Commenting on this passage and recalling that for Lacan, as well, "the notion of unconscious fantasy . . . is supported only by taking a detour via the ego," Silverman observes that "although at the deepest recesses of its psyche the subject has neither identity nor nameable desire, the fantasmatic and the *moi* together work to articulate a mythic but determining version of each" (*Male Subjectivity at the Margins* 5–6).

whereas the two remembered forms—the "objective" and the "voyeuristic" forms, as Freud calls them—would correspond respectively to the pornographic text and the pornographic text viewed by the subject. The structural analogy of conscious and unconscious fantasies, remarked by Laplanche and Pontalis, and brought close to home by Anna Freud's contrastive analysis of her patient's "nice stories" and masturbatory fantasies ("Beating Fantasies and Daydreams" 149–53), does not collapse the distinction between them. The point is that "the subject" is *both* conscious and unconscious. In fact, Butler's own argument suggests as much.

"Fantasy is the very scene which *suspends* action and which, in its suspension, provides for a critical investigation of what it is that constitutes action" (113), she states, adding that, insofar as it opens up "interpretive possibilities" (113), she sees "the pornographic text as a site of multiple significations" (114). Surely the subject of such critical investigation is much closer to the conscious end of the fantasy spectrum than to the unconscious one. The *interpretation* of a text's or a scene's multiple significations is the work of analysis, of secondarization, whose subjective purpose *is* mastery and self-possession. And these, I suggest, acquire all the more weight in the interpreter's confrontation with a "pornographic" text (the representation of a sexual scene) which by its very content (the sexual scenario) is likely to engage directly the subject's unconscious (repressed) fantasy and thus present the threat of fragmentation and undoing of the interpreter's ego. In other words, Butler's is not a silly notion of the nature of fantasy, but it is still an optimistic, or rather a voluntaristic, one. For, in asserting that fantasy suspends action by fostering at the same time a disruption of identity and a critical distance in the viewer of pornography, Butler would have her cake and eat it too: fantasy (pornography) can do no harm. In part, this may derive from her taking the other side in the "political" opposition against the anti-pornography feminists represented in her text by "Dworkin." (I put this name between quotation marks to indicate that I am not referring to the person or the author Andrea Dworkin but to the character in Butler's fictional dialogue, the antagonist in her argument. I thus hope to indicate as clearly as possible that, in objecting to Butler's argument, I am neither "defending" "Dworkin" nor—much less—supporting the arguments made by the actual Andrea Dworkin.)

> Indeed, if pornography is to be understood as fantasy, as anti-pornography activists almost invariably insist, then the effect of pornography is not to force women to identify with a subordinate or debased position, but to provide the opportunity to identify with the entire scene of debasement, agents and recipients alike. . . . The pornographic fantasy does not restrict identification to any one position, and [Andrea] Dworkin, in her elaborate textual exegesis, paradoxically shows us how her form of interpretive mastery can be derived from a viewing which, in her own view, is supposed to restrict her to a position of mute and passive injury. (114)

Butler's polemic against "Dworkin" misses its target by ignoring the obvious, if contradictory, fact that feminist analysis and politics have always proceeded concurrently with—indeed have been prompted by—the social injury suffered by women, but the strength of feminism, or what social power it may have, does not disprove that injury. When Butler suggests that the argumentative power or "interpretive mastery" of a feminist critique of pornography can derive only from an identification with the pornographic fantasy and its representation of aggression, I want to think it is because she, too, simply transposes the theory of the psychoanalytic subject of fantasy to the viewer of a public, industrially produced representation. In equating the pornographic text with the pornographic fantasy, or pornography with fantasy, she conflates fantasy with representation and disregards the different relations of production of fantasy that obtain for the subject in a private or analytic situation, on the one hand, and for the subject in a public context of representation, on the other. In the end, Butler's equation of (pornographic) representation with (unconscious) fantasy is the obverse of the move to equate pornographic representation with action. One side ignores the possibly heterogeneous effects of fantasy within the subject vis-à-vis representation; the other side disregards the contradictions within the subject and denies the effects of fantasy with regard to action, which (after all) is an important dimension of the political. While both pornographic representation and action do have an intimate relation to fantasy, and to each other, in the realm of the senses and in that of the law, in sexual practices as well as in the juridical-legislative domain, nevertheless, it seems to me, retaining the distinction among the three terms—representation, action, and fantasy—is important, not only theoretically but also politically.

Quite correctly, in my opinion, Butler reads "Dworkin's" interpretive mastery as a form of feminist sociopolitical subjecthood; but she does not acknowledge that subjecthood—conscious, affirmative, even willful, and based on a political and collective identity—is not the same as subjectivity, which is permeated by repression, resistance, ambivalence, and contradiction. Obviously, subjectivity and subjecthood are never dissociated in the subject, just as the psychoanalytic subject is always a social subject, but the two terms stand to each other in a conceptual relationship analogous to that of private or subjective representation (fantasy) to public representation. By not distinguishing between fantasy and representation, or between the psychoanalytic subject of (unconscious) fantasy and the social or the political subject, what Butler loses sight of, ironically, is precisely the imaginary (unconscious?) force of fantasy in "Dworkin's" subjectivity. For it is the hold of a socially constructed and subjectively internalized identification with the victim's or "feminine" position, I would speculate, that prevents "Dworkin" from fantasizing herself in the other place and taking up the aggressor's or "masculine" position which Butler projects onto her. It is that imaginary identification with the victim's position that both limits the interpretive possibilities for "Dworkin" as viewer of the pornographic text and makes her feel constricted in a fantasy scenario that her subjecthood will not accept as hers. I would speculate, therefore, that it is not, as Butler suggests, that "Dworkin's reading draws its strength and mastery" from "an identification and redeployment of the very representation of aggression [the 'masculine' position] that she abhors" (115), but rather that "Dworkin" resists seeing herself in the mass-produced pornographic fantasy, in which yet she does see herself. In short, what Butler sees as masculine aggression, to another may look more like feminist resistance.

Again, as I objected to Cowie's reading of *Now, Voyager* in "Fantasia," the problem is that no one spectator's reading of, or identification in, a text or represented scene can be generalized as a property of the text, and that the heterogeneous, special effects of fantasy in the viewer of a representation are contingent on that viewer's subjectivity and subjecthood. Thus Butler's view of the pornographic text as a site of multiple or concurrent identifications is contingent on a viewer's capacity to distance herself from it (or to de-subjectivize herself, as happens in the original—unconscious—fantasy recovered in analysis). That "Dworkin" may not be capable of such distance, or that her political subjecthood and need for self-possession may militate against it, is a possibility Butler does not admit.

At any rate, "Dworkin" does not lend support to Butler's theory that "fantasy does not restrict identification to any one position." This is so, I have suggested, because "Dworkin" is neither the subject nor the producer of the fantasy in question; because the pornographic text is not her fantasy but a fantasy (representation) produced by others, which, as she sees it, interpellates her and solicits her identification with a particular scenario in which she does not, will not, or cannot find her place, a scenario whose specified positions (victim or aggressor) she will not or cannot occupy—much in the same way that "Dora" and the unnamed girl of "Psychogenesis" resisted Freud's interpretation of their wish in the Oedipal scenario. And in the same way a spectator may refuse to enter or to identify in a film's scenario. For the self-representations and constructions of identity—imaginary and symbolic, subjective and social—that one brings to the viewing of a film and any other representation or "ready-made fantasy" not only overdetermine but also restrict one's path through its "multiple significations."

Ideology is a quaint word now, in disuse, but its effects are still at work in the spectator-subject of public fantasy, as is secondarization in the psychoanalytic subject. The work of unconscious fantasy, important as it is for our understanding of psychic contradiction and divisions in the social subject, cannot simply replace the complex intersections of conscious and unconscious processes in the subject of fantasy. Nor can a theory of film spectatorship, a theory of representation, collapse the social into the subjective by equating representation with fantasy. Finally, the theory of fantasy I have been discussing should not serve to legislate spectatorial identification and desire. Its value resides, I have tried to argue, in the possibility it offers for a more nuanced understanding of the heterogeneous and often contradictory effects of representation in the subject. This in turn reaffirms the historical, particular situatedness of the spectator in a given configuration of the social field, and makes spectatorship an important site of articulation of individual subjectivity with social subjecthood and of fantasy with representation.

Chapter 4

The Seductions of Lesbianism: Feminist Psychoanalytic Theory and the Maternal Imaginary

Metaphors of maternity and mothering and nurturing had acquired a disturbing centrality to discussions of female creativity and "women's culture." . . . More recently, however, it has come to seem that lesbians too are everywhere, particularly in critical texts about modernist literary practice written by women and men who are not lesbians about women who may or may not have been.
—Meryl Altman (501)

A Discourse on Love

In a book whose title I adapted for this chapter, the argument is advanced that both psychoanalytic theory and practice hinge on a logic of seduction. In the theory, psychoanalytic explanation of sexual subjectivity rests on the structure of deferred action (*Nachträglichkeit*), a distinctive articulation of present, past, and future by which a forgotten event can be recovered and understood only after some other event has acquired a causative function. The chronologically first event, whether real or fantasized, is of the nature of a seduction; the second event, whatever its nature, becomes understood (as attached to the first) through a particular form of discursive interaction between patient and analyst which is itself a kind of seduction. In naming transference (*Übertragung*) the process by which a patient's forgotten sexual thoughts and feelings belonging to the past are (re)invested in the person of the analyst, Freud identified at the therapeutic core of psychoanalysis a mechanism for eliciting the patient's production of memories, dreams, and/or fantasies. Thus the very nature of the "talking cure" makes for an eroticization of the analytic situation itself as a discourse on love. Both in theory and in practice, therefore, psychoanalysis "must welcome all the storms and stresses of violent antagonism, of infatuation, of tears, laughter and forgetting. It welcomes these because it lives off the *analysis* of the immediate 'reality' of these states. . . . Yet all these states must be dissolved into the fictionality proper to analysis," and the psychoanalytic contract is both "the means for instigating these states" and "the means for containing them" (Forrester, *The Seductions of Psychoanalysis* 5).

Already in his early *Studies on Hysteria* (1895) Freud identified the analytic process of transference, which Forrester aptly calls "contracting the disease of love" (30):

> In one of my patients the origin of a particular hysterical symptom lay in a wish, which she had had many years earlier and had at once relegated to the unconscious, that the man she was talking to at the time might boldly take the initiative and give her a kiss. On one occasion, at the end of a session, a similar wish came up in her about me. She was horrified at it, spent a sleepless night, and at the next session, though she did not refuse to be treated, was quite useless for work. . . . What had happened therefore was this. The content of the wish had appeared first of all in the patient's consciousness without any memories of the surrounding circumstances which would have assigned it to a past time. The wish which was present was then, owing to the compulsion to associate which was dominant in her consciousness, linked to my person, with which the patient was legitimately concerned; and as the result of this *mésalliance*—which I describe as a "false connection"—the same affect was provoked which had forced the patient long before to repudiate this forbidden wish. . . . The patients, too, gradually learnt to realize that in these transferences on to the figure of the physician it was a question of a compulsion and an illusion which melted away with the conclusion of the analysis. (*SE* 2: 302–303)

But the psychoanalytic contract involves two contracting agents, and the analyst is not immune to the disease, though curing it is precisely his task. As Freud admits some twenty years later in one of his papers on technique,

When a woman sues for love, to reject and refuse is a distressing part for a man to play; and, in spite of neurosis and resistance, there is an incomparable fascination in a woman of high principles who confesses her passion. It is not a patient's crudely sensual desires which constitute the temptation. These are more likely to repel, and it will call for all the doctor's tolerance if he is to regard them as a natural phenomenon. It is rather, perhaps, a woman's subtler and aim-inhibited wishes which bring with them the danger of making a man forget his technique and his medical task for the sake of a fine experience. ("Observations on Transference-Love" [1915], *SE* 12: 170)

The psychoanalytic scenario, with its original cast of characters—young female patient and older male doctor—engaged in the passionate fiction of a mutual seduction, repeats in its fictionality, its compulsion and its illusion, the scene of paternal seduction that the theory thematizes as original trauma, first, and as original fantasy subsequently. In a permutation of the classical Oedipal scenario, in which the boy child would seduce his young mother, here the young woman's seduction of the doctor-father is both instigated and contained by his authority and "ethical" responsibility under the psychoanalytic contract. Compelled into the field of language, elevated from her "crudely sensual desires" (which do not tempt him anyway) to the discursive realm of confession and aim-inhibited wishes, the daughter's seduction is made at once non-threatening and permanent (for the duration of the analysis). Conversely, if the analyst-father can exercise "a lasting seduction upon the hysteric," as Gallop writes glossing Irigaray, it is because the seduction he "exercises refuses her his body, his penis, and asks her to embrace his law" instead (*The Daughter's Seduction* 75).

"The father's law is a counterphobic mechanism," Gallop further suggests. It protects him from his desire for the daughter, and patriarchy from "the potential havoc of the daughter's desirability. Were she recognized as desirable in her specificity as daughter, not as son ('little man') nor as mother, there would be a second sexual economy," one not predicated on "the phallus's desire for itself" (76). Thus the father must guard against his desire for the daughter; he "protects himself from her desire for his body, protects himself from his body. For it is only the law—and not the body—which constitutes him as patriarch" (77), securing his place in the structure of symbolic exchange (of women) between men.[1] Ironically, this emphasis on a desire for and of the body seems to me less germane to "the psychoanalytic father," of whom Gallop here ostensibly speaks, than to the real father in the many past and present situations of incest; although the latter does not "protect himself from his body," he does act upon his desire for the daughter's body precisely "in her specificity as daughter," then publicly denies his physical contact with her body in order to retain his patriarchal place in the family and in society.

In the psychoanalytic scene, Gallop's emphasis on a desire for/of the body rather obscures the two-way character of analytic transferential seduction, as described by Freud, where the contract of transference-love is binding to both parties. Here it is "the seductive function of the law itself" (*Speculum* 41)—the doctor's very authority vested in his body, rather than that body—which succeeds in eliciting and refocusing the patient's desire, *if* the transference works (for "Dora" and the girl of "Psychogenesis" it did not work; and why some transferences work while others do not is another issue). Similarly, her power of seduction is not that of the body's "sensual desires" but rather a filigree of *aim-inhibited* wishes, a gossamer of symptomatic projections on the screen of memory, phantoms of another scene. Such is the structure of desire, of mutual seduction, that subtends the analytic interaction and its two agents: it is only by denying both the "fine experience" that the contract underwrites seduction as the structure of their exchange, however uneven. As Freud put it in another context, "a man's love and a woman's are a phase apart psychologically" (*SE* 22: 134).

This may not be the "second sexual economy" auspicated by Gallop, which could not exist in any case for the "daughter" within the patriarchal or androcentric kinship structure of compulsory heterosexuality; but it is nonetheless distinct from the sexual economy of familial incest, where the young girl has no margin of safety, no room to withstand the father's desiring body, and especially no space to speak her desire. On the other hand, while not disallowing

---

1. Gallop's argument follows and glosses Irigaray's reading of Freud in *Speculum* (1974). The same point and a similar fantasy—a daughter's wish to seduce the father who rejects her—are expressed, in the form of letters by a woman patient to her analyst, in Erika Kaufmann's *Transfert*, an epistolary novel published in Italy in the same year and apparently translated into French in 1975, according to Jardine (79).

the reality or the occurrence of familial incest (a reality that is much more consistently denied or covered up by the very institution in which it occurs—the family itself), psychoanalysis has produced and circulated a representation of woman as subject of fantasy and of desire. It is the fantasy of incest, with its psychic and discursive reality, rather than the physical reality of incest, that sustains the seductions of psychoanalysis and its adepts' passionate fictions, Freud's first of all and those of many others, men and women, after him. In this sense, he never abandoned his "seduction theory" but rather refined it, reworked it through self-analysis, and made it the core of the analytic method. And in this sense is his notion of fantasy, of the psychic reality of fantasy, among Freud's major contributions to contemporary cultural theory.

Thus what has been taken by many, feminists and others, as a self-serving equivocation, on Freud's part, between actual incest and fantasized incest, leading to an opportunistic denial of the reality of incest (Masson) or to a betrayal of Dora and of himself (Frank), seems to me instead one of the reasons why the theory—and, if much more conditionally, the practice—of psychoanalysis has been so appealing to women. Even to feminists. Martha Evans, for example, is captivated by the daughter's powers of seduction and seems to reproach the psychoanalytic father for not yielding to them. But first, following Masson's "evidence," she argues that the term *seduction* [*Verführung*], increasingly used by Freud in place of *attacks* [*Angriffen*] and *abuse* [*Abusus*], is "a cover for rape and incest" ("Hysteria and the Seduction of Theory" 82): by implying "the use of persuasion in the sexual corruption of another individual" (74), the term *seduction* served to dissimulate "the blatant exercise of sexual power by fathers with respect to their young daughters" (82). Subsequently, Freud's bad faith in absconding the reality of incest would carry through into the analytic scene; there, it would reappear in the analyst's self-protective distance and his invocation of superior knowledge and technique "against the traumatic effects of a devastating encounter with a female subject of desire" (79). At this point of Evans's argument, in other words, the presumed recipient of paternal/analytic abuse is also subject of the desire that seduces/abuses her; she is herself a seducer. For when paternal incest is transformed into the seductive function of theory in the analytic situation, the analyst-father is confronted with a patient-daughter who is somehow no longer a passive victim but rather a tease ("what the French call an *allumeuse*"), one who will not stay in the position of the object of his desire but will seduce him and then not "follow through"; and "the seduction ends when the hysteric insists on subjectivity, on her status as a subject" (78).

Evans's notion of an "autonomy of female desire" (81, 82) that manifests itself in the hysteric parallels Gallop's notion of a "second sexual economy," but neither critic explains where that autonomous desire would come from (from what it would be autonomous), how it is configured in relation to the Oedipal scenario, or what fantasy sustains it. Indeed both critics very nearly collapse analytic, transferential seduction, and its fantasy of incest, with actual father-daughter intercourse. Nevertheless—and this is the point of my discussing them—the figure of woman as subject of (heterosexual) desire appears for them only in the analytic interaction, in the figure of the hysteric, and in what Evans decries as "the paradigm of hysteria as a heterosexual love story" (77).

The conclusion I draw from such feminist arguments against Freud, as surely as from those in favor, is that psychoanalysis has managed to envisage at least some women—the hysterics, the psychically deviants—as both sexed subjects and subjects of desire, albeit a desire unsatisfiable under the given conditions. Not by coincidence, then, feminist theory has addressed itself to Freud from the start, rereading him critically and with greater or lesser gain depending, in part, on the particular forms of institutionalization of psychoanalysis in diverse cultural contexts and on the epistemological frameworks feminists employed. Where subjectivity and desire were emphasized, the gain to feminist theorizing has been greater (Irigaray, Mitchell, etc.); where subjecthood and social agency were first on the agenda, the gain has seemed negative (Millett, etc.). What I would suggest to the proponents of the latter view is that the figure of the young female patient in the psychoanalytic scenario, the hysteric or the deviant, is also endowed with symbolic agency, as well as desire. She plays opposite the father in the scene of seduction, and on her role, her speech, and her response depend his own role and his theory. Theirs is a symbolic exchange as well as an imaginary one, and the structure of their exchange is mutual seduction. This is the case neither with incest or rape, nor with the socially sanctioned pretty picture of daddy and his little girl. "Was will das Weib," therefore, is not an idle question but the founding impulse of the psychoanalytic method and its original fantasy; it is, to paraphrase Laplanche and Pontalis (19), one major enigma to which the myth of psychoanalysis would provide a solution.

It may be just this characteristic feature of psychoanalysis, the possibility for the woman to be an agent, a sexed and desiring subject, even a protagonist, in its particular form of symbolic exchange—a possibility denied women by all juridical, scientific, and philosophical discourses at the time of Freud, and still denied today within the institutional structures of compulsory heterosexuality—that has attracted women and feminists to psychoanalysis in the various roles of patients, analysts, theorists, interlocutors, translators, muses, or all of the above. The seductions of psychoanalysis for women can be documented: from Anna O., alias Bertha Pappenheim, who named it "the talking cure" (*SL* 2: 30) and outlived it to become a Jewish-feminist activist, to Anna Freud, "true daughter of an immortal sire" (as her rejected suitor, Ernest Jones, patronizingly memorialized her dedication to psychoanalysis in dedicating to her his biography of Freud), to the contemporary feminist scholars who have embraced it and in growing number have been entering training analysis.[2]

Freudian psychoanalysis grants women the power of seducing *and of being seduced*, being—in the latter case as well—sexed and desiring subjects, if only within the terms of its contract, its particular scenario. Outside of that, in the regime of compulsory heterosexuality, women's power of seduction (touted in folk wisdom and eulogized by philosophers from Nietzsche to Baudrillard) is the flip side of their powerlessness as objects of seduction (incest); in either case they are not the subjects of a desire of their own. Everywhere

---

2. An initial effort toward historical and biographical documentation in feminist perspective is the compelling if uneven collection of profiles from Anna O. to Irigaray edited by Vegetti-Finzi, *Psicoanalisi al femminile*. See also Chodorow's interview study of gender consciousness in early women psychoanalysts, "Seventies Questions for Thirties Women" (*Feminism and Psychoanalytic Theory* 199–218), which includes useful statistical information and biographical references in notes 7 and 8 (269–70). Trasforini's excellent sociological study documents the steady growth of women's membership in the psychoanalytic profession in Italy and in the Italian psychoanalytic societies (Freudian and Jungian) since the 1970s, and its consistent acceleration since the early 1980s (*La professione di psicoanalista*, esp. 85–96). Lastly, some rather inchoate thoughts on feminism and psychoanalytic transference are offered in Jardine, "Notes for an Analysis."

outside the Freudian scenario of analytic transference-love, even in feminist theory and in much psychoanalytic theory as well (cf. Lacan's view of "the hysteric's desire" I discuss in chapter 2), what one finds again and again is, in Rose's poignant phrase, "the impossibility of subject *and* desire" ("Dora" 146).

Now, as the title of this chapter suggests, I am going to speculate that lesbianism performs, within feminist theory and vis-à-vis the question of female subjectivity and desire, a role analogous to that of psychoanalysis as I have just outlined it—but without the heavy costs of the mortgage to patriarchy that the Freudian transferential contract entails.[3] And for this reason, I suggest, feminist psychoanalytic theory has reclaimed homosexuality as a prerogative or a component of female sexuality while, in so doing, equivocating on the specificity of lesbian sexuality and eliding its psychic and social differences from heterosexuality.

Like the hysteric in the analytic scenario, the figure of the lesbian in contemporary feminist discourse represents the possibility of female subject *and* desire: she can seduce and be seduced, but without losing her status as subject. That is to say, unlike the hysteric, she is both—even at once—desiring subject and desiring object; and given the existence of other lesbians, her desire is—in principle—satisfiable. Surely, not all women are lesbians, many women desire men. But then, not all women are hysterics, and not all women are in analysis, either. *What I am referring to is not the reality, the psychic and/or social reality, of lesbianism but its fantasmatic place and figuration in feminist theory:* a place from where female homosexuality figures, for women, the *possibility* of subject and desire. To the extent that all women may have access to that place, female homosexuality—like hysteria, to which it is often linked (e.g., in feminist

---

3. Not the least of those costs is to have one's work, as well as one's love, rejected, ignored, or underrecognized by the theoretical father. See Sabina Spielrein's diary of her analysis and relationship with Carl Gustav Jung, and her correspondence with Jung and Freud published in Carotenuto. In 1911, at one of the Wednesday night meetings at Freud's house, Spielrein presented a paper arguing for a destructive impulse in the drive for the preservation of the species ("Die Destruktion als Ursache des Werdens"). Although Freud later acknowledged this paper as having anticipated "a considerable portion" of his own speculations on the death drive in *Beyond the Pleasure Principle* (*SE* 18: 55), at the time he effectively took it to represent the work of Jung and recommended that it be heavily edited for publication in the psychoanalytic *Jahrbuch*, then edited by Jung himself, who agreed and further belittled the paper and its author (see Molfino 252–57 and Sprengnether 92–93 and 124–27).

readings of "Dora") and occasionally assimilated (Grosz, "Lesbian Fetishism?")—guarantees women the status of sexed and desiring subjects, wherever their desire may be directed. In other words, regardless of its objects or actual satisfiability, the desire expressed in the figure, the trope, of female homosexuality may be predicated unconditionally of the female subject; it becomes one of her properties or constitutive traits (as desire is of the male subject). But unlike the hysteric's desire, it need not be confined in the patriarchal frame of "a heterosexual love story."

Here is one of several examples I will adduce to illustrate my hypothesis. In reflecting on the seductiveness of psychoanalysis for feminist theorists, Mary Ann Doane suggests that it has to do with an "erotico-theoretical transference" (the phrase is Michèle Le Doeuff's) to the discourse of "pure difference" or "in-difference" propounded by influential male theorists such as Barthes, Foucault, and Lacan (see Schor, "Dreaming Dissymmetry"). To Doane herself, it is Rose's articulation of Lacanian psychoanalysis as a theory of "the constant failure of sexual identity, its instability or even its impossibility," that is "the most seductive"; but she admits that "insofar as patriarchy seems to work—and to have worked for a long time— [sexual identity] cannot be seen as either a failure or an impossibility" (Doane, "Commentary: Post-Utopian Difference" 76). Thus Doane would retain the notion of "a feminine specificity or sexuality" as a strategic move in feminist politics: "Identity at the level of the social may be oppressive, and identity at the level of the psychical may be fictional, but what about identity at the level of the political? One's identity as a feminist, for instance. . . . Identities must be assumed if only temporarily" (76–77), with the stipulation that all identities be strictly provisional. In the perspective of Barthes's "utopia of pluralities," she adds—exemplifying the theoretical transference mentioned above—"the opposition between homosexuality and heterosexuality should falter as well" (77).

This latter point serves as the lead to a brief comment on Heather Findlay's "Is There a Lesbian in This Text?," a reading of Derrida's *Spurs* against Wittig's *The Lesbian Body* (see chapter 5 below), which is the occasion for Doane's "Commentary." She concedes that Findlay is right to insist on the necessity (for Doane, only political) "of delineating a specifically 'lesbian theory' as a first stage in dismantling the hegemonic heterosexual regime," but immediately warns her that such a theory "activates an identity which is already marked for destruction" (77). In other words, Doane allows that a certain fixing of identity and desire in the theorization of a *lesbian* specificity has a tactical value in the *feminist* struggle against the heterosexual hegemony and in preserving "any explanatory power that psychoanalysis may have for feminism"—that is to say, in sustaining one's feminist identity and erotico-theoretical transference. But she sees the articulation of a specific *lesbian* identity or sexuality as the "first stage" of a conceptual project whose aim should be to self-destruct, in the interest of *feminist* politics and theory.[4]

However, homosexual difference is not less relevant to lesbian subjectivity than the more "visible" sexual difference between female and male, which is the mainstay of feminism. And many feminists, unlike Doane, appear to be aware of this. For them, therefore, the question is, How can the difference between heterosexuality and lesbianism be negotiated in order for all women to accede to the place of a female homosexuality that could guarantee female desire? I have already suggested in chapter 2 that the road of access lies in the pre-Oedipal relation to the mother. Feminism would have the mother as protagonist either next to or instead of the father in the psychoanalytic scenario. The trouble is, psychoanalysis has already assigned a role to the mother, although with a certain flexibility built in to accommodate a variety of stagings, from the bit part the mother plays in Freud's to her leading role in Klein's.

The latter, then, would seem more likely to appeal to feminists concerned to trace a female lineage, an erotic and symbolic derivation from the mother. And indeed the influence of Klein and object-relations theory on feminist psychological writings has been proportionately greater than Freud's. However, the erotic constitution of the maternal body in Klein's theory is entirely dependent on the father's penis it contains and jealously guards, creating problems of envy in the daughter; and with these feminism has found it difficult to come to terms.[5] For this reason, perhaps, those drawn to a

---

4. Doane's objection to Findlay, in other terms and times, repeats the history of struggles over lesbianism in the early days of the women's movement from the Lavander Menace's intervention onward. For two opposite accounts of that history, see Echols and Miriam.

5. As Nunziante Cesaro concludes her critico-biographical profile, "Melanie Klein, invisible to her father who preferred her sister and unrecognized by Freud who

Kleinian scenario have downplayed desire and sexuality as such in favor of gender identity construction and what is called "the self in relation" (Chodorow, *Feminism and Psychoanalytic Theory,* chapters 5, 9, et passim; for a critical discussion of the "new psychology of women," see Westkott). In the Freudian staging, on the other hand, the mother's secondary part turns out to have greater potential, for, in the end, an unexpected twist in the plot gives her the role of primary agent of seduction. Before advancing further in my speculations and discussing other views of the maternal relation through which is posited the access to a fantasmatic place of female homosexuality, I must retrace my steps to Freud's seduction theory which, I stated, he never really relinquished.

The Mother's Seduction

As a matter of fact, Laplanche points out, Freud never stopped looking for factual clues about what happened in his patients' childhood or wondering whether the primal scene was actually witnessed by a subject (e.g., the "Wolf Man") or fabricated from later events. In spite of the momentous discovery of fantasy and the formulation of the pivotal category of psychic reality, Freud "found himself caught in an alternative which, in recent years, we have attempted to go beyond: that between the real, on the one hand, the reality of a lived memory whose trace can be detected in an almost sleuthlike manner, and, on the other hand, the imaginary, traditionally conceived of as a lesser entity" (*Life and Death in Psychoanalysis* 33). Because of this ambiguity and the consequent oscillation in his use of such terms as *reality, pure imagination,* and *retrospective reconstruction,* Laplanche argues, Freud did not fully elucidate the notion of psychic reality, "something which would have all the consistency of the real without, however, being verifiable in external experience" (33). His incessant search for "the *fact* of seduction" led him, at the end of his work, to find it in "a quasi-universal datum":

---

put his daughter Anna first, hides the father inside the female body of the mother enthroned in the fantasmatic scene" (130; my translation).

Beyond any seduction scenes by the father, and beyond any openly genital seductions, [Freud] refers to seduction through maternal care as his *primary model*. Such care, in focusing on certain bodily regions, contributes to *defining* them as erotogenic zones, zones of exchange which demand and provoke excitation in order subsequently to reproduce it autonomously, through *internal* stimulation. . . . But here, we should go a step further and not restrict ourselves to the pure materiality of stimulating actions. . . . Beyond the contingency and transiency of any specific experience, it is the intrusion into the universe of the child of certain meanings of the adult world which is conveyed by the most ordinary and innocent of acts. The whole of the primal intersubjective relation—between mother and child—is saturated with these meanings. Such, we maintain, is the most profound sense of the theory of seduction. (44)

This emphasis on the mother-child, pre-Oedipal dyad comes in the context of Laplanche's brief discussion of Klein and Ferenczi (who, incidentally, had been Klein's first analyst and whom Freud reproached for "playing a tender mother role" with his patients [quoted in Forrester 60]). Whether Laplanche wants to provide a corrective to Freud's belated and insufficient interest in the mother's active part in a subject's psychosexual development, or whether he wants to stress the constitutive role of the parental fantasies in the subject's fantasmatic structuration ("the father is present from the beginning, even if the mother is a widow: he is present because the mother herself has a father and desires a penis" [46], Laplanche flatly remarks), his conclusion rewrites Freud's seduction theory retroactively, anticipating Foucault's theory of sexuality:

What is described schematically and in almost caricatural fashion as an *event* in the Freudian theory of the *proton pseudos* [first lie or primal deceit, i.e., the hysteric's claim of paternal seduction] should be understood as a kind of implantation of adult sexuality in the child. We believe that it should be reinterpreted, not as an event, or as a datable lived trauma, but as a factor which is both more diffuse and more structural, a more primal factor as well in the sense that it is so linked to the process of humanization that it is only through abstraction that we can suppose the existence of a small human "before" that seduction. For, to be sure, to speak of a child who was initially "innocent" would be to forge a myth exactly symmetrical to the myth of seduction. (*Life and Death in Psychoanalysis* 46)

In other words, with or without an actual event of material seduction—be that deliberate incest or unwitting stimulating actions by the adults in charge of the child—there is always something "real" in the subject's fantasy of seduction, even if only as an effect of parental or societal fantasies.

It may be worth observing that my rephrasing of what I take to be the significant contribution of Laplanche to the seduction theory, or the seduction fantasy, of psychoanalysis, purposely avoids calling seduction a myth, as he does (losing by that very phrase some of the terrain he gained over Freud's own ambiguity). I have preferred the seeming oxymoron *there is always something "real" in the fantasy of seduction* because this seems to me the sense of Laplanche's argument or, perhaps better, this is the sense in which I find it productive to read it: seduction is not just a myth (a fantasy in the traditional sense of fabrication or a made-up story, as opposed to reality) but rather, again paraphrasing him, something which has all the consistency of the real, and has very real effects in subjectivity, without being necessarily traceable to specific material events.

But a second observation is in order. Laplanche emphasizes, even more than Freud does, the real seduction (the "materiality," "the *fact* of seduction") of maternal care over and against an equivalently material, paternal seduction. About the latter he merely proffers Freud's objections, one "of fact—the impossibility of ever rediscovering *the* 'scene'—and [one] of principle: the impossibility of admitting that paternal perversion is *that* frequent and, above all, the inability to decide whether a scene discovered in analysis is true or fantasied" (32). Thus, while Laplanche, like Freud, does not exclude the possible occurrence of paternal incest, he sharply distinguishes between a real, "quasi-universal" or inevitable seduction by the mother and a possible, numerically circumscribed or contingent seduction by the father (paternal perversion cannot be *that* frequent). The latter, then, if and when it takes place, would be deliberate, and hence "perverse," whereas the former, owing to the necessity of maternal care, is presumably unintentional, although, with reference to Klein's work, Laplanche notes that "the mother has libidinal designs on her own child and, *beyond* him, on the penis she desires. These truths . . . are verified daily in the psychoanalysis of women, but . . . are all too easily forgotten when the children of these same women are in question" (46). He does not further specify whether the mother's libidinal designs are unintentional (unconscious) or deliberate (incestuous).

In any case, here Laplanche seems to shift the weight of seduction, and hence the "implantation" of sexuality in the child, squarely onto the mother; her material seduction (through unavoidable maternal care) and her "verifiable" desire for the penis would then determine the fantasmatic and erotic structuration of each child more fundamentally than any paternal seduction could later on. This overcorrection of Freud, it seems to me, tilts the balance toward a real event of seduction (maternal seduction as the counterpart of Freud's early belief in paternal incest), making that event not only foundational and inevitable but also more insidiously phallocentric in its unqualified reduction of the mother's libidinal designs to "the penis she desires." Finally, then, Laplanche himself comes close to forging another "symmetrical myth of seduction" and losing most of the terrain he gained in redefining seduction as the effect of *parental fantasies* on the subject's psychic reality ("something which would have all the consistency of the real without, however, being verifiable in external experience" [33]). Moreover, if the mother's fantasies, in her desire for the penis, are homologous to the father's, then the specificity of maternal seduction in Laplanche would remain confined, as it is in Freud, to the "pure materiality of stimulating actions," to the realm of the real; and the parental fantasies would amount to a single fantasy, that of phallic seduction. This would mean that "the figure of the mother at the site of the origin of the fantasies drops out," as Julia Erhart observes of the trajectory of Freud's theory of seduction. While paternal seduction begins in the realm of the real but then crosses over into that of fantasy and representation, maternal seduction "remains anchored to reality . . . locked within the terms of 'pre-1897' thought"; nothing is said about "under what conditions it occurs, what role it can play in future symbolic representing":

> Not fantasized, not imagined, the mother becomes, in Freud,
> literally unimaginable, unspeakable. Moreover, I believe the
> problem of maternal erasure is double-edged: not perceived as the
> result of little girls' fantasies, the maternal scenario is unable to
> serve in the symbolic structuring of future fantasies either. Not
> spoken by seduction discourse, the maternal is also unable to
> speak there. Thus what is effaced along with the fact of maternal

presence . . . at the fantasies' origins is the possibility of symbolic activity that begins with the mother, of maternally generated representation. ("Representation and the Female Symbolic: What's Lesbianism Got to Do with It?" 26–27)

The task of feminist psychoanalytic theory, the passage implies, is not only a rewriting of the mother as symbolic agent, a theory of her agency and role in the symbolic, but especially an account of her role in symbolic seduction, in the transmission of specifically maternal or female fantasies, and finally the representation of the mother as a site, figure, or actor in the fantasies of the female subject (the daughter). As I go on to consider some of the ways in which feminists have rewritten the maternal role within the psychoanalytic scenario, I will try to answer the provocative question in Erhart's subtitle by reflecting further on the figuration or the fantasmatic place of lesbianism in feminist theorizing.

The Maternal Imaginary

The idea of a "maternal discourse" emerging from pre-Oedipal relations is adumbrated in Madelon Sprengnether's thesis that "the body of the (m)other provides its own sources of signification" (*The Spectral Mother* 234). Seeing the mother's body "as a locus of difference and estrangement, instead of the privileged place of unity and fulfillment" (233), Sprengnether reads castration as separation from the mother, and hence the mother's body as the place where division occurs. Thus, in her view, the function of the father ("to divide the mother from her infant" [236]) becomes unnecessary since the mother's body already contains "the lack that fuels desire" (234) and "propels the process of signification" (245). The critic's concern is "to account for femininity in both biological and cultural terms" (223) but avoiding the drift toward essentialism she finds in the writings of Cixous, Kristeva, and Irigaray, as well as Chodorow and Stoller. Steering a zigzag course between the overpresence of the pre-Oedipal mother in object-relations theories, her absence in Lacan, and her closeness to the imaginary in the French "psychoanalytic feminists," Sprengnether sketches a hybrid figure of pre-Oedipal mother that seems literally to embody the Lacanian symbolic:

her body is not just *in* the symbolic but is itself the symbolic (it is a "locus of difference and estrangement" that has "its own source of signification" and "propels the process of signification").

In putting the body of the mother in the place of the name of the father, Sprengnether reverses the Freudian hierarchy where the pre-Oedipal, seductive, and "phallic" mother was banished or subordinated to the Oedipal father. And not only by Freud: "Neither object relations theory nor Lacanian psychoanalysis . . . succeeds in transforming the implicit meaning of femininity as subversion," she challenges, because both theories "fail to question her subordination within the Oedipal-preoedipal hierarchy" (183). But the pre-Oedipal mother will reappear as a "spectral figure" throughout Freud's work, most obviously in "The Uncanny," where "the infant's relation to the feminine threatens the structure of masculine development" (183).

> Freud's attempts to theorize the preoedipal period, if not the role of the preoedipal mother herself, in *Beyond the Pleasure Principle* and *Inhibitions, Symptoms and Anxiety* reveal both his fascination with this subject and his ultimate inability to integrate it smoothly into his Oedipal construct. If anything, the dyadic mother-child relationship threatens to subvert the triangular Oedipal structure. The concepts of repetition compulsion and the death instinct appear to give the lie to the progressive model of development based on the paternal threat of castration and the male child's renunciation of desire for his mother. Instead they memorialize a prior sense of loss, instituting a form of mastery that seeks its own undoing. . . . The meaning that attaches to femininity, as a result, is subversion. (182–83)

This brilliant insight captures quite well the characteristic ambivalence of Freud's thought and his oscillation between what I have called his passionate fiction—the Oedipal scenario, seen from the point of view of Oedipus—and the awareness of another scene in which the subject is dispersed across several points of identification; an ambivalence also constitutive of the various dualities, tensions, and contradictions that pervade his theory (pleasure principle and death drive, primary and secondary processes, normal sexuality and perversion, and so forth). Sprengnether's insight, however, and with it the productive contradictions in Freud's writings are undercut by her substitution of a symmetrical (pre-Oedipal *instead of* Oedipal) model where "the mother's body as the fleshly

origin of human subjectivity" (236) replaces the father as sole causative principle of signification and desire. For, once the father has
been ousted from the scene, (the mother's) femininity appears to be
less a "subversion within patriarchy" (183) than a successful coup
d'état. (In this respect, one cannot be altogether surprised by *The
Spectral Mother*'s closing project: "what we need is a whole new
metaphysics beginning here" [246].) Moreover, in reversing the Oedipal–pre-Oedipal hierarchy, Sprengnether also reverses the psychoanalytic point of view from the child to the mother.[6] The subject
for whom femininity, not unlike Kristeva's *le sémiotique*, acts as
"subversion" of the paternal symbolic is not the child, male or
female, but the mother herself. Ironically, therefore, in reclaiming
the subversive status of femininity for women through the figure of
a symbolically empowered pre-Oedipal mother, Sprengnether
comes to equate woman with mother, rejoining the more
conservative view of female sexuality within feminism and
subscribing to what may be called its maternal imaginary. Her pre-
Oedipal mother, in whose body are produced division, signification,
and desire without interference by the father or the phallus,
proposes itself as the figure of a maternal symbolic; but its
imaginary nature is apparent precisely in its substitutive and all-
encompassing function: where the name of the father was, there
shall the mother's body be.

By maternal imaginary I do not mean a simple notion of matriarchal power sustaining a utopian sisterhood of women, or a dream of
pre-Oedipal fusion whose uncontrasted bliss would be superseded
by divisions and contradictions due to the intervention of patriarchy, the phallus, or whatever. I mean an equally idealized if composite construct or, in Domna Stanton's phrase, a maternal metaphor,

---

6. "When mothers write . . . they unravel the fiction of mother-infant symbiosis
which underlies the object relations view of development, not to mention Lacan's
conception of the Imaginary. [A mother] does not experience a total fusion of self
with Other, an absolute identity with her infant. . . . The concept of *mother*-infant
symbiosis is an obvious absurdity" (233). The disappointment with psychoanalysis
for not being "a maternal discourse" has been voiced most clearly by Marianne
Hirsch: "One of the barriers to a theory and a practice of maternal discourse is the
feminist reliance on psychoanalysis as a conceptual framework. . . . In all psychoanalytic writing, *the child* is the subject of both study and discourse. While psychoanalytic feminisms have added the female child to the male, they have not succeeded in
inscribing the perspective of adult women. The adult woman who is a mother, in
particular, continues to exist only in relation to her child, never as a subject in her
own right" (*The Mother/Daughter Plot* 167).

in which the mother stands for what women have in common as women—for better or for worse. This mother does not necessarily have an erotic or fantasmatic role in female sexuality, although in many instances it does, but it always stands as the figure of individual and collective female empowerment. Even when articulated as the structure of a female symbolic (most forcefully and originally by the Milan Women's Bookstore Collective in *Sexual Difference*, where the symbolic mother is the term that guarantees sociosymbolic relations between women), the maternal metaphor subtends an imaginary relation in that its proponents devalue or ignore the paternal function and replace it with the maternal as the origin and cause of female subjectivity. In some instances, the feminist configuration of the mother-daughter relationship rejects most of Freud and Lacan as phallocentric and aims to go beyond the theory of the drives (Chodorow, *Feminism and Psychoanalytic Theory* 114–53), but then replaces the name of the father with the metaphor or, in Sprengnether, the body of the mother—without, however, questioning whether or how a female sexual specificity might derive from this symbolic, as well as physical, sexual difference or what relation that sexuality might have to female subjectivity. In these works, the female sexed subject is conceived of in relation to the maternal only as it effects social or gender reproduction, and not as it affects sexuality and desire, whether heterosexual or lesbian.[7]

Other configurations of the maternal metaphor, however, are centrally concerned with female sexuality and situate themselves within the perspective of Freudian metapsychology, seeking to refocalize it on feminist issues. As I stated in chapter 2, discussing Rose's and other feminist readings of "Dora," the importance of the mother for female sexuality rests on the pre-Oedipal postulate—the particu-

---

7. When, as I suggested earlier, sexuality, the drives, the unconscious, and the Oedipus are bypassed to focus on the self-in-relation and gender identity construction (as in Chodorow, Benjamin, Flax, Hartsock, and others), it becomes relatively easy to move forward, or rather backward, to the old humanist (and pre-feminist) view of a neuter or non-sexed subjectivity, one that is independent even from gender: "We are not always and in every instance determined by or calling upon these gendered and sexualized psychological experiences. Gender and sexuality are situated in, as they help to create, *life in general*" (Chodorow, *Feminism and Psychoanalytic Theory* 198; emphasis added). On the Milan Collective's work, its conceptualization of the symbolic mother, its originality as a theory of social-symbolic practice, and its equivocation on the question of sexuality, see my introductory essay "The Practice of Sexual Difference and Feminist Thought in Italy" (*Sexual Difference* 1–21).

lar relation of the female child to the mother from which would derive a specific feature of all female sexuality, its so-called "homosexual factor." In the course of a woman's psychosexual development, and indeed throughout her life, this pre-Oedipal attachment would remain active, causing a strong tendency toward bisexuality, a labile or oscillating pattern of identifications and object-choices, and a forever unachieved feminine sexual identity. That these characteristics are to be found in hysteria underscores the homology between the female homosexual and the hysteric in relation to desire: both are sexed and desiring subjects, although the latter is so only within the limits of the transferential contract and setting (for what may happen to her when the contract expires, see the story of Sabina Spielrein [note 3 above] recounted by Molfino). Thus the seductions of lesbianism begin to transpire in the homosexual-maternal metaphor. But before considering it further, I want to show how they may be glimpsed as well between the lines of Sprengnether's text.

The closing paragraph of *The Spectral Mother* addresses "each of us, male and female" (245):

> Each of us enters the world through the body of a woman—a carnal enigma that has virtually baffled our systems of understanding. Rather than fleeing, condemning, or idealizing the body of the (m)other, we need to recognize her in ourselves. "I am the lover and the loved," Adrienne Rich writes in "Transcendental Etude," "home and wanderer, she who splits / firewood and she who knocks, a stranger / in the storm" (*Dream of a Common Language* 76). If the sense of estrangement and familiarity which we choose to name subjectivity resides in our very flesh, then what we need is a whole new metaphysics beginning here. (246)

The reference to Rich is apparently motivated by the "carnal enigma," which is most effectively encapsulated in the title of Rich's *Of Woman Born*. The work by Rich that Sprengnether cites, however, is a lesbian love poem, no less so marked than the "Twenty-One Love Poems" that constitute the previous section of *The Dream of a Common Language*. It is not only its dedication to Michelle Cliff that identifies this poem as lesbian, but the very stanza from which Sprengnether excerpts her quote and paraphrases her conclusion. To facilitate the reader's following of my comments, I reproduce that stanza (marked C) and the two previous ones (marked A and B).

(A) But in fact we were always like this,
   rootless, dismembered: knowing it makes the difference.
   Birth stripped our birthright from us,
   tore us from a woman, from women, from ourselves
   so early on
   and the whole chorus throbbing at our ears
   like midges, told us nothing, nothing
   of origins, nothing we needed
   to know, nothing that could re-member us.

(B) Only: that it is unnatural,
   the homesickness for a woman, for ourselves,
   for that acute joy at the shadow her head and arms
   cast on a wall, her heavy or slender
   thighs on which we lay, flesh against flesh,
   eyes steady on the face of love; smell of her milk, her sweat,
   terror of her disappearance, all fused in this hunger
   for the element they have called most dangerous, to be
   lifted breathtaken on her breast, to rock within her
   —even if beaten back, stranded again, to apprehend
   in a sudden brine-clear thought
   trembling like the tiny, orbed, endangered
   egg-sac of a new world:
   *This is what she was to me, and this
   is how I can love myself—
   as only a woman can love me.*

(C) *Homesick for myself, for her*—as, after the heatwave
   breaks, the clear tones of the world
   manifest: cloud, bough, wall, insect, the very soul of light:
   homesick as the fluted vault of desire
   articulates itself: *I am the lover and the loved,
   home and wanderer, she who splits
   firewood and she who knocks, a stranger
   in the storm,* two women, eye to eye
   measuring each other's spirit, each other's
   limitless desire,
                     a whole new poetry beginning here.
                     (Rich 75–76)

   While "the homesickness for a woman, for ourselves" of stanza B
re-images the loss of the female body—the mother's, one's own, and
other women's, described in stanza A ("Birth stripped our birthright
from us, / tore us from a woman, from women, from ourselves / so
early on")—here the poet, after "a sudden brine-clear thought / trembling like the tiny, orbed, endangered / egg-sac of a new world," has

apprehended the meaning of that loss and, at the same moment, in a single thought, a single image, has also apprehended the fragile wonder of recapturing the female body—the mother's, her own, and other women's—with a woman lover: *"This is what she was to me, and this / is how I can love myself— / as only a woman can love me."* Now, after the epiphanic moment, the stanza in question (C), in repeating *"Homesick for myself, for her,"* links the homesickness *for her* both to the lost mother of stanzas A and B (*"This is what she was to me"*) and, by the use of italics, to the woman who now loves her (*"as only a woman can love me"*). The next repetition of *"homesick"* (line 4 of stanza C), also in italics, occurs under "the fluted vault of desire," and the lines quoted by Sprengnether (also italicized) are in fact the articulation of a "limitless desire" between two women, each of whom is at once the lover and the loved, desiring subject and desiring object.

One has to wonder why these lines were chosen (extracted from the immediately adjacent ones) and not, for instance, those of stanza B which re-image the loss specifically of the mother's body ("her heavy or slender / thighs on which we lay, flesh against flesh, / eyes steady on the face of love; smell of her milk, her sweat, / terror of her disappearance . . . "). After all, the images of *"home and wanderer, she who splits / firewood and she who knocks"* are not nearly as suggestive of pre-Oedipal motherhood as the ones I have just cited. And the recurrence of the word *desire* twice in the second part of the stanza, first as a vault and then limitless, unconstrained, releasing the homesick heart into the storm, should leave no doubt as to the nature of *this* carnal enigma.[8] But apparently it does not, since another reader of the poem also manages to miss it, in spite of demonstrating an otherwise keen sense of poetic language. "When Rich's 'Transcendental Etude' speaks of homesickness," writes Mary Jacobus, "the term is synonymous with desire ('the vaulted flute [*sic*] of desire'). Desire for the mother is desire doubled—'two women, eye to eye / measuring each other's spirit, each other's limitless desire' " ("Freud's Mnemonic" 137). (Mis)taking the doubled desire

---

8. Sprengnether makes no mention of lesbianism; her index entry for homosexuality refers to the Leonardo and Schreber case histories, the Freud/Fliess relationship, and of course "Dora." Rich's "Compulsory Heterosexuality and Lesbian Existence" is footnoted merely as "offer[ing] a searching critique of Freud's heterosexist bias" (155). Indeed.

to be a desire for the mother, instead of the lover, Jacobus reads the poem as "a mnemonic for the will to change, or feminist politics in its retrospective, nostalgic mode" (138). In the face of such obstinate resistance by the poem to be read as a lesbian love poem, I will spend a little more time with it.

The image Jacobus reads as a desire for the mother ("two women, eye to eye . . . ") can hardly conjure up a maternity scene, if for no other reason than the poem has already inscribed that scene quite differently in the previous stanza (B), with the child lying on the mother's thighs or "lifted breathtaken on her breast, to rock within her." But, besides the different visual logistics of the two images or scenes (think where you would put the camera in filming them), the critic also disregards the temporal, mnemonic movement of the poem from the past of childhood (*"This is what she was to me"*) to the present ("I am *the lover and the loved"*); an inattentiveness which is more surprising in a critical essay devoted to the psychoanalytic reading of the text of memory, and thus more telling of the overdetermination and fantasmatic projection that constitute all reading and all writing.[9] Uncannily, having just analyzed Freud's autobiographical screen memories, Jacobus does not notice that the two scenes in stanzas B and C—linked together semantically by "homesickness"/"*homesick*" and apprehended by the poet's mind in one "sudden brine-clear thought"—articulate the psychic structure that Freud called deferred action (*Nachträglichkeit*) and that describes the operating mechanism of primal fantasies, in particular of the seduction fantasy. By deferred action, an earlier scene (here, the child and the mother) is recovered or remembered in light of a later one (here, the present scene of "two women, eye to eye"), which thus acquires a causative function.

To read the latter scene as "desire for the mother," then, is to collapse the psychic movement of fantasy from present to past to

---

9. Without making too much of what could be either a telltale slip of the author's pen or a printer's error, I will simply remark on the transcribing (transcoding) of Rich's image "the fluted vault of desire" as "the vaulted flute of desire" on p. 137 of Jacobus's article. Here again it is the visual image in the vehicle of the metaphor, the literal (textual) signifier of desire, that marks the difference between the poem and Jacobus's reading. The difference in representing desire as a fluted vault or as a vaulted flute is one whose decoding I confidently leave to the reader's visual and linguistic proficiency.

future into a retrospective, static tableau, and to reduce the fantasmatic, dynamic triangulation of the subject's desire between the
other woman, the mother's body, and her own to the fixity of a fro-
zen memory. On the contrary, the "limitless" desire of the present
scene lives inscribed across and sustained on (Freud's *Anlehnung*,
anaclisis) the fantasy scenario of the maternal female body, which is
a fantasy precisely because *that* body is always lost. This is not will
or feminist politics or myth, but lesbian desire. Perhaps Jacobus
does not see it as desire, can see it only as nostalgia, because she
misses the "third term," the paternal phallus, which is indeed not
present in the scene. But I would argue (although I cannot do so
until later, when I return to the question of lesbian desire in chapter
5) that the signifier of desire *is* present and, like Poe's stolen letter,
quite legible on the surface of the text, underscored in the very lines
partially quoted by Sprengnether and partially by Jacobus:

> *I am the lover and the loved,*
> *home and wanderer, she who splits*
> *firewood and she who knocks, a stranger*
> *in the storm,* two women, eye to eye
> measuring each other's spirit, each other's
> limitless desire.

The fantasmatic relation to the mother and the maternal/female
body is central to lesbian subjectivity and desire, as Rich's poem
exemplifies, although seldom expressed in so direct a manner. For
this reason I find it necessary to examine the maternal metaphor in
feminist writings in order to analyze its differential construction
and effects in heterosexual and lesbian representations of the
daughter-mother relation. Jacobus's and my respective readings of
one poem highlight the stakes of such a project, showing that they
are not a matter merely of interpretation, of agreeing to disagree on
the meaning or the reading of a text, but effectively entail the elision—in the one case—or the representation—in the other—of an
actual sexual difference. My argument with what I call the maternal
imaginary in feminist scholarship, therefore, is motivated by a long
history of equivocation on a sexual difference between women that
not only orthodox psychoanalysis but also the greater part of feminist theory persistently disallows—perhaps because they simply
cannot see it.

A most influential figure in the development of feminist psychoanalytic discourse has been Julia Kristeva, in spite of her explicit
disidentification with feminism; and one of the most powerful
works of feminist psychoanalytic theory is Kaja Silverman's *The
Acoustic Mirror*, which, reading Kristeva through feminism and
even against herself, presents another configuration of the maternal
metaphor, with a significant variant. Refreshingly, Silverman finds
the pre-Oedipal mother vastly overrated, as I do, and instead proposes the figure of an Oedipal mother, inscribed within the paternal
symbolic but nonetheless determining in the construction of female
subjectivity, as well as feminist identity. More important, she, too,
poses the question of the maternal and its relation to female sexuality and desire as a question of fantasy. Her point of departure is
what she calls "the *choric* fantasy," derived from Kristeva's essays
"Place Names," "Motherhood According to Giovanni Bellini" (in *Desire in Language*), and "Stabat Mater."

> Within Kristeva's writing, the image of the child wrapped in the
> sonorous envelope of the maternal voice is not only a fantasy
> about pre-Oedipal existence, the entry into language, and the
> inauguration of subjectivity; it is also a fantasy about biological
> "beginnings," intrauterine life, and what she calls the "homosexual-
> maternal facet." The primary term with which she conceptualizes
> that fantasy is, of course, the *chora*, a word she borrows from
> Plato, who uses it to designate "an unnameable, improbable,
> hybrid [receptacle], anterior to naming, to the One, to the father,
> and consequently, maternally connoted." (*Acoustic Mirror* 101–102)

While Kristeva's fantasy is located in the pre-Oedipal, Silverman's
reading will recover an Oedipal and quite different mother, one less
inimical but more equivocal as the figure of a "homosexual-maternal" imaginary. Because such theoretical trajectory is rather complex, I must discuss it at some length.

Analyzing the polyvalence of the term in Kristeva's writings,
Silverman points out that the fantasy of the maternal *chora* works
differently for the mother of a son and for the mother of a daughter—differently, I may add, according to the standard rules of sexual
difference in psychoanalysis. Kristeva writes:

> For a woman, the arrival of a child breaks the auto-erotic circle of
> pregnancy . . . and brings about *what, for a woman, is the difficult*

account of a relationship with an other: with an "object" and with
love [my emphasis, added to underscore the idea of woman as
narcissistically oriented and unable to love an other]. . . . The
mother of a son (henceforth the generic "infant" no longer exists)
is a *being* confronted with a *being-for-him* [Kristeva's emphasis].
The mother of a daughter replays in reverse the encounter with
her own mother: differentiation or leveling of beings, glimpses of
oneness or paranoid primary identification phantasized as
primordial substance. (*Desire in Language* 279, quoted by
Silverman 107)

In quoting this, Silverman rightly remarks how Kristeva's theory
works "primarily to disenfranchise the daughter" (108), but she nevertheless attempts to give a feminist interpretation of what seems to
me an unambiguously orthodox, and orthodoxly heterosexist, view
of female subjectivity. I ask myself, What is at stake in Silverman's
project? Her thesis is that Kristeva's account "functions in some very
profound way as the *libidinal* basis of *feminism*" (102; emphasis
added). She argues that "the *choric* fantasy"—the scenario of a "maternal *enceinte*," a "homosexual-maternal scene," an autoerotic and
"undifferentiated community of women" which the female subject
must renounce in order to recognize the father and thus enter the
hierarchies of the sociosymbolic realm—points to the presence in
Kristeva of a repressed, unconscious desire for the mother.

On her part, Kristeva does not acknowledge (Silverman says that
she "resists") this alleged "desire for a corporeal union of mother
and daughter" (110): she flatly denies that the mother could ever
symbolically authorize or erotically empower the daughter and, on
the contrary, insists that the latter can rejoin the mother only when
she becomes a mother herself, that is, when she subjects herself to
the father's law and bears his child. Silverman retorts: "Although
Kristeva goes so far [in "Motherhood According to Giovanni Bellini"] as to acknowledge the homosexual basis of the union she seeks
with the mother, she also repeatedly denies that 'homosexual' means
'homo*sexual*' " (110). All the same, in spite of Kristeva's denial of the
sexual in relation to the mother, Silverman claims that the eroticism
displayed in her analysis of Bellini's madonnas is but a displacement
onto the son of "the desire which cannot be openly expressed with
regard to the daughter" (111). It is as if, in order to recover "the
choric fantasy" for feminism, Silverman must engage in a close

reading of Kristeva's writings that more and more comes to resemble a psycho-analysis, inclusive of what I take to be the transference of Silverman's own fantasy into "the Kristevian fantasy" (107), and signaled by phrases such as "the libidinal bases of Kristeva's analysis" (111), "the mother who is the object of Kristeva's unconscious desire" (119), or such unguarded wording as "if we penetrate the Kristevian fantasy . . . " (109). Eventually the transference is broken, and Silverman goes on to other texts which might give stronger support to her own version of "the *choric* fantasy," that is, the image of a symbolic, Oedipal mother who can authorize the daughter's "passionate desire" and "erotic investment in the mother" as the mainstay of female subjectivity.

Silverman's reading of Kristeva and their respective fantasies of the maternal raise some nagging questions that have serious implications for a theory of the female-sexed subject. What is at stake for Silverman, a feminist, when she tries to reclaim Kristeva's anti-feminist and patently reactionary view of motherhood? Why does she go to such lengths to persuade us that the *choric* fantasy "speaks to an erotic desire which is completely unassimilable to heterosexuality" (102), when the texts she uses rather suggest the contrary? Or again, why does Silverman want to read "homo*sexual*" in Kristeva's passing comment about the pregnant woman "actualiz[ing] the homosexual facet of motherhood" (*Desire in Language* 239, quoted by Silverman 110) when Kristeva makes it clear that she means *homo* but not *sexual*? To me, it seems clear enough that she means a homosocial, woman-to-woman, intrafeminine relationship, for which the term *homosexual* is used either ingenuously or ingeniously to mean, literally, "of the same anatomical/biological sex"— a common practice among French and Italian feminist intellectuals (including lesbians, by the way)—and not at all a homosexual-lesbian one.

Furthermore, if Silverman is concerned with theorizing a female desire that is not heterosexual, that is (I emphasize) "*completely* unassimilable" to heterosexuality, why is she so put off by Irigaray's scenario of a female-specific sexuality based in the female body? "In her determination to tear female sexuality free from the economy of the phallus," Silverman writes, "she *even* characterizes the insertion of the penis into the vagina as an interruption of woman's natural pleasure, an unwelcome intrusion into her erotic domain" (*Acoustic Mirror* 144, emphasis added). The paraphrase comes from "This Sex Which Is Not One" (24), one of the few essays by Irigaray that have been read (wrongly, in my opinion, but see also Grosz, "The Hetero and the Homo") as outlining a theory of lesbian sexuality. But regardless of whether Irigaray was intending to do that, or whether her work does lend itself to such a theory (and I believe it does not), the characterization of the penis as an intrusion into a woman's body or into her erotic pleasure is hardly shocking, especially if one is trying to theorize an erotic desire "completely unassimilable to heterosexuality." As it happens, Irigaray also hypothesizes a desire for the mother that is, she thinks, non-phallic.

In glossing Freud's "Femininity," Irigaray imagines that a little girl might wish to conceive a female child with her mother: "Engendering a girl's body, bringing a third woman's body into play, would allow her to identify both herself and her mother as . . . *two* women, defining each other as both like and unlike, thanks to a third 'body' that both by common consent wish to be female" (*Speculum* 35). This fantasy would imply, she states, "a positive representation of femininity (not just maternity) in which the little girl can inscribe herself as a woman in the making" and "would mean that the little girl, *and her mother also, perhaps,* want to be able to represent themselves as women's bodies that are both desired and desiring—though not necessarily 'phallic' " (36; emphasis added to mark what seems to me the inscription of a second subject, perhaps the author, into the girl's fantasy). The problem is, of course, that such a fantasy writes (hetero)sexual difference out of the scenario and thus reconfirms Freud's argument that, since conceiving children—male or female—requires two sexes, the girl's fantasy is a refusal to accept castration. This girl, he would surely rebut, is thinking of herself as phallic and will likely grow up to be a feminist, that is, either a hysteric or a lesbian.

Silverman might not have in mind this particular fantasy of mother-daughter desire; but then, how is one to understand her "homosexual-maternal" fantasy? If my readers can bear with me a little longer, I will come back to these questions and attempt to tease out some of their implications. But to that end I must first (briefly) give my own understanding of the maternal fantasy in Kristeva's "Stabat Mater."

The Lost Continent

Maternity is the "fantasy of a lost continent," Kristeva writes, thinking of Freud, no doubt—and perhaps also, one may wonder, of all the West's colonial possessions long gone by? She warns feminists that, by refusing to look more closely at the function of maternity, they risk making women "vulnerable to the most frightful forms of manipulation" (150), for maternity is "an idealization of the—unlocalizable—*relationship* between [the primitive mother] and us, an idealization of primary narcissism"; and feminism, "because it rejects this image and its abuses, sidesteps the real experience that this fantasy obscures" (99).[10] Then she proceeds with an apology of Maternity as represented to Western Christendom by the Virgin Mother of Christ (the capitals are Kristeva's), "one of the most potent imaginary constructs known to any civilization" (101).

That representation, Kristeva explains, has served the purpose of providing social stability, not only by calming men's anxiety about their power to create, since the appropriation of the maternal by men is "a necessary precondition of artistic or literary achivement" (to wit: "Henry Miller's claim to be pregnant or Artaud's imagining himself to be like 'his girls' or 'his mother' " [100]). But it has also served "to satisfy a woman, in such a way that the community of the sexes is established beyond, and in spite of, their flagrant incompatibility" (101). The "virginal maternal," she suggests, is an imaginative and effective way for society to cope with "female paranoia": onto the Virgin a woman can project her paranoid desire for power, her denial of the other sex, her impulse to murder or devour, even her masochism, for the Virgin attaches a positive value to suffering ("*stabat mater dolorosa*" are the first words of the Catholic chant that glorifies the grieving [*dolorosa*] mother of the man-god, fixed in her role of icon, outside of time [*stabat*], at the foot of the cross). Above

---

10. By the time the essay appeared in English, nearly ten years after it was written, Kristeva's warning had been heeded and, as I believe this chapter shows, much more was to come that would support her views. "Stabat Mater" was originally published with the title "Héréthique de l'amour" in *Tel Quel* 74 (1977); it was first published in English translation in *Poetics Today* 6.1–2 (1985) and then reprinted in Susan Suleiman, ed., *The Female Body in Western Culture* (1986); a different version subsequently appeared in the English translation of Kristeva's *Histoires d'amour* (Denoël, 1983), *Tales of Love* (1987), where "Stabat Mater" is dated 1976. The version I cite from is in Suleiman.

all, for a woman, the Virgin eliminates by foreclosure the hostility or rivalry toward "the other woman," that is to say, the hostility between mother and daughter, since the Virgin Mother is "alone of all her sex" (the title of Marina Warner's book on the cult of Mary, to which Kristeva here is largely indebted): she is unique among women as well as men, and as such inimitable, incomparable, anyway. And even though that uniqueness is attained only at the cost of an "exacerbated masochism," it points the way to the reformulation of the West's ethical tradition, to a new heretical ethics or "herethics" of love (*"Héréthique de l'amour"*), which Kristeva proposes as the appropriate role for women in the modern world: "Women imbued with the desire to reproduce (and to maintain stability); women ready to help our verbal species, afflicted as we are by the knowledge that we are mortal, to bear up under the menace of death; mothers" (117–18).

When the potent effect of Kristeva's rhetorical mastery has subsided, one must begin to see that the heresy in her ethics is very tame indeed. In one sense, she assumes and glorifies, as only a Christian can, Freud's version of the traditional modern view of femininity as motherhood. The female (bi)sexuality—which Freud superimposed onto the anodyne or demonic, yet asexual, image of Victorian woman—achieves its sublimation in the personal and social power granted by motherhood, as the woman's (male) child becomes for her the phallus she could never otherwise possess. It is easy to hear Kristeva echo Freud's condemnation of women's masculine protest ("she was in fact a feminist," he had said of his recalcitrant homosexual patient) when she decries women's rejection of the other sex—a rejection that today's women (read: feminists) justify not in the name of the child ("the third, the non-person, God") but rather by a counterinvestment in intellectual and public activities, in "blue-chip shares," as she calls them, "redeemable tokens of power": "Feminine psychosis today sustains itself through passion for politics, science, art, in which it becomes engrossed" (117).

At the same time, Kristeva's self-possessed assurance of the value of motherhood gives it a categorical positivity that Freud (not being a mother himself, one must infer) was always a little hesitant to assert, as if aware that it *might be* a fantasy, a projection, an imaginary construct. Not so for Kristeva, whose claim to the personal, direct, experiential knowledge of motherhood is conveyed in the "different" text printed in boldface here and there on the left side of the page, adjacent to the main text. But for all its rhetorical sophistication, its lyrical and philosophical ambiguity, its will to have it both ways, this "different" text is not any more reliable, unmediated, spoken from the body—not any more "semiotic" or any less "symbolic"—than any other piece of language, and thus does not succeed in either masking or supporting the fundamental essentialism of her fantasy.[11] "[A] woman rarely, I do not say never, experiences passion—love or hate—for another woman, without at some point taking the place of her own mother—without becoming a mother herself" (116). In other words, women can experience passion and desire only through the male's penis and the child it produces in them, Kristeva believes; this is why women need men. And hence her strenuous defense of heterosexuality and the penis as ramparts to be industriously re-erected against death.

Or are they instead, heterosexuality and the penis, a narcissistic denial of the mother, as Silverman suggests? Not the mother a woman may become, thereby gaining the phallus, but the one she was not loved by long ago, whose body in the service of the phallus became to the daughter a "lost continent" buried under the ravages of man's civilization. This hypothesis would certainly account for that "female paranoia" that Kristeva observes but cannot see for what it is, behind heterosexuality and the phallus: "civilization" and its contents. Just as certainly, however, and quite aside from such psychologizing, her textual scenario of a *virgin* mother, *single* bearer (the son—Christ—is merely her phallus) of a *feminine* (more emphatically than Christian) ethics of compassion and connectedness, which replaces both the ineffectual Oedipal scenario of the nativity scene and the all-male cast of the trinity, would account for the appeal of Kristeva's maternal imaginary to feminists of various persuasions.

And yet the homophobic, heterosexist subtext remains. Creeping about more or less discreetly in this essay, the suggestion that lesbianism may be the feminist form of female paranoia is raised to the

---

11. A similar point is made by Mary Russo in her reading of Kristeva's reading of Céline: "The accumulated horror and contempt that these descriptions of the maternal body suggest generate a subliminal defense of the maternal, which then re-emerges in Kristeva as an idealized category far from the realities of motherhood, either as a construction or as a lived experience" (220).

status of a death sentence elsewhere in the same volume, *Histoires d'amour,* and not coincidentally in an essay subtitled "On Male Sexuality": "Could one imagine an erotics of the purely feminine?" Kristeva asks rhetorically. I report her answer in some detail, highlighting here and there, but abstaining from further comments that could not prove my argument better than she does herself.

> Lesbian loves comprise the delightful arena of *a neutralized, filtered libido, devoid of the erotic cutting edge of masculine sexuality.* Light touches, caresses, barely distinct images fading one into the other, growing dim or veiled without bright flashes into the mellowness of *a dissolution, a liquefaction, a merger.* . . . It evokes *the loving dialogue of the pregnant mother with the fruit,* barely distinct from her, that she shelters in her womb. Or the light rumble of soft skins that are iridescent *not from desire* but from that opening-closing, blossoming-wilting, an in-between hardly established that suddenly collapses in the same warmth, that slumbers or wakens within *the embrace of the baby and its nourishing mother.* . . . Relaxation of consciousness, daydream, language that is neither dialectical nor rhetorical, but peace or eclipse: nirvana, intoxication, and silence. When such a paradise is not *a sidelight of phallic eroticism, its parenthesis and its rest,* when it aspires to set itself up as absolute of a mutual relationship, the *nonrelationship* that it is bursts into view. Two paths are then open. Either they take up again, yet more fiercely, the *erotic mania* along with *the havoc of the "master-slave" game.* Or else, and often as a consequence, death . . . : *lost identity, lethal dissolution of psychosis,* anguish on account of lost boundaries, *suicidal call of the deep. (Tales of Love* 81; emphasis added)

The motivation of psychosis in Kristeva's view of lesbianism is directly tied to the maternal body to which the subject clings melancholically in her rejection of the paternal phallus with its "cutting edge." As Judith Butler sees it, the flip side of this view of female homosexuality as "a culturally unintelligible practice, inherently psychotic," is the mandate of "maternity as a compulsory defense against libidinal chaos" (*Gender Trouble* 86). Thus Kristeva's view of the maternal body as prediscursive *chora* or "pre-paternal causality" is "fundamentally inverted" with respect to a Foucaultian view, Butler observes: "the discursive production of the maternal body as prediscursive is a tactic in the self-amplification and concealment of those specific power relations by which the trope of the maternal body is produced." In other words, the fantasy of the maternal body would be the effect of "a system of sexuality in which the female body is required to assume maternity as the essence of its self and the law of its desire" (92). On further consideration, then, it is difficult to see why any feminist would want to salvage something out of this dismal view of female subjectivity as structured by paranoia, exacerbated masochism, ever-lurking psychosis, and absolute dependence on the fruit of the penis. In fact, Silverman's fantasy of a symbolically empowering Oedipal mother, emblem of "a female collectivity [based] upon a primary and passionate desire for the mother" (139), stands in direct opposition to it, as I will presently show. Meanwhile the question lingers, Why Kristeva? What does Kristeva offer such a feminist fantasy?

The Oedipal Mother

Drawing on Lampl–de Groot's analysis of the negative Oedipus complex in girls (i.e., the girl's phallic attachment to the mother during and after the Oedipal phase), Silverman argues that for the girl as well as for the boy, "desire for the mother is initiated only through *symbolic castration,* i.e., only through the entry into language" (122), that is to say, at the time of language acquisition. In this Lacanian perspective, symbolic castration would occur long before the child's awareness of anatomical sexual difference and the consequent onset of the castration complex as Freud envisioned it. Here, then, Silverman goes against Freud's view of the asymmetrical outcomes of the Oedipus complex in the two sexes, but she also goes against the predominant feminist view that ties the mother-daughter bond to the pre-Oedipal period and effectively presents it as pre-sexual or unrelated to adult sexuality. Instead, she proposes that the girl's libidinal investment in the mother may continue after the resolution of the Oedipus complex, as it does for the boy, except that then the female subject would be split (unlike the male subject) between the desire for the mother and the desire for the father.

> The female subject is thus split, in some profound way, between two irreconcilable desires, desires which persist in her unconscious long after the Oedipus complex has ostensibly run its course. . . . I

> say "irreconcilable" because within the present symbolic order,
> desire for the mother can never be anything but a contradiction of
> the daughter's much more normative and normalizing desire for
> the father. . . . Whereas the latter is a libidinal investment in the
> phallus, and hence in the symbolic order, the former is a libidinal
> investment in everything which that order disvalues. (123)

This conclusion sounds rather more optimistic than Lampl–de Groot's, for whom the split or oscillation between heterosexual and homosexual attachments results in an *inhibition* of sexuality and sexual gratification *of any kind* (see my discussion of Lampl–de Groot in chapter 2). At any rate, in situating "the daughter's passion for the mother" within the Oedipus complex, and bringing "the homosexual axis of mother and daughter" (123) within the symbolic, castration, and lack, Silverman accomplishes two things. First, she avoids the essentialist pitfall of what Kleinians have called primary femininity; second, she intimates that a different symbolic order, female or feminist, can valorize the mother as object of libidinal investment. But how would such a symbolic redefine female sexuality?

The articulation of a female symbolic is, of course, the project of Irigaray's more recent work and, in her wake, the work of Luisa Muraro and the Milan Women's Bookstore Collective.[12] And, if it is the case that "the female symbolic depends upon a female imaginary," as Margaret Whitford argues of Irigaray, and vice versa "the imaginary is an *effect* of the symbolic; it is the symbolic which structures the imaginary" ("Rereading Irigaray" 118–19), then one may also want to know what kind of imaginary is effected by a female or maternal symbolic. There are, in other words, two interrelated questions: Which fantasies or phantoms does the symbolic order of the mother generate? And conversely, What imaginary gives rise to the notion of a symbolic or feminist mother? The first question may be answered by recent works of feminist

---

12. For Irigaray, see especially *L'éthique de la différence sexuelle* and *Sexes et parentés*. Reflecting further on the notion of symbolic mother developed in the Milan Women's Bookstore Collective book *Sexual Difference* (see note 7 above), of which she was one of the authors, Muraro's recent book *L'ordine simbolico della madre* [*The Symbolic Order of the Mother*] regressively collapses the symbolic mother back onto the real mother who thus becomes, in lieu of the father, the sole structural agent of linguistic and symbolic mediation in the "maternal continuum" (54) that defines women's culture.

psychoanalysis such as Sprengnether's *Spectral Mother* or Vegetti Finzi's *Il bambino della notte* [*The Night Child*]. The latter, from the analysis of two young girls, hypothesizes an essential or foundational unconscious fantasy of maternity in the female child, which would be at the root of female subjectivity and self-realization—an idea similar and indebted to the Kleinian notion of primary femininity but inflected by the current feminist doxa of women's creative-maternal power and already achieved enfranchisement from men.[13] The answer to the second question, What imaginary underlies the maternal symbolic?, may be found in the texts that instigate and contain the seductions of lesbianism; that is to say, the fantasmatic-theoretical construct of a female homosexuality, much like Freud's notion of bisexuality deriving from the early attachment to the mother, which would be foundational in female subjectivity and lead to an unstable or uneasily achieved sexual identity. This lingering or subterranean homosexuality would find its symbolic and affective resolution in feminism—but not specifically in lesbianism. Indeed, that term is signally absent from these works. I will pursue this conundrum a little longer.

I have quoted from Silverman's *Acoustic Mirror* at some length to show how insistently the terms *homosexual, erotic investment, passion,* and *desire* recur in her description of the daughter's relations to the mother. These are the terms she sought in vain to find in Kristeva's maternal fantasy, and whose absence she attributed to repression. Yet the fantasy scenario remains the same: the mother-daughter (or rather, the daughter-mother) relationship requires what Silverman calls "the positivity of the *chora,* its promise of a female *enceinte*" (125), with its two meanings of "protective wall" and "pregnant woman." The *enceinte,* she states, "represents one of the governing fantasies of feminism, a powerful image both of women's unity and of their at times necessary separatism," and she will go so far as to say that "without activating the homosexual-maternal fantasmatic, feminism would be impossible" (125). In other words, the homosexual-maternal fantasy is the necessary

---

13. "Feminine identity," Vegetti Finzi states, is a "long process that leads from being female to becoming woman" (13). The book's subtitle further specifies that process as "Becoming Woman Becoming Mother" (my translation).

imaginary of feminism; activated by feminism as sociosymbolic form, it subtends women's relations to women in (what used to be called) feminist practice. But what are the sociosexual implications of this seduction fantasy?

The phrase "homosexual-maternal," used earlier with regard to the daughter-mother relation, and this time used à propos of (adult) feminists, comes very close to suggesting that the connections between women in feminism hinge on an erotic attachment, a sexual investment (cathexis) in women which would be carried over, in the female subject, from the "passion" for the mother that she felt during the years of the Oedipus complex and that has persisted, albeit unconscious, from then on. In this sense, the girl's negative Oedipus complex would be equivalent to the boy's positive Oedipus complex and thus, by implication, would determine for her a female object-choice just as it does for him (since his libidinal investment in the mother is also given up, but persists in his unconscious, after the resolution of his positive Oedipus complex, and that is what determines, according to Freud, his "normal" heterosexual development). According to this logic, then, all feminists would be either lesbians or consistently bisexual. But this is neither the letter nor the spirit of Silverman's argument, I believe, and not just for the factual reason that many feminists live and love heterosexually but also because, in the psychoanalytic theory of female sexuality, a woman's homosexual object-choice is customarily explained precisely as an enduring, active, and phallic attachment to the mother (or a regression to the phallic phase, for Lampl–de Groot and Deutsch) consequent upon the disappointment of her Oedipal love for the father (according to Lampl–de Groot, Deutsch, Jones, and Lacan, among others). In other words, the notion of the Oedipal mother cannot be meant to account for lesbianism (which, in fact, is not mentioned in *The Acoustic Mirror*), since psychoanalysis has already accounted for it in very similar terms, whereas Silverman's project is to provide a *revised* account of female subjectivity, and one that would be *inclusive of all women*.

What the Oedipal mother accounts for, finally, is the feminist anti-patriarchal fantasy of a woman-identified community based on the imaginary projection of a mother both narcissistically and symbolically empowering. This is a novel mother figure in psychoanalytic theory from Freud and Klein to Lacan and Kristeva, a figure that now challenges the dominance of the pre-Oedipal mother in feminist psychoanalytic discourse. This, then, may provide something of an answer to the question I asked myself, What is at stake in Silverman's feminist reading of Kristeva? And why is it to Kristeva that she turns for inspiration, even as she recasts the Kristevian fantasy of a masochistic maternal body into a narcissistically and symbolically empowering one? For Silverman's is not a "virginal maternal" but a sexual, and affirmatively heterosexual, maternal image; one that does not reject, disauthorize, or replace the male sex or the paternal phallus, and yet asserts, next to it, the presence and the power of a symbolic mother constructed in and through feminism, and able to provide the daughter with a specular measure of enhanced femininity. The latter, I suggest, is the very image that Kristeva's writings do not include but forcefully *project*. It seems to me, finally, that Silverman's Oedipal mother figures the *authorial persona* of Kristeva—she who, alone of all her sex, can claim at once the symbolic, phallic mastery of language and the unquestionable femininity of the mother of man.

This is the image that Silverman claims for feminism. And a highly seductive image it is. But such a maternal fantasy, grounded as it is in Kristeva's texts, entails as a liability the paternal-phallocentric structure of her thought. Not the least effect of that liability, I shall endeavor to show, is the assimilation of feminism to lesbianism and the confusion of lesbian sexuality and desire with the maternal imaginary under the equation, as Kristeva puts it, of "lesbian loves" to "the embrace of the baby and its nourishing mother" (*Tales of Love* 81). It may now be more apparent why I thought it important to belabor this point, which is implicit in Silverman's argument, if never stated or argued as such. It is important because the fantasy of a sexually empowered and empowering mother is, of course, a common feminist fantasy, though almost no one else articulates it so lucidly in psychoanalytic terms.[14]

One notable exception is Jessica Benjamin's "A Desire of One's

---

14. As another critic sees it, "Silverman's reading of the negative Oedipus complex brings to the realm of high theory the feminist notion of 'women-identified women' popular in the 1970s. While they could not be more unlike in other ways, Silverman's analysis . . . acquires some of the contours of the 'lesbian continuum' proposed by Adrienne Rich as informing a wide spectrum of female relationships" (Mayne, *Woman at the Keyhole* 153–54).

Own," which also argues for a less clear-cut separation between the pre-Oedipal and Oedipal periods, and for an identification with the mother on the part of the girl that would exist in the former period concurrently with her "ideal love" for the father (who is taken as ego-ideal by children of both sexes). The problem is that, since only masculinity embodies active desire, and since she is denied identification with the father because of her gender, later on the girl-woman can have no active desire. Hence, Benjamin urges, "the need for a mother who *is* articulated as a sexual subject, who is an agent, who does express desire" (89); but this need remains unfulfilled in society as presently structured and, I would add, in feminist psychoanalytic theories that tend to evade the question of female heterosexual desire or look for alternative models (Benjamin proposes "intersubjectivity" [92]). If I understand the argument correctly, then, the problem is less how to make fathers more nurturing and less distant from their female children (which Benjamin at one point seems to suggest as a solution) than how to represent the mother as a sexual agent, how to articulate her desire in such a way that it may appear to be not in the service of the father's but in her own.

Whether or how female heterosexual desire can be represented and narcissistically revalorized as a desire for the penis and/or the paternal phallus, as psychoanalysis construes it, is a question that feminists have been most reluctant to address. Instead, their efforts to valorize femininity and to provide women with an enhanced image of female sexuality have been directed toward the mother, seemingly the path of least resistance, and have seen in the mother or the mother's body the most effective "site of feminism's libidinal struggle against the phallus" (*Acoustic Mirror* 154). I would argue, however, that the mother-daughter bond dear to feminist object-relations theorists, the bisexuality theorized by Sarah Kofman, the convergence of desire and narcissistic identification proposed by Silverman, or the fluidity of boundaries generally said to characterize female sexuality, going as far back as de Beauvoir's notion of a "natural" homosexuality of women (*The Second Sex* 454), are all themes of a popular feminist fantasy which *projects onto female sexuality certain features of an idealized feminist sociality*—sisterly or woman-identified mutual support, anti-hierarchical and egalitarian relationships, an ethic of compassion and connection, an ease with intra-gender affectionate behavior and emotional sharing, and a propensity for mutual identification. The relatively recent emphasis on differences between and among women, as well as the oppositional, polarizing character of debates internal to feminism, especially with regard to race and sexual choice, are evidence of a strong pull toward a collective and generalized woman-identification that is necessary to feminism even as it must be constantly resisted by stressing differences and individual or group autonomy.

Feminine Narcissism and the Envy of Desire

What *The Acoustic Mirror* painstakingly articulates is the feminist fantasy of woman-identification and its relation to feminine (secondary) narcissism. This can then be appreciated as the empowering counterpart, owing to feminism, of the melancholia (paranoia, hysteria, and masochism) endemic to the female subject subjected to the father's desire (in the positive Oedipus scenario). But the valorization of female sexuality through a narcissistic identification with the mother entails, in Benjamin's words, a mother "articulated as a sexual subject"; that is to say, they entail posing, for woman, the possibility of being subject of desire. I believe that the homosexual-maternal imaginary is both a response to that problem and an attempt to resolve it theoretically, or rhetorically, by the trope of a feminine homosexuality; by intimating, in the figure of female homosexuality (or the hysteric in a homologous role), the possibility of subject *and* desire—while at the same time not disowning the psychoanalytic tenet that her desire is only an imposture, a phallic posturing. But psychoanalytic theory thrives on ambiguity, which is one of its enabling seductions for feminists, myself obviously included. The ambiguity in the homosexual-maternal metaphor I have been persistently exploring in these pages tropes on the terms *homosexual* and *desire*.

I have argued that the notions of a "homosexual factor" inherent in all female sexuality since the pre-Oedipal attachment to the mother (Rose), of women's inherent bisexuality (Kofman) or bisexual oscillation (Adams), are an equivocation on the term *homosexuality*. In a similar vein, Silverman's argument that feminine narcissism goes hand in hand with *desire* for the mother—that narcissistic identification with the mother is continuous with the "passionate desire" which characterizes the girl's phallic phase—equivocates on the meaning of the term *desire*. For, although desire could be meant in a sense less stringent than sexual desire, her text emphatically inscribes it with the uniquely *sexual* connotations of the term *object-choice*, citing supporting evidence from Freud's essay on narcissism; namely, "certain later forms of object-choice which are predicated in some way upon identification" and which he classifies as narcissistic (153).[15] However, as I read it, "On Narcissism" describes (a) male homosexual narcissistic object-choice and (b) certain forms of feminine heterosexual object-choice (or object-love) that seem to be anaclitic, in that they display an object-relation, but are actually narcissistic in that the object in question is either part of the subject's own body (her child) or a reminder of her own pre-pubertal masculine identification.[16] Nowhere does Freud suggest that those choices have to do with the female subject's narcissistic identification with the mother.

Practically, finally, what does "desire for the mother" mean when predicated of a (feminist) woman? It is not only in my admittedly off-center or deviant perspective that this phrase appears nonsensical with regard to heterosexual female sexuality. It is so, as well, in the neo-Freudian psychoanalytic perspective, where feminine desire is either the desire to be desired, and that is feminine narcissism, or the desire to desire, and that is the rivalry with male desire or "the

---

15. On Freud's typically ambiguous statements on narcissism and his equivocation between the terms *object-choice* [*Objektwahl*] and *object-love* [*Objektliebe*], see my discussion in chapter 3. However, on the meaning of object-cathexis he states unequivocally: "not until there is object-cathexis is it possible to discriminate a sexual energy—the libido—from an energy of the ego-instincts" (*SE* 14: 76).

16. (a) "We have discovered, especially clearly in people whose libidinal development has suffered some disturbance, such as perverts and homosexuals, that in their later choice of love-objects they have taken as a model not their mother but their own selves. They are plainly seeking *themselves* as a love-object, and are exhibiting a type of object-choice which must be termed 'narcissistic' " (*SE* 14: 88). (b) "Even for narcissistic women, whose attitude towards men remains cool, there is a road which leads to complete object-love. In the child which they bear, a part of their own body confronts them like an extraneous object, to which, starting out from their narcissism, they can then give complete object-love. There are other women, again, who do not have to wait for a child in order to take the step in the development from (secondary) narcissism to object-love. Before puberty they feel masculine and develop some way along masculine lines; after this trend has been cut short on their reaching female maturity, they still retain the capacity of longing for a masculine ideal—an ideal which is in fact a survival of the boyish nature that they themselves once possessed" (*SE* 14: 89–90).

envy of desire," in Lacan's phrase (*"à l'envi du désir,"* aptly translated by Rose in *Feminine Sexuality,* for it thus conveys the sense that this is the *neo*-Freudian, up-to-date version of penis envy). Taking this latter view of woman's relation to desire as her guiding premise in *The Desire to Desire,* Doane argues that both psychoanalysis and cinema consign the female subject to a place of excessive proximity to the body and of overidentification with the image, from which she lacks the distance prerequisite for desire. Unable to desire, she can only desire to desire, she can find her *jouissance* only in rivalry with man's desire, in "the envy of desire." Doane quotes Lacan:

> Far from its being the case that the passivity of the act corresponds to this desire, feminine sexuality appears as the effort of a *jouissance* wrapped in its own contiguity (for which all circumcision might represent the symbolic rupture) to be *realised in the envy of desire,* which castration releases in the male [pour se *réaliser à l'envi du désir* que la castration libère chez le mâle] by giving him its signifier in the phallus. ("Guiding Remarks for a Congress on Feminine Sexuality," in *Feminine Sexuality* 97 [Lacan, *Ecrits* 735], quoted by Doane 12; emphasis added)[17]

What Doane does not say—and the omission is significant in light of my present argument—is that the passage comes from a section of Lacan's paper subheaded "Feminine Homosexuality and Ideal Love," where Lacan is discussing Ernest Jones's own foray into the unusual field of female homosexuality (and both are having a field day of it). Since I already presented Jones's views on the matter in chapter 2, here I will merely summarize their conclusions. Despite some difference of opinion as to whether it is an identification with the father that makes her a lesbian, or whether what makes her so is her taking up the challenge of "excelling" in what she doesn't have (i.e., gratifying her partner sexually better than a man would), Lacan and Jones concur in granting that her erotic interest is less in

---

17. In very similar terms Benjamin speaks of Freud in "A Desire of One's Own": "for woman desire is constituted by the effort to get the missing phallus, an effort that leads her irrevocably into the passive position of being the object for the father, the male subject. In this sense, woman has no active desire; instead, she is doomed to *envy the embodiment of desire,* which forever eludes her since only a man can possess it. *Desire in women thus appears as envy, and only as envy.* For Freud, what woman lacks is a desire of her own" (84; emphasis added). Another version of this essay appears in chapter 3 of Benjamin's *The Bonds of Love* under the subhead "Woman's Desire."

the penis or phallus than in the female body—and here they are obviously right. But they also agree that, first, this interest is "of an essentially secondary and defensive nature" (Jones, "The Early Development of Female Sexuality" 469) due to "a demand for [the father's] love thwarted in the real" (Lacan, *Feminine Sexuality* 96); second, her erotic interest in her partner is sustained by the fantasy of "the man as invisible witness" of her sexual prowess (Lacan 97; cf. "the hand of an unseen man" in Jones 468)—and here is her "rivalry" with male desire. In more familiar words, the lesbian must imagine herself a man in order to desire. Thence, Lacan goes on to make his statement on the relation of feminine sexuality to desire quoted by Doane. He does not say whether he means feminine *homo*sexuality or feminine sexuality *tout court*. Nor, consequently, does Doane, who thus, perhaps unwittingly, adds to the confusion.[18] Jones, more thorough in covering the field, adds a footnote about the homosexual woman's partner who, like Havelock Ellis's "womanly woman" or feminine invert, turns out to be "nearer to the normal" in that she obtains gratification of her "feminine desires" by means of the penis surrogates employed by the other, "such as the tongue or finger" (Jones 468).

To sum up: for Jones, what any woman wants, in one way or another, is the father's penis (on Jones's characteristic literalism, see chapter 2); and what a woman desires, according to Lacan, is to desire herself *and* or *as* the paternal phallus. In this conceptual framework, then, a woman's "desire for the mother" can be understood only as either a homo*sexual* (phallic) desire or a desire to desire herself in the phallus (a phallic mother).[19] Both of these desires

---

18. Unwittingly or not, Doane similarly reproduced the cliché of the lesbian-who-would-be-man in citing, you guessed it, Kristeva (see note 19 of chapter 3). As another critic comments, "In this heterosexual logic, woman's desire for woman is masculine" (Roof, *A Lure of Knowledge* 49).

19. Glossing Lacanian desire through Kristeva's notion of a primary narcissism, or non-sexual love, in the child's identification with the imaginary (pre-Oedipal) father, Cynthia Chase adds another twist: "What the infant reads in maternal care, according to Kristeva, is the mother's desire for the phallus. The infant identifies with that desire. . . . Kristeva follows Lacan in conceiving identification with the phallus, with the signifier of desire, as the first key condition of the emergence of the subject [which] is then situated in the identification with the desire *of* the mother, rather than with the desire *for* the woman. Such would be an account of the so-called preoedipal dimension of Dora's or the witty butcher's wife's case that would stress precisely the *questionable* nature of the maternal function, of 'maternal' 'desire,' rather than counter Freud's and Lacan's insistence on desire's masculine identification with an

are narcissistic, although in differing degrees and with very different psychic and social consequences. I would not for a moment deny that both may be widely operational in feminism, even though the latter is seldom avowed and the former is disparaged as masculine. (In chapter 5 I will try to show how they may be reconceptualized as perverse or fetishistic.) What the homosexual-maternal metaphor accomplishes, by joining the two terms *desire* and *identification with the mother,* is to negate both lesbianism and narcissism while at the same time installing them at the core of female subjectivity and of feminism. As the two terms *desire* and *identification with the mother* slide into each other, the masculine (lesbian) connotation of *desire* is assimilated to the feminine (narcissistic) connotation of *identification;* and both the lesbian and the narcissistic connotations, which are socially disparaged or disapproved, become muted under the strong positive connotations of a *maternal* feminine identification. Whether that maternal identification is Oedipal or pre-Oedipal, reconstructed or primary, does not alter the operation of the metaphor a great deal. Thus to make desire for, as well as identification with, the mother a *sine qua non* condition of feminism continues to blur the already fraught distinction between heterosexual feminism and lesbian feminism, to say nothing of the far more consequential differences between lesbian sexuality or subjectivity and heterosexual female sexuality or subjectivity.[20]

The Lesbian Metaphor

The storm of criticism and the furor of consensus that have accompanied Adrienne Rich's notion of a lesbian continuum since it appeared in "Compulsory Heterosexuality and Lesbian Existence" (1980, written in 1978) give an idea of the stakes that feminists of various colors and sexual identities have in the trope of woman-

insistence on the daughter's primary, unmediated identification with the mother's body" ("Desire and Identification in Lacan and Kristeva" 79–80).

20. These arguments ground my objections to the lesbian readings of *All about Eve* and other films in chapter 3, and to other authors (e.g., Fuss) whose assimilation of identification and desire does not carefully articulate their respective implications for lesbian and heterosexual female sexualities.

identification, and how deeply those stakes are planted in a fantasy of lesbianism. The reception of the essay is a transparent example of the seductions of lesbianism and of its metaphorization in feminist thought and writing.[21] I will not go into "the lesbian continuum debate" here, except to say that the most common and popular interpretation of this essay—that lesbian and heterosexual women have much in common and differ merely in what is taken to be their contingent or "optional" sexual "preferences"—is also the most simplistic and self-serving to all those whose interest lies, whatever their reasons and purposes, in blurring the distinction I want to clarify. Certainly, the text lends itself to different interpretations and allows the translation of *lesbian* with *woman;* but what concerns me here is how often, how widely, *woman* has been read in it instead of *lesbian*.

Rich is positing (as her title states) lesbian *existence* across diverse historical periods and sociogeographical locations, regardless of what dominant discourses might have construed it to be, or what records might or might not be available to prove it. Her "continuum," it seems to me, is a conceptual space in which lesbian existence can be envisioned, rather than a sociological hypothesis to be verified. It is a theoretical construct and a metaphor, a concept and a conceit, as are "female desire," "female spectatorship," or Rich's own "motherhood," and, like them, has both discursive and material implications; but it is less in the realm of what is than in the realm of what if, less a factual description than a passionate fiction. It is not about who could or should be called a lesbian, but about imagining the existence of lesbians in spite of all that conspires to obliterate, deny, or make it unimaginable.

The feminist political fantasy of a diasporic and yet continuous community of women, at once lovers and mothers to one another, may be or have been Rich's own enabling fiction (as the positive Oedipus complex was Freud's). Just as "the homesickness for a

---

21. Urging feminist critics "to examine the status of metaphor within our own discourse," Meryl Altman sees lesbianism used "as a stand-in for certain kinds of purely formal, purely textual 'subversiveness.'" Some years ago, she observes, "metaphors of maternity and mothering and nurturing had acquired a disturbing centrality to discussions of female creativity and 'women's culture.' . . . More recently, however, it has come to seem that lesbians too are everywhere, particularly in critical texts about modernist literary practice written by women and men who are not lesbians about women who may or may not have been" (501).

woman" links lesbian desire to a fantasy of the maternal body in "Transcendental Etude," here lesbian existence occurs within a female continuum that sustains the trope of woman-identification and aligns it with what I have been calling the maternal metaphor.[22] Nevertheless, in the late 1970s (when Kristeva was writing "Stabat Mater"), it was *lesbian* and not *woman* or *mother* that expressed Rich's vision, that signified women's resistance to marriage and to the institution of heterosexuality, asserted their subjective and social agency in relation to one another, and, as I have been saying, conveyed the possibility of subject *and* desire. It still does today. These considerations, and the importance of configuring lesbianism as a sociosymbolic form at a time when it was seen as psychosis or sexual aberration, have been all but eclipsed in the popular version of "the lesbian continuum." On the contrary, the essay has been most often used to blur or to "traffic" (as Donna Haraway suggested to me) the distinction between feminism and lesbianism, making the latter more respectable and the former more radical, thrilling yet safe; and the continuum has been invoked less often to articulate further the conditions and the many other modes of lesbian existence than to metaphorize lesbianism into the sign of an implicitly heterosexual female resistance and desire. Ironically, therefore, while recognizing the existence of "lesbian women," the popular interpretation makes lesbianism still unimaginable today by obliterating its specific sexual and social differences.[23]

Here is one non-lesbian feminist with an atypical feminist agenda:

> An intelligible continuum of aims, emotions, and valuations links lesbianism with the other forms of women's attention to women; the bond of mother and daughter, for instance, the bond of sister and sister, women's friendship, "networking," and the active struggles of feminism. . . . Thus the adjective "homosocial" as applied to women's bonds (by, for example, historian Carroll

---

22. In suggesting the kinship of these two texts, I am indebted to a conversation with Myriam Díaz-Diocaretz, one of the most perceptive readers and translators of Rich's poetry (into Spanish).

23. As Rich herself would realize only one year after the essay's publication, the notion of lesbian continuum "can be, is, used by women . . . as a safe way to describe their felt connections with women, without having to share in the risks and threats of lesbian existence. What I had thought to delineate rather complexly as a continuum has begun to sound more like 'life-style shopping' " (*Blood, Bread, and Poetry* 73).

Smith-Rosenberg) need not be pointedly dichotomized as against "homosexual"; it can intelligibly denominate the entire continuum. The apparent simplicity—the unity—of the continuum between "women loving women" and "women promoting the interests of women," extending over the erotic, social, familial, economic, and political realms, would not be so striking if it were not in strong contrast to the arrangement among males. (Sedgwick, *Between Men* 2–3)

The "simplicity" of female bonding and the "unity" of straight women and lesbians in social interactions, as Sedgwick would have it (no matter what lesbians have been saying to the contrary), is intelligible by comparing them with men; for, she explains, a continuum between "men-loving-men" and "men-promoting-the-interests-of-men" is made impossible by patriarchal institutions such as heterosexual marriage and their necessary consequence, homophobia. As if heterosexual marriage did not apply to women or homophobia to lesbians.[24] I already remarked (in chapter 3) on the absence of sexuality and desire among the terms of "women's attention to women" in this passage. I will add only that the asymmetry it describes between women and men, and between lesbians and gay men, reverses the actual sociohistorical causality by making feminism the epiphenomenon of an imagined female homosociality (idealized as it is in the passage above) instead of its cause, or rather instead of the ground of its idealization. The fact is, "the patriarchy" does not like lesbians any better than gay men, but some women, straight and lesbians, have produced a feminism (some say several feminisms) while men, straight or gay, have not produced one. So the comparison is not intelligible, except in the terms of that reversal and its revocation of both feminism and lesbianism as forms of cultural production and social change.

More responsive to the seductions of a "lesbian continuum" is Haunani-Kay Trask's *Eros and Power*. Although "Compulsory Heterosexuality and Lesbian Existence" is not cited, Rich is a major

---

24. Revisiting the "lesbian continuum" in a later work, Sedgwick attributes to it, as the dominant "lesbian interpretive framework," the different arrangements between women and between men that she had earlier attributed to patriarchal institutions: "According to that framework, there were essentially no valid grounds of commonality between gay male and lesbian experience and identity; to the contrary, women-loving-women and men-loving-men must be at precisely opposite ends of the gender spectrum" (*Epistemology of the Closet* 36).

point of reference for the "feminist eros" which Trask opposes to "male power" in the two parts of the book. The other main influence, also reflected in the title, is Herbert Marcuse. While Part I ("Male Power") is organized by disciplines, with chapters on Ideology and Ontology, Sociology, History, and Psychology, Part II ("Feminist Eros") is organized by the thematic subheadings "Love" and "Power," each of which is further subdivided into "The Return to the Mother" and "The Return to the Body." I note this organizational symmetry internal to Part II—in contrast to the asymmetry between Parts I and II, which I take to reflect the asymmetry between "Male Power" and "Feminist Eros," or between men and women—because this author, unlike Sedgwick, acknowledges the particular contributions of lesbian thought and writings to feminism; yet she also includes lesbians in a continuum of "feminist eros" for which she uses the predominant maternal metaphor, the "return to the mother."

That Trask's discussion of lesbianism occurs with chiastic symmetry in the opening chapter of Part II ("Love—The Return to the Mother") and again in the closing chapter of the book ("Power—The Return to the Body") further embeds the feminist eros within what seems to be its obvious matrix, lesbianism. However, this is not what the author means. Both the return and the eros are meant at once literally and symbolically, and a continuum encompasses both modes and equalizes them:

> For feminists in movement toward a new Eros, this "return to the mother" is both literal and symbolic. It is literal for those feminists who identify wholly with women: lesbian feminists. And it is less physical but nevertheless affectionate and nurturant for feminists who identify with women as part of a family of sisters: women in sisterhood. In both groups, the tender, symbiotic relationship between mother and infant is the conscious foundation upon which the identification between women is built. (103)

The continuum of feminist eros from the literal to the symbolic is represented by "Moraga's triumphant love for her mother" (114), at one end, and at the other, by Robin Morgan's "reliving" with her husband "the life-encouraging, life-protecting love" given her by her mother.

There is a certain irony in the fact that the theoretical paradigm employed to argue for this continuum, and thus to account for lesbian eros, as well as heterosexual eros, is Nancy Chodorow's *The Reproduction of Mothering* (1978), if one considers that the index of that book gives one page entry for lesbianism: "Lesbian relationships do tend to recreate mother-daughter emotions and connections, but most women are heterosexual," is Chodorow's laconic pronouncement on the topic (200). The pertinent footnote refers us to Helene Deutsch's *Psychology of Women,* with no further comment. (As my discussion of Deutsch's essay in chapter 2 may suggest, some further comment would seem in order to one not altogether unconcerned with the issue.) After a brief index search, one finds that Chodorow's second book, *Feminism and Psychoanalytic Theory* (published some ten years later, in 1989), also has no entry for lesbianism or homosexuality, although it has, like the first, several entries for heterosexuality. But there is, to be sure, one entry for "lesbian continuum," and that refers us directly to a footnote containing the familiar popular interpretation, in minimalist format: "Adrienne Rich calls this need for closeness and feeling of identification with women the 'lesbian continuum'" (223). This is the extent of Chodorow's concern with lesbianism, and would present no problem in itself, since she makes no pretense of having any such concern and simply repeats the commonplace. It does become a problem, however, when her theory of the mother-daughter bond is invoked by feminists specifically to account for lesbian relationships and, worse still, desire or eros.

It is difficult to imagine how one could be more explicit than Cherríe Moraga or Audre Lorde—the two feminists of color on whom Trask mostly relies—about the sexual (literal *and* symbolic) nature of their love for women; how the physical relation to women and the imaginary/symbolic relations to the mother stand, for them as lesbians, in a most complex and deeply conflicted relation to one another; and how, moreover, the complexity and the depth of that relation is differently overdetermined, for each of them, by their sociocultural positions as a Chicana and a Black American respectively (for Moraga, see especially *Loving in the War Years* and *Giving Up the Ghost;* for Lorde, *Sister Outsider* and *Zami*). It may well be the case that all relations between women go back in some way to the (pre-)Oedipal relations to the mother, but, if they do, surely they "return" in different ways and, what is more, they "return" to different mothers. I would argue that those differences are precisely the ones that make sisterhood just as impossible in some circumstances as they do, in others, make it possible. Were it not so, there would have been no history of homophobia, silencing, and outright discrimination against lesbians by feminists in communities both white and of color. Amazingly, however, Trask suggests that the contrary is true.

In a tone between pleading and accusatory, she states that "lesbian theorists must accept" the heterosexuality of most feminists as "the major reality, not merely as one stop on women's continuing journey toward lesbianism," for "separatism as a necessary but temporary strategy should always be available, but it cannot be convincingly argued as a realistic alternative for the majority of women" (115). At this point one realizes that Trask is speaking of political lesbianism, which has much less to do with eros than with feminist politics (actually, with feminist politics in the 1970s). As she puts it, "love cannot spring from theory," and "much of lesbian theory" is really quite removed from most women's lives. While no one would or could disagree with the latter part of the statement (about the former, I am not so sure: perhaps *love* does not spring from theory, but *desire?*), the question remains, What is the feminist eros, if it is neither lesbian eros nor feminist politics? Trask responds indirectly by raising the stakes of the argument to a global level and taking an unassailable position: the debate around "sexual preferences," she states, "threatens to divert feminist energy from more serious problems such as the death-nature of American culture, the grotesque exploitation of people of color, and the destruction of the living earth." And her answer to these enormous, incommensurate problems is utopian sisterhood: "The 'return to the mother' speaks to the promise of a creative, nonpossessive kind of love: the love between sisters" (116).

While this conclusion is consonant with Sedgwick's view of the feminist continuum, Trask's particular focus on eros makes it clear that the special contribution of lesbianism to feminism is its erotic charge, the overtly sexual empowerment of that "more physical" ("literal") image of female eros in relation to the female body that lesbianism represents, rightly or wrongly, in contemporary North America. That is not, however, the "tender, symbiotic" love of a mother for her child, which is life-enhancing precisely in that it is not "sexual," in the common sense of the term (and psychoanalysis would essentially agree, finer distinctions about the meaning of "sexual" notwithstanding). Rather, it is the explicitly sexual and desiring aspect of women's relation to women that lesbianism does, and sisterhood or feminism does not, carry, even as it carries a socially empowering image of women. I am once again suggesting that what the popular interpretation of the *"lesbian* continuum" makes available to all women is a *fantasy* of female seduction. (But most women are heterosexual.)

Looking over the various configurations of the maternal imaginary inscribed in feminist texts, from Kristeva's homophobia at one end to global sisterhood at the other, I have described a composite figure of symbolic mother, Oedipal, pre-Oedipal, or feminist, which—more or less emphatically, with greater or lesser rhetorical sophistication, by explicit or ambiguous phrases ("lesbian continuum," "homosexual-maternal"), strongly connoted words (*passion, desire, erotic attachment, libidinal investment*), and symptomatic citations—gestures toward lesbianism. More often this maternal figure casts its feminist mantle protectively over lesbianism, but at times, especially in those psychoanalytic texts concerned with the question of female sexuality and desire, it dresses up in drag and seems perversely to subsume feminism under lesbianism. I have suggested that this may be an unexpected effect of the conceptual frame of orthodox psychoanalysis, which does not recognize female desire if not as homosexual (or hysteric) and phallic—that is to say, in heterosexual terms. Hence the ambiguity or oscillation in feminist psychoanalytic theory: on the one hand, female sexuality is defined with the ambiguous concept of "the envy of desire" or "the desire to desire" (which, we recall, is imaged by Lacan and Jones in "the hand of an unseen man"); on the other, it is emphatically linked to the maternal as the non-phallic par excellence. In the latter case, the maternal image is diffracted and multiplied into a collectivity of woman-identified women, with the "homosexual factor" evenly distributed across all female sexuality, which must be carefully *not* qualified as lesbian—because indeed it is not, nor is it meant to be. Or, when so qualified as in "the lesbian continuum," then the lesbian qualifier must be carefully taken as a metaphor.

A few years back, noting the trend toward hypostatizing the maternal common to feminists in Western cultures, Domna Stanton

remarked that "the metaphorization of the mother/daughter relation has provided an important vehicle for speaking the Lesbian relation in an enduringly homophobic hegemony" ("Difference on
Trial" 177). I hope to have succeeded in arguing that, since "the Lesbian relation" has been most often spoken only as a maternal metaphor, that hegemony appears to be more enduring than feminists
like to think, and we can foresee it enduring as long as feminism
remains unwilling to dig up and confront its deeply ambivalent
stakes in lesbianism. I would even suggest that the maternal imaginary is dangerous for women, in this troubled end of a century
which could again mark the end of feminism—dangerous, first of
all, because reducing female sexuality to maternity, and feminine
identity to the mother, whether imaginary or symbolic, erases a history of women's political and personal struggles for the affirmation
of a difference of and between women vis-à-vis hegemonic institutions and cultural formations in many countries; and dangerous, as
well, because reclaiming maternity and maternal power on the
ground of an ambiguous theoretical premise (a "homosexual factor"
or a "homosexual-maternal" latent in every woman) in turn erases
the history of individual and social struggles for the affirmation of
lesbianism as a particular relation between women that is not only
sexual but also sociosymbolic; that is to say, a relation between
women that entails a different production of reference and meaning, if not always in the terms of feminism.

To Have and to Keep, to Be or Not to Be

I want to close this chapter by returning to a specifically psychoanalytic reflection on the maternal fantasy, but this time in relation
to sexual difference between women and a different textual inscription of the maternal. In her essay "Birthmarks and Blind Spots,"
Victoria Smith offers an insightful reading of Gayl Jones's novel *Corregidora* through a comparative analysis of Hortense Spillers and
Luce Irigaray. The work of each of these theorists, Smith argues, can
be read as "an intervention into the project of the other" (3). Spillers
"short circuits a totalizing impulse on the part of Irigaray that often
leaves historical, racial and sexual contexts unexamined," while the
latter's critique of the phallocentric "economy of the same" can be

usefully brought to bear on the feminist analysis of racial and sexual differences between women. In Spillers's "Mama's Baby, Papa's Maybe: An American Grammar Book," Smith sees the radical figure of a racially and historically gendered female body which offers the possibility of conceptualizing "horizontal relations among women, including the mother-daughter relationship, as well as other geometries . . . in the face of an economy of *colorless sameness*" (8) that has marred white feminist theory.

Spillers's "Mama"—the term's familiar, affective connotations at once doubled and undercut by the social devaluation that attaches to the privatized, infantile, familial, and here subservient inflection of *mother*—refers to the African woman in America during the period of slavery and to her direct descendant, the African American woman of today. In the symbolic order of this particular "American grammar" (where the term *grammar* "plays off the kinship/grammar nexus shared by structuralism and psychoanalysis" [Smith 8], and hence alludes to the structural complicity of sexuality, social reproduction, and Name of the Father), the axiomatic certainty of maternity takes on a multiply layered thickness of ironic meanings. In the first place, the slave mother has no right to her children: these are a property of the white master, who can take them from her, use them, or sell them at his convenience. She has no property right in them, but also none of the affective rights that are socially recognized for the white mother. Secondly, the father is not only uncertain but often is that very master who, however, does not recognize his paternity of the children he has procreated in raping the slave woman; and indeed these children inherit from the mother their condition of slavery, their non-humanity. Therefore, the Name of the Father (or of the white master, since the African slave man also has no rights with regard to the children he generates) defines neither the African woman nor the African man in slavery, for they do not have the status of social subjects or even of human subjects.

Whereas the white mother has both affective rights to her children and a social worth, if only as vehicle of a social and human status transmitted in the name of the father, the slave mother has neither affective rights nor social worth; but at the same time she is the one who passes on, together with physical existence, the social non-existence, indeed the non-humanity, of the beings who thus are and are not *her* children. Her body is not the locus of man's reproduction (the physical and social reproduction of "mankind"), as is the white mother's, but rather the point of "passage" from the human to the non-human. It is not body but "flesh," says Spillers, and hence, Smith rejoins, the African American mother is outside the categories of gender and nomination, outside symbolic legitimation. As a consequence of what Spillers aptly calls the "theft of the body" in her history, the African American woman does not fit into the white feminist analysis of gender and sexuality; and her relation to the mother and to the female body is necessarily other: it makes for a different positionality of the subject vis-à-vis kinship, the name of the father, and a maternal and female body that is always already expropriated and lost. It is this loss, according to Smith, that constitutes the thematics of Jones's *Corregidora* (and of Toni Morrison's *Beloved*), whose writing attempts precisely to re-member, re-find, or reconstitute a female-sexed body as a body for the subject and for her desire.

Reading two contemporary lesbian writers, Judith Roof also finds that the place of the mother is empty, or rather, structured by an absence. To the protagonists of Rita Mae Brown's *Rubyfruit Jungle* and Jane Rule's "This Is Not for You," she observes, the mother is unknown, inaccessible, unreachable even through memory. What this absent mother generates is not fantasies of plenitude or a dream of pre-Oedipal bliss but rather the consciousness of a loss which is and will remain unrecoverable; an emptiness, a void, a lack on which is constituted the daughter's subjectivity. In the fantasmatic scenario of the two texts, the mother's absence from the place of origin and the impossibility of identifying with maternal desire produce in the daughter a desire that is absolutely unrealizable, and hence must consist in the desiring itself. Roof contrasts these texts with Kristeva's and Chodorow's theories of the maternal. In their heterosexual perspective, she states, the process of differentiation from the mother that takes place through the Oedipus complex and the encounter with sexual difference leaves as a residue the nostalgic wish to return to the undifferentiated fusion of the pre-Oedipal period; henceforth the female subject will oscillate between a fantasy of maternal union and the desire to become herself a mother, which is the meaning of sexual difference for woman. "Nostalgia for the mother becomes an unfulfillable desire that is . . . displaced into a fulfillable wish—the desire for a child" or in "an illusory dream of heterosexual fulfillment." Both Kristeva and Chodorow, therefore, project the maternal phantasm as a "memory of mother/daughter unity in the place of desire" (Roof, *A Lure of Knowledge* 107).

In the lesbian stories, on the other hand, that place is marked not by an identification with the mother but by her absence. The narratives "recreate the scenario of maternal loss whereby the daughters cease to be the desire of the mother," and refigure that loss in a desire sustained by its impossibility, that is to say, a desire to desire: "Whereas the heterosexual accounts privilege the illusion of a desire fulfillable via maternity, lesbian stories situate desire as fulfillable only by desire itself" (116). According to Roof, these are not two different structurations of desire but rather two different positions within the same structure (116). And indeed, equating "the absent mother [with] the absent and inaccessible phallus," her interpretation of the texts rests on the imaginary structure of Lacanian desire, where the positionalities of desire are two—the masculine, to have the phallus; the feminine, to be the phallus—and both designed "to sustain the father's desire."

In reading the daughter's (the protagonist's) desire for desire as "an identification with the desire of another woman" (116), Roof is following Lacan's reading of the dream of the Witty Butcher's Wife in Freud's *Interpretation of Dreams*, which "elaborates the desire for desire in terms of a woman's identification with the desire not for a phallus, but for a woman" (114). There seems to be some confusion between (a) identification with the desire *of* another woman (ultimately, with the mother's desire for the phallus) and (b) identification with the (husband's) desire *for* another woman.[25] In (a) the identification is with the phallus in the sense of wanting to be it; in (b) the identification is with the phallus in the sense of wanting to have it. So we run again into an old problem: if we say that the desire to desire is a desire for the phallus—whether to have it or to be it—how do we distinguish lesbian desire from masculine desire or from feminine desire? (Psychoanalysis, of course, does not, but I am assuming that Roof would want to.) And how do we factor in (so to speak) the fantasy of the female body that is so much a part of lesbian desire?

---

25. In this regard, see Chase's discussion of the same dream [I refer to it in note 19 above], which appears in a volume co-edited by Roof.

Finally, then, Roof's formulation of lesbian desire as "the desire for desire"—which echoes the title of Doane's book, *The Desire to Desire*, and recalls the trope of feminine *jouissance* as "the envy of desire" (on which I commented earlier)—shows once again the limits of a feminist theory schooled by Lacan: even though it poses the questions of sexuality and desire more consistently than any other branch of feminist psychoanalytic thought, it does not manage to escape from a conceptual schema axiomatically centered on the paternal phallus. Nevertheless, Roof's is an important attempt to grasp the working of a maternal fantasy in relation to lesbian subjectivity. Amid the rhetorical and conceptual convolutions that any Lacanian reading inevitably generates, she comes very close to suggesting that a woman's desire is directly related to another woman's desire—she thinks, by identification, because she works inside the scenario designed by Lacan and redecorated by Kristeva. I will try to argue otherwise and outline another scenario in the following chapter.

Chapter 5

The Lure of the Mannish Lesbian: The Fantasy of Castration and the Signification of Desire

Whereas castration is clearly negated [in Wittig's *The Lesbian Body*], it is also affirmed *in a new sense*.
—Heather Findlay (68)

Desire for these objects is, then, not really desire for the objects themselves, but rather for the presence of that object whose absence they both designate and deny.
—Leo Bersani and Ulysse Dutoit (67)

Still following the yellow brick road of my own fantasies, I start out on this leg of my journey from two texts that inscribe the lesbian body within a fantasy of dispossession. I think it can be usefully read as a fantasy of castration. Lest this opening statement be taken as unnecessarily provocative or perverse (Why, of all things, read castration in a lesbian text? To what end can that be useful?), I hasten to add that I fully intend what I am about to say to be perverse but, while it may well be provocative, it is not unnecessarily so.

In chapter 2, discussing Diane Hamer's suggestive speculations on lesbianism and psychoanalysis, I disagreed with her revision of "the meanings attached to castration," yet expressed the view that a psychoanalytic theorization of lesbian sexuality must account for a concept so pivotal to Freudian theory as is castration, since to reject it altogether or to refuse to rethink its terms is to leave the lesbian subject without symbolic means to signify desire. I now keep my promise and take up the challenge of rethinking lesbian desire in relation to the meaning(s) of castration. Perversely, I intend to reappropriate the notions of castration and the phallus for lesbian sexuality, but in the perspective of Freud's (negative) theory of sexuality as perversion outlined in chapter 1. I will propose *a model of perverse desire* based on the one perversion that Freud insisted was not open to women—fetishism. And I will thus argue that the lesbian subject neither refuses nor accepts castration, but rather disavows it.[1]

The Texts

Radclyffe Hall's *The Well of Loneliness* and Cherríe Moraga's *Giving Up the Ghost* span nearly a century of lesbian literary self-representation and, in many ways besides chronology, stand at the remotest distance from each other, at the beginning and the end of the twentieth century. *The Well of Loneliness* was published in 1928 but written in the pre-modernist, Victorian style of the British novelistic tradition, the style of George Eliot and the Brontës rather than, say, the Woolf of *Orlando*, published that same year, or *To the Lighthouse*, published the year before. The story of Stephen Gordon's life is roughly contemporary with Radclyffe Hall's: she was forty-eight when the book was published, and it is well known that the novel and its larger-than-life protagonist, "the mythic mannish Lesbian," as she has been called, are largely an autobiographical projection.[2] A pre-feminist text, drawing its view of homosexuality from the late-nineteenth-century sexology of Krafft-Ebing and Havelock Ellis, it was intended, and in the main received, as a plea for social acceptance or toleration of sexual deviance cast in terms of divine compassion and liberal humanism.

Moraga's play *Giving Up the Ghost* was first published in 1986

---

1. In her discussion of an earlier version of this chapter published in Dutch translation ("De verwonding en het litteken"), Renée Hoogland misses the distinction I want to make between a lesbian or perverse desire based on disavowal (*Verleugnung*) and Hamer's appropriation of the masculinity complex based on the rejection or repudiation (*Verwerfung*) of femininity (see Hoogland, "Fallische perversie"). I hope that the more detailed articulation of my argument in this and the following chapters will make the distinction clearer.

2. The most informative, if at times annoyingly condescending, biography to date is Baker, *Our Three Selves*. Of the numerous critical essays on the novel, Stimpson's "Zero Degree Deviancy" and Newton's "The Mythic Mannish Lesbian" remain the most incisive, the latter including a concise survey of prior criticism. Among recent criticism, see Ruehl, Barale, and O'Rourke for a partial study of the novel's reception.

and has since continued to be revised with each successive stage production. Set in East Los Angeles in 1980, the story of Marisa, a Chicana in her late twenties, and of her younger self, nicknamed Corky, at ages eleven and seventeen, is also to some extent an auto-biographical projection—or so one can infer, for Moraga was born in Los Angeles in 1952 and was twenty-eight in 1980. The play is written in English and Spanish, in the style favored by contemporary Chicanas and other writers of color who self-identify politically and unapologetically as lesbians within U.S. Third World feminism; a style that, from the title of one major exemplar (Anzaldúa), may be called borderland style, *estilo fronterizo*—a kind of writing that combines prose with poetry and fiction with biography and oral history, crisscrossing borders between languages, genres, and sociopolitical locations.[3]

Giving Up the Ghost

The ghost to be given up in Moraga's play is Corky, the *pachuca*, Marisa's adolescent self whose experience of racist and sexist oppression, rape, and social rejection still haunts Marisa as a pain that stiffens her legs between the ankle and the knee—a symptomatic, bodily hurt that only self-love can begin to heal, a self-love gained in the struggle for political, Chicana, and feminist consciousness. The play is about the struggle of Marisa/Corky to remember and express, to come to terms with the ghosts of a past still very much alive and kicking, as it were. In a sense—though this is most certainly my own reading of the play, the partial or even idiosyncratic view of a white, European, middle-class, and middle-aged lesbian reader and spectator, mindful of the formal experiments of Brecht's epic theater (later taken up by, for example, El Teatro Campesino)—the play can be seen as a kind of psycho-epic, with the audience as the analyst/Other in the guise of a community of women (the audience appears as "THE PEOPLE" in the list of characters on the first page of the text).

3. The best example of this style in Moraga's work is her widely cited *Loving in the War Years: Lo que nunca pasó por sus labios*. Critical works on *Giving Up the Ghost* are still comparatively few, but see Yarbro-Bejarano. On the uses of autobiographical writing in the political construction of lesbian identity in Moraga and others, see Biddy Martin.

The fourth and last character in the play, and another ghost haunting Marisa, is Amalia, a Chicana/Mexicana in her late forties whom Marisa loves but cannot really have, because Amalia's own ghosts possess her; she is herself disempowered, dispossessed of her sexual womanhood by age, exile, and the death of her man. Marisa's and Amalia's passion is fraught with pain, their love with dissatisfaction; their fantasies are inextricably caught up in an imaginary of sexual difference in which the body, as it was for Stephen Gordon despite their enormous differences of class, race, culture, and sociohistorical location, is either male or female.

As Corky ("quirky"? "queer"?) is inside Marisa, a part of her experiential history and a component though not strictly causal element of her fantasy, Amalia is outside, desired and unattainable, as the object of desire properly is. But they are both actors and actants (roles) in the scenario of desire, the original fantasy that runs through the history of the subject that is Marisa. Their interrelation is set up in a process of deferred action at the play's opening, when Marisa is remembering Amalia, and the first association, the first ghost she sees, is the man, Amalia's man ("I always see that man—thick-skinned, dark, muscular. / He is a boulder between us" [3]). Then, suddenly, Corky appears: she's seventeen. At her next appearances, interspersed with those of Amalia throughout the two acts, Corky is younger still, as the play weaves back and forth between Marisa's present time and other times/events whose memory surfaces in her, on stage, in the manner of an anamnesis. The passage I selected is part of a very long monologue of Corky's, in her last appearance, who tells The People how she was raped in the seventh grade by the custodian of her Catholic school.

> *"Don't move," he tells me.*   *In English.*   *His accent gone.*
> *'n' I don'.*
> *(SHE moves right down the center of THE PEOPLE).*
> *From then on all I see in my mind's eye . . .*
> were my eyes shut?
> *is this screwdriver he's got in his sweaty palm*
> *yellow   glass   handle*
> *shiny   metal*
> *the kind my father useta use to fix things around the house*
> *remember how I'd help him*
> *how he'd take me on his jobs with him*

'n' I kept getting him confused in my mind this man 'n' his arm
with my father   kept imagining him my father returned
come   back
the arm was so soft   but this other thing . . .
hielo   hielo   ice
I wanted to cry "papá papá" 'n' then I started crying for real
cuz I knew I musta done something real wrong to get myself
in this mess.

. . . .

By the time he gets my chonas down to my knees
I suddenly feel like I'm walking on air
like I been exposed to the air   like I have no kneecaps
my thing kinda not attached to no body
flapping in the wind like a bird
a wounded bird.

. . . .

Y ya 'stoy lista for what long ago waited for me
there was no surprise
"open your legs" me dijo otra vez
'n' I do cuz I'm not useta fighting
what feels
like resignation

. . . .

'n' I open my legs wide wide open
for the angry animal that springs outta the opening
in his pants 'n' all I wanna do is have it over
so I can go back to being myself 'n' a kid again.

Then he hit me with it
into what was supposed to be a hole
that I remembered had to be one Norma had found it
once wet 'n' forbidden 'n' showed me too
how wide 'n' deep like a cueva
hers got when she wanted it to
only with me she said   (pause)
"Only with you, Corky."

But with this one
there was no hole
he had to make it
'n' I saw myself down there like a face
with no opening
a face with no features
no eyes no nose no mouth
only little lines where they shoulda been
so I dint cry
I never cried as he shoved the thing

> *into what was supposed to be a mouth*
> *with no teeth*
> *with no hate*
> *with no voice*
> *only a hole.   A Hole!*
> (gritando)
> *HE MADE ME A HOLE!*
> Black out. (40–43)

At the play's close Marisa is again alone, remembering Amalia long since gone and their passionate lovemaking. Her last words have the force of a performative statement: "It's like making familia from scratch / each time all over again . . . with strangers / if I must. / If I must, I will. / I am preparing myself for the worst, / so I cling to her in my heart, / my daydream with pencil in my mouth, / when I put my fingers / to my own / forgotten places" (58). In the process of remembering, reelaborating, and working through her ghosts in writing ("my daydream with pencil in my mouth"); in the effort of recovering a voice, of speaking out to The People, "making familia from scratch . . . with strangers"; and in the struggle to reconstitute a family no longer patriarchal but political, feminist and anti-racist, the healing process has begun for Marisa by the end of the play. What is renewed with it is the possibility of self-love, primary narcissism, and autoeroticism—a recovery of that "mythical moment," we might say with Laplanche and Pontalis, when "hunger and sexuality meet in a common origin" and are thereafter forever disjoined.

Like the disjuncture between sexuality and hunger, the disengagement of the subject from the first, real object of satisfaction takes place in the painful experience of the absence of that object, which henceforth will be hallucinated or reconstructed in fantasy ("I cling to her in my heart . . . when I put my fingers / to my own / forgotten places"). The movement from need to desire, which passes through the impossible demand for love made to a mother herself dispossessed of her body and so unable to love and nourish her female child, is accomplished by the enactment, the restaging, of an original fantasy of castration, of bodily dispossession—a fantasy which is not the object but (here, literally) the "stage setting of desire" (Laplanche and Pontalis, "Fantasy and the Origins of Sexuality" 26). It is of crucial significance that that restaging, the performance, is accomplished *for* and *with* "The People," a Chicana community who act as both the play's point of address and the point of Marisa's transference: for it is their presence, their participation in the staging, and their recognition of the fantasy that provide the Chicana subject with a meaning and a narcissistically empowered image of herself.

The Well of Loneliness

From its obscenity trial in London in 1928 to well into the 1970s, Radclyffe Hall's classic novel of female sexual inversion has been the most popular representation of lesbianism in fiction. Thus it needs no other introduction, except a word of warning: my reading of a crucial passage in the text—crucial because it inscribes a fantasy of the female body that works against the grain of the novel's explicit message—is likely to appear far-fetched. This is so, I suggest, because my reading also works against the heterosexual coding of sexual difference (masculinity and femininity) which the novel itself employs and in which it demands to be read.

The passage I selected from *The Well of Loneliness* occurs during Stephen's love affair with Angela Crosby, at the height of her unappeased passion and jealousy for the woman who, Stephen correctly suspects, is having an affair with Roger, her most loathed rival. The only things in which Stephen is superior to Roger are social status and, even more relevant to Angela, wealth: Stephen is an independently rich woman at twenty-one and someday will be even richer. Though bothered by this "unworthy" thought, Stephen nevertheless seeks to use her money and status to advantage; to impress Angela, she buys her expensive presents and orders herself "a rakish red car" as well as several tailor-made suits, gloves, scarves, heavy silk stockings, toilet water, and carnation-scented soap. "Nor could she resist," remarks the narrator, "the lure of pyjamas made of white crêpe de Chine [which] led to a man's dressing-gown of brocade—an amazingly ornate garment" (186). And yet, "on her way back in the train to Malvern, she gazed out of the window with renewed desolation. Money could not buy the one thing that she needed in life; it could not buy Angela's love." Then comes the following short section (book II, chapter 24, section 6), which I will call "the scene at the mirror":

That night she stared at herself in the glass; and even as she did so she hated her body with its muscular shoulders, its small compact breasts, and its slender flanks of an athlete. All her life she must drag this body of hers like a monstrous fetter imposed on her spirit. This strangely ardent yet sterile body that must worship yet never be worshipped in return by the creature of its adoration. She longed to maim it, for it made her feel cruel; it was so white, so strong and so self-sufficient; yet withal so poor and unhappy a thing that her eyes filled with tears and her hate turned to pity. She began to grieve over it, touching her breasts with pitiful fingers, stroking her shoulders, letting her hands slip along her straight thighs—Oh, poor and most desolate body!

Then, she, for whom Puddle was actually praying at that moment, must now pray also, but blindly; finding few words that seemed worthy of prayer, few words that seemed to encompass her meaning—for she did not know the meaning of herself. But she loved, and loving groped for the God who had fashioned her, even unto this bitter loving. (186–87)

The typographical division that separates the last sentence of the first paragraph, describing the movement of Stephen's hands and fingers on her own body, from the second and last sentence of the second paragraph cannot disguise the intensely erotic significance of the scene. At face value, the paragraph division corresponds to the ideological division between body and mind, or "spirit," announced in the first paragraph ("all her life she must drag this body of hers like a monstrous fetter imposed on her spirit"), so that the physical, sexual character of Stephen's unappeased love and thwarted narcissistic desire is displaced onto an order of language which excludes her—the prayer to a distant, disembodied God by one who can pray to him because she also has no body, i.e., Puddle, Stephen's tutor and companion, and her desexualized double. While in the first paragraph Stephen "stares" at her own body in the mirror, in the second she is blind, groping—a sudden reversal of the terms of vision which recalls the "nothing to see" of the female sex in psychoanalysis and, in a rhetorical sleight of hand, forecloses its view, its sensual perception, denying its very existence.

But a few words belie the (overt) sublimation and the (covert) negation of the sexual that the second paragraph would accomplish: "Then," the first word in it, temporally links the movement of the hands in the preceding paragraph to the final words of the second,

"even unto this bitter loving," where the shifter "this" relocates the
act of loving in a present moment that can refer only to the culmina-
tion or conclusion of the scene interrupted by the paragraph break;
that is, the scene of Stephen in front of the mirror "touching her
breasts with pitiful fingers, stroking her shoulders, letting her hands
slip along her straight thighs . . . [and, if we might fantasize along
with the text, watching in the mirror her own hands move down-
ward on her body] even unto this bitter loving." No wonder the next
paragraph must rush in to deny both her and us the vision of such
an intolerable act.

If Marisa's were "forgotten places" that can be "remembered" as
the healing begins, Stephen's are not only forgotten or repressed,
but virtually foreclosed or repudiated, the effect of an even greater
and more final repression.[4] "She did not know the meaning of
herself." Her groping blind and wordless toward an Other who
should provide the meaning, but does not, only leads her back to the
real of her body, to a "bitter" need which cannot accede to
symbolization and so must remain, in Lady Gordon's words, "this
unspeakable outrage that you call love" (200, emphasis added). As
the passage anticipates, the narrative resolution and Stephen's
eventual "healing" can be cast only in terms of renunciation and
salvation, in an order of language that occludes the body in favor of
spirit and, with regard to women specifically, forecloses the
possibility of any autonomous and non-reproductive sexuality. The
text's inability to articulate a lesbian sexual difference, and its
consequent reinscription of lesbianism in hom(m)osexuality or
sexual indifference, are the effects of that foreclosure. Stephen's
"sacrifice" of her love for Mary—and, more gruesome still, of Mary's
love for her—which concludes Radclyffe Hall's "parable of
damnation" (in Stimpson's memorable phrase) will ironically
reaffirm the repudiation of lesbianism as such; that is to say, the
novel cannot conceive of an autonomous female homosexuality and

---

4. For the distinction between repression (*Verdrängung*) and repudiation or foreclosure (*Verwerfung*), see Ned Lukacher, *Primal Scenes* 149–51. While the repressed
contents are theoretically accessible to consciousness and to be worked over, for example in analysis, what is repudiated is permanently repressed, lost to memory, or, in
Lacan's translation, "foreclosed." *Verwerfung*, Lukacher argues, "is Freud's explanation of the patient's failure of memory. . . . For the Wolf-Man, as well as for Freud, [it
is] a mechanism to explain one's inability to raise a question [specifically the question
of castration]—which is to say, one's inability to articulate difference" (151 and 153).

thus can only confirm Stephen's view of herself as a "freak," "nature's mistake"—a masculine woman.

The passage, however, contains another, ambiguous message. Like Corky's monologue in *Giving Up the Ghost*, this scene in *The Well of Loneliness* speaks a fantasy of bodily dispossession, the fantasy of an unlovely and unlovable body, but the terms of reference differ. Stephen's body is not feminine or maternal, not narcissistically cherished, fruitful, or productive, nor, on the other hand, barren (as the term goes) or abject, but simply imperfect, faulty and faulted, dispossessed, inadequate to bear and signify desire. Because it is not feminine, this body is inadequate as the object of desire, to be desired by the other, and thus inadequate to signify the female subject's desire in its feminine mode; however, because it is masculine but not male, it is also inadequate to signify or bear the subject's desire in the masculine mode. I want to argue that, however different, both these fantasies of bodily dispossession are subtended by an original fantasy of castration, in the sense elaborated by Laplanche and Pontalis, with the paternal phallus present and visible in the dark, muscular, thick-skinned man of Marisa's reverie and in the white, muscular, athlete's body of Stephen who "dares" to look so like her father. It is the paternal phallus, inscribed in her very body and as a ghost in Marisa's fantasy scenario, that imposes the taboo which renders the female body (the mother's, other women's, and their own) forever inaccessible to Stephen and Marisa, and thus signifies their dispossession, their castration. But before discussing the ways or even the sense in which the notion of castration may be reformulated in relation to lesbian subjectivity and representation, I want to stress how the two fantasy scenarios differ with respect to their sociohistorical settings.

In the novel as in the Victorian imaginary, the body is given by God and nature; culture seemingly has no say. By her own admission, Stephen is a "freak of a creature," "some awful mistake—God's mistake," to the point that her own mother is *naturally* repulsed by her child's body and later made physically sick by that body's alien, *unnatural* sexual urge. In the play, it is not nature but culture in its patriarchal mode, as understood in contemporary feminist terms, that brands certain bodies with the marks of race and gender. Stephen's body is not feminine, on the Victorian model of femininity that is her mother Anna: it is "ardent and sterile," and its taut muscular strength, whiteness, and phallic self-sufficiency make Stephen wish to maim it, to mark it with a physical, indexical sign of her symbolic castration, her captivity in gender, and her semiotic disempowerment ("she did not know the meaning of herself") by the Other, the God who made her "a freak of a creature." For she can worship the female body in another but never be worshiped in return. Thus, if she hates her naked body, it is because that body is masculine, "so strong and so self-sufficient," so phallic. The body she desires, not only in Angela but also autoerotically for herself, the body she can make love to and mourns for, is a feminine, female body. Paradoxical as it may seem, the "mythic mannish lesbian" (in Esther Newton's wonderful phrase) wishes to have a feminine body, the kind of female body she desires in Angela, later in Mary—a femme's body. How to explain such a paradox?[5]

On the contrary, Corky's body has been made feminine, but that, to her, means vilified, diminished ("He made me a hole!" she shouts). It has been *reduced* to a female body, with all the specific consequences that entails for the racially subaltern subject, first and foremost that of being a body *for* the other—the male, white, prepossessing master. For the "pachuca," the young Chicana butch, this is the mode of apprehension of "sexual difference." As the "hungry animal that springs outta the opening" of the man's pants makes a hole in her body, it also makes a hole *of* her body, turns her into a hole; and she can never "go back to being myself 'n' a kid again." The difference between rape and seduction—rape by a man whose screwdriver resembles her father's, and seduction by Norma, a prefiguration of the later, maternal, character Amalia—corresponds to the perceived distinction and dissociation between the female body articulated as sexual in relation to the phallus and the female body articulated as sexual in relation to autoerotic or female-erotic drives. The dissociation produces a paradox in this subject as well,

---

5. I want to point out how the paradox in the scene at the mirror contradicts, or at least complicates, the more immediate and traditional reading of Stephen's masculinity complex. For on the one hand, Stephen's sense of herself depends on a strong masculine identification; yet, on the other hand, it is precisely her masculine, phallic body which bears the mark of castration and frustrates her narcissistic desire. So, in this case, it is not possible simply to equate the phallic with the masculine and castration with the feminine body, as psychoanalysis would have it. And hence the question that this singular passage in the novel raises for me: What does castration mean in relation to lesbian subjectivity and desire?

the paradox of two different and mutually exclusive holes in Corky's perception of her body: one made by the man and the other, previously discovered by Norma, which can expand and deepen "when she wanted it to," but ceases to be one when the man hits her "into what *was supposed to be* a hole" (for, with him, she says, "there was no hole / he had to make it"). In force of this paradox, one might say, the female sex is in effect a hole which is not one.

The different inscription of femininity in these two texts, which in many respects are located at each other's sociocultural antipodes, can be better appreciated by referring to another work by Moraga, *Loving in the War Years,* in particular the section "A Long Line of Vendidas." There, the experience of growing up as a woman in Chicano culture, with its Mexican and native Indio components and its historical burden of socioeconomic and racist subjection, is unavoidably linked to the powerful figure of the cultural imaginary that is Malinche (Malintzin Tenepal), the Aztec woman accused of betraying her race by collaborating with the white conquistador, Hernán Cortés, learning to speak his language, acting as his interpreter, and bearing his progeny (on Malinche, see also Alarcón).

> You are a traitor to your race if you do not put the man first. The potential accusation of "traitor" or "vendida" is what hangs above the heads and beats in the hearts of most Chicanas seeking to develop our own autonomous sense of ourselves, particularly through sexuality. Even if a Chicana knew no Mexican history, the concept of betraying one's race through sex and sexual politics is as common as corn. . . .
>
> If the Chicana, like her brother, suspects other women of betrayal, then she must, in the most profound sense, suspect herself. How deep her suspicions run will measure how ardently she defends her commitment, above all, to the Chicano male. As obedient sister/daughter/lover she is the committed heterosexual, the socially acceptable Chicana. Even if she's politically radical, sex remains the bottom line on which she proves her commitment to her race. (Moraga, *Loving in the War Years* 103 and 105)

Although recently reclaimed by some Chicana feminists as a figure of female resistance to patriarchy and the mother of the new mestiza race, in the Chicano cultural imaginary Malinche is the sellout (*la vendida*), the traitor, the whore, the vilest of the vile. The association with her is most compelling and most grievous for a feminist or a lesbian, who are doubly disparaged as women and as women who love women (perhaps even white women) at the expense of the men of *la raza*, and hence of the race as a whole.

But if the mark of gender and the effects of patriarchy and heterosexism are accountable for Marisa/Corky's pain, they cannot be extricated from a femininity that is also, concurrently and indissociably, marked by racism: Corky's rape by the Chicano janitor, who speaks Spanish to approach her and obtain her cooperation but then rapes her in English, is preceded in Act I by another "memory" of a traumatic event, an incident of not sexist but unequivocally racist humiliation that occurred when Corky was eleven.[6] This incident is also recounted in a long monologue by Corky (17–19), which is formally symmetrical to the rape monologue in Act II. Marisa's symptomatic cramps are clearly overdetermined by the contents of both these repressed memories; that is to say, by the traumatic effects physical and psychical of her living under historical conditions of gender, race, and class oppression.

I stress the discontinuity, the incommensurability, of the experience of lesbian subjectivity inscribed in my two texts because, when I speak of the fantasy of dispossession that they both inscribe, and of an original fantasy of castration that subtends it, I do not want to give the impression that the two subjects of the fantasy are one and the same or interchangeable. That would deny the sociosexual specificity of each subject's subject-ion, the historicity of the texts, and the conditions of representation of two altogether distinct forms of lesbian subjectivity. Nevertheless, it is possible to argue, or I am willing to take the risk of arguing, that the two fantasies are similarly structured in relation to an original fantasy of castration and that such fantasy is a lesbian fantasy, or better, a fantasy that structures some of the settings, some of the scenarios, of lesbian desire. Before I do, however, I must first reconsider the possible meaning and function of castration in relation to lesbian desire.

---

6. My impression that the janitor was an Anglo man pretending to be Chicano was corrected by Moraga in a private communication. I am grateful to her for her generous comments on an early draft of this chapter.

Castration and the Paternal Phallus

How can the notion of castration serve us in this project? one may well ask. How can the concept of castration as a psychic structure, a subjectively introjected mode of social cognition that rewrites in the symbolic order what may be purely an imaginary content of the patriarchal unconscious, namely, the so-called difference between the sexes—how can such a notion, formulated by Freud and others as the castration complex (see Green), in a precise, determined relation to the human male anatomy and physiology (presence or absence of the penis and its consequences for sexual pleasure), as well as to their assumptions about gender, their ideological (if not crassly self-serving) attributions of gender made on the basis of a particular Western/European/Victorian vision of the social good—how can such a notion as castration, the very name of which evokes an alien or unfamiliar or perhaps even unknown bodily shape—how can such a notion pertain, explain, or gain us knowledge of female, let alone lesbian, sexuality today?

The difficulty of this notion of castration for feminist theory is too well known to be rehearsed once again. To sum it up in one sentence, that difficulty is in the definition of female sexuality as *complementary* to the physiological, psychic, and social needs of the male, and yet as a *deficiency* vis-à-vis his sexual organ and its symbolic representative, the phallus—a definition which results in the exclusion of women not from sexuality (for, on the contrary, woman is the locus, the lure of the sexual), but rather from the field of desire. However, there is another paradox here because the very effectiveness of castration as a psychic structure—the internalized prohibition or inaccessibility of the first (lost) object of desire that is the mother's body—consists precisely in allowing access to desire itself, the phallus representing at once the mark of difference and lack, the threat of castration, and the signifier of desire. But only for the male. The female's relation to castration does not allow her entry into the field of desire except as its (his) object.

This is so, Freudians and Lacanians join forces in saying, because women lack the physical property that signifies desire: not having a penis (the bodily representative and support of the libido, the physical referent which in sexuality, in fantasy, becomes the signifier, the sign-vehicle, or the bearer of desire), females are effectively castrated, in the sense that they lack—they do not have and as females can never hope to have, in either the symbolic or the imaginary register—the means of access to the first object of desire, represented by the paternal phallus. Whereas it is the potential for losing the penis—a potential loss which subjects the male to the Law of the Father and structures his relation to the paternal phallus as one of insufficiency (also called lack)—that gives the male the possibility, in both the symbolic and the imaginary registers, that his penis may attain the value and the stature of the paternal phallus. Having nothing to lose, in other words, women cannot desire; having no phallic capital to invest or speculate on, as men do, women cannot be investors in the marketplace of desire but are instead commodities that circulate in it (see Irigaray, "Women on the Market" and "Commodities among Themselves," in *This Sex Which Is Not One*).[7]

Some feminist theorists, following Lacan, have sought to disengage the notion of castration from its reference to the penis by making it purely a condition (and a structure) of signification and thus making the "entry into desire" accessible to women concurrently with "the entry into language." Silverman, for example, argued that "one of the crucial features of Lacan's redefinition of castration has been to shift it away from this obligatory anatomical referent [the penis] to the lack induced by language" ("Fassbinder and Lacan" 79; she has subsequently revised her opinion of the penis-phallus relation, as will be noted shortly). She would distinguish Lacanian or symbolic castration from Freud's castration complex because "it is the former rather than the latter which ush-

---

7. In a similar vein Jean-Joseph Goux speaks of the phallus as "the general equivalent for the objects of the drives, and thus as the signifier-standard of *jouissance*" by comparing it to other master signifiers such as money, gold, and speech ("The Phallus" 71–72): "With money, exchange-value becomes autonomous, appearing independent of any effective transaction. . . . Money (always on the condition of being imagined as incorruptible or stable—a fantasy that *gold* long satisfied) appears to be a self-sufficient value: the abstract *jouissance* of its indeterminate virtualities of appropriation . . . can eclipse the pleasure promised by the finite use-value of an object" (69–70). Homologously, "the post-traditional phallus founds and erects itself in the space left by the breaking of matrimonial barter" (70). And "just as the financial sign is nothing but the indefinite inscription and circulation of a debt by means of accounting, a writing game, without reference to any real goods," so is the Lacanian phallus "the hyperbolic hypothesis of an absolute mediation with nothing to mediate" (72). However, this sounds too optimistic to me. For, if the master signifiers are merely chips in a writing game, still the game has high stakes, those stakes being precisely the terms and conditions of the mediation itself, who does it and for whom.

ers in the first phase of the Oedipus complex" (*The Acoustic Mirror* 156): "desire for the mother is initiated only through *symbolic castration*, i.e., only through the entry into language. It is, after all, impossible for either subject [female or male] to enter into desire until linguistic immersion, since it is only through the consolidation of the signifier that the lack necessary to desire's functioning is opened up" (122). Silverman charges Freud with "projection" (16) when he insists that "the term 'castration complex' ought to be confined to those excitations and consequences which are bound up with the loss of the *penis*" (*SE* 10: 8). Instead, she favors an expanded view of castration that includes prior divisions or separations of the subject from its own body, such as feces, or from the mother's breast at weaning; these are "the various, pre-Oedipal castrations catalogued by Lacan, castrations which are realized only retroactively, with the entry into language. These castrations produce a subject who is structured by lack long before the 'discovery' of sexual difference" (16).

Juliet Mitchell sees it differently. For Lacan as for Freud, she states, "the castration complex is *the* instance of the humanisation of the child in its sexual difference. Certainly it rejoins other severances, in fact it gives them their meaning." But if the specific threat of *phallic* castration is discounted, then there is nothing that explains the difference between the sexes: "If castration is only one among other separations or is the same as the dread of the loss of sexual desire common to men and women alike (Jones's *aphanisis*), then what distinguishes the two sexes?" ("Introduction—I" 19). Or, put otherwise, what distinguishes the desire that constitutes the female subject as such, and thus must follow upon the perception of sexual difference, from the pre-Oedipal, non-gendered attachment to the mother? For Jacqueline Rose, "castration means first of all this—that the child's desire for the mother does not refer *to* her but *beyond* her, to an object, the phallus" ("Introduction—II" 38), which is the representative of the paternal law and the object of the mother's desire. If sexual difference is assigned according to anatomical difference, according to "whether individual subjects do or do not possess the phallus," it is not because "anatomical difference *is* sexual difference," Rose underscores, but rather because "anatomical difference comes to *figure* sexual difference. . . . The phallus thus indicates the reduction of difference to an instance of visible perception, a *seeming* value" (42), but is not to be "crudely" identified with the order of the visible or the real.

And yet, others contend, the semiotic bond between the significa-tion of the phallus and the "real" penis remains, crudely or not, in-dissoluble. To wit, Stephen Heath: "No one has the phallus but the phallus is the male sign, the man's assignment. . . . The man's mas-culinity, his male world, is the assertion of the phallus to support his having it" ("Joan Riviere and the Masquerade" 55). And Jane Gallop: "Lacanians would simply separate the symbolic phallus from the penis. But is this separation possible? Or is it merely a fantasy? Of course, the signifier *phallus* functions in distinction from the signi-fier *penis*. It sounds and looks different, produces different associa-tions. *But* it *also* always refers to *penis*" (*Thinking through the Body* 126). And Teresa Brennan: "Feminists influenced by Lacan have stressed that both sexes can take up the masculine and feminine places; these shift and slide—no one has the phallus. Yet the tie be-tween phallus and penis exists, and persists" (*Between Feminism and Psychoanalysis* 4). And Charles Bernheimer, in a self-styled "ma-terialist, feminist-informed, straight male reading of male sexuality" ("Penile Reference in Phallic Theory" 118), has this to say: "For La-can, the phallus, originating principle of this mobility [of the signi-fying chain], refers to no body. But he is wrong: the link between signifier and signified in the sign cannot be severed and produces an effect of reference that inscribes bodily experience into the uncon-scious. The phallus's pretense to universality and transcendence thus is challenged in the unconscious by the penis's claim to histori-cal specificity" (120–21).

A similar criticism, if more painstakingly argued and understated ("there is a good deal of slippage in Lacan not only between the phal-lus and the penis, but between the phallus in its symbolic capacity, and the phallus in its imaginary capacity" ["The Lacanian Phallus" 97]), is made by Silverman in a recent essay that appeared next to Bernheimer's in "The Phallus Issue" of the journal *d i f f e r e n c e s* and that she qualifies as "a feminist account of the Lacanian phallus" (85). Both Silverman and Bernheimer advance what each seems to consider a novel interpretation of the phallus as (1) intrinsically bear-ing a "penile" reference and (2) having an intimate relation, not only symbolic but also imaginary, to the paternal metaphor, the Name of the Father. In other words, both observe that the phallus's privileged status as master signifier derives from its kinship with the penis and with the authority of paternal law, and both want to diminish that status in psychoanalytic theory (a contention which, in feminist or feminist-informed readings, is hardly news). But whereas Bernheimer argues for the penis as phallic *signified* in order to counter "the body's strangulation by the signifying chain" (130), Silverman wants to dislodge the phallus "from its privileged position" as signifier of desire (113), consistently with her interpretation of symbolic castration (noted above) as prior to sexual difference and not predicated on the phallus or the Name of the Father but rather on the "entry into language." This allows her to postulate that the female child enters desire before the phallus appears on the scene, and presumably enters as subject (in glossing Lacan's reading of *Hamlet,* she speaks of Gertrud's desire for Claudius's penis [103]). Her conclusion, therefore, is the exact opposite of Bernheimer's: "The only immutable law of desire is . . . the Law . . . of Language" (Silverman 114).

In these learned disquisitions, however, nearly everyone fails to note that the Lacanian framing of the question in terms of having or being the phallus is set in the perspective of normative heterosexuality (which indeed both psychoanalytic practice and theory strive to retrieve or induce in their subjects), with the sexual difference of man and woman clearly mapped out and the act of reproductive copulation firmly in place. As Lacan himself puts it,

> The phallus is the privileged signifier of that mark in which the role of the logos is joined with the advent of desire. It can be said that this signifier is chosen because it is the most tangible element in the real of sexual copulation, and also the most symbolic in the literal (typographical) sense of the term, since it is equivalent there to the (logical) copula. It might also be said that, *by virtue of its turgidity, it is the image of the vital flow as it is transmitted in generation.* ("The Signification of the Phallus," *Ecrits* 287; emphasis added)

That the heterosexual perspective in this much-quoted passage goes regularly unnoticed or unremarked by Lacan's sophisticated exegetes is surely the sign of a deeply buried wish not to see it, if psychoanalysis is to be believed. Freud himself remarked on this long ago, in a 1915 addition to the *Three Essays on the Theory of Sexuality:*

A choice of an object independently of its sex . . . is the original basis from which, as a result of restriction in one direction or the other, both the normal and the inverted types develop. Thus from the point of view of psycho-analysis the exclusive sexual interest felt by men for women is also a problem that needs elucidating and is not a self-evident fact. (*SE* 7: 146)

And in "The Psychogenesis of a Case of Homosexuality in a Woman" (1920), he actually suggested a practical reason for psychoanalysis's disavowal of what, on the other hand, is rather self-evident:

The girl was not in any way ill (she did not suffer from anything in herself, nor did she complain of her condition) and . . . the task to be carried out did not consist in resolving a neurotic conflict but in converting one variety of the genital organization of sexuality into the other. Such an achievement—the removal of genital inversion or homosexuality—is in my experience never an easy matter. . . . One must remember that normal sexuality too depends upon a restriction in the choice of object. In general, to undertake to convert a fully developed homosexual into a heterosexual does not offer much more prospect of success than the reverse, except that for good practical reasons the latter is never attempted. (*SE* 18: 150–51)

That one might undertake analysis as a cure for heterosexuality is a radical suggestion, but what practitioner or theorist of psychoanalysis has ever thought of that?

Yet it is useful to keep in mind that, as I pointed out in chapter 1, the very notion of a normative sexuality, a normal psychosexual development, and a normal sexual act are inseparable, in Freud's work from the *Three Essays* on, from the detailed consideration of its aberrant, deviant, or perverse manifestations and components. It bears reiterating that the whole of Freud's theory of the human psyche, the sexual instincts and their vicissitudes, owes its material foundations and developments to psychoanalysis, his clinical study of the psychoneuroses—that is to say, those cases in which the mental apparatus and instinctual drives reveal themselves in their processes and mechanisms, which are "normally" hidden or unremarkable otherwise. The question whether a normal instinct, phylogenetically inherited, preexists its possible deviations (in psychoneurotic individuals), or whether instinctual life is but a set of transformations, some of which are then defined as normal (that is, non-pathogenic and socially desirable or admissible), is far from closed.

What if, then, one were to reframe the question of the phallus and the fantasy of castration in this other perspective provided by Freud's negative theory, so to speak, of the perversions? With regard to my immediate project, let me restate that the two lesbian texts under discussion speak fantasies of castration; but they also, and very effectively, speak desire; and thus they are fully in the symbolic, in signification. Yet the desire they speak is not masculine, nor *simply* phallic. But again, if the phallus is both the mark of castration and the signifier of desire, then the question is, What acts as the phallus in these lesbian fantasies? *Pace* Freud and Lacan, I will propose that it is not the paternal phallus, or a phallic symbol, but something of the nature of a fetish, something which signifies at once the absence of the object of desire (the female body) and the subject's wish for it. I am indebted in this venture to Leo Bersani and Ulysse Dutoit's reading of Freud's paper on "Fetishism."

Toward a Model of Perverse Desire

In "Fetishisms and Storytelling" (in *The Forms of Violence*), Bersani and Dutoit delineate a "formal model of desire's mobility" (72). I find it compellingly suggestive, in conjunction with my reading of Freud's negative theory of sexuality as perversion, toward a reconceptualization of possibly both gay and lesbian sexualities. On my part, I will attempt to elaborate the model in relation to the latter, with reference to the two texts introduced earlier, and will call the result a model of perverse desire.

Freud's theory of desire as an activity of fantasy aimed at repeating a past experience of satisfaction, and hence dependent on an internalized, primary, and absent object of desire for which all others are merely derivative substitutes, may be seen as "intrinsically fetishistic," Bersani and Dutoit remark: "that is, a theory determined to *have* a founding object of desire, to repudiate its absence just as the fetish repudiates the absence of a penis in women" (67). However, with their perverse discussion of the fetishist as "a hero of uncertain desire" (71), they mean to use Freud's very notion of fetishism against him, or at least against the fetishistic theory of desire that can be read, and has been read, in his texts; in its stead, they propose a formal model in which desire is no longer attached to a privileged object, nor dependent on the phallus as its privileged signifier, but able to move on to other images and objects.

In the accepted or clinical view of fetishism, the perversion is related to the subject's disavowal of the mother's castration, which occurs by a splitting of the ego as a defense from the threat of castration. Disavowal implies a contradiction, a double or split belief: on the one hand, the recognition that the mother does not have a penis as the father does; and yet, on the other hand, the refusal to acknowledge the absence of the penis in the mother. As a result of this disavowal, the subject's desire is metonymically displaced, diverted onto another object or part of the body, clothing, hair, etc., which acts as "substitute" (Freud says) for the missing maternal penis. In this way, to the child who is to become a fetishist "the woman *has* got a penis, in spite of everything; but this penis is no longer the same as it was before. Something else has taken its place, has been appointed its substitute, as it were, and now inherits the interest which was formerly directed to its predecessor" (*SE* 21: 154). In this *diversion* consists, for Freud, the *perversion* of the sexual instinct, which is thus diverted or displaced from its legitimate object and reproductive aim onto some other, non-reproductive object— though not diverted, of course, from the aim of pleasure (on Freud's contradictory statements with regard to the existence or non-existence of a "legitimate" object of the sexual instinct and its relation to aim, see my discussion of the *Three Essays* in chapter 1).[8] But since the whole process, the disavowal [*Verleugnung*] and the displacement [*Verschiebung*], is motivated by the subject's fear of his own possible castration, what it brings into evidence is the fundamental role in fetishism of the *paternal* phallus (that which is

---

8. Here I will recall only Freud's more conspicuous passages: "Experience of the cases that are considered abnormal has shown us that in them the sexual instinct and the sexual object are merely soldered together—a fact which we have been in danger of overlooking in consequence of the uniformity of the normal picture, where the object appears to form part and parcel of the instinct. . . . It seems probable that the sexual instinct is in the first instance independent of its object; nor is its origin likely to be due to its object's attractions" (*SE* 7: 147–48); and "a choice of an object independently of its sex . . . is the original basis from which, as a result of restriction in one direction or the other, both the normal and the inverted types develop" (*SE* 7: 146).

missing in the mother).[9] Which is why, Freud states, fetishism does not apply to women: they have nothing to lose, they have no penis, and thus disavowal would not defend their ego from an "already accomplished" castration.

However, argue Bersani and Dutoit, Freud places too much emphasis on the paternal phallus. "The fetishist can see the woman as she is, without a penis, because he loves her with a penis somewhere else," they say. (This is the sense in which they read Freud's statement that for the child who is to become a fetishist "the woman *has* got a penis, in spite of everything, but this penis is no longer the same as it was before. Something else has taken its place, has been appointed its substitute, as it were, and now inherits the interest which was formerly directed to its predecessor" [*SE* 21: 154].) They elaborate:

> The crucial point—which makes the fetishistic object different from the phallic symbol—is that the success of the fetish depends on its being seen as authentically different from the missing penis. With a phallic symbol, we may not be consciously aware of what it stands for, but it attracts us because, consciously or unconsciously, we perceive it *as* the phallus. In fetishism, however, the refusal to see the fetish as a penis-substitute may not be simply an effect of repression. The fetishist has displaced the missing penis from the woman's genitals to, say, her underclothing, but we suggest that if he doesn't care about the underclothing resembling a penis it is because: (1) he knows that it is not a penis; (2) he doesn't want it to be only a penis; and (3) he also knows that *nothing* can replace the lack to which in fact he has resigned himself. (68–69)

Ironically, they point out, it is because the subject has resigned himself to castration that desire can be "cut off" from its object, the

9. Freud insists that the special characteristic of the phallus in fetishism is its being the maternal phallus. But, in effect, the missing maternal phallus is what the mother would have were she not castrated; and that is to say, the same phallus the father has. In other words, the maternal phallus differs from the paternal phallus in that the former is a fantasy object without the symbolic and imaginary valences that constitute the latter as the agent of castration and the signifier of desire. Or again, the difference between the paternal phallus and the maternal phallus is not the difference between two kinds of phalluses but a difference between presence and absence of the phallus as such (i.e., the paternal phallus); that difference which indeed, for psychoanalytic theory, is alone responsible for sexual difference. And hence Freud: "In conclusion we may say that the normal prototype of fetishes is a man's penis, just as the normal prototype of inferior organs is a woman's real small penis, the clitoris" (*SE* 21: 157).

mother, and move on to other objects. Thus, to the fetishist, the fetish does much more than *re-place* the penis, "since it signifies something which was never anywhere": what it does is "derange his *system of desiring*," even as far as "deconstructing and mobilizing the self." Unlike a phallic symbol, which stands for an actually perceived penis, the fetish is a "fantasy-phallus," "an inappropriate object precariously attached to a desiring fantasy, unsupported by any perceptual memory" (69). Thus fetishism, they conclude, outlines a model of desire dependent on "an ambiguous negation of the real. . . . This negation creates an interval between the new object of desire and an unidentifiable first object, and as such it may be the model for all substitutive formations in which the first term of the equation is lost, or unlocatable, and in any case ultimately unimportant" (71).

Discussing this work by Bersani and Dutoit, Parveen Adams objects (on the authority of Joyce McDougall) that the psychic process from which they derive such a mobility of desire usually leads to the pathological rigidity and compulsive repetition of clinical or classic fetishism. "Of course they are aware that . . . the clinical fetishist still believes in the paternal phallus," she condescends, but perhaps not aware enough; or rather, she is doubtful as to what extent the fetishist's desire, with its rigid scenarios and compulsive repetition, may serve as a formal model of desire freed from, as she puts it, "the penile representation of the phallus" ("Of Female Bondage" 258).[10] As I read it, Bersani and Dutoit's argument is more radical than Adams realizes, for the mobility of desire they theorize is not a freedom from the penile representation of the phallus but a freedom

---

10. Adams cites McDougall's *A Plea for a Measure of Abnormality* (four times, without any page numbers), but an earlier work of McDougall's makes the point just as well. While "activities which are commonly regarded as perverse—voyeurism, fetishism, exhibitionism, interest in a diversity of possible erotic zones—all might form part of the experience of a normal love relation," what characterizes the pervert, she emphasizes, "is that he has no choice; his sexuality is fundamentally compulsive. He does not choose to be perverse and cannot be said to choose the form of his perversion" ("Primal Scene and Sexual Perversion" 371). Adams's recasting of the "clinical" view of "the pervert" is as follows: "One could say that the pervert is all right so long as things go according to plan. The trouble is that he finds his own plans compelling and has little ability to change them" ("Of Female Bondage" 259). Neither one stops to reflect on the equally compulsive quality of the sexuality of the "normal" heterosexual, who also "has no choice" in whatever turns her or him on, also finds her or his own plans quite compelling, and has just as little ability to change them. It is in such unself-conscious statements that psychoanalytic theorists reveal the pathologizing impulse of "clinical" psychoanalysis and its drive to normativity, alongside the operations of what Wittig has aptly called *The Straight Mind*.

from the phallus itself. For Adams, "the paternal phallus exacts its price. In spite of the construction of the fetish the pervert [is still under the sway] of the paternal phallus" (259). On the other hand, as if to anticipate this "clinical" objection, Bersani and Dutoit resolutely emphasize: "What goes 'wrong' in clinical fetishism is perhaps *an insufficient degree of castration* . . . an inability to detach oneself from the phallus itself" (71–72)—and they are speaking, I believe, not only of the subject but of the "fetishistic [phallic] theory of desire" as well. In other words, what is wrong with psychoanalytic theory may also be an insufficient degree of castration, and hence its holding on for dear life to the paternal phallus.

In spite of her principled objection, Adams, too, relies on Bersani and Dutoit to advance her own argument, as I am doing, but with different ends in mind. Hers are to account psychoanalytically for what she calls "new sexualities," and in particular lesbian sadomasochism—sexualities which would be "divorced from gender positions" (250; notice the metaphor: heterosexuality rearing its normative head even as she speaks of something quite unlike it). Driven by this pressing concern to "divorce" sexuality from gender, Adams's argument for lesbian s/m runs aground on the totally unsupported claim that "the homosexuality of the lesbian sadomasochist . . . is quite differently organized from that of the lesbian who is not a pervert," the latter being, in her opinion, "fundamentally similar to the traditional heterosexual woman" (263). Confident in the truth of the master's words and with a flourish of arrogance wedded (one might say) to psychoanalytic fundamentalism, she pronounces: "For both these women the paternal phallus is the signifier of desire and nothing changes this" (263).[11]

My interest in Bersani and Dutoit's model, on the contrary, is to understand how lesbian homosexuality, subjectivity, and desire are *not* similar to heterosexual female sexuality, subjectivity, and desire; they are not similar precisely in that they are organized in a differ-

---

11. To my knowledge, the proponents, practitioners, and/or theorists of lesbian s/m in the United States have not engaged with the abundant psychoanalytic literature on perversion and sadomasochism in particular. "Daughter of the Movement," the first psychoanalytically informed study of lesbian s/m fiction and of the role of feminism in the scenarios of lesbian s/m fantasy, is the work of Julia Creet, a Canadian. See also Monika Treut, "Perverse Bilder," introducing the book of lesbian s/m photographs by the German Krista Beinstein, *Obszöne Frauen.*

ent relation to the phallus, and to the penis. While lesbian s/m may be the current vacation spot of Feminists for Sexual Indifference, I am less interested in locating rare specimens of non-phallic sexual organization or new brands of sexuality than in figuring out a theory of sexuality non-heterosexual and non-normatively heterosexual, perhaps a theory of sexuality as perversion, that may account for my own sexual structuring and perverse desire.[12] For these purposes, the point made by Bersani and Dutoit stands: that "the process which *may* result in pathological fetishism can *also* have a permanent psychic validity of a formal nature" (71, emphasis added). For if (and admittedly it is a big if, but not a speculation alien to or unprecedented in psychoanalytic theory)[13] the psychic process of disavowal—the ambiguous negation of castration in women—that detaches desire from the paternal phallus in the fetishist can *also* occur in other subjects, and if it can have enduring effects or formal validity as a psychic process, as Bersani and Dutoit suggest, then their formal model of desire's mobility does recommend itself as applicable, at least preliminarily and *mutatis mutandis*, to lesbian sexuality.

Consider the following three paraphrases from their essay cited above, with the word *lesbian* in lieu of the word *fetishist:* (1) the lesbian can see the woman as she is, without a penis, because she loves her with a penis somewhere else; (2) the lesbian also knows that nothing can replace the lack to which in fact she has resigned herself; (3) the lesbian's desire is sustained and signified by a fetish, a fantasy-phallus, an inappropriate object precariously attached to a

---

12. As should be clear from chapter 1, I do not equate *perverse* with *pathological*, for these terms, like *normal*, are discursive shifters —terms whose semantic boundaries depend on the social conceptualization and institutional regulation of behaviors. Those are historically specific and based in the medical, juridical, moral, and popular discourses, and the relations of power and knowledge of any particular epoch. Today, *perverse* and *pathological* are no longer fully coextensive terms. (Cf. Laplanche and Pontalis, "Perversion," in *The Language of Psycho-Analysis*.)

13. Juliet Mitchell also extrapolates from disavowal and fetishism a more general, formal model of the constitution of the subject: "Freud ended his life with an unfinished paper: 'Splitting of the Ego in the Process of Defence' (XXIII, 1940). It is about the castration complex and its implication for the construction of the subject. It describes the formation of the ego in a moment of danger (of threatened loss) which results in a primary split from which it never recovers. Freud offers the reaction to the castration complex when a fetish is set up as its alternative, as an exemplary instance of this split. In this paper we can see clearly the position of Freud's to which Lacan is to return. A primordially split subject necessitates an originally lost object" ("Introduction—I" 25).

desiring fantasy, unsupported by any perceptual memory; she knows that it is not a penis, and she does not want it to be a penis. And now compare them with the following statement:

> For me, the erotic essence of the butch-femme relationship was the external difference of women's textures and the bond of knowledgeable caring. I loved my lover for how she stood as well as for what she did. Dress was a part of it: the erotic signal of her hair at the nape of her neck, touching the shirt collar; how she held a cigarette; the symbolic pinky ring flashing as she waved her hand. I know this sounds superficial, but all these gestures were a style of self-presentation that made erotic competence a political statement in the 1950s. . . . Deeper than the sexual positioning was the overwhelming love I felt for [her] courage, the bravery of [her] erotic independence. (Nestle, *A Restricted Country* 104–105)

In other words, what the lesbian desires in a woman ("the penis somewhere else") is indeed not a penis but a part or perhaps the whole of the female body, or something metonymically related to it, such as physical, intellectual, or emotional attributes, stance, attitude, appearance, self-presentation—and hence the importance of clothing, costume, performance, etc. in lesbian subcultures. She knows full well she is not a man, she does not have the paternal phallus (nor would her lover want it), but that does not preclude the signification of her desire: the fetish is at once what signifies her desire and what her lover desires in her. It is both an imaginary or fantasmatic "object," a cathected signifier, whose erotic meaning derives from its placement in a subjective fantasy scenario; and a symbolic object, whose meaning derives from a sociohistorical context of cultural *and* subcultural discourses and representations. In short, then, the lesbian fetish is any object, any sign whatsoever, that marks the difference and the desire between the lovers: say, "the erotic signal of her hair at the nape of her neck, touching the shirt collar" or, as Joan Nestle also suggests, "big-hipped, wide-assed women's bodies" ("The Fem Question" 236).[14] It could be the

---

14. A sign, of course, has to be socially coded in order to be one. So when I say any sign whatsoever, I mean any sign that is so constituted in a particular cultural or subcultural context, a particular set of social discourses, representations, and practices. Nestle's "signs," for example, are clearly embedded historically in the United States urban and working-class lesbian subculture of the 1950s that she describes. See also Davis and Kennedy's summary of the Buffalo Oral History Project, Lorde's

masquerade of masculinity and femininity of the North American butch-femme lesbian subculture, or what Newton calls the "male body drag" of Stephen Gordon in *The Well of Loneliness*, but it can also be, as I will argue shortly, the image of a white flower.

The Signification of the Fetish

The object and the signifier of desire are not anatomical entities, as are the genitals, the vagina and the penis, with which they are usually associated in a simplistic notion of (hetero)sexuality. They are fantasmatic entities, objects or signs that have somehow become "attached to a desiring fantasy" and for that very reason may be "inappropriate" to signify those anatomical entities (or "inappropriate for sexual purposes," as Freud says of the fetish) and precarious—not fixed or the same for every subject, and even unstable in one subject.[15] But if there is no privileged, founding object of desire, if "the sexual instinct is in the first instance independent of its object" (*SE* 7: 148), or if "the objects of our desires are always substitutes for the objects of our desires" (Bersani and Dutoit 66), nevertheless desire itself, with its movement between subject and object, between the self and an other, is founded on difference—the difference and separateness of one from the other. And what signifies desire is a sign which both elides and remarks that separation in describing *both the object and its absence*. This sign, I am arguing, is a fetish.

Because the term *object* may be equivocal, let me clarify the sense in which I am using it here. The phrase I emphasized just

---

account of New York Village gay subculture in *Zami,* and Jenny Terry's counterhistory of deviant subjectivity in her analysis of Henry's influential *Sex Variants: A Study of Homosexual Patterns,* which resulted in the medicalization of homosexuality in the 1930s.

15. "What is substituted for the sexual object is some part of the body (such as the foot or hair) which is in general very inappropriate for sexual purposes, or some inanimate object which bears an assignable relation to the person whom it replaces and preferably to that person's sexuality (e.g. a piece of clothing or underlinen). Such substitutes are with some justice likened to the fetishes in which savages believe that their gods are embodied" (*SE* 7: 153). Recalling Freud's predilection for his collection of archaeological statuettes, one must remark once again on the presumption of white "civilized" man; but one may ask, as well, whether the difference between the erotic fetish and the diffuse fetishism of collecting is a qualitative difference or one of degree. I will return to this question in chapter 6.

above comes from the section "Fantasy and the Origins of Sexuality" (discussed in chapter 3) where Laplanche and Pontalis are retracing, through several of his texts, Freud's theoretical model of desire, which they also call "the Freudian fiction (*Fiktion*)"; namely,

> an analytic "construction," or fantasy, which tries to cover the moment of *separation* between *before* and *after*, whilst still containing both: a mythical moment of disjunction between the pacification of need (*Befriedigung*) and the fulfilment of desire (*Wunscherfüllung*), between the two stages represented by real experience and its hallucinatory revival, between the object that satisfies and the sign [*] which describes both the object and its absence: a mythical moment at which hunger and sexuality meet in a common origin. (24–25)

The asterisk I inserted after the word *sign* marks the place where the authors add the following terse footnote: "The breast, wrongly named 'object of desire' by psychoanalysts" (34). With that footnote they want to make even clearer the distinction between the object (the real object, the milk, in the first stage) and the sign (the breast, in the second stage of hallucinatory revival) which describes the now absent or, better, *lost* object (the breast with milk). In the first stage, the child is with the mother; in the second, it is alone. It is in the second stage that fantasy and desire are instantiated together, by separation and in memory, in the child's first wishing after the loss of the object ("The first wishing [*Wünschen*] seems to have been a hallucinatory cathecting of the memory of satisfaction" [Freud, *SE* 4–5: 598, quoted by Laplanche and Pontalis, "Fantasy and the Origins of Sexuality" 33]).

Thus the term *object*, commonly used in psychoanalytic theory in such expressions as *object-choice, object of the drive*, and so on, designates more properly a sign, or something that functions as a sign, a signifier, even when it in fact refers to a person or a physical object, as may be the case with the fetish; in other words, the object always functions in desire as a sign, since it stands in for a lost object. I also use *object* in this sense, consistently with psychoanalytic usage, to indicate its general or structural function in the process of desire, as distinct from its contingent particularity in an individual psychic configuration. But in saying that the fetish is a sign that signifies the desire for an originally lost object, I must specify that the object of perverse desire—the wished-for object whose absence is represented in the fetish—stands for something that never existed in perception, or for which there is no perceptual memory; and in this sense it is an originally lost object. That is to say, the lost object of perverse desire is not necessarily the lost object par excellence, the breast with milk or the mother's womb, for which there may be a perceptual memory, but *an entirely fantasmatic object,* as is the maternal penis in Freud's definition of fetishism. In lesbian perverse desire, however, the fantasmatic object is the female body itself, whose original loss in a female subject corresponds, as I shall argue, to the narcissistic wound that the loss of the penis represents for the male subject.

If the term *castration* designates the paternal (patriarchal) prohibition of access to the mother's and/or female body, with its fantasy of unity and plenitude, and if the term *phallus* designates the sign that signifies the subject's desire to recapture that plenitude through (hetero)sexual union, then that notion of castration and *some* notion of phallus—some notion of signifier of desire—are necessary to understand the processes and forms of subjectivity. However, while psychoanalysis insists that the signifier of desire is *the paternal phallus* alone, presuming that sexuality is normatively heterosexual and reproductive, Bersani and Dutoit say it is *a fantasy-phallus,* "an inappropriate object precariously attached to a desiring fantasy, unsupported by any perceptual memory" (69). By a different route and for purposes different from, though not antithetical to, mine, Judith Butler proposes the deconstructive trope "the lesbian Phallus."[16] I prefer to call the signifier of perverse desire *a fetish* in order to avoid the unavoidable semantic complicity of phallus with penis, even at the risk of evoking the negative (reductive) connotations that the term *fetish* also currently carries. The reason why some such term is necessary to a theory of lesbian sexuality is not just that the texts which reinscribe the original fantasies give both castration and the

---

16. Through a deconstructive reading of Freud's and Lacan's naturalization of the phallus as pertaining to the morphology of the male bodily ego, Butler's project is to displace the hegemonic, heterosexist concept of sexual difference and to promote an alternative erotic imaginary. She argues that the phallus as signifier of desire is an idealization, and thus a transferable or expropriable property: "The displaceability of the Phallus, its capacity to symbolize in relation to other body parts or other body-like things, opens the way for the lesbian Phallus, an otherwise contradictory formulation" ("The Lesbian Phallus and the Morphological Imaginary" 158).

signification of desire a pivotal place in lesbian subjectivity, as I have tried to show. It is also that what I am calling a fetish, in contradistinction to the paternal penis-phallus, serves as the sign or signifier of prohibition, difference and desire, without which the lesbian lovers would be simply, so to speak, two women in the same bed.

This may be the right place to answer a question put to me by Paula Bennett in hearing a lecture version of this chapter back in 1990: Why not say that the clitoris, instead of the penis-phallus or any symbol thereof, is the signifier of female desire? Since then, Bennett has articulated her question in a well-argued essay by the menacing title of "Critical Clitoridectomy: Female Sexual Imagery and Feminist Psychoanalytic Theory." As the title indicates, her critique is addressed to feminist and especially lesbian critics who are, like me, "contaminated" by the Freudian and Lacanian theoretical frameworks. Because I take her charge to be very serious, as well as representative of the suspicion that other lesbian readers have expressed of preliminary versions of my argument in this chapter (see de Lauretis, "Perverse Desire: The Lure of the Mannish Lesbian"), I must consider Bennett's article with attention.

By a compelling reading of nineteenth-century American poets such as Emily Dickinson, Amy Lowell, Lydia Huntley Sigourney, and Harriet Prescott Spofford, Bennett makes a very convincing case for their "clitorocentric" self-representation of female sexuality and autoeroticism. While vaginal and uterine symbology is widely used in Western literature and art to suggest female sexual power, Bennett argues, a primarily clitoral symbolism was employed by women poets to evolve a "separate but equal" female erotic discourse at a time in which white middle-class women were confined to the separate sphere of domesticity and motherhood.

> Profoundly influenced by a cultural ideology that gendered nature's transient beauties as female, they used the popular erotic symbolism of their day—flowers and, above all, buds—as "natural" symbols for the difference they sought to inscribe. In the sexual symbology that developed from this set of identification, difference between men and women still produced meaning; where women were concerned, however, the clitoris (not the penis-which-they-lacked) was the primary signifier. The clitoris was that which was

present, and it was men who were erased or conceptualized as
other, whether as "herald Spring" or "dark March." (247)

Bennett carefully documents how the sexual subtext of the so-
called Language of Flowers, which by a long Western tradition associated women with flowers, was readily "familiar to bourgeois men,
women, and children" (242) at the time; Dickinson and other
women poets exploited it as a semiprivate code through which clitoral images—"buds, berries, seeds, and small compact flowers such
as snowdrops and crocuses" (243)—could express "the utter self-
containment, the complete autonomy, of clitorally based female sexuality" (246). The prevalent sexual subtext of the poems Bennett
analyzes is masturbation: men are casual allusions, babies are altogether absent, and the poetic meaning conveyed is "the power of
inwardly felt and directed desire" (248). (One of the poems, Lowell's,
refers to two women; I will return to it shortly.) While it is not surprising that most of these poems never made it into the canon, or
did so in literally excised, neutered form (e.g., Dickinson's edited by
Thomas Johnson [239]), and were generally belittled by male critics
as sentimental and imitative, Bennett remarks, yet they clearly show
that the clitoris "can supply an alternative and autonomous site for
definition of female pleasure and desire," and why then has feminist
psychoanalytic theory been so reluctant to discuss it? "No feminist
psychoanalytic theorist with whom I am familiar has taken the clitoris's symbolic potential seriously, let alone attempted to theorize its
relation to desire" (248). Bennett believes that such silence, which
"neither female sexual symbolism nor the female sexual response in
themselves supports," is merely in deference to or in compliance
with the psychoanalytic fathers.

Her argument, I think, is both right and wrong. It is right in that
the poems' sexual symbolism and female sexual response are, as she
says, clitoral, and insofar as the clitoris is indeed an autonomous
site of sexual *pleasure*. It is not right in implying an equivalence between orgasmic pleasure and desire, and in proposing the clitoris as
the theoretical and physical term of female *desire*. As I have indicated on several occasions throughout this book, I believe that desire is never "utterly self-contained" or "autonomous" as sexual
pleasure and masturbation can be. Even as it is perceived as a quality of the self, the support of one's being, and although it can exist

only through fantasy, desire is a tension toward the other(s), a drive toward something or someone outside the self. The signification and representation of that tension necessitates a signifier, "the sign which describes both the object and its absence" (in Laplanche and Pontalis's words); it is this sign that signifies, for the subject, the object's existential otherness, difference, and distance from the self. Or so it seems to me, not in deference to psychoanalytic theory but by the long-meditated intellectual conviction that Freud's theory of desire, for the most part and as I now understand it, does account for my experience.

Of course, since I maintain that the signifier of desire is contextual to a particular fantasy scenario and contingent upon each singular sociohistorical subjectivity (and therefore call it a fetish), I see no reason why the clitoris could not, in a particular fantasy or in a certain representation, signify female or lesbian desire; I will be suggesting in a moment that this is exactly what it does in the Lowell poem. But to theorize the clitoris, as such, as the primary or unique signifier of female desire is to make the clitoris (merely) the equal of the penis in the psychoanalytic imaginary that we all find so inadequate. Both the clitoris and the penis being anatomical entities, their capacity to signify desire depends on their representation; thus, to the extent that the clitoris is imaged erect, a bud, a little seed, a spear, hooded, sheathed, pulsing, thrusting upward, and so forth, as it is in the poems cited by Bennett (248), the clitoris is indeed "the real little penis of the woman," as Freud described it, offending so many women. (On the other hand, if one shares, as I do, Dickinson's feeling that small is beautiful and Bennett's comment that "the little could also be great" [236], then Freud's description might not be so offensive.) Bennett herself suggests the equivalence of penis and clitoris when, citing Laqueur, she writes that Freud's theory of the vaginal orgasm "in effect, 'castrates' women" (249).

But is a clitoris/penis really what one needs to signify female or lesbian desire? In arguing against the psychoanalytic homologation of the latter to male heterosexual desire (the so-called masculinity complex), I have attempted to show that neither the penis nor its symbolic inscription in the paternal phallus is *the* signifier of lesbian desire, and instead suggested *fetish* as a more useful general term to signify the working of a non-phallic, non-heterosexual, or perverse desire. Insofar as the clitoris functions in representation like a penis (that is, with the same attributes and function in sexual arousal and pleasure, if without the symbolic valence of the paternal phallus), it too cannot assume the role of privileged or absolute signifier of lesbian desire, although it can assume that role in a given representation. For example, in the Amy Lowell poem cited by Bennett:

> I put your leaves aside,
> One by one:
> The stiff, broad outer leaves;
> The smaller ones,
> Pleasant to touch, veined with purple;
> The glazed inner leaves,
> One by one
> I parted you from your leaves,
> Until you stood up like a white flower
> Swaying slightly in the evening wind.
>   ("The Weather-Cock Points South" [1919] 211)

The white flower with its purple-veined outer leaves and its glazed inner leaves, symbolizing the female sex, is the object and the sign of the poet's desire. If we imagine two people in the scene (that is, if the "you" is not only a clitoris but also, metonymically, the woman in whose body the clitoris stands up *like* a white flower), then the difference, distance, and separateness of the poet—identified as a woman by her signature—from the other woman is marked by their respective positions of subject and object of desire.[17] Then, even as it stands for an anatomical entity, the "you" refers beyond that to the subject's desire for the female body in another woman (here, in the other woman who is her lover). And in this sense the

---

17. In the lines quoted by Bennett, it is also possible to read the "you" as the poet's own clitoris, which would make the sexual subtext of this poem (masturbation) the same as the other poems'. But this reading is weaker, less satisfying to me as well as, apparently, to Bennett, who does not consider it at all. The pleasure of masturbation may be associated through fantasy with the most diverse objects and scenarios of desire, and it is the latter that signify or represent the subject's desire (cf. my reading of the masturbation scenes in *The Well of Loneliness* and *Giving Up the Ghost*). I may be guilty of literalism, but it seems to me that only when sexual pleasure is fantasmatically linked, for the subject, to another woman or another female body—whether in actual physical proximity, in memory, or in fantasy—can we speak of lesbian desire. This is the sense of my assertion that it takes two women, not one, to make a lesbian: however similar, the bodies are two, not one and the same. Their difference is what enables desire.

flower in Lowell's poem, or the clitoris it symbolizes, is what I would call a lesbian fetish. For, while each of the two women in the poem (presumably) has a clitoris, yet only one clitoris has the function of object and signifier of desire in this erotic scene, which the past tense ("I *parted* you from your leaves") represents as a memory—and thus endows with the dimension of fantasy. It is in acknowledging the absence or loss of that other female body that the subject's desire is (re)constituted through language and inscribed in the poem. (Similarly, it was the sense of a fantasmatic rememoration of lost female bodies—the minds, works, or names remain—emerging from the project of Judy Chicago's *The Dinner Party* that, for me, conferred a strong erotic fascination to the installation itself.)

In Lowell's flower, lesbian desire is expressed and representable. In another, more famous flower image, "the match burning in a crocus" of Virginia Woolf's *Mrs. Dalloway*, as Judith Roof has observed, it is not. I concur with Roof, though my reading and reasons are not hers. Bennett, on the other hand, while commending Roof's "moving and eloquent tribute to lesbian sexuality," reproaches her for providing only a glimpse of the "hidden but radiant other-than-phallus" (Roof, "The Match in the Crocus" 114) by which lesbian desire is dimly alluded to in Woolf's novel but not expressed, not represented. "By refusing to name the clitoris," Bennett concludes, Roof's effort to critique phallocentric representation ends up reconfirming "the phallus's dominance as signifier of difference" ("Critical Clitoridectomy" 251). What Roof sees in the burning crocus image is Woolf's attempt to represent "lesbian sexuality in other-than-phallic terms" (114). Her reading is thus germane to my own thesis and calls for another brief digression.

The passage in question is part of Clarissa Dalloway's interior monologue in her attic bedroom where her husband "insisted, after her illness, that she must sleep undisturbed. And really she preferred to read [Baron Marbot's *Memoirs*] of the retreat from Moscow. He knew it" (46). By her narrow, virginal bed, Clarissa reminisces about her girlhood and then about the moment when, she realizes, she had failed her husband.

> She could see what she lacked. It was not beauty; it was not mind.
> It was something central which permeated; something warm
> which broke up surfaces and rippled the cold contact of man and

woman, or of women together. For *that* she could dimly perceive.
She resented it, had a scruple picked up Heaven knows where, or,
as she felt, sent by Nature (who is invariably wise); yet she could
not resist sometimes yielding to the charm of a woman, not a girl,
of a woman confessing, as to her they often did, some scrape,
some folly. And whether it was pity, or their beauty, or that she was
older, or some accident—like a faint scent, or a violin next door (so
strange is the power of sounds at certain moments), she did
undoubtedly then feel what men felt. Only for a moment; but it
was enough. It was a sudden revelation . . . an illumination; a
match burning in a crocus; an inner meaning almost expressed.
But the close withdrew; the hard softened. It was over—the
moment. (*Mrs. Dalloway* 46–47)

The inner meaning is *almost* but not quite expressed. Whether by
scruple or by nature, Clarissa lacks the "something central" that es-
tablishes a warm contact between the self and another, man or
woman. She lacks desire: "there was an emptiness about the heart of
life; an attic room" (45); "a virginity preserved through childbirth
which clung to her like a sheet" (46). But in those brief moments
when she did yield "to the charm of a woman," then she did feel,
Woolf can only say, "what men felt" toward women. The objective
correlative Woolf gives for that feeling is "a match burning in a
crocus."

Roof reads this image as a double phallic symbol (while Bennett
reads it as a clitoral symbol) because of its shape, and interprets it to
be one solution offered by Woolf to the problem of representing lesbian sexuality—to represent it "as an assumption of the phallus," a
"double masquerade" (102).[18] The other solution, contained in the
phrase immediately following ("an inner meaning almost
expressed"), would be

the paradoxical representation of both women and lesbian
sexuality as unrepresentable. Enfolded as a present yet hidden and
invisible third term in the phallic register of representation, this
solution, modeled after female genitalia seen other than as lack, re-

18. As I am writing this, in the city of Amsterdam and during the week of late-
winter school recess that the Dutch call *krokus vakantie* (crocus vacation), I must
confess that I actually went for a walk to look at the crocuses, now beginning to
bloom in virtually every available bit of soil. This field research proved to me and my
companion that both Roof's and Bennett's readings of the image are supported by the
shape of the crocus, depending on its stage of bloom.

creates the conditions of its own representational impossibility: it can be there, but it cannot be seen in its own terms since such terms do not exist. ("The Match in the Crocus" 103)

One cannot but agree that Clarissa's inner response to "the charm of a woman" never quite reaches expression, remains only *almost* expressed by the ambiguous objective correlative—which would not be ambiguous if brought forth by a man. But I am not convinced that the "representational impossibility" is to be attributed to Woolf's lack of "other-than-phallic" terms with which to express lesbian desire (adequate terms were found by Amy Lowell and other writers before her, all the way back to Sappho). I think it may be more a question of Clarissa's lack of desire, her "constricted vitality" (Abel 38), than of Woolf's lack of terms. I suggest that what Woolf is brilliantly representing is not the unrepresentability of lesbian sexuality but rather Clarissa's "lacking"—that "emptiness about the heart of life" which makes her run hot and cold toward her husband and Peter Walsh, as well as Sally and the other unnamed women, and makes her prefer to read of the retreat from Moscow.

What strikes me in the passage is how Woolf accounts for the feeling in Clarissa whose meaning must remain inchoate: "whether it was pity, or their beauty, or that she was older, or *some accident— like a faint scent, or a violin next door* (so strange is the power of sounds at certain moments), she did undoubtedly then feel what men felt." These dim sensory perceptions, accidents rather than narrated events, evoke an unremembered fantasy, an unstaged scenario, whose contours and figures the sudden, fleeting illumination is insufficient to define. These almost-fetishes, almost-signifiers of another scene, also suggest the "lacking" in Clarissa, her difficulty in making contact with her phantasms, with sexuality, with the lost object(s) of desire. A similar observation is made by Elizabeth Abel in relation to the figure of Sylvia, a "seemingly gratuitous" character and "an exaggerated echo of Clarissa's own split experience." Her brief mention in the novel, Abel writes, has the effect of "a story intentionally withheld . . . written both into and out of the text" (*Virgina Woolf and the Fictions of Psychoanalysis* 33). This seems to me an apt description of the way in which Woolf represents, or rather *almost* represents, Clarissa's feeling toward women—less an oscillation than a "vacillation" (Abel 43) between two equally shadowy forms of sexuality, heterosexuality and homosexuality.[19] Which, in turn, may have prompted in Roof the strange equation of "women and lesbian sexuality" under the same representational paradox.

The Scar and the Wound, Fetishism and Narcissism

Returning, at long last, to the two texts this chapter started from, it may now be possible to see the fantasy of bodily dispossession they inscribe as related to a somewhat different notion of castration. Let me recall for you the passage in *The Well of Loneliness* where, in describing Stephen's purchase of clothes intended to impress Angela—and they are, as we know, masculine-cut or mannish clothes— the narrator tells us: "Nor could she resist the lure of pyjamas made of crêpe de Chine [which] led to a man's dressing-gown of brocade— an amazingly ornate garment" (186). Now, we can be almost sure that Angela would never see those pyjamas and dressing gown. And yet Stephen *could not resist* their *lure*. Then, in the immediately following scene at the mirror, she hates her *naked* body and wants to "maim" it (to inscribe it with the mark of castration) precisely because it is masculine, "ardent and sterile," "so strong and so self-sufficient"—so phallic—whereas the body she desires, wants to make love to, and mourns for is a feminine, female body. In other words, just as she hates her masculine body naked, so does she respond to the lure of masculine clothes; and we may remember, as well, the intensity with which both Stephen Gordon and her author Radclyffe Hall yearned to cut their hair quite short, against all the contemporary appearance codes.

This paradox, I noted, contradicts or at least complicates the traditional reading of Stephen's "masculinity complex," a reading that the novel as a whole and its author's well-known ideological convictions certainly sustain. What the paradox suggests to me is that masculine clothes, short hair, the insistence on riding astride, and all the

---

19. In her psychological reading of the novel, Abel suggests that Clarissa's "constricted vitality" is due to a "developmental impasse," an unachieved passage from the pre-Oedipal domain of female bonds and her adolescent love for Sally Seton to the Oedipal attachment to men demanded by adult life. Thus "*Mrs. Dalloway* outlines the [female's] developmental sequence Freud was plotting simultaneously" (36); but by the end of the day Clarissa has succeeded in letting go of the hold of the past "to embrace the imperfect pleasures of adulthood" (40).

other accoutrements and signs of masculinity, up to the war scar on her face, are not a phallic pretension but rather a fetish. It is this fetish—analogous in function to the phallus in Lacan's model but emphatically not a substitute for it—that signifies Stephen's desire for the (lost) female body.

Consider, if you will, this scene at the mirror as the textual re-enactment of the Lacanian mirror stage. A pivotal moment in the constitution of the human subject, the mirror stage coincides with the formation of primary narcissism and is exemplified in the ex-perience of the six- to eighteen-month-old child upon first seeing its reflection in a mirror and recognizing its body as a whole in relation to surrounding objects and persons. The child's "jubilant assumption of his specular image," writes Lacan, is *"an identifica-tion*, in the full sense that analysis gives to the term: namely, the transformation that takes place in the subject when he assumes an image [*imago*]" (*Ecrits* 2). Because this identification far exceeds the child's still-limited motor and sensory capacities, the primor-dial form of the ego it produces is a fictional or imaginary one; a *mis*recognition of its body-ego in an image that is superior to and in discordance with the reality of social determinations, as the child will soon apprehend them in the symbolic order. The mirror stage thus constitutes the fictional matrix or first outline of the ego, as well as "an essential libidinal relationship with the body-image" ("Some Reflections on the Ego" 1). As Laplanche and Pontalis summarize it,

> The establishment of the ego can be conceived of as the formation of a psychical unit paralleling the constitution of the bodily schema. One may further suppose that this unification is precipitated by the subject's acquisition of an image of himself founded on the model furnished by the other person—this image being the ego itself. Narcissism then appears as the amorous captivation of the subject by this image. Jacques Lacan has related this first moment in the ego's formation to that fundamentally narcissistic experience which he calls the *mirror stage*. ("Narcissism," *The Language of Psycho-Analysis* 256)

What Stephen sees in the mirror (the image that establishes the ego) is the image of a phallic body, which the narrator has taken pains to tell us was so from a very young age, a body Stephen's mother found "repulsive."[20] Thus, since "the other person" who serves as model of bodily desirability is Stephen's mother, the image of herself that Stephen sees in the mirror does not accomplish "the amorous captivation of the subject" or offer her a "fundamentally narcissistic experience," but on the contrary inflicts a narcissistic wound: that phallic body-image, and thus the ego, cannot be loved, cannot be narcissistically invested *because* it is *phallic*. In respect of psychoanalytic theory, this is another paradox, for the relation of narcissism to the castration complex is predicated on the valued presence of the phallus in the subject's body-image:

> A second theoretical characteristic of the castration complex is its impact upon narcissism: the phallus is an essential component of the child's self-image, so any threat to the phallus is a radical danger to this image; this explains the efficacity of the threat, which derives from the conjunction of two factors, namely, the primacy of the phallus and the narcissistic wound. ("Castration Complex," *The Language of Psycho-Analysis* 57)

However, the scene at the mirror in *The Well of Loneliness* suggests that the phallus—as representative of the penis—is not an essential component of the female subject's body-image; what is essential is what the mother desires, and Stephen's narcissistic wound consists in not having a body such as the mother desires it. Psychoanalysis theorizes that the child's wish to be the object of the mother's desire is a wish to be the phallus, as the latter is assumed to be the mother's only object of desire. But in this case the relation of castration to the narcissistic wound in the daughter appears to be based on another maternal fantasy, namely, the mother's narcissistic wish for a feminine body (in the daughter as in herself).

---

20. As Newton remarks in her reading of the novel, the mother's rejection and fear of Stephen's body is strongly remarked by the narrator: during her childhood, the mother's "eyes would look cold, though her voice might be gentle, and her hand when it fondled would be tentative, unwilling. The hand would be making an effort, and Stephen would be conscious of that effort" (*The Well of Loneliness* 15). As an adolescent, "Stephen was suddenly outspoken: 'It's my face,' she announced, 'something's wrong with my face.' 'Nonsense!' exclaimed Anna, and her cheeks flushed a little . . . then she turned away quickly to hide her expression" (73). Or again, as Stephen sleeps, "Anna would stare at that splendid young body, and would feel, as she did so, that she looked on a stranger. . . . [Then she] would stoop and kiss Stephen, but lightly and very quickly on the forehead, so that the girl should not be awakened. So that the girl should not wake and kiss back" (82–83).

In sum, the fantasy of castration in this text is explicitly associated with a failure of narcissism as the lack not of the phallus as such, but of a (female) body the mother can love. Failing the mother's narcissistic validation of the daughter's body-image, castration means the lack or loss of the female body; that is to say, the castration complex rewrites in the symbolic a narcissistic wound, a lack of being (Lacan's *manque-à-être*), already established in the imaginary matrix of the body-ego; it rewrites it in terms of anatomical ("natural") sexual difference, refiguring as lack of a penis what was first and foremost lack of a lovable body. Then, the defense of disavowal, the splitting of the ego, and the ambiguous negation of the real (I don't have it, but I do/can have it) do not derive from the lack or loss of a penis but rather from the earlier lack and its consequent damage to the subject's libidinal relationship with her body-image.[21] What is formed in the process of disavowal, for this female subject, is not a phallic symbol, a penis substitute (indeed Stephen hates her phallic body), but something of the nature of a fetish—something that would cover over or disguise the narcissistic wound (the loss of the female body), and yet leave a scar, a trace of its enduring threat.

Thus Stephen's fetish, the signifier of her desire, is the sign of both an absence and a presence, as the denied and wished-for female body is both displaced and re-presented in the visible signifiers and accoutrements of masculinity: the desire for the female body is displaced onto the fetish (the masculine clothes whose lure Stephen cannot resist) and at the same time resignified by it through the

---

21. The question of temporality may of course be raised here. If the psychoanalytic model is understood in developmental terms as a chronological succession of stages, the mirror stage precedes the Oedipal stage and the castration complex, whereas my argument collapses them together. But insofar as both the mirror stage and the castration complex are fantasmatic instances, they are governed by the psychic structure of retroactivity (*Nachträglichkeit*) and partake of the atemporality or endless repeatability of fantasy's "mythical moment." In this sense my argument is not inconsistent with Laplanche's definition of sexuality as "*a movement which deflects the instinct, metaphorizes its aim, displaces and internalizes its object, and concentrates its source on what is ultimately a minimal zone, the erotogenic zone. . . . These zones focalize parental fantasies* and above all *maternal fantasies*" (*Life and Death in Psychoanalysis* 23–24). And although I do not wish to consider or rely on object-relations theory, I will note Phyllis Greenacre's argument that, in spite of marked similarities, an infantile fetish and Winnicott's transitional object ultimately differ in that the former issues from a "faulty development of the body image" caused by severe disturbances in the mother-child relationship.

most strongly coded of cultural conventions, gender. For, while other objects/signs of lesbian desire certainly exist, as I hope this book begins to demonstrate, by far the most common in modern Western cultures, heavily dichotomized by gender and anatomical-body differences, is some form of what is coded as masculinity. The reason seems too obvious to belabor: not only is masculinity associated with sexual activity and desire, imaged in the erect penis and its symbolic or ritual representation in the phallus; but, more to my immediate point, in a cultural tradition pervasively homophobic, masculinity alone carries a strong connotation of sexual desire for the female body. *That* is the lure of the mannish lesbian—a lure for her and for her lover. The fetish of masculinity is what both lures and signifies her desire for the female body, and what in her lures her lover, what her lover desires in her *and with her.* Unlike the masculinity complex, the lesbian masculinity fetish does not refuse castration but disavows it; the threat it holds at bay is not the loss of the penis in women but the loss of the female body itself, and the prohibition of access to it.

In this respect the mobility of desire auspicated by Bersani and Dutoit seems rather less free than they hypothesize. In their model, "desire is 'cut off' from its object [the phallic mother] and travels to other objects. Thus the very terror of castration can initiate us into those psychic severances which guarantee the diversification of desire" (69). On the basis of this and other lesbian texts, it seems to me that, if indeed any number of fetish objects, images, or signs can lure and signify lesbian desire, the (lost) object which they displace and resignify in many different ways is always the female body itself. Thus perverse desire is indeed "cut off" from its original object (the breast with milk, the mother's body) and moves on to other images/objects/signs, but the latter do refer metonymically to one and the same instance, the female body itself, whose loss in the mother could mean, to the female subject, a loss of her body-ego. The fantasy of castration reinscribes this loss in the paternal law that prohibits her access not only to the mother but to the female body in herself and in other women. In the male subject of perverse desire, the fantasy of castration and the psychic process of disavowal would obviously have different effects.

To Marisa, in *Giving Up the Ghost,* the female body is equally denied, if in a different way. It has been vilified, made into a hole, into a body *for* the master, and so literally dispossessed of its capacity for pleasure, its autoerotic and narcissistic drives. In this text as well, the fantasy of castration is associated with a failure of narcissism, although the latter is not induced by "nature" or "God's mistake" but by a patriarchal culture in which white racism compounds the effects of sexism in Chicana life. Here, the failure of narcissism also derives from the lack or loss of a lovable female body, not only in the subject but also in the mother, for she is also dispossessed and vilified as merely a body. Corky's masculine identification is obviously a denial of that dispossession, which the mother's preference for the son all but reconfirms to the daughter perhaps as effectively as any cultural image can. Her rape further confirms that dispossession and deepens the denial, forcing her dissociation from her female body, which is then fantasmatically projected onto an unattainable maternal figure (as Amalia is to Marisa). But if at the play's opening it is Marisa's symptoms that "speak" the castration, the dispossession and symbolic disempowerment, which she has "forgotten" and therefore cannot speak, as soon as the performance begins, Corky and the other ghosts appear—and they do speak it out: they embody those repressed events and fantasies whose memory surfaces in Marisa, on stage, in the manner of an anamnesis. By the end of the play, her healing has begun, and so has her writing, a writing of which the play itself is a result ("It's like making familia from scratch . . . my daydream with pencil in my mouth"). Thus the ending of the play circles back to its beginning when, just before the ghosts come to visit her, Marisa's voice offstage tells the audience: "I'm only telling you this to stay my hand" (3). Which makes the entire play a daydream, and the performance a staging of Marisa's fantasies.

The possible meanings of this obscure pronouncement cannot be grasped until after the play is over. *To stay* means "to brace, support or prop up   2. To strengthen or sustain mentally or spiritually; to comfort   3. To rest or fix on for support" (*The American Heritage Dictionary of the English Language*). *Telling you this* must refer to the play itself, to what Marisa tells the audience sitting in the theater, but also, and more likely, "THE PEOPLE" who appear in the list of characters as "Those viewing THE PERFORMANCE," although they never speak or actually appear on stage. *I'm only telling you this to stay my hand,* then, may mean that telling THE PEOPLE (and incidentally the audience) will strengthen, sustain, or support her writer's hand, comfort her as she writes about her pain. However, if we relay these words to the last words of the play, with which Marisa describes herself daydreaming and writing ("I am preparing myself for the worst, / so I cling to her in my heart, / my daydream with pencil in my mouth, / when I put my fingers / to my own / forgotten places"), then *to stay my hand* acquires an openly sexual meaning: the telling of her experience, pain, loss, and desire will serve to brace, prop up, or sustain her own self-loving and healing. In sharing them with THE PEOPLE, she can love herself: *I'm only telling you this to stay my hand.*[22]

It seems to me, therefore, that the staging of Marisa's fantasy of castration functions as a performative reenactment of the mirror stage, in which the audience within the play, the Chicana people to whom Marisa and Corky tell their stories, silently act as the "other person" in the mirror. I take this to be the significance of "THE PEOPLE," a character so designated but who never speaks: it is the Other on whose image the subject's ego is (re)modeled. The image they send back to Marisa, the image which constitutes the fictional matrix of the ego, is that of an empowered female Other, at once imaginary *and* symbolic in that the Chicana feminist, politically conscious, rewriting of history and myth, is the discursive production of an emerging social subject, and hence a production of symbolic as well. By assuming or identifying with this image, Marisa establishes a new libidinal relationship with her body-image and, by the end of the play, begins to write.

With the rewriting of herself in relation to an empowered and empowering female Other, and the "fundamentally narcissistic experience" it provides, the healing process begins for Marisa.[23] The performance enacts her simultaneous recrossing of the "stages" of psychic development toward subjectivity and subjecthood ("making

---

22. I will only note, as an interesting coincidence, Newton's comment on a detail in *The Well of Loneliness*, when seven-year-old Stephen is reproached by the maid Collins for having dirty fingernails and runs to scrub them. "After this episode, thinking of Collins makes Stephen 'go hot down her spine,'" Newton remarks: "The invert's hand is a sexual instrument, but it's polluted" ("The Mythic Mannish Lesbian" 572).

23. Whereas Stephen Gordon's "bitter need" could not accede to symbolization in the discourse of her Other, the Catholic God, and thus remains to the end of the novel an *"unspeakable"* outrage," Marisa's can be expressed, and her wound partially healed, through the discourse of an Other, the Chicana PEOPLE, whose imaginary and symbolic order are unavailable to Stephen.

familia from scratch / each time all over again"), from primary
narcissism and autoeroticism to the disavowal of castration and a
new body-ego. Castration is no longer denied, since the fantasy has
been represented and become conscious, but neither is it accepted
or acquiesced to; instead, it is disavowed by the formation of a
fetish, self-writing and a publicly affirmed and valorized self-image,
which both sustains and signifies her perverse desire ("I cling to her
in my heart, / my daydream with pencil in my mouth, / when I put
my fingers / to my own / forgotten places"). Through it, Marisa's
healing can be transferred to her lover and, beyond her, back to the
fantasized mother Amalia represents: "and just as I pressed my
mouth to her, I'd think . . . / *I could save your life*" (57). In a
sociocultural context where sexuality and fantasy are not confined
or privatized in the separate sphere of the Victorian middle-class
household, but more publicly expressed and imbricated with other
issues at stake in the community, Marisa's fetish, the signifier of her
desire, is her activist-writer self-image, the openly transgressive,
politicized image of the Chicana butch as lover and healer of the
women of her race.

I suggested earlier that an important point of reference for Chicana subjectivity in Moraga's writing is the figure of Malinche.
Though cursed as a traitor of the race, vilified as the conqueror's
whore, and reduced to a hole (like Corky), a body for the white master, Malinche can nevertheless be reclaimed in a Chicana feminist
rewriting of history and mythology as the mother of a new mestiza
race. I now suggest that Marisa's self-image is both fashioned on this
powerful cultural icon and a recasting of it. In her "cyborg manifesto," Donna Haraway also sees a connection, a symbolic lineage,
between the figure of Malinche and Moraga's authorial figure, as the
latter's use of English and Spanish in her writing replicates the former's use of Spanish, in addition to her native Aztec language, as
Cortés's translator, mistress, and advisor. Their symbolic lineage is
based on their transgressive use of language in violation of patriarchal law.

> Moraga's writing, her superb literacy, is presented in her poetry as
> the same kind of violation as Malinche's mastery of the conquerer's
> language—a violation, an illegitimate production, that allows
> survival. Moraga's language is not "whole"; it is self-consciously

spliced, a chimera of English and Spanish, both conqueror's languages. . . . Malinche was mother here, not Eve before eating the forbidden fruit. ("A Manifesto for Cyborgs" 199)

In Haraway's cyborg myth, Malinche's violation, to which Moraga is heir, leads to the illegitimate production of children and ensures the survival of her racially mixed progeny, the new "bastard race" of cyborgs, "stripped of identity" but endowed with "the power of the margins" (200). Haraway's fantasy of bodies without mothers, of sex without difference, of writing without desire, of subjectivity without memory and loss, makes the postmodern subjects of her myth literally "etched surfaces," indefinitely recombinable, survivors in a world without beginning and without end: "a world without gender," she writes, "is perhaps a world without genesis, but maybe also a world without end" (174–75). Where does Moraga fit in this myth? I ask myself. What manner of survival can her writing, her illegitimate production, ensure in such a world? Are the two forms of violation and their effects really the same in kind? And how are her passion, her desire for the women of her race, her pain in their rejection—when it does occur, and it does—to be accounted for?

On the one hand, Malinche's transgression of the patriarchal property law, its ownership of women's bodies and speech, does not unsex her; her children are not produced parthenogenically or by biotechnical intervention but in the old-fashioned way, by reproductive sexual coupling, except that she determines when and how, and pays the price (also in the old-fashioned way). On the other hand, the violation of patriarchal law in Moraga's writing is its inscription of her desire for women; her mastery of language does not lead to the production of illegitimate progeny—her illegitimacy is her loving women—but to the production of a language, an imaginary and symbolic order in which the new mestiza, unlike Haraway's cyborg subject, is sexed and indeed female-embodied. If Malinche is mother to her, then, it is not only in the symbolic power of her literacy but also, ironically, as a phallic mother in a perverse origin myth—a mother whose fantasized phallus is not the paternal phallus, with its patriarchal and oppressive power, but rather the sign of an enduring spiritual and erotic mestiza strength.[24]

---

24. "The cyborg has no origin story," Haraway maintains. "An origin story in the 'Western,' humanist sense depends on the myth of original unity, fullness, bliss and

In the "daughter's" (re)writing, in Marisa's self-image as Chicana butch, Malinche does not merely replace the illiterate mother's body but takes it on and empowers it with both language and desire. Defiance and sexual autonomy, pain and self-determination are the attributes of the female body this mother offers her daughter(s) for survival, a survival not only social and political but psychical as well—survival as a desiring subject in spite of the paternal phallus. The illegitimacy of this "Malinche" is her desire for a denied and wished-for female body, her loving and warring with it, and representing it empowered by perverse desire. I would argue, further, that it is this empowered signification of the body in Moraga's writing, rather than her mastery of the conquerors' languages, that lures and seduces her wide, heterogeneous feminist audience as much as, if not more than, political affinity. In disavowing castration, the social and psychic reality of her bodily dispossession, this lesbian subject transgresses the boundaries of gender and sexual embodiment without giving up her claim in the female body that is the object and the sign of her perverse desire, the very ground of subjectivity and of any relations she may form with others—and thus of their, as well as her own, possibility of survival.[25]

> It makes you feel so good,
> like your hands are weapons of war
> and as they move up into el corazón de esta mujer
> you are making her body remember
> it didn't hafta be that hurt, ¿me entiendes?
> It was not natural or right
> that she got beat down so damn hard.
> (*Giving Up the Ghost* 57–58)

Without this emphasis on the signification of the body as fantasmatic and symbolic production, on sexuality as the reciprocal heal-

terror, represented by the phallic mother from whom all humans must separate, the task of individual development and of history, the twin potent myths inscribed most powerfully for us in psychoanalysis and Marxism. . . . The cyborg skips the step of original unity" (175). This means, of course, that the cyborg does not have the dimension of fantasy and hence, in the terms of my argument, has no sexuality. For this reason, I believe, the notion of "cyborg writing" ill suits Moraga's writing, and *Giving Up the Ghost* least of all.

25. In this sense, the public staging of Marisa's fantasy of castration can be seen as an analogue of the scene of mutual seduction that constitutes the transferential contract in psychoanalysis (discussed in chapter 4), empowering the audience as Other and, by identification with Marisa, as subject of desire.

ing of wounds even as it is a weapon of war, Moraga's writing would lose its specificity as an inscription of lesbian subjectivity and desire; it would thus lose, I believe, much of its transgressive, seductive, and political force.

The Third Woman

In the two texts I have been considering, different and discontinuous as they are in their conditions of production and forms of address, the lesbian body is inscribed in a fantasy of dispossession which, I have argued, is an original fantasy of castration. Both fantasies speak a failure of narcissism: I cannot love myself, says the subject of the fantasy, because the (M)Other does not love me (the Victorian mother was repulsed by her daughter's body, the Chicana mother preferred her son). I want another to love me, and to love me sexually (the genital emphasis is remarked in both texts: by the masturbation scene barely disguised in the first and more explicit in the play, as well as Corky's seduction by Norma). This lover must be a woman—and not a faulty woman, dispossessed of her body (like me), but a woman embodied and self-possessed as a woman, as I would want to be and can become only with her love. In this regard, consider the Rich poem discussed in chapter 4, where the fantasy of dispossession is most explicitly linked to the subject's loss of the female body in the mother, in herself, and in other women: "Birth stripped our birthright from us, / tore us from a woman, from women, from ourselves" ("Transcendental Etude," *The Dream of a Common Language* 75).

Rich recapitulates the entire fantasy in three lines, telescoping its multiple temporalities and textualities into a dense poetic present, an epiphanic moment in which the subject apprehends at once past, present, and future (like the unconscious, it seems, poetry knows only the present):

> *This is what she was to me, and this*
> *is how I can love myself—*
> *as only a woman can love me.* (76)

The three characters in the poem—*she* [the fantasized mother], *I*, and *a woman*—have been read by critics as two, mother and daughter, with the third character, *a woman*, elided and metaphorized into an attribute (femaleness) common to *she* and *I*, mother and daughter. The difference between the maternal imaginary presupposed by this interpretation and the lesbian maternal imaginary of the poem—an imaginary that subtends the fantasy of dispossession in the other texts as well—is precisely the elided third term, the other woman. While the relation of the subject to the mother is one of loss and lack, the relation of the subject to the other woman is made possible by the disavowal of that lack. In Rich's words, "knowing it makes the difference" (75). The signifier of desire is the signifier of the difference that desire articulates between *"the lover and the loved"*:

> *homesick* as the fluted vault of desire
> articulates itself: *I am the lover and the loved,*
> *home and wanderer, she who splits*
> *firewood and she who knocks, a stranger*
> *in the storm,* two women, eye to eye
> measuring each other's spirit, each other's
> limitless desire. (76)

"Home and wanderer, she who splits / firewood and she who knocks, a stranger / in the storm": these, emphasized by the poet, are the terms of the fantasy scenario in which the poem inscribes the difference and the desire between the lesbian lovers, and the "limitless" desire that is *within* each of them.

As I have tried to show, the terms of difference and the signifiers of desire vary from text to text and from lesbian subject to lesbian subject, but they always refer to one fantasmatic instance—the doubling of the originally lost object (the mother's body) by another originally lost object (the female body), and the displacement of the latter onto the signification of desire itself. Thus, Freud's statement that "the finding of an object is in fact the refinding of it" (*SE* 7: 222) may be true of a successfully Oedipalized subject; but to the subject of perverse desire, "the objects of our desires are always substitutes for the objects of our desires" (Bersani and Dutoit 66). For this reason, I would argue, the lesbian subject's desire is "limitless": in a repeated process of displacement and reinvestment, her desire is a movement toward objects that can conjure up what was never there, and therefore cannot be refound but only found or, as it were, found again for the first time ("But in fact we were always like this, / rootless, dismembered: knowing it makes the difference").

I may recall here Roof's insight that the desire inscribed in the two lesbian texts she examined was a desire "fulfillable only by desire itself" (*A Lure of Knowledge* 116). The problem with her formulation, I suggested in chapter 4, was its Lacanian framework, in which the protagonist/daughter's "desire for desire" was defined by identification either with the desire *of* another woman (the mother) for the phallus or with (the husband's) phallic desire *for* another woman. What I found most suggestive in Roof's reading was the idea that lesbian desire is directly related to another woman's desire, but it seemed to me that her account of that relation foundered on the notion of identification, or rather the confusion of desire with identification. In light of my own reading of other lesbian texts, I now suggest that Roof's "desire for desire" is akin to Rich's "limitless desire": both describe an unending displacement and reinvestment of the drive from an originally lost object, the female body, onto the signifiers of desire itself; these are the fetish objects that re-present and allow the recathecting of the subject's own body-ego.

In my view, then, lesbian desire is not the *identification* with another woman's desire, but the *desire* for her desire as signified in her fetish and the fantasy scenario it evokes. What one desires is her lover's perverse desire; her fetish, in which her castration or lack of being is both acknowledged and denied, also mediates the other's fantasmatic access to her originally lost body. Provided their fantasy scenarios are compatible, both subjects can find together, always for the first time, that fantasmatic body for themselves and in each other. (In other words, as in McLaughlin's film, the seduction and castration fantasies are mutually constitutive or complementary.) While this accounts for my claim that it takes two women, not one, to produce lesbian desire, it does not presume to account for the success or even the viability of a lesbian sexual relationship. Experience shows that, contra Foucault, sex and desire are often as much at odds with one another as bodies are with pleasures. Under the current state of sexuality, none of these four terms is unitary, self-evident, or independent of the others. Part of the problem is the complexity of fantasy in its unconscious, as well as conscious, processes. For subjectivity, I maintain, is as effectively involved in what we call sexuality as are the apparati and mechanisms of the social technology of sex.

One last observation, in closing. Reading *The Lesbian Body* as a deconstructive text that actually exceeds not only the opposition femininity/masculinity but also the philosophical "bisexuality" theorized by Derridian feminists, Heather Findlay points out how Wittig's rewriting of the myth of Isis and Osiris "refuses to believe in the she-Osiris's castration. Yet lack and loss are disseminated over the lesbian body of Osiris." Unlike the Egyptian myth, where the thirteenth piece, the penis, is missing, in Wittig's lesbian version of the body "there are thirteen pieces which are constantly lost and found. Whereas castration is clearly negated, it is also affirmed *in a new sense*" ("Is There a Lesbian in This Text?" 68).

> The thirteen pieces of Osiris's fragmented body, for example, reappear in Wittig's text as the average of thirteen poems between each page of boldfaced, listed lesbian body parts. The images of Osiris's split subject [remarking the bar that divides Wittig's subject pronoun *j/e* throughout the text] reappear in almost every poem as the lovers tear each other apart and exhibit one another in exoscopy. The stability of the lesbian body is seen as fundamentally precarious: every moment of bodily reconstruction is accompanied by destruction[:] After Isis completes her search and reassembles her lover, Osiris is done and "undone" at once; *"toi alors m/on Osiris m/a très belle tu m/e souris défaite epuisée"* [Wittig, *Le corps lesbien* 87] ("m/y Osiris most beautiful one you smile at m/e undone exhausted"). (Findlay 68–69)[26]

The negation of castration and its affirmation in a new sense in the inscription of the lesbian body is what I also read in several other texts throughout this chapter, and called it disavowal. Findlay's observation about the dissemination of lack and loss across the

---

26. Findlay takes issue with Elizabeth Berg's elaboration of Derrida's "affirmative woman" as a figure of philosophical bisexuality and therefore, for Berg, most suitable to subversive femininity and feminism. She argues that Berg's and Derrida's "third woman" is constructed as an alternative to passive femininity (the first woman, woman as untruth) and to lesbian feminism (the second woman, woman as truth); especially the latter, who "serves as the philosopher's and the psychoanalyst's proof of castration, particularly because she refuses to believe in it" (68). It is against this heterosexist feminine typology that Findlay proposes Wittig's text as a more truly deconstructive one. The third woman of my title for this section is obviously not a deconstructive trope but rather the figure of an elision—the elision of lesbianism—that deconstruction shares with other feminist critical practices.

textual body in Wittig corroborates my own that the originally lost object, the one that was never anywhere, can be conjured up and recathected only in the signifying or the representing of desire itself. This would account for the centrality, the apparently necessary repetition, of the figure of loss and dispossession that yet sustains subjectivity and desire in *The Lesbian Body,* as it does in Rich's poem; and its persistence in Stephen and Corky/Marisa, who end up still dispossessed in spite of having had women lovers. While the sense of belonging to "one's own kind," the political presence of a community (the distant "thousands" and "millions" like her for whom Stephen implores God at the close of the novel, and Marisa's "making familia . . . with strangers / each time all over again" at the close of the play), can soothe the pain and provide what Radclyffe Hall calls "that steel-bright courage . . . forged in the furnace of affliction," nevertheless the narcissistic wound remains, live under the scar that both acknowledges and denies it ("I am preparing myself for the worst," says Marisa, "so I cling to her in my heart, / my daydream with pencil in my mouth . . . "). If the wound and the scar, castration and the fetish, are the twin elements of a fantasy that is represented—inscribed or reenacted in different scenarios—in lesbian writing and in lesbian eros, it may well be because that fantasy is not only representative but in effect constitutive of perverse desire.

PART THREE

Toward a Theory of Lesbian Sexuality

I find myself for a moment in the interesting position of not knowing whether what I have to say should be regarded as something long familiar and obvious or as something entirely new and puzzling. But I am inclined to think the latter.
—Sigmund Freud ("The Splitting of the Ego," *SE* 23: 275)

Chapter **6**

Perverse Desire

Etwas-Haben-Wollen
—Anna Freud to Max Eitingon,
February 19, 1926 (quoted by Young-
Bruehl 133)

In the preceding chapter, through the reading of diverse literary
and critical texts, I have proposed a model of perverse desire based
on Freud's notion of disavowal and an unorthodox reading of fetishism. Before considering how other recent discussions of fetishism
may or may not corroborate or parallel my own, I will bring together the main threads of my argument, which has been advanced
in a somewhat tortuous and discontinuous manner.

It may be proper to remark at the outset that neither the materials
I considered nor my purposes in considering them are of a clinical
nature. Of course, a distinguished precedent for analyzing literary or
written texts for theoretical purposes, and quite apart from any
clinical knowledge about their author, exists in Freud's own work.
But my business with psychoanalytic theory is not an end unto itself,
nor intended as a contribution to the development of clinical psychoanalysis, as Freud's undoubtedly was. Nor, on the other hand, do I
wish to account psychoanalytically for (vulgarly put, to psychoanalyze) either the texts or the authors I discuss. For one thing, I do not

think that the object of my attention—lesbian sexuality and perverse desire—is, in and of itself, a psychic illness or that it would, therefore, benefit from analytic therapy. For another, I do not take psychoanalytic theory as a stable conceptual grid to be applied or deployed toward a "deep" or even an adequate literary interpretation (on the mutually implicative relations of literature and psychoanalysis, their being not subordinated to, but "enfolded within," each other, the definitive statement remains Shoshana Felman's in *Literature and Psychoanalysis*). As I already indicated, I think that Freud's theory of sexuality is best read as a passionate fiction, if one perhaps most appealing to a particular generation and sociocultural formation. My own critical effort, here, to articulate some of the processes of lesbian subjectivity should also be read in that light.

Two characteristics of Freud's thought that I find particularly congenial are (1) its ambivalence or systematic instability which, while pursuing a theoretical object—be it the concept of fantasy, sexuality, the ego, or seduction—is less interested in fixing its definition than in registering its transformations or alterations under, so to speak, one's theoretical eyes; and (2) its retroactivity, the returning over time to prior formulations and reframing them through a perspectival shift. Such is the kind of thinking that has led to the two successive models of the psychic apparatus, one topographical (in *The Interpretation of Dreams*) and the other structural (in *The Ego and the Id*); to the radical reformulation of the nature of the drives (in *Beyond the Pleasure Principle*); to the late 1920s and 1930s revisions in his theory of female sexuality; or to the reconsideration of fetishism itself, from the *Three Essays* edition of 1915 to the "Fetishism" paper of 1927 and finally the two papers of 1938.

Toward the very end of his life (at 82 and dying of cancer), Freud returned to the concept of disavowal in the unfinished "Splitting of the Ego in the Process of Defence" (1940 [1938]) and "An Outline of Psycho-Analysis" (1940 [1938]); there, again exemplifying it by reference to fetishism, he specifically linked disavowal to ego defenses, a question with which he was most concerned at the time possibly through discussions with his daughter Anna Freud, who had just published her own major work, *The Ego and the Mechanisms of Defence* (1936).[1]

---

1. In Freud's new formulation of the splitting of the ego, as the *Standard Edition* editors note, "the topic links up with the wider question of the 'alterations of the ego'

In "An Outline of Psycho-Analysis," the disavowal of portions of the external world and the psychical split consequent upon holding two contrary beliefs are recast as a general psychic process obtaining in psychoses and neuroses as well:

> The childish ego, under the domination of the real world, gets rid of undesirable instinctual demands by what are called repressions. We will now supplement this by further asserting that, during the same period of life, the ego often enough finds itself in the position of fending off some demand from the external world which it feels distressing and that this is effected by means of a *disavowal* of the perceptions which bring to knowledge this demand from reality. Disavowals of this kind occur very often and not only with fetishists. . . . The disavowal is always supplemented by an acknowledgement; two contrary and independent attitudes always arise and result in the situation of there being a splitting of the ego. Once more the issue depends on which of the two can seize hold of the greater intensity. (*SE* 23: 203–204)

Freud then goes on to say that, in the case of neuroses, one of the two attitudes belongs to the ego and the other, which is repressed, to the id. The difference between these two instances of ego splitting, neurosis and fetishism, then, "is essentially a topographical or structural one, and it is not always easy to decide in an individual instance with which of the two possibilities one is dealing." But in both cases, "whatever the ego does in its efforts of defense, whether it seeks to disavow a portion of the real external world or whether it seeks to reject an instinctual demand from the internal world, its success is never complete and unqualified"; for, he concludes, "little of all these processes becomes known to us through our conscious perception" (204).

The passage calls for several considerations. First, it indirectly reproposes, now in relation to ego defenses, the tropical image of neurosis and perversion as the respective positive and negative of each other, which was elaborated in the *Three Essays* in relation to sexuality (see chapter 1). Second, it reiterates in this new context the

---

which is invariably brought about by the processes of defence. This, again, was something with which Freud had dealt recently—in his technical paper on 'Analysis Terminable and Interminable' (1937*c*, especially in Section V)—but which leads us back to very early times, to the second paper on the neuro-psychoses of defence (1896*b*) . . . and to the even earlier Draft K of the Fliess correspondence (1950*a*)" (*SE* 23: 274).

impossibility of making a formal distinction between normal and pathological effects of disavowal, even within a single individual (earlier on, in "Fetishism," Freud had stated that "though no doubt a fetish is recognized by its adherents as an abnormality, it is seldom felt by them as the symptom of an ailment accompanied by suffering" [*SE* 21: 152]). Third, both repression and disavowal are presented as ego defenses, on a par with one another if with different outcomes. Indeed it can be argued that, whereas repression was the cornerstone of psychoanalysis "as the defense mechanism that gave the greatest insight into the structure of the psychic apparatus," the new emphasis on disavowal as general defensive strategy shifts the focus in Freud's understanding of psychic reality: "the generality of disavowal can change our view of the 'external' world, just as repression had changed our view of the 'internal' world" (Bass 320).

Fourth, the ego is no longer the undivided seat of consciousness. The process of a splitting of the ego in disavowal, Freud writes, "seems so strange to us because we take for granted the synthetic nature of the processes of the ego. But we are clearly at fault in this. The synthetic function of the ego, though it is of such extraordinary importance, is subject to particular conditions and is liable to a whole number of disturbances" (*SE* 23: 276). Seen in light of the second model of the psyche—where the subject's internal world is comprised of ego, id, and superego—the ego is no longer coextensive and cannot be identified with the agency of consciousness. Rather, as I have argued in chapter 1 and as Freud's emphasis on perception here remarks, it is a "body-ego," a frontier and a site of incessant negotiations between the demands of id and superego, on one front, and those of external reality on the other; that is to say, between the subject's internal or psychic reality and the external world. Similarly, the two agencies Cs. and Ucs. are no longer sealed off from each other by the threshold of censorship (repression) as they were in the earlier conceptualization of the psyche; here, they both and equally incessantly engage the ego in its dealing with the external world.

In chapter 1 I suggested an analogy between this formulation of the ego's relations to id and superego, and the relative position of "normal" sexuality (i.e., the projection of a successfully Oedipalized sexuality) vis-à-vis perversion and neurosis. If the ego, in effect, appears to consist in its defenses from the instinctual demands of id and superego, *and* from the external world—defenses that are characterized by varying degrees of repression or whose modalities are conscious and unconscious—then sexuality can be seen to consist of positive and negative perversions, depending on the degree of repression involved. I would now extend the analogy and suggest that, just as the ego, by dint of its various processes of internal and external defense, is subject to continuous alterations, so can sexuality be understood as a series of alterations, a succession of instinctual investments in object-cathexes (some of which will be called normal and others perverse in a given sociocultural context). In this sense, sexuality appears less a stable structure, set in place once and for all in the Oedipal or pubertal period, than a relatively open-ended *process of sexual structuring*, overdetermined by vicissitudes and contingencies in the subject's internal *and* external worlds.

Thus, for instance, according to Whitney Davis, the passage from the prefetishism of "the normally neurotic, preperverse mode of masculinity that Freud labels 'aversion to the female genitals'" ("HomoVision" 97) to fetishism proper, in a given subject, would consist in a second denegation, a further compromise formation or a reinforcement of the first compromise, under a continuing or stronger threat of castration. In other words, the difference between perversion and normal neurosis, with respect to disavowal, would be a matter of degrees, of more or less disavowal, and thus of the contingencies of one individual history. Davis's exploration of fetishism in its relation to (repressed) male homosexuality is only tangentially relevant to my project, but his argument that disavowal also occurs in the "prefetishist—the normally neurotic, preperverse male" (97), does converge with Freud's view of disavowal as a general psychic process, not limited to one particular perversion. The hypothesis I have advanced, on a suggestion by Bersani and Dutoit, is that disavowal is the psychic process that sustains a perverse desire, detaching it from both the mother's body and the paternal phallus, and reorienting the drive toward other objects; a perverse desire that specifically operates in lesbianism as a particular form of subjectivity. Whether or not it may sustain other forms of female subjectivity is a question I will raise later but leave for others to consider more fully, if they wish.

Lesbian desire, I have argued, is constituted against a fantasy of castration, a narcissistic wound to the subject's body-image that redoubles the loss of the mother's body by the threatened loss of the female body itself. Failing the mother's narcissistic validation of the subject's body-image, which constitutes the imaginary matrix or first outline of the ego, the subject is threatened with a loss of body-ego, a lack of being. The castration complex, in establishing the paternal prohibition of access to the female body (to the female body in the mother: incest; in oneself: masturbation; and in other women: perversion), as well as the "inferiority" of women, inscribes that lack in the symbolic order of culture, in the terms of sexual difference, as a biological, "natural," and irremediable lack—the lack of a penis. Confirmed by the subject's own perception ("I do not have a penis") and reiterated by virtually all cultural representations in both the symbolic and the imaginary orders of the external world, this lack (of a penis) is reluctantly acquiesced to and accepted by the subject herself, if with continued resistance, in lieu of the other lack, which is registered subjectively, in her internal world, on an imaginary or fantasmatic level (although it may also have symbolic expression through verbal statements); and which, moreover, is disconfirmed by perception ("I do, after all, have a female body—and yet . . . "). Such recalcitrant acceptance (but acceptance nevertheless) may then provide the "evidence" for what has been called penis envy, a term that translates—incorrectly—the sense of lack or dispossession acknowledged by many women privately and in public. (Thus, for instance, Freud believed that women reproach their mothers for not having endowed them with a penis.) The importance of the castration complex in female subjectivity, therefore, is not to be underestimated.

The psychic mechanism of disavowal is directly connected with the castration complex. But if, to the female subject of perverse desire, castration means first and foremost a lack of being in her body-ego consequent upon the narcissistic wound, and only secondarily the lack of a penis, then it is the former—the lack of a libidinally invested body-image, a feminine body that can be narcissistically loved—that threatens the subject most deeply. And it is against this threat that the mechanism of disavowal intervenes to defend the ego by producing the compromise fantasy "I don't have it but I can/will have it";[2] or, turning the narcissistic lack onto

---

2. In Isaacs's view, such fantasy would be unconscious (see note 19, chapter 2 above), and indeed its singular representation in that peculiar passage of *The Well of*

the mother, the first exemplar of the female body, "She doesn't have it but I can/will have it" (which might be read as "The mother is castrated but I am not"). "Phantasy," as Susan Isaacs puts it, "is the operative link between instinct and ego mechanism" (89). As distinct from the mechanisms or methods of functioning of mental life (her example is "introjection"), unconscious fantasies (her example, "the phantasy of incorporation") are "the primary content of unconscious mental processes" (96); they "are primarily about bodily aims, pains and pleasures" (90). What the female subject of perverse desire must disavow, then, is not the perception of a missing maternal penis (actually a non-perception), toward which she could not have bodily aims and which, therefore, would have no fantasmatic value to her, but rather the absence (also a non-perception) of a female body-image. This (non-)perception, I suggest, is homologous to the (non-)perception of the missing penis in Freud's male fetishist, and its disavowal serves a similar function of ego defense and validation of the body-ego.

Freud's understanding of castration and disavowal was explicitly cast in relation to the male body and its aims, pleasures, and pains— which led him to the logical conclusion that fetishism could not occur in women. I would argue instead that through the mechanism of disavowal, the female subject of perverse desire displaces the wish for the missing female body and the (non-)perception of its absence onto a series of fetish objects or signs that signify at once the wish and the absence (loss), and re-present the absent (lost, denied) and wished-for female body. If the lesbian fetishes are often, though certainly not exclusively, objects or signs with connotations of masculinity, it is not because they stand in for the missing penis but because such signs are most strongly precoded to convey, both to the subject and to others, the cultural meaning of sexual (genital) activity and yearning toward women. Such signs can also most effectively deny the female body (in the subject) and at the same time resignify (her desire for) it through the very signification of its prohibition. In this sense one can translate in psychic terms Foucault's thesis that the discourses on homosexuality, inversion, psy-

---

Loneliness that I have called the scene at the mirror—a brief scene which seems to contradict Stephen's self-understanding and characterization throughout the entire novel—suggests as much.

chic hermaphrodism, and so forth made possible not only the construction and control of perversion but also "the formation of a 'reverse' discourse: homosexuality began to speak in its own behalf, to demand that its legitimacy or 'naturality' be acknowledged, often in the same vocabulary, using the same categories by which it was medically disqualified" (*The History of Sexuality,* vol. 1: *An Introduction* 101).

Where Freud fixes the creation of the fetish to a single specific moment in the subject's developmental history ("the last impression before the uncanny and traumatic one is retained as a fetish" [*SE* 21: 155]), I would use his own notion of retroactivity to argue that the lesbian fetish is often constructed retroactively and by a kind of reverse discourse in which the subject makes use of the very categories, male/female and masculinity/femininity, by which sexuality is socially constructed and subjectively apprehended. For the function of the fetish, I will stress, is not dependent on the particular fetish, masculinity, from which I have developed my argument through the analysis of two primary texts. These were chosen for the reason that the signs of masculinity are the most visually explicit and strongly coded by dominant discourses to signify sexual desire toward women, and hence their greater visibility in cultural representations of lesbianism, which correlates to their greater effectivity in a political use of reverse discourse (on *The Well of Loneliness* as deliberate political intervention, see Ruehl). And yet, I argue, to the lesbian subject, those signs of masculinity signify something quite other and much more consequential for a female body-ego than the wish for a penis: beyond what may be (has been) read as the wish for a penis is the wish for a lost or denied female body. The latter, however, can also be signified by another reverse discourse, that of a quintessential, empowered, and exclusive or absolute femininity.

The exaggerated display of femininity in the masquerade of the femme performs the sexual power and seductiveness of the female body when offered to the butch for mutual narcissistic empowerment. The femininity aggressively reclaimed from patriarchy by radical separatism, with its exclusive reference and address to women, asserts the erotic power of the unconstricted, "natural," female body in relations between women. Similarly, it is the fantasy of a femininity at once constrained and defiant that is revalorized in the popular imagination of all-female sociosexual spaces, amazonic or matriarchal, ranging from girls' schools to prisons and from alternative worlds to convents and brothels. Here the female body is the site of a sexuality that is both incited and forbidden or regulated, but in either case female-directed and female-centered. The elaborate scenarios of lesbian sadomasochism, too, hinge on the power and control of the sexual female body by and for women. In spite of the different emphases on sexual "style" or of the oppositional claims as to which groups "have" what kind of "sex," in all these cases perverse desire is sustained on fantasy scenarios that restage the loss and recovery of a fantasmatic female body. Even when they take the form of a return to the mother—and thus may appear as ineffectual political nostalgia for a non-Oedipal, prepatriarchal world, or as a regressive retreat from the "realities" of sexual conflict (which the straight mind presumes to be necessarily heterosexual and traditionally views as the "battle of the sexes") to a nurturing, anodyne, maternal body—the fetishized scenarios of an empowered and exclusive femininity have less to do with mothering or with the mother's body as such than with restaging the subject's own loss and recovery of the female body. Though seemingly antithetical to the fetish of masculinity, they also serve to disavow castration as a sexual difference that deprivileges the female ego and its instinctual demands by making the female body a property of men and a vehicle of their social reproduction.

In sum, I am arguing that the disavowal of castration is a force that propels the drive *away* from the originally lost object (the mother) and toward the objects/signs that *both acknowledge and deny* a second, more consequential, narcissistic loss (the subject's own libidinally lost body-image), thus keeping at bay the lack of being that threatens the ego. This "displacement of value" (*SE* 23: 277) or transfer of affect onto the fetish allows the subject to reinvest libidinally in the female body, in other women, through its fantasmatic or intrapsychic image, of which the fetish is a metonymic sign.[3] This means, however, that the process of disavowal which articulates and sustains perverse desire is dependent on an

---

3. In Freud's example, the fetishist "did not simply contradict his perception and hallucinate a penis where there was none to be seen," which would be "a turning away from reality," a form of psychosis; instead "he effected no more than a displacement of value—he transferred the importance of the penis to another part of the body" (*SE* 23: 277).

underlying fantasy of castration (dispossession, lack of being). And indeed the latter's persistence in the unconscious and its constitutive role in subjectivity are thematized in one and legible in the other of the two lesbian texts discussed in chapter 5; they are remarked by Freud, as well, in his account of the boy fetishist in "Splitting of the Ego." Although the boy's successful way of dealing with external reality (in his case, the prohibition of masturbation) by the creation of a fetish "almost deserves to be described as artful" (*SE* 23: 277), he nevertheless developed a slight symptom, "an anxious susceptibility," that expressed his internal acknowledgment of the enduring threat of castration. It is as if, Freud writes, "in all the to and fro between disavowal and acknowledgement, it was nevertheless castration that found the clearer expression . . . " (278). (Everything considered, one cannot help but comment that a certain susceptibility to anxiety is a slight price to pay for one's desire.)

To this explanation of the instability of the subject, split and compromised in its desire by the lack of being that threatens the body-ego, one more observation can be added. Distinguishing between the *fetish-image* ("what is remembered as the last wished-for perception . . . a purely intrapsychic object, a constructed memory-fantasy") and the *fetish-effigies* ("the many transient external objects which could attract a fetishist's erotic interest"), Whitney Davis observes that the latter can only approximate metonymically, but never wholly replace or embody, the fetish-image. For this reason, "in fetishistic practice the fetishist is doomed to *Ichspaltung*—a division of his interest—and to continual sexual disillusionment and repetition" (110). He concludes that, if "the fetish-effigy is *nothing but* a first impression," nevertheless one "finds it momentarily exciting because the fetish-effigy always works as the absolute first impression, with no past and no future" (111).

I would certainly contest the word *doomed,* and less because of its tone of religious condemnation than because it misrepresents as a specific quality of fetishistic desire what is in fact a quality of all desire—its being subject to "continual sexual disillusionment and repetition." But much as I contest the word, I think the statement does describe the process of perverse desire as I have tried to articulate it. In its repeated process of displacement and reinvestment, perverse desire is a movement toward objects that can conjure up what was never there; a displacement of the drive from the originally lost object, the female body, onto the signifiers of desire itself and its reinvestment in the fantasmatic body they hold up as a promise, a representation of fulfillment. That "absolute first impression, with no past and no future," seems to me an apt interpretant of the various narrative and poetic signifiers in which I have traced perverse desire throughout this book: from the war scar of the mythic mannish lesbian to the writing hand of the activist-invert; from the plastic image of two women looking at each other, etched against the limitless horizon of their desire, to the white flower swaying in the southern wind; from the way she holds a cigarette to the pinky ring flashing as she waves her hand.

Masquerades and Other Fetishisms

In her "Female Fetishism," Naomi Schor observes the recurrence of a fetishistic scenario in the novels of George Sand, the eroticization of wounds. Interestingly, in view of my own terms of analysis, Schor also remarks on "the mobility of the fetish, its aptitude to press into service any wound inflicted on the female body." Although the subjects of fetishistic desire are embodied in male characters, her argument that they represent a female form of fetishism is built on the reading of authorial desire. "The fact that the female fetish par excellence in Sand should be a wound is not insignificant, for wounds *per se* are not generally fetishized by men" (366); and, of course, the masculine signature of the author only thinly disguises a woman writer, if one notorious for her masquerades—a woman writer, I might add, of whom lesbian literary historians have been eager to note "the pronounced masculinity of her always semi-autobiographical heroines" (Foster 127) as well as her own often masculine dress, feminist views, and unconventional behavior with both male lovers and female "friends" (Faderman 263–64).

Schor explains both the masquerade of masculinity and female fetishism in Sand's fiction as a textual strategy of "perverse oscillation" and names it *"bisextuality"* after Sarah Kofman's thesis of feminine bisexuality (in *The Enigma of Woman*): "what is pertinent to women in fetishism is the paradigm of undecidability that it offers. By appropriating the fetishist's oscillation between denial and recognition of castration, women can effectively counter any move to

reduce their bisexuality to a single one of its poles" (368). This interpretation is elegant but not convincing. For if bisexuality is a possible, perhaps even a probable, account with regard to Sand,
nevertheless the argument for female fetishism must rest on the
meaning of castration. Regrettably, Schor's reliance on Kofman's
Derridian reading of fetishism (in " 'Ça cloche' ") does not allow her
to go very far either in subverting Freudian orthodoxy or in the specification of a female fetishism; moreover, it brings her to align herself, albeit reluctantly, with what I call the discourse of sexual
(in)difference: "the wounds inflicted on the female protagonist's
body as a prelude to her sexual initiation [by a man] are the stig-
mata . . . of a refusal firmly to anchor woman—but also man—on
either side of the axis of castration" (369).

What is at issue, to be sure, is not the fact that the characters
inflicting the wound and eroticizing it as a fetish are men, since the
point of Schor's argument is authorial desire. What is at issue is the
theoretical perspective in which the latter is read: that is, first,
Kofman's view of bisexuality or "feminine oscillation" as, on the one
hand, the constitutive feature of femininity and, on the other, a fem-
inine/feminist *strategy;* second, and on that basis, her "feminization"
of fetishism—the rhetorical troping or metaphoric extension of a
specific psychic process into a feminine but sexually indifferent
"generalized fetishism" (" 'Ça cloche' " 117–18).[4] Schor's insistence
on *female* instead of *feminine* suggests, already in the title of her
essay, a certain unease with Kofman's theory and a doubt about its
validity. That doubt is stated explicitly at the end of the essay when
Schor, suddenly putting into question her own speculation on the
nature of female fetishism, concludes: "To forge a new word
adequate to the notion of female fetishism, what we need now is . . .
a new language" (371).

Were I to offer an account of the wound as female fetish in Sand,
I would likely argue away from the theoretical placebo of bisexuality

---

4. As Emily Apter notes, "Kofman succeeds in demasculinizing fetishism through
theory but in the process dispenses almost entirely with sexual difference. Female
fetishism, insofar as it could even be epistemologically distinguished according to
her terms, is subsumed within the neutered modalities of textual indeterminacy"
(*Feminizing the Fetish* 110). On her part, Apter proposes a female fetishism based on
loss and "the transgressively eroticized mourning of missing love objects" (122) that
are gender-specific and indeed maternal, as in Mary Kelly's *Post-Partum Document.* I
shall return to it shortly.

and more in the direction I have been pursuing here.[5] For it seems to me that to postulate female (bi)sexuality as an oscillation of desire or sexual identity between the "poles" of masculinity and femininity does not call into question the fulcrum of that "axis of castration" on which is balanced the seesaw of such a subjectivity, that is to say, the paternal phallus. Thus Kofman's generalization, or feminization, of fetishism does not spell "the end of the privileged phallus" ("'Ça cloche'" 133), but rather confirms it as the master term par excellence. Indeed Schor herself wonders, at the close of her paper, whether the notion of female fetishism she has hypothesized for Sand is not in fact "the latest and most subtle form of 'penis-envy'?" (371). This possibility, which would account for Sand's masculine masquerades in the most classic of terms, the masculinity complex, is perfectly consistent not only with the theory of "oscillation" but also with the conceptual frame in which the feminine is predicated on the masculine, and oscillation on a phallic axis. In remarking that troubling complicity, Schor's doubt—her own critical habit of theoretical consistency and intellectual honesty—virtually collapses Kofman's theory like a house of cards, cautioning against facile or voluntaristic appropriations of sexual differences whether by women or by men.

While the notion of oscillation is gaining currency in the theorizing of heterosexual female subjectivity (see also Adams's "Per Os(cillation)" and my discussion of it in chapter 2), for some of us, women and men, subjects of perverse desire, more castration is better than less castration, as Bersani and Dutoit cleverly put it. We need not just to refuse to anchor ourselves *firmly* on one or the other side of the paternal phallus, but to loosen ourselves from it altogether, and to really follow through the idea of a mobility of fetishistic or perverse desire by giving up the convenience of notions such as oscillation and undecidability. As for the relations of fetishism to masquerade, just as there are many fetishisms—that is, different ways of conceptualizing and using the term *fetishism*—so are there several masquerades. Which kind of masquerades Sand's may have been depends on how one reads her fetishism. And vice versa.

---

5. In my reading of authorial desire in *The Well of Loneliness*, the fetish is a scar rather than a wound, but the wound and the scar are two mutually referential points in one psychic trajectory: fetishizing the wounds in another, from a certain point of view, could be equivalent to fetishizing the scar in oneself.

The connection between (male) fetishism and (female) masquerade was first suggested by Joan Riviere in "Womanliness as a Masquerade" and subsequently reformulated by Lacan. For Riviere, the masquerade of femininity is an exaggerated, compulsive display of womanly behavior; the flirting and coquetting with men in social intercourse serves to disguise the heterosexual woman's masculinity complex and her competitiveness with men. Since her achievement in a masculine profession is tantamount to stealing the penis from the father, she must propitiate all "father-figures" by wooing their favor and offering herself sexually to them after each one of her intellectual performances. Following the doctrinal positions of Jones and Klein, who have both been her analysts, Riviere's analysis of one patient (who appears to have remarkable similarities to Riviere herself) is typically based on the credo of penis envy and sadistic-aggressive impulses toward the mother.[6] On a cue from Jones's "The Early Development of Female Sexuality" (discussed in chapter 2 above), Riviere surmises in her patient a latent or unconscious homosexuality as envious contempt of men, but insists on her successful performance in heterosexual intercourse as the determination to surpass the (frigid) mother and to prove herself the equal of men in sexual potency: "In effect, sexual enjoyment was full and frequent, with complete orgasm; but the fact emerged that the gratification it brought was of the nature of a reassurance and *restitution* of something lost, and *not ultimately pure enjoyment*. The man's love gave her back her self-esteem" (38; emphasis added). Thus, for Riviere, narcissism is central to the woman's masquerade of femininity, while fetishism is the province of its analogue in men, the man's masquerade of femininity, as in her male homosexual patient who could attain sexual gratification (presumably "pure" or not restitutive) only when crossdressed as his sister (39–40).

For Lacan, on the other hand, the fetish is the specific value conferred upon woman by the masquerade, because her purpose in masquerading is to be(come) the phallus:

---

6. In the biographical notes that introduce his essay on Riviere, Heath also speculates on a possible love affair between Riviere and Jones. As for the possible autobiographical basis of her theory of masquerade, no one should be surprised who has any familiarity with the lives of the rich and famous in psychoanalysis, from Freud himself to Anna Freud, Klein, Bonaparte, Jones, and so forth.

Paradoxical as this formulation may seem, I am saying that it is in order to be the phallus, that is to say, the signifier of the desire of the Other, that a woman will reject an essential part of femininity, namely, all her attributes in the masquerade. It is for that which she is not that she wishes to be desired as well as loved. But she finds the signifier of her own desire in the body of him to whom she addresses her demand for love. Perhaps it should not be forgotten that the organ that assumes this signifying function takes on the value of a fetish. ("The Signification of the Phallus," *Écrits* 289–90)

Referring to Jones (rather negatively), but not mentioning Riviere, Lacan nonetheless takes from her the notion of mask, and uses it pointedly in "The Signification of the Phallus" in the context of an incidental remark on female homosexuality:

Male homosexuality, in accordance with the phallic mark that constitutes desire, is constituted on the side of desire, while female homosexuality, on the other hand, as observation shows, is orientated on a disappointment that reinforces the side of the demand for love. . . . The function of the mask . . . dominates the identifications in which refusals of demand [for love] are resolved. (290–91)

Like Jones and Riviere (and Freud and Deutsch, among others), Lacan also believes that female homosexuality derives from the disappointment of the subject's Oedipal love for the father; and like them (but unlike Freud or Deutsch) he speaks of female homosexuality and heterosexuality without solution of continuity. Quite appropriately, therefore, Judith Butler glosses this passage with the question, "Is it the mask of the female homosexual that is 'observed'?" (*Gender Trouble* 49). Indeed, who is refusing whom? It is not clear whether Lacan is saying that the homosexual woman refuses the man, as Butler suggests (he "takes lesbian sexuality to be a refusal of sexuality *per se* only because sexuality is presumed to be heterosexual, and the observer, here constructed as the heterosexual male, is clearly being refused"), or whether he is saying that the woman is homosexual, or identifies with the male phallus, because her demand for the father's love has been refused, and she has resolved his refusal by identifying with him. In either case, however, the feminine woman, too, identifies with the phallus in order to be loved, which neatly ties up the theorem of the phallus: women can either try to have it or try to be it.

Lacan cites Jones again—this time from "The Early Development of Female Sexuality," a paper entirely devoted to female homosexuality and the one cited by Riviere—in "Guiding Remarks for a Congress on Feminine Sexuality" (written the same year as "The Signification of the Phallus," 1958), and again with regard to homosexuality (*Feminine Sexuality* 96–97). Here Lacan is concerned with the "perversions in the woman": "Since it has been effectively demonstrated that the imaginary motive for most male perversions is the desire to preserve the phallus . . . then the absence in women of fetishism, which represents the virtually manifest case of this desire, leads us to suspect that this desire has a different fate in the perversions which she presents" (96). Her fate, it turns out, is "the envy of desire," or Lacan's version (*père-version* might be suitable here) of penis envy that I discussed in chapter 4: "such a love prides itself more than any other on being the love which gives what it does not have, so it is precisely in this that the homosexual woman excels in relation to what is lacking to her," he states, adding: "Jones clearly detected here the link between the fantasy of the man as invisible witness and the care which the subject shows for the enjoyment of her partner" (96–97).

This casts further ambiguity on the fetishistic value of the "organ that assumes [the] signifying function" in "The Signification of the Phallus." For whom does that organ take on the value of a fetish? For the heterosexual woman masquerading as phallus, or for the homosexual penis-envying and -simulating woman? Since the fate of both, it seems, is to be(come) the phallus, one might conclude—from a certain point of observation—that the organ takes on the value of a fetish for the theory itself. Which is what makes Lacan's, much more than Freud's, a "fetishistic theory of desire" (Bersani and Dutoit 67). But while it may be fetishistic because it is dependent on a narcissistic and exclusive investment in the penis-phallus, such theory is, however, not *perverse* because, in fact, by the collusion of the respective male and female investments in the penis-phallus, the "normal" or reproductive aim of the sexual instinct remains on track and can be fully attained.[7]

---

7. Clinical views of perversion that oppose Lacan's "phallic sexual monism" and Freud's emphasis on the castration complex attribute fetishism to pre-Oedipal "separation anxiety and the inability to renounce primary identification with the mother," according to Chasseguet-Smirgel ("Reflections on Fetishism" 83–85). Her own theory is a compromise between the two views: "the fetish is an anal phallus which attempts

Others have commented on the multiple intersections of fetish-ism and masquerade. In "Versions of Masquerade" John Fletcher observes that just as Lacan rewrites Freud's theory of fetishism, so is Riviere's masquerade rewritten in the Lacanian and Nietzschean femininities of masquerade (woman as phallus) that are now popu-lar in feminist and film theory: "Lacanian and feminist uses of the concept of fetishism have extended its reference, from a minority clinical perversion to a generalised structure that governs the con-stitution of the woman's image as object of desire" (51).[8] And Emily Apter, in *Feminizing the Fetish*, thus summarizes the theory of feminine masquerade prominent in feminist psychoanalytic writings: "With Lacan's formulation, we come full circle from male fetishism as female masquerade *manqué* [in Riviere] to women masquerading as fetishes, that is, as false phalluses that permit the imaginary phallus which both sexes want, but which neither sex has, to continue functioning as a *manque à être* ('lack in being') that generates desire" (94). Against this view of femininity as a masquerade by which the (heterosexual) woman turns herself into a simulacrum, a "semblance of womanliness superimposed on a pretend masculinity" (92–93), Apter proposes an approach that allows her to theorize female subjectivity and female fetishism together "in terms of an aesthetics of ornamentation without immediate recourse to a compensatory emphasis on phallic cover-up" (97–98).

Starting from a little-known remark of Freud's to the effect that all women are clothes fetishists, and drawing on descriptions of fe-male fetishism both literary and psychoanalytic, Apter reads women's penchant for clothes as a "sartorial female fetishism"

---

to exclude the genital penis from the sexual stage. [The fetishist is] trying to foil his castration complex by likening it to his previous experiences of separation . . . and the primal scene is mimed as a pregenital relationship" (87).

8. For example Victor Burgin, reading Freud with Laplanche to the effect that "all human sexuality is deviant," in the sense of not natural or reducible to the biological function of species reproduction, argues that the fetishistic "overvaluation of the phallic metaphor in patriarchy" expressed by the naked female body (in a Helmut Newton photograph) is "perfectly normal—but only when we fetishize it, only when we isolate it from the space within which it is situated." In contrast to fetishism, which demands coherence and a fixed framing of the object isolated in the visual field, the space of Newton's photograph is "perverse" precisely in that it is mobile, encumbered with "elements which are normally excluded" (e.g., the photographer and his wife, looking on), and without fixed aim, like the drives, thus representing "the fundamental incoherence of sexuality" ("Perverse Space" 137).

which reinforces feminine narcissism by a kind of prosthesis, en-hancement, or self-valorization of their "corporeal superego."[9] By the addition of what she calls "an ethic of sartorial presence" (frankly, the ethical dimension escapes me) to the aesthetics of clothing, Apter would "unmask" the phallic theory of masquerade and replace it with a "projected affirmation of female ontology" (97–98). *Feminizing the Fetish* argues that female fetishism is compensatory, not to phallic lack but to an unspecified "female loss," and is represented in the "feminine collecting" of objects, relics, keepsakes, etc. that eroticize and mourn the subject's lost objects: "Whether standing in for lover, parent, child, or female double, the female fetish belongs to an erotic economy of severance and disappropriation, itself less fixed on a fiction of castration anxiety" (121).

It must be clear from my analysis in this and the preceding chap-ter that I concur with Apter in seeing an intimate relation between fetishism and narcissism, and in locating fetishism, at least par-tially, in an erotic economy of loss. (The other aspect of the fetish, which should not be overlooked, is its erotic power, its performative character of exploit noted by Metz in *The Imaginary Signifier*—"an exploit that underlines and denounces the lack [while it] consists at the same time of making this absence forgotten" [74]—and encapsu-lated in Nestle's "I can spot a butch thirty feet away and still feel the thrill of her power" [*A Restricted Country* 100].) But I am skeptical about a solution that implies yet another form of generalized fetish-ism: if feminine narcissism automatically results in female fetish-ism, then the latter would equally apply to all forms of female subjectivity. Moreover, by severing the fetish from the castration complex (which she assumes to be necessarily phallic) and ground-

---

9. "Corporeal superego" is a phrase from Béla Grunberger's "Outline for a Study of Narcissism in Female Sexuality," which Apter cites from the French "Jalons pour l'étude du narcissisme dans la séxualité féminine," providing her own translation (the English version gives "body self" [70]). However, her argument that "Grunberger's notions of physically extended subjectivity and 'material support' *literalize* sartorial figures of speech as they recode them within the rhetoric of feminist psychoanalysis" (97), *and therefore eschew the traditional compensatory phallic emphasis,* seems to me altogether unwarranted by Grunberger's essay and his Lacanian thesis that women's narcissistic autonomy is reached by their becoming the phallus: "The woman who is loved thereby possesses in her unconscious a phallic equivalent. She sometimes be-comes this phallus herself and thus achieves a state of narcissistic autonomy by ca-thecting herself narcissistically: becoming beautiful, charming, and desirable" ("Outline for a Study of Narcissism in Female Sexuality" 75).

ing it in a generic "female loss" (of lover, parent, child, etc.), Apter loses sight of disavowal as a defense against the specifically sexual loss or threat signified by castration. With disavowal and castration gone, female fetishism is now gendered but no longer sexual. While correcting Kofman's metaphorization of femininity by an exclusive emphasis on gender—exclusive, that is, of sexuality and sexual object-choice—Apter's own feminization of the fetish also dilutes the theoretical value of fetishism as the specification of a particular form of sexuality, or of perverse desire. (For other accounts of fetishism in non-sexual or non-psychoanalytic terms, see Pietz.)

In my reading of Radclyffe Hall's Stephen Gordon and Moraga's Marisa/Corky, the masquerade of masculinity in the mannish drag or the contemporary butch persona, although it operates as a fetish, is not a phallic symbol, a substitute for the penis, or a pretentious claim to the paternal phallus. A fetish-object and signifier of desire, it is constituted through the disavowal of castration, but with the fundamental specification that in lesbian subjectivity the ultimate meaning of castration as narcissistic wound is not the lack of a penis but the loss of the female body; and consequently, the *threat* of castration threatens a lack of being in the subject's body-ego. With and against Freud, I argued that the fetish, a "memorial" to that threat (*SE* 21: 154), does not stand in for the maternal phallus (psychoanalysis's own imago of the paternal phallus), but rather for the denied and longed-for female body. That is the lesbian's "object of desire"— the intrapsychic or fantasmatic image of a body lost by castration but found again and again in the metonymic fetish-signs to which her perverse desire attaches itself contingently and precariously. In the perspective I have been elaborating, then, the phallus itself could be a fetish, in its various incarnations from the erect penis to the dildo and other representations of its symbolic power, including the phallic mother; but it would be only one among other possible— contingent and "inappropriate"—signifiers of perverse desire.

This is how the butch and mannish lesbian's drag, recast in terms of perverse desire, differs from the standard interpretation of her "masculinity complex" couched in normatively heterosexual terms as the wish for a penis. And how it differs, as well, from that other form of drag, the masquerade of femininity, the excessive display of the signifers and accoutrements of femininity, by which the heterosexual woman disguises her own "masculinity complex" and penis envy in her relations with men (Riviere) or masquerades as phallus for the man (Lacan). A third case, in which the masquerade of femininity is performed by the femme and addressed to the butch in a lesbian subcultural context, was exemplified by the character Jo in McLaughlin's film *She Must Be Seeing Things*, discussed in chapter 3 (see also Case, "Towards a Butch-Femme Aesthetic," and Nestle, "The Fem Question").[10] In all three cases, the masquerade is a matter of per-forming; that is to say, of a public display or presentation of self to others in a given sociocultural and sociosexual context. Thus the form and mode of address—what form the masquerade takes and to whom it is addressed—are part and parcel of its psychosexual content, and in-form the subjectivity of its wearer. In other words, the distinction in address between the three forms of masquerade also entails a distinction in instinctual aim and object-choice: how sexual pleasure is attained, by means of what fetish, and whether the subject's libidinal investment is in the female body or in the phallus.

FIGURE 1

subject	form of masquerade	address	object-choice	libidinal aim
		sociosexual	psychosexual	
Stephen Gordon Marisa/Corky	masculine	women/men	female	fantasmatic female body
Jo	feminine	women	female	fantasmatic female body
in Riviere and Lacan	feminine	men	male	phallus

Considering the masquerade in relation to the fetish, and taking fetishism specifically as a psychosexual and sociosexual form of subjectivity, rather than in an extended, literary-philosophical, metaphoric, or generic sense, Figure 1 summarizes these three types of masquerade.

---

10. My topic being lesbian subjectivity, I consider only instances of masculine and feminine masquerade by women. For various forms of crossgender masquerade by men, see Newton, *Mother Camp*, and Garber's comprehensive, up-to-date survey in *Vested Interests*.

Not represented in Figure 1 is the homosexual woman in Lacan, whose "mask" he does not actually describe, although he evokes it by reference to Jones (who does describe her even as far as the details of her lovemaking practices). But a description of this fourth type of masquerade is made available by an extraordinary occurrence in psychoanalytic writing: a feminist working with Lacanian theory has considered fetishism in relation to lesbian sexuality. Elizabeth Grosz's "Lesbian Fetishism?" proposes that, Freud notwithstanding, both heterosexual femininity and female homosexuality may be seen in feminist sociopolitical terms as forms of fetishism, a disavowal of women's social reality, and that lesbianism in particular is one of the forms that female fetishism takes. But Grosz is ambivalent toward her own thesis. Torn between psychoanalysis ("female fetishism is psychically inconceivable") and feminism ("in another, more strategic and political sense, it seems plausible to suggest, as Naomi Schor does in her analysis of George Sand, that there *can* be a form of female fetishism"), Grosz foregrounds in her title the questionable nature of the project and, like Schor, reiterates her ambivalence at the close of her essay. Yet she will pursue the question, and will do so within the parameters of orthodox Freudian and Lacanian theory, but "strategically harnessed for [feminist] purposes for which they were not intended" (40): "Like the fetishist," she teases, "I want to have it both ways" (39).

The argument proceeds from two premises. One is that the three paths of post-Oedipal female development outlined by Freud—femininity, hysteria, and the masculinity complex—are not the "normal" consequences of the female castration complex, as they are described by Freud, but rather "result from the girl's disavowal of her own castration" (47). Let it be stressed: what the girl disavows is not the mother's castration but her own. If this first premise seems out of line with the classical Freudian theory of female sexuality, it is because Grosz's second premise is in line with Lacan's definition of femininity and masculinity as symmetrical positions vis-à-vis the phallus: masculinity is to have it and femininity, to be it. Thus while all women disavow castration, they do so differently, by taking up one or the other position: in femininity, the woman masquerades as phallus, "effects a phallicization of the whole of her body"; in hysteria, "she hystericizes, that is to say, phallicizes, not the whole of her body, but a hysterical zone" (49); and the masculine woman "takes an external love-object—another woman" (51), who represents the phallus.

In all three cases, disavowal would function as "a strategy of self-protection" against "personal debasement and the transformation of her status from subject to object" (49–50). But in the first case, Grosz argues, reading Freud's femininity by way of Lacan's, the heterosexual narcissistic woman pampers and overvalues her body, "treating it as if it were the phallus"; through makeup, artifice, and dissimulation, she seduces the male lover, becoming his love object and securing through him "a mode of access to the phallic" (48). In this manner the narcissistic woman "compensate[s] for her genital deficiency, which she is able to disavow through her narcissistic self-investment" (48–49). Not unlike the hysteric, who also rebels against the passivity of normal femininity and who—Dora to wit—hystericizes (phallicizes) only a part of her body: "the difference between the hysteric and the narcissist is the difference between the displacement of the phallus onto a part or onto the whole of the subject's own body" (49).

In other words, the narcissistic femininity of masquerade is not the "normal" femininity, the contented acquiescence to the passive, vaginal, maternal role of the woman who has adjusted to her "sexual inferiority" and made peace with castration, as Freud sometimes imagines her. It is a femininity that is founded, instead, on disavowal, on the concurrent affirmation and negation of her "genital deficiency" vis-à-vis the male. But once again, just like the disavowal of Freud's male fetishist, this female disavowal is also one that supremely valorizes the phallus. Although antithetical to the classic masculinity complex of the woman who would be man, the femininity of masquerade is quite as much an effect of the primacy of the phallus. Moverover, both concepts—the masculinity complex and the femininity of masquerade—must be understood in the perspective of heterosexuality, whether that be the bona fide, "normal," heterosexuality of Freud, where sexual difference is predicated on the phallus as signifier but on the mother's body (the *reproductive* female body) as object of desire, or whether that be the sexually indifferent heterosexuality of Lacanian theory, where the phallus alone is both signifier and object of desire (of male, as well as female, desire).

The place where the valorization of the phallus in Lacanian theory and in Grosz's account of lesbian fetishism most clearly differs

from my reading of lesbian texts in the perspective of perverse desire, is her discussion of the third form of female disavowal, the
masculinity complex. When Freud writes that "a girl may refuse to
accept the fact of being castrated, may harden herself in the conviction that she *does* possess a penis, and may subsequently be compelled to behave as though she were a man" (*SE* 19: 253); or when he
"describes her as behaving like a chivalrous male lover, displaying
many of the characteristics attributed to the anaclitic or masculine
type," Grosz states,

> it seems clear that [Freud] certainly describes at least one kind of
> lesbian relation, that which seems to replicate the structural
> position of a patriarchal heterosexuality, distinguishing a
> narcissistic (feminine) lover from an anaclitic (masculine) lover.
> Here the latter disavows her castration, while the former accepts
> her castration but refuses to convert her love object from maternal
> to paternal. (50)

In the latter case, therefore, in the feminine lesbian who "accepts
her castration," there is no disavowal. Whereas the former, "the
woman suffering from the masculinity complex," disavows her own
castration and, like the fetishist, "takes on a substitute for the phallus, an object outside her own body," namely, another woman, "and
through this love-object is able to function as if she *has*, rather than
is, the phallus" (51). In light of this formulation, the fourth type of
masquerade can now be included in Figure 2.

FIGURE 2

subject	form of masquerade	address	object-choice	libidinal aim
		sociosexual	psychosexual	
Stephen Gordon Marisa/Corky	masculine	women/men	female	fantasmatic female body
Jo	feminine	women	female	fantasmatic female body
in Riviere and Lacan	feminine	men	male	phallus
in Grosz and Lacan	masculine	women/men	female	phallus

But for the conceptualization of libidinal aim, the terms of Grosz's description of lesbianism are uncannily resonant with the conceptual universe of *The Well of Loneliness*. Had she been able to avail herself of Lacanian theory, Radclyffe Hall might well have concluded that Stephen Gordon had the phallus in her Mary, and therefore Mary need not be sacrificed after all. But as far as contemplating the possibility of a non-heterosexual or perverse lesbian desire, Lacanian theory does no better than the discourse of Radclyffe Hall's Catholic God. In spite of Grosz's valiant efforts to stretch the parameters of orthodox psychoanalysis "beyond the limits of their tolerance" (39; the word *tolerance* itself recalls Radclyffe Hall's plea to science and society, in the name of God), her argument remains mired in the paradox of sexual indifference, and her critical fetishism, her wanting psychoanalysis both ways, ricochets against that rock which in the Lacanian tautology is by definition a hard place. Nevertheless, the essay contains several intriguing implications that I would like to draw out with regard to the theoretical cluster of masquerade, castration, fetishism, and disavowal.

In Grosz's reading, the first two terms remain unchanged, couched in the standard psychoanalytic frame (castration is the lack or loss of the penis) or in the French-Freudian revision (woman masquerades as phallus/fetish in order to be desired: the penis, you may recall, "takes on the value of a fetish" in Lacan). The next two terms have undergone a displacement from the realm of the psychic to that of the social: disavowal is a strategy women employ in self-protection, not against a specifically sexual threat but against their socially debased status as sexual objects; and fetishism names, in general, the mode of a political (feminist) resistance to social reality. In particular, however, fetishism names a form of female homosexuality in which the fetish—the lesbian's loved object, the other woman—results from not "a fear of femininity but a love of it" (51). This incidental remark, almost an aside, is most suggestive to me. Not only does it give another brief glimpse of that shadowy and elusive figure, the feminine lover, of whom we have been told only that she "accepts her castration but refuses to convert her love object from maternal to paternal" (50). More important, the statement's hint at a love of femininity suggests a possible convergence with my own understanding of perverse desire. In the hope of finding support for my theory, I speculate.

Which—whose—femininity does the masculine lesbian love, and what manner of femininity? Is it the masquerade of the (heterosexual) narcissist, or could it be instead the fantasmatic image of a feminine body lost/denied by castration and recovered through the fetish, through another woman? At first, it seems ironical that, among the general repudiation of castrated femininity common to masculine, hysteric, and narcissistic women, the only exception should be a lesbian—that is, the (masculine) lesbian's feminine lover; she who, in accepting her castration but loving another woman, provides the solitary figure of a non-problematic (to herself) and desirable (to her lover) femininity. On second thought, she appears to be something of a dream figure, more a projection, a fantasy, than a real woman. For her alone there is no need for disavowal; her temporary, early attachment to the father (during a brief positive Oedipus complex) is quickly and smoothly transferred to a "phallic" woman ("a woman precisely . . . with a masculinity complex" [51]); she retains her maternal love object, but without persisting in the phallic phase, and thus without developing a masculinity complex (which might compete with her masculine lover's). The more I think about her, the more she reminds me of Radclyffe Hall's Mary, a fictional figure that might well be every lesbian's dream lover—woman and woman-identified, -loving, -devoted, and -admiring; most of all, undemanding. She is, in sum, the ideal and most convenient object, but hardly a subject, of desire. Indeed, she is a fetish—an object on which is projected, and which can make good, the subject's fantasmatic lack. Whether or not such a woman or such a femininity exists, it is not the femininity of masquerade or any other contemplated by psychoanalysis; not even the passive, maternal femininity of Freud, which is entirely cathected on the child rather than on the sexual partner.

Regretfully, my speculations find no confirmation in the text. Grosz's own speculation on "the possibility of 'lesbian theory'" (40) reaches no further than a "strategic" answer and a "cultivated ambivalence" (51–52). Thus, to the question her title asks of the reader, "Lesbian Fetishism?" I would have to reply that the distribution of lesbians into masculine and feminine women, respectively having and being the phallus, cannot but uphold the latter and all it stands for in psychoanalysis and in the culture at large; consequently it colludes with the heterosexual and patriarchal purposes for which psychoanalytic orthodoxy was and is intended, and most immediately the foreclosure of lesbian sexuality.

A whole other set of questions is raised by Grosz with the observation that feminism may be regarded as a defensive strategy, a political disavowal of the reality of women's social oppression. This, too, is worthy of consideration. For, if one agrees that the sociopolitical changes brought about by First and Third World feminisms, and the very conception of a global feminist project, are made possible by a concerted action that defies what does appear as women's social reality, then disavowal could effectively explain the feminist refusal to accept the reality of an oppression we acknowledge as ours. But is the disavowal of social reality that is necessary for political self-empowerment under oppression immediately translatable in psychosexual terms? Let us assume for the sake of argument that the psychosexual process of disavowal may be translatable into a sociosexual one. Is this latter of the fetishistic, perverse kind that deranges the subject's system of desiring, or is it like the disavowal acted out in the heterosexual masquerade of femininity, strategically self-protective but ultimately on track, in keeping with the "normal" aims of society? Or again, is feminism after a fetish in the classic sense, the restoration of the phallic mother, or is it after a bold, contingent design of social "perversion"? (The latter two questions are in part explored in two feminist works of lesbian theory, respectively Julia Creet's reading of Pat Califia's *Macho Sluts* in "Daughter of the Movement" and Sue-Ellen Case's performative meditation on ontology and desire in "Tracking the Vampire.")

Conversely, if one grants that a feminist political identity can deeply affect the subject's psychosexual reality, what would be the fetish of a heterosexual feminist? The boundary between straight and inverted women seems easily fordable in the social terrain of feminist alliances, and perhaps more so in the borderlands of U.S. Third World feminism, but is it really open to the traffic of sexual desire? According to my reading of her play, Moraga would say that it is. But that is precisely Marisa's fantasy, one particular lesbian's fetish, not generalizable as any lesbian's; whereas it seems unlikely that a heterosexual feminist's object of desire—fetish or not—were anything but the penis-phallus. This is not to say that sexual restructuring, the complex and overdetermined experiential passage from straight to perverse desire, cannot occur at any point during a woman's life. It can and does, perhaps more often in feminism than elsewhere. But insofar and as long as a woman is straight (and able to choose), her sexual object-choice will be a heterosexual one, and vice versa.

This last statement seems reasonable enough, in fact tautological. And yet it has been contested in feminist psychoanalytic writings on the grounds (discussed in chapter 4) of women's greater sexual mobility, their fluid, unbounded, polymorphous, or bisexual disposition; their oscillation or bi-positional structuration in relation to the phallus; the continuity of maternal identification and object-choice, and so on. At the same time, somehow, the issue of female heterosexual desire is as carefully avoided in feminist psychoanalytic writings as it is systematically and normatively propounded in the writings of women analysts from the 1930s onward. An unusually candid feminist statement on this issue reads:

> By insisting on the penis, I was looking for some masculine body, some other body, some bodily object of female heterosexual desire, trying to find not just the institution of heterosexism but also the experience of heterosexuality. I cannot disintricate the penis from the phallic rule but neither is it totally synonymous with the transcendent phallus. At this point in history I don't think they can be separated, but to insist on a bodily masculinity is to work to undo the heterosexist ideology which decrees the body female, to be dominated not by a male body (too disorderly to rule) but by an idealized, transcendent phallus. I want to render that idealization impossible. (Gallop, *Thinking through the Body* 131–32)

Is the penis, object of such insistence, a fetish? Or, put otherwise, does my model of perverse desire apply to forms of female sexuality that are apparently heterosexual? I leave the question to others more concerned or better qualified to consider it, and go back to my main topic, lesbian sexuality and perverse desire.

The Practice of Love

On several occasions throughout this book, I have asserted that it takes two women, not one, to make a lesbian. I was not thinking solely of object-choice, but of the fact that lesbianism is a sexual practice, as well as a particular structuration of desire. Since the fantasies that ground it and the fetish signs that signify it may differ both culturally and individually, perhaps the single defining condition of lesbian sexuality and desire is that their subject and their object are both female-embodied. Whatever other affective or social ties may be involved in a lesbian relationship—ties that may also exist in other relations between and among women, from friendship to rivalry, political sisterhood to class or racial antagonism, ambivalence to love, and so on—the term *lesbian* refers to a sexual relation, for better or for worse, and however broadly one may wish to define *sexual.* I use this term in its psychoanalytic acceptation to include centrally—beyond any performed or fantasized physical sexual act, whatever it may be—the conscious presence of desire in one woman for another. It is that desire, rather than woman-identification or even the sexual act itself (which can obviously occur between women for reasons unrelated to desire), that specifies lesbian sexuality.

As defined in Laplanche and Pontalis's authoritative *Vocabulaire de la psychanalyse,*

> Sexuality does not mean only the activities and pleasure which depend on the functioning of the genital apparatus: it also embraces a whole range of excitations and activities which may be observed from infancy onwards and which procure a pleasure that cannot be adequately explained in terms of the satisfaction of a basic physiological need (respiration, hunger, excretory function, etc.). . . . As opposed to love, desire is directly dependent on a specific somatic foundation; in contrast to need, it subordinates satisfaction to conditions in the phantasy world which strictly determine object-choice and the orientation of activity. (*The Language of Psycho-Analysis* 418 and 421–22)

Desire, not love or need, is specific to sexuality. But then, what of my title? What do lesbian sexuality and desire have to do with the *practice of love?*

The passage just quoted states that desire is (unlike love) *directly dependent* on a somatic or instinctual foundation, but instinctual satisfaction is (unlike need) dependent on fantasy, which in turn *strictly determines* object-choice and orientation of activity, or instinctual aim. I have argued earlier that the object to which the drive attaches itself, the so-called object of desire, *represents* a *fantasmatic object*, an intrapsychic image; in other words, desire is dependent on a fantasy scenario which the object evokes and from which the object acquires its fantasmatic value, acquires the ability to represent the fantasmatic object. With the word *love* (rather than sex) I want to stress this *fantasmatic* quality of sexuality and the dependence of lesbian desire, specifically, on what is ultimately a *demand for love* inscribed in a fantasy of the female body, a fantasy of dispossession. Where does such fantasy come from?

In Freudian psychoanalysis, fantasy—conscious and unconscious—is understood as a psychic process structuring subjectivity: prompted by the loss of the first object of satisfaction, it is initially shaped by the parental fantasies (see "The Mother's Seduction" in chapter 4 and my reading of the scene at the mirror in *The Well of Loneliness* in chapter 5) and subsequently acts as a dynamic grid through which external reality is adapted or reworked in psychic reality.

> It is the subject's life as a whole which is seen to be shaped and ordered by what might be called, in order to stress this structuring action, "a phantasmatic" (*une fantasmatique*). This should not be conceived of merely as a thematic—not even as one characterised by distinctly specific traits for each subject—for it has its own dynamic, in that the phantasy structures seek to express themselves, to find a way out into consciousness and action, and they are constantly drawing in new material. (*The Language of Psycho-Analysis* 317)

As the new material includes events and representations occurring in the external world, one may add that fantasy is the psychic mechanism that governs the translation of social representations into subjectivity and self-representation, and thus the adaptation or reworking of public fantasies in private fantasies (see chapter 3). However, the parental fantasies and other sociocultural representations of the body as sexual are transmitted to the subject not only discursively but also through practices familial and institutional which, Laplanche and Foucault concur, "implant" sexuality in the body as both source and effect of the subject's desire. The word *practice* in my title is meant to emphasize the material, embodied component of desire as a psychic activity whose effects on the subject's bodily ego constitute a sort of habit or knowledge of the body, what the body "knows"—or better, has come to know—about its instinctual aims.

In one sense, then, "The Practice of Love" is intended to convey that lesbian perverse desire is articulated from a fantasy of dispossession or lack of being through the personal practices that disavow it and resignify the demand for love. But in another sense it means to suggest that the specifically sexual and representational practices of lesbianism, in providing a (new) somatic and representational ground for the work of fantasy, can effectively (re)orient the drives. How specific objects become attached to a desiring fantasy has been exemplified through the reading of fictional texts in chapter 5; in the last chapter I will attempt to articulate the general process by which objects become assigned to the instinct, as Freud puts it, "in consequence of being peculiarly fitted to make satisfaction possible" (*SE* 14: 122). Here I want to consider how practices may affect instinctual activity. In the term *practices* I include personal as well as interpersonal or social practices, what Foucault has described as practices or "technologies" of the self, as well as the practices issuing from institutions and discourses deployed in the "technology of sex," and whose effect is to produce the subject as a sexual subject according to culturally specified categories such as male or female, normal or deviant, healthy or pathological, heterosexual or homosexual, and so forth. A psychoanalysis is an instance of practice that is at once individual and interpersonal; a practice of self, on the part of the analysand, but one whose connection with the socioinstitutional technologies of sexuality, represented by the trained and licensed analyst, is rendered explicit by the essential function of transference. I must recall, in this regard, my discussion of a paper by Helene Deutsch in chapter 2 (58–65 and 70–76).

From the analysis of several, and in particular two, cases of female homosexuality, Deutsch produces a description that diverges in several respects from the classic picture. Having already summarized the salient points in which her deviation from Freud's Oedipal narrative, ironically, approaches what I call his negative theory of sexuality—sexuality as perversion—I will now reconsider them in light of my theory of lesbian sexuality and perverse desire. First, Deutsch sees active female homosexuality ("genuine inversion") as a "return to the mother" detoured and reactivated through the positive Oedipus complex. Such "return," however, is not actually a return to the pre-Oedipal relationship, which is prephallic and pregenital, and solely characterized by oral and sadomasochistic drives. While the latter are prominent in active female homosexuality, they are not so to the exclusion of the phallic or genital drives, which, in effect, are the condition of "genuine" inversion. For without them, Deutsch remarks—and without the passage through the positive Oedipus complex, which entails the recognition of sexual difference and the function of the father as the symbolic agent of castration—the "return" to the mother would need remain sexually inactive in the adult subject and would be symptomatic of "psychic infantilism" ("On Female Homosexuality" 509).

According to the teleological, reproductive assumption that the positive Oedipus complex must altogether replace its negative version—and thus, for the female subject, a male object-choice must replace the infantile female object-choice—Deutsch sees female homosexuality as a regressive object-relation. However, by her own account, "genuine inversion" actually goes beyond the sexual passivity of the feminine position in the positive Oedipus complex in that it is at once both Oedipal and genital, and also able to reactivate the instinctual drives typical of the pregenital relation to the mother, *but redirecting* them toward another female object-choice ("The wish for activity belonging to the phallic phase is carried along in the regression, and reaches its most satisfactory fulfillment in the homosexual relationship" [507]). Were it not for the assumption of reproductive teleology, in other words, "genuine inversion" would be a perfectly satisfactory *resolution* of the female Oedipus complex: its active sexual character is defined primarily by the component instincts but includes genital drives, if not necessarily genital primacy; and its relation to the third term, the father, and hence to the structure of castration, is not denied but recognized and acknowledged. In short, were it not for the presumption of normative heterosexuality, there would be nothing wrong with this picture.

In the perspective of perverse desire, of a theory of sexuality that is non-heterosexual or non-normatively heterosexual (non-reproductive), the picture looks somewhat different. The difference concerns the object-choice which, contrary to Deutsch, I believe is not a maternal one, not a mother substitute. What she understands as "pregenital urges" in the sexual attraction of one woman to another—and consequently construes as a return to the mother instantiated by castration and the disappointment of the wish for the father's child—take on another valence in light of disavowal. The fantasmatic object represented by lesbian object-choice is not the mother, I maintain, but the subject's own body-image, the denied and wished-for female body which castration threatens with nonexistence, and disavowal makes attainable by a compromise fantasy. For, as I have argued, when the disavowal of castration is predicated of the female subject of perverse desire, then what is disavowed must be the loss of something of which her body has knowledge, pain, and pleasure; something toward which she has instinctual aims. That something is not, cannot be, a penis but is most likely to be her body itself (body-image and body-ego), although the symbolic structure of castration rewrites that loss as lack of a penis. For her, then, disavowal produces the ambivalent or contradictory perception of having and yet not having a body: having a body designated as female, and yet not having a female body that can be narcissistically and libidinally invested.

If the narcissistic wound dates back to the pregenital period of the mirror stage and the formation of the first outline or matrix of the ego, and is only subsequently—retroactively—resignified as castration, then the "pregenital urges" seem all the more important to recover and reactivate. But the process of disavowal, through which the compromise fantasy is produced, allowing the reactivation of *all* instinctual drives, entails the displacement of the drives from the first lost object, the mother, to the new objects/signs that both acknowledge and deny the second and most consequential object-loss; that is to say, the subject's own libidinally lost body-ego. This is how I would account for Deutsch's therapeutic success in overcoming her patients' "narcissistic standstill," the symptomatic blocking of affect that kept them passive vis-à-vis their homosexual partners or caused their homosexual relations to be inactive or sublimated. The "standstill in the pendulum swing of the libido," manifested in these patients' "bisexual oscillation between father and mother" (505), is resolved by a freeing of the drives which can then move on to other objects better "fitted to make satisfaction possible," in Freud's words. But how are the drives released from their oscillatory standstill? Deutsch's case histories contain two important indications: one is the role of the positive Oedipus complex and the function of castration, or better the symbolic function of the father; the other is her notion of a "consent to activity."

I have already pointed out how important the castration complex and the role of the father are in Deutsch's view. While the analytic transference allows the patient to recover a positive libidinal cathexis toward the mother, it is only the analytic reworking of the Oedipal relation to the father that reactivates the repressed genital and phallic drives ("not one of my cases failed to have a very strong reaction to the castration complex" [508], and the phallic tendencies are "usually the most urgent" [506] with them). Counterintuitive as that may be, it is the castration complex, with its instantiation of *sexual* difference and its genital emphasis, that turns the pre-Oedipal libidinal investment in the mother into the genital cathexis on another woman that characterizes "genuine homosexuality." The latter, then, requires a passage through the Oedipal wish for the father's child—a wish Deutsch sees reactivated later on in the homosexual relationship: there the father's child would act as a third term between the subject and the mother, to whom the subject "returns" through her homosexual relationship. In the Lacanian revision of the Oedipal structure, the symbolic equivalence of father and father's child is subsumed in the function of the phallus, which also mediates the sexual relation as signifier of desire.

In my reading of perverse desire, however, the mediating term, the signifier of desire, is not the paternal phallus but the fetish. Produced in the disavowal of castration, the fetish retains the active— phallic and genital—valences acquired by the drives in the subject's passage through the complete Oedipus complex (negative and positive) and the apprehension of sexual difference; but fetishistic or perverse desire goes beyond the Oedipus complex and in its own way resolves it. For the instinctual investment represented by the fetish is an investment not in the mother (negative Oedipus) or in the father/father's child (positive Oedipus), but in the female body itself, ultimately in the subject's own body-image and body-ego, whose loss or lack it serves to disavow. I would therefore speculate that the dream images produced by Deutsch's second patient—Anna Freud in masculine clothes and Helene Deutsch herself with a smoldering cigar (pure psychoanalytic camp, one might say)—are fetish images; and, moreover, that they are produced in direct response to the promptings of analytic practice.

What I am suggesting is that it is quite possibly the analyst's belief in the positive Oedipus, her own passionate fiction, and her insistence on representing the function of the father to her patient
that prompt the latter's unconscious fantasy to surface in the
dreams; or that perhaps elicit in the patient a similar, though significantly modified, version of the Oedipal fantasy. The significant modification is that, instead of the father, the patient dreams of phallic
women: a subject of perverse desire, she produces the fetish of masculinity in lieu of the phallic signifier. My divergence from Deutsch
on this point bears restating: as a result of her successful analysis,
the patient does not "return to the mother" empowered by phallic
and Oedipal drives but effectively resolves the complex, with its
"pendulum swing of the libido," and exits the Oedipal stage.[11]
Analysis, in this lucky case, releases the drives from their oscillation
within the two terms of the Oedipus complex and frees them to
move on to other objects better "fitted to make satisfaction
possible." In other words, the analytic promptings instigate in the
patient a practice of the self that, in rewriting or working through
the Oedipal fantasy, produces an active sexuality, one of the
conditions of the practice of love.

Granted, I am speculating. But while Deutsch does not say how
her patients were cured, only that they were later able to live out
their homosexuality successfully, another famous case of analytic
mothering does encourage the hypothesis that an external prompting or analytic suggestion can produce in the subject a fantasy potent enough to release the affective block and reorganize the
instinctual cathexes. I am referring to Melanie Klein's analysis of
"Little Dick," endorsed by Lacan as "precious because it is the text of
a therapist, of a woman of experience," and reported by Felman in
Jacques Lacan and the Adventure of Insight (105–14).

> She sticks symbolism into him, little Dick, with the utmost
> brutality, that Melanie Klein! She begins right away by hitting him
> with the major interpretation. She throws him into a brutal
> verbalization of the Oedipus myth, almost as revolting to us as to

---

11. Similarly, I register my disagreement with Fletcher's view of lesbianism as "a
restorative strategy which seeks to *repair* the losses, denigrations, thwartings that a
patriarchal culture inflicts on the girl in her primary relation to the mother" ("Freud
and His Uses" 105).

any reader whatever—*You are the little train, you want to fuck your mother.* . . . But it is certain that, as a result of this intervention, something happens. (Lacan, *Le Séminaire* I.81, quoted by Felman 107–108)

What does happen? Felman asks on her part. What has the analyst actually done? "Nothing other than to provide verbalization. She has symbolized an effective relation, the relation of a being, named, with another." In response to that, little Dick speaks for the first time, asks for his nurse, and displays anxiety; he "produces a reaction of appeal," a "verbalized address" that entails an answer, thus entering the symbolic. The analyst's prompting ("Dick—little train, Daddy—big train, Dick is going into mummy"), Felman states, "does not function *constatively* (as a truth report, with respect to the reality of the situation) but *performatively* (as a speech act)" (114), providing the structure by which the child will henceforth relate to other human beings (I have commented on this in chapter 3, note 26).

It is this performative quality of psychoanalytic "interpretation" that makes analytic practice an *effective* discourse, a representation of the sexual that has effects, that effects a structuring—in Dick's case, more exactly an implantation—of sexuality in the subject ("she sticks symbolism into him"); or, as I speculate of Deutsch's patients, that may overdetermine a restructuring, a reconfiguration of the drives. While both analysts deploy one and the same Oedipal fantasy, the contingent sociosexual locations and personal histories of the respective patients cause the latter to rework or recast that fantasy and produce individual modifications (though little Dick may have had little room for maneuver), even in a direction the analyst has not intended. And so I have come to Deutsch's second suggestion: that psychoanalytic practice may work as a "consent to activity," granting permission or authorization to sexual practices and instinctual gratifications "which had been impossible in the past" (506), prohibited and/or repressed (her example is masturbation, mine is lesbianism).

How unique this contribution of Deutsch is to the psychoanalytic discourse on female homosexuality can be verified by comparing it with a more recent work by Joyce McDougall (1964) which, while converging with Deutsch's view in many respects, is replete with pathologizing and chastising statements such as "it is only in her relation to a man that a woman feels herself to be sexually a woman and complementary to her mate" ("Homosexuality in Women" 173); "the homosexual pays dearly for a fragile identity which is not truly her own" (210); or "the price she must pay for her homosexual identity is the renunciation of all feminine sexual desire as well as of the children she consciously longs for" (211). No less pathologizing is a long essay by M. Masud R. Khan, "The Importance of Infantile Sexuality and Early Object Relations in Female Homosexuality," first published in 1963 and later included in his influential *Alienation in Perversion*. He explicitly relies on Deutsch but, unlike her, insists that anything but a temporary "acting out" of homosexuality is a form of psychopathology. Characteristically, Khan's argument is made from the case history of one young woman who, as a result of the "homosexual acting out" of her (pre-)Oedipal conflicts by means of a temporary lesbian relationship and of working through said conflicts in a transference neurosis while in analysis with him, succeeded in reaching heterosexual orgasm and being "happily married" ever after (62). He does report, however, in all honesty, that the patient had stated up front that she was not a lesbian.

Much more rigidly than Deutsch, both Khan and McDougall insist that only normative heterosexuality counts as a successful outcome of analysis, reiterating in a "serious" context what pop psychoanalysis in the United States was dispensing to the avid readers of pulp fiction at approximately the same time (see, for example, Robertiello's *Voyage from Lesbos*).[12] In light of Deutsch's suggestion that analytic practice should provide a "consent to activity," there can be no surprise at the near-unanimous rejection of psychoanalysis by contemporary gay studies, for she is clearly unique among orthodox practitioners. The importance of her essay toward a theory of lesbian sexuality owes as much to her singular awareness of the effective, performative character of analytic practice as it does to the singularity of the clinical practice she describes as a "consent to activity."

I have already said that the nature of such consent may be discursive and symbolic, as it can be only in a therapeutic setting, as

---

12. I am indebted for this reference to Yvonne Keller's original study of what she defines as the "lesbian pulps" genre in American popular fiction of the 1950s and 1960s. For the reference to Masud Khan's work, I am grateful to Maria Antonietta Schepisi.

well as bodily or physically sexual in the context of an actual lesbian relationship. But the implications of such notion of consent exceed both analytic practice and the practice of sex between female partners. For sexuality and desire exist in the realm of fantasy, which trespasses beyond the couch, beyond the bedroom, into the public spaces of representation. Thus the public representation of lesbianism, including most importantly lesbian discursive and performative practices, can be an equally effective discourse, yielding "multiple effects of displacement, intensification, reorientation, and modification of desire itself" (Foucault, *The History of Sexuality,* vol. 1: 23). The conjunction of new symbolic forms with a performative consent or authorizing (authoritative) discourse on lesbian sexuality can result not only in a different knowledge of the body or what the body-ego can know about its instinctual aims, but also in what I will call new habits or habit changes; that is to say, a different production of reference and meaning. How representational, performative, or directly sexual practices can inflect instinctual and psychic organization through a subject's perceptions of her body-ego will be the topic of the next chapter.

This book has been about representations of lesbian sexuality and desire, private and public forms of fantasy, individual and collective passionate fictions. Only a minimal part of the wide range of writings and other forms of cultural production by lesbians has found a place in what had to be a tight and thorough argumentation with and through feminist and psychoanalytic writings on the subject, not merely in order to counter their elisions, equivocations, assimilations, or appropriations, whether in naive good faith or with the insouciance of heterosexual presumption, but more constructively in order to articulate a formal model of desire that may account for the sociopsychic processes of lesbian subjectivity as I see it represented in the works of lesbians. That my own critical practice of subjective, dialogic engagement with the texts I cite is itself a practice of love and the exposure of a passionate fiction, should be by now quite apparent: it is only by generic and rhetorical conventions that this book does not read like an autobiography. But I would like to close with bits of a conversation between two lesbians about their own practice of love. I select this particular text, published in 1981, not as paradigmatic of the many and diverse ways in which lesbian sexuality is lived and can be represented, but because the words of the speakers resonate with the texts on which this study is based.

(1) A: My fantasy life is deeply involved in a butch/femme exchange. I never come together with a woman, sexually, outside of those roles. It's saying to my partner, "Love me enough to let me go where I need to go and take me there. Don't make me think it through. Give me a way to be so in my body that I don't have to think; that you can fantasize for both of us. You map it out. You are in control."

(2)   It's hard to talk about things like giving up power without it sounding passive. I am willing to give myself over to a woman equal to her amount of wanting. I expose myself for her to see what's possible for her to love in me that's female. I want her to respond to it. I may not be doing something active with my body, but more eroticizing her need that I feel in her hands as she touches me.

(3)   I begin to imagine myself being the *woman that a woman always wanted.* That's what I begin to eroticize. That's what I begin to feel from my lover's hands. I begin to fantasize myself becoming more and more female in order to comprehend and meet what I feel happening in her body. I don't want her not to be female to me. Her need is female, but it's butch because I am asking her to expose her desire through the movement of her hands on my body.

(4)   I am making every part of my body accessible to that woman. I completely trust her. There's no place she cannot touch me. My body is literally open to any way she interprets her sexual need. My power is that I know how to read her inside of her own passion.

(5) B: From an early age . . . I didn't really think of myself as female, or male. I thought of myself as this hybrid or somethin. I just kinda thought of myself as this free agent until I got tits. Then I thought, oh oh, some problem has occurred here. . . . For me, the way you conceive of yourself as a woman and the way I am attracted to women sexually reflect that butch/femme exchange—where a woman believes herself so woman that it really makes me want her.

(6)   When I was making love to her . . . every pore in her body was entrusting me to handle her, to take care of her sexual desire. This look on her face is like nothing else. It fills me up. She entrusts me to determine where she'll go

sexually. And I honestly feel a power inside me strong enough to heal the deepest wound.

(7)   To be butch, to me, is not to be a woman. The classic [stone butch] stereotype is the woman who sexually refuses another woman to touch her. It goes something like this: She doesn't want to feel her femaleness because she thinks of you as the "real" woman and if she makes love to you, she doesn't have to feel her own body as the object of desire. She can be a kind of "bodiless lover."

(8) A: You see, I want you as a woman, not as a man; but, I want you in the way *you* need to be, which may not be traditionally female, but which is the area that you express as *butch*. Here is where in the other world you have suffered the most damage. Part of the reason I love to be with butches is because I feel I repair that damage. . . . I feel that as a femme I get back my femaleness and give a different definition of femaleness to a butch. That's what I mean about one of those unexplored territories that goes beyond roles, but goes through roles to get there.

(9) B: How I fantasize sex roles has been really different for me with different women. . . . I am seriously attracted to butches sometimes. . . . I know there's a huge part of me that wants to be handled in the way I described I can handle another woman. I am very compelled toward that "lover" posture. I have never totally reckoned with being the "beloved" and, frankly, I don't know if it takes a butch or a femme or what to get me there.

(10)   I remember being fourteen years old and there was this girl, a few years older than me, who I had this crush on. And on the last day of school, I knew I wasn't going to see her for months! We had hugged good-bye and I went straight home. Going into my bedroom, I got into my unmade bed and I remember getting the sheets, winding them into a kind of rope, and pulling them up between my legs and just holding them there under my chin. I just sobbed and sobbed because I knew I couldn't have her, maybe never have a woman to touch. It's just pure need and it's whole. It's like using sexuality to describe how deeply you need/want intimacy, passion, love. (Hollibaugh and Moraga 398–402)

The speakers, A and B, self-identify and speak from the respective positions of femme and butch, but their statements, which I have excerpted and very slightly rearranged in fragments 1–10 (hereafter cited in parenthesis in the text), equally support my reading of perverse desire. Its instinctual investment in the female body, I suggested earlier, can be attained only with another woman: A's "let me go where I need to go and take me there" in fragment 1 is echoed by B's "I don't know if it takes a butch or a femme . . . to get me there" in fragment 9. Or, to repeat my catch phrase one last time, it takes two women, not one, to make a lesbian. When A says, "Give me a way to be so in my body that I don't have to think; that you can fantasize for both of us" (1); when she opens her body to the need she feels in the other's hands, and wants "to see what's possible for her to love in me that's female" (2), A is expressing her own instinctual aim, as well; she is also striving after the fantasmatic female body, the intrapsychic image that is the lovers' common object of desire, the female body they can find together, always for the first time.

The denied and wished-for female body of the "bodiless" butch lover (7) is recovered in the gaze of the other woman whose entrusted body fills B with the power "to heal the deepest wound" (6 and 7)—her own wound, the other woman's, or perhaps both? To this power corresponds the femme's seemingly complementary power to "repair the damage" suffered by the butch "in the other world" (8)—the damage of dispossession, devaluation, or degradation of her body-ego and body-image that is female castration. But their powers are only seemingly complementary because, for both, for A as well as B, the power to heal, to momentarily make whole the body-ego, is female-sexed and female-embodied. Indeed, if A knows the damage suffered by her lover, if she can "read her inside of her own passion" (4), it is because her body also knows that wound, that "pure need," that demand for love (10): "Love me enough to let me go where I need to go and take me there" (1). And for that very reason she can eroticize her own body *for* the other: "I *begin* to fantasize myself *becoming* more and more female *in order to comprehend and meet* what I feel happening in *her* body" (3; emphasis added).

Erotic power, wound, need, hands: these are the signifiers of desire, the fetish signs that disavow—acknowledge and deny—the damage, castration, the loss of a libidinally invested body-image, the lack of being in the female body-ego. They may be represented by different sociosexual masquerades, by mannish or feminine styles of self-presentation, but as A remarks, "It's not that I have to have spike heels on in order to fantasize who I am. Now that's a lot of classist shit, conceiving of a femme in such a narrow way" (399). By fantasizing herself the object of her lover's desire ("the *woman that a woman always wanted*" [3]), A conjures up and elicits a desire she knows ("My power is that I know how to read her inside of her own passion" [4]) and whose source is her own body ("I am asking her to expose her desire through the movement of her hands on my body" [3]). She is as much the subject of that desire as she is its object; she is at once desiring subject and desiring object. The wish to be at once the lover and the loved, in Adrienne Rich's words, is also expressed, if more tentatively, by B: "I have never totally reckoned with being the 'beloved.' . . . I am seriously attracted to butches sometimes" (9).

The erotic rules of butch and femme that so unquestionably shape the fantasy scenarios of the two speakers' desire are at the same time reaffirmed and deconstructed in this exchange. They are strongly coded signs, markers of difference that each must go through to reach, beyond them, "a different definition of femaleness" (8). As B self-searchingly concludes, "Frankly, I don't know if it takes a butch or a femme or what to get me there" (9).

Chapter 7

Sexual Structuring and Habit Changes

> I am much more interested in problems about techniques of the self and things like that. . . . Sex is boring.
> —Michel Foucault, Interview in *Vanity Fair* (1983), quoted by Martin, Gutman, and Hutton 8

Having advanced the idea that the body-ego (with its conscious and unconscious defenses: disavowal, repression, etc.) is subject to continuous negotiations with both the internal and external worlds, I must refer to an earlier work in which I sought to articulate the relations of the subject to the world of signs and to locate subjectivity, through the concept of experience, in the area of theoretical overlap between semiotics and psychoanalysis ("Semiotics and Experience," *Alice Doesn't* 158–86). My concern in that book was with representation, and its primary emphasis fell on semiotics as a theory of signs, of signifying systems as well as of the conditions of sign production. However, in proposing that the subject of semiotics is at once producer and interpreter of signs, and thus "physically implicated or bodily engendered in the production of meaning, representation and self-representation" (183), my study reached toward the domain of psychoanalysis: the psychic apparatus with its primary and secondary processes, the drives and their vicissitudes, and the unconscious and conscious defenses that constitute the subject as a bodily ego were an integral, though as yet unintegrated, part of the terrain I began to map out in that book for a semiotic approach to subjectivity.

I now would like to look more closely at the conceptualization of the subject in Freud's theory of sexuality and Charles Sanders Peirce's theory of semiosis, two theories that are roughly contemporary chronologically but seem otherwise quite distant, if not incompatible. My purpose in doing this is to articulate more precisely the join of the psychic to the social by focusing, this time, on sexuality as one particular instance of a more general process that links subjectivity to social signification and material reality. In *Alice Doesn't*, drawing on Peirce's theory of interpretants, in particular the concept of habit-change, I redefined experience as a complex of habits, dispositions, associations, perceptions, and expectations resulting from the continuous semiosic interaction of the self's "inner world" with the "outer world." The Peircian worlds—most obviously the former—are not strictly coterminous with the ego's internal and external worlds in Freud's second model of the psyche, but are homologous to them; for in both theories the epistemological function of the notions of inner and outer, and internal and external worlds is to account for the constructedness of subjectivity and its overdetermination by the social (on Peirce's semiotic view of subjectivity, see Colapietro).

What bridges or connects Peirce's outer and inner worlds is the chain of interpretants, an ongoing series of semiotic mediations linking objects, signs, and events of the world to their "significate effects" in the subject—a subject that can thus be said to be "the place in which, the body in whom, the significate effect of the sign takes hold and is real-ized" (*Alice Doesn't* 182–83). Freud's ego, I have argued here, is a frontier creature, a site of negotiations—an open border, so to speak—between internal or instinctual pressures and external or societal demands. In a semiotic perspective, then, the ego's alterations resulting from its defenses may be seen as an ongoing series of mediations which the ego performs or which are performative for the ego in relation to its internal and external worlds. In this perspective, the ego's mechanisms of defense appear homologous to Peirce's interpretants: they have a similarly constitutive function vis-à-vis the ego as the interpretants have vis-à-vis the subject in semiosis. To clarify this statement I briefly summarize the argument of my earlier work.[1]

Peirce names interpretant the dynamic structure that supports the nexus of object, sign, and meaning, as well as the process of mediation itself. A series of interpretants, or "significate effects" (I insist on this term which conveys the processual and open-ended nature of meaning), sustains each instance of semiosis, each instance of the unending process of mediations or negotiations between the self and the world; that is to say, each moment of what, for the subject, is an imperceptible passage from object (or event, in the outer world) to sign (mental or physical representation) to meaning effect (in the inner world) is conceptualized by Peirce as an interpretant. Interpretants are not only mental representations: there are, of course, "intellectual" interpretants (concepts), but there are also "emotional" and "energetic" interpretants. For example, the significate effect produced by a sign such as the performance of a piece of music may be only a feeling; such a feeling is an *emotional interpretant* of that sign. However, through the mediation of the emotional interpretant, a further significate effect may be produced, which may be a mental or a "muscular exertion"; this would be an *energetic interpretant*, for it involves an "effort," whether mental or physical. The third type of effect that may be produced by the sign is a *"habit-change"*: "a modification of a person's tendencies toward action, resulting from previous experiences or from previous exertions" (*Collected Papers* 5.491). This is the final or "ultimate" significate effect of the sign, Peirce writes, designating it the *logical interpretant:* "The real and living logical conclusion [of the series of mediations that makes up this particular instance of semiosis] *is* that habit." But he quickly qualifies the designation "logical":

> The concept which is a logical interpretant is only imperfectly so. It somewhat partakes of the nature of a verbal definition, and is as inferior to the habit, and much in the same way, as a verbal definition is inferior to the real definition. The deliberately formed, self-analyzing habit—self-analyzing because formed by the aid of analysis of the exercises that nourished it—is the living definition, the veritable and final logical interpretant. (5.491)

---

1. The discussion of Peirce in this and the following paragraphs builds on pp. 172–83 of *Alice Doesn't*, occasionally borrowing a phrase or a sentence verbatim, but the comparison with Freud that I am about to elaborate was no more than suggested there (181).

Therefore, as I argued in *Alice Doesn't,* the final interpretant is not logical in the sense in which a syllogism is logical, or because it is the result of an intellectual operation such as deductive reasoning, but rather because it makes sense out of the emotion and muscular/mental effort that preceded it by providing a conceptual representation of that effort. Peirce uses the term *habit* rather widely, to include "associations" and even "dissociations," although he does at one point join habit to belief and conscious purposefulness: "A practical belief," he states, "may be described as a habit of deliberate behavior"; but he qualifies the statement by adding, "The word 'deliberate' *is hardly completely defined* by saying that it implies attention to memories of past experience and to one's present purpose, together with self-control" (5.538; emphasis added). The purposefulness of habit, in other words, is not merely rational or willful; if its attentiveness to "memories of past experiences" makes me think of Freud's association of screen memories with fantasy, Peirce's own use of *habit* to denote "such a specialization, original or acquired, of the nature of a man, or an animal, or a vine, or a crystallizable chemical substance, or anything else, that he or it will behave, or always tend to behave, in a way describable in general terms upon every occasion" (5.538), recalls or resonates with Freud's notion of phylogenetic or hereditary factors in mental life (*SE* 17: 121).

In "Instincts and Their Vicissitudes" Freud distinguishes between external stimuli and instinctual stimuli. The latter, originating from within the organism, cannot be mastered, like the former, by a purposeful or "expedient" muscular movement (cf. Peirce's "muscular exertion") but require the nervous system "to undertake involved and interconnected activities by which the external world is so changed as to afford satisfaction to the internal source of stimulation." However, there is nothing to prevent us, he concludes, from "supposing that the instincts themselves are, at least in part, precipitates of the effects of external stimulation, which in the course of phylogenesis have brought about modifications in the living substance" (*SE* 14: 120). Elsewhere, elucidating the separate developments of the libido and the ego-instincts, he writes that both "are at bottom heritages, abbreviated recapitulations of the development which all mankind has passed through from its primaeval days over long periods of time" (*SE* 16: 354); and the primal fantasies themselves are "a phylogenetic endowment" (*SE* 16: 371).

My intention here is not to trace easily arguable parallels in Peirce's and Freud's epistemological assumptions or backgrounds, but rather to stress that Peirce's habit is not a purely mental, rational, or intellectual result of the semiosic process. While it is a mental representation, it is so in the sense in which Freud speaks of mental life as psychic reality, a domain where the mental is always implicated with the somatic. Put another way, habit or habit-change is the final interpretant or representative of a somatic-mental process (semiosis) not unlike the way in which the drive becomes perceptible in its representations or signifiable through its representatives. Thus, while Freud's specific elaboration of the unconscious is quite absent from Peirce's work, one may nevertheless, today, re-read the notion of habit-change as the end result of mental processes that may be in part or wholly unconscious; in turn, habit might be thought of as one element involved in, for example, repetition compulsion. Indeed, when Laplanche and Pontalis explain that in Freud "unconscious wishes tend to be fulfilled through the restoration of signs which are bound to the earliest experiences of satisfaction" and that the "restoration operates according to the laws of primary processes" (*The Language of Psycho-Analysis* 481), I see no reason why it would be wrong to infer that those early experiences could have resulted in signs whose final interpretants were unconscious habits. Unconscious wishes, therefore, might be thought of as the significate *effects* of those early experiences as well as *causes* for the re-presentation—be it through symptom-formation, hallucination, dream images, or fetishes—of the *signs* that fulfill(ed) them.

On the other hand, Lacan absolutely denies the kinship of the unconscious with instinct as "archaic function" (Freud's phylogenesis). Although an idea of the unconscious as "veiled presence of a thought to be placed at the level of being before it is revealed" existed long before Freud (Edward von Hartmann first used the term in his *Philosophie des Unbewussten* in 1869), Lacan insists that "whatever reference Freud makes to it . . . has nothing to do with the Freudian unconscious, nothing at all, whatever its analytic vocabulary, its inflection, its deviations may be" (*The Four Fundamental Concepts of Psycho-Analysis* 126). In his "new alliance with the meaning of the Freudian discovery," Lacan programmatically declares himself concerned only with "the Cartesian subject," the subject who is an effect of "speech," and not of any "substance," "pathos," "suffering," etc.; he thus excludes from his purview the instinctual, somatic, and material components of Freud's drives and, ironically, of Peirce's semiosis as well. But, as Laplanche remarks citing Freud, the drive leans or is propped up on a "bodily function essential to life" (16). Thus, when the Peircian notions of habit and habit-change are evoked or explicitly invoked by those Lacanian theorists concerned with the efficacy of analytic practice and interpretation (Felman, *Jacques Lacan and the Adventure of Insight* 125 and 140) or with the real as cause of psychic reality (Copjec 239), one may suppose that they do so because Peirce's interpretant and habit-change, in joining subjectivity to the social as a confrontation with material reality, also confer upon the subject a historical dimension. (For a fuller discussion of this point and a comparison of Peirce's and Lacan's formulations of the subject's relation to, respectively, the sign and the signifier, I must refer the reader to *Alice Doesn't* 178–81.)

It is these particular aspects of the concept of habit-change as I have elaborated it—the somatic, material, and historical dimensions it inscribes in the subject—that are especially important to me in conceptualizing sexuality as a *process of sexual structuring*, a process overdetermined by both internal and external forces and constraints. The homology I see between the subject of semiosis and Freud's bodily ego allows me to envisage sexuality itself as a semiosic process in which the contingencies of both a personal and a social history produce the subject as their shifting point of intersection. Or, looking at it another way, sexuality appears as a semiosic process in which the subject's desire is the result of a series of significate effects (conscious and unconscious interpretants, so to speak) that are contingent upon a personal *and* a social history; where by history I mean the particular configurations of discourses, representations, and practices—familial and broadly institutional, cultural and subcultural, public and private—that the subject crosses and that in turn traverse the subject, according to the contingencies of each subject's singular existence in the world. I want to argue that sexuality is one form of (self-)representation, and fantasy is one specific instance of the more general process of semiosis, which enjoins subjectivity to social signification and to reality itself.

One might ask, at this point, whether the concept of semiosis is a useful analogy, a useful theoretical interpretant, for intrapsychic processes in Freud's internal world, as well as for the ways in which external factors influence and shape, from its very beginning, the subject's *sexual* existence. With regard to the internal world, consider Laplanche's description of the infantile subject's relation to the object.

> *On the one hand there is from the beginning an object, but . . . on the other hand sexuality does not have, from the beginning, a real object.* It should be understood that the real object, milk, was the object of the function, which is virtually preordained to the world of satisfaction. Such is the real object which has been lost, but the object linked to the autoerotic turn, the breast—become a fantasmatic breast—is, for its part, the object of the sexual drive. Thus the sexual object is not identical to the object of the function, but is displaced in relation to it. . . . The object to be rediscovered is not the lost object, but its substitute by displacement; the lost object is the object of self-preservation, of hunger, and the object one seeks to refind in sexuality is an object displaced in relation to that first object. From this, of course, arises the impossibility of ultimately ever rediscovering the object, since the object which has been lost *is not the same* as that which is to be rediscovered. (*Life and Death in Psychoanalysis* 19–20)

Compare this with Peirce's distinction, à propos of the relation of sign to object, between "the Dynamical Object" and "the Immediate Object." The former is external to the sign and corresponds to the referent in linguistics or to the real object in common language (it is, he writes, "the Reality which by some means contrives to determine the Sign to its Representation"), whereas the latter is a representation internal to the sign ("the Object as the sign itself represents it, and whose Being is thus dependent upon the representation of it in the Sign") (4.536). The difference between dynamic and immediate objects is given by the latter's relation to "the ground of the representation" (the setting or context which makes pertinent certain features of the object in/for the representation).[2] Umberto Eco explains the distinction thus:

---

2. "A sign, or representamen, is something which stands to somebody for something in some respect or capacity. It addresses somebody, that is, creates in the mind of that person an equivalent sign, or perhaps a more developed sign. That sign which it creates I call the *interpretant* of the first sign. The sign stands for something, its *object*. It stands for that object, not in all respects, but in reference to a sort of idea, which I have sometimes called the *ground* of the representamen" (Peirce 2.228).

> Signs have a direct connection with Dynamic Objects only insofar
> as objects determine the formation of a sign; on the other hand,
> signs only "know" Immediate Objects, that is, meanings. There is a
> difference between *the object of which a sign is a sign* and the
> *object of a sign;* the former is the Dynamic Object, a state of the
> outer world; the latter is a semiotic construction. ("Peirce and the
> Semiotic Foundations of Openness" 193)

The difference between dynamic object and immediate object is
analogous, I suggest, to the one Laplanche postulates between the
breast with milk (the object of hunger or self-preservation) and the
fantasmatic breast (the sexual object, the lost object one seeks to
refind in sexuality), a difference that he describes as a substitution
by displacement: the two objects "are in a relation of essential *conti-
guity* which leads us to slide almost indifferently from one to the
other, from the milk to the breast as its symbol" (20). (Similarly, by
the way, the immediate object, transposed in the Saussurian system
and equated to the signified, is often assimilated and made to slide
into the referent, the dynamic object.) Both the sexual object constructed in fantasy and the immediate object constructed in semiosis are contiguous but displaced in relation to the real; and hence
the homology of fantasy (in sexuality) and semiosis with regard to
the subject's relation to the object of representation.

Freud, too, stresses the instinct's *displacement* in relation to the
object and the latter's mutability in the course of the former's vicissitudes.

> The object [*Objekt*] of an instinct is the thing in regard to which or
> through which the instinct is able to achieve its aim. It is what is
> most variable about an instinct and *is not originally connected with
> it, but becomes assigned to it only in consequence of being peculiarly
> fitted to make satisfaction possible.* The object is not necessarily
> something extraneous: it may equally well be a part of the subject's
> own body. It may be changed any number of times in the course of
> the vicissitudes which the instinct undergoes during its existence;
> and highly important parts are played by this displacement of
> instinct. (*SE* 14: 122–23; emphasis added)

In the phrase *becomes assigned* one can read a sort of motivation for
the object, namely, its fitness or suitability to provide satisfaction:
an(y) object—a real object, so to speak—can become the object of

the instinct, can become a sexual object, by virtue of that (real) object's fitness to provide satisfaction. It seems to me that a very similar notion of motivation informs Peirce's notion of *ground* as that which underlies the semiosic passage from dynamic object to immediate object and determines the suitability of the latter; that semiosic passage or movement is, in effect, a displacement of the real object into its representation in the sign.

Indeed Laplanche's definition of sexuality—a recasting of Freud's four-term articulation of the concept of drive in "Instincts and Their Vicissitudes," premised with the crucial comment that "the drive properly speaking, in the only sense faithful to Freud's discovery, *is* sexuality" (23)—reads like the description of a semiosic process: "Sexuality, in its entirety, in the human infant, lies in a movement which deflects the instinct, metaphorizes its aim, displaces and internalizes its object, and concentrates its source on what is ultimately a minimal zone, the erotogenic zone" (23). The kind of movement rendered by *deflects, metaphorizes, displaces,* and *internalizes,* I suggest, is quite akin to the representational work of interpretants; for them, as for the sexual drive, the real object is lost and *is not the same* as the one which is found or resignified in semiosis. Thus the dynamic structure of semiosis can usefully account—is a useful interpretant—for intrapsychic processes. Does it also offer a useful interpretant for the external or interpsychic factors that overdetermine a subject's experience of sexuality?

After examining the drive's relation to the object, Laplanche turns to elaborating its source in the erotogenic zones. These, "a kind of breaking or turning point within the bodily envelope," bear "the principal biological exchanges" (feeding, evacuation, etc.) and are thus zones of exchange and of attentive maternal care (23–24).

> These zones, then, attract the first erotogenic maneuvers from the adult. An even more significant factor, if we introduce the subjectivity of the first "partner": these zones *focalize parental fantasies* and above all *maternal fantasies,* so that we may say, in what is barely a metaphor, that they are the points through which is *introduced into the child that alien internal entity* which is, properly speaking, *the sexual excitation.* (24)

At the subjective, intrapsychic, and most concrete bodily level, this psychoanalytic view corresponds to Foucault's historical view of sexuality as "an implantation of perversions" in the subject by the discursive and institutional practices (familial and more broadly social) that constitute the technology of sex. In a semiotic view or in the terms of my argument, the child's placement vis-à-vis parental fantasies may be seen to constitute the *ground* of the subject's first apperception or rudimentary representation of the sexual; say, the representational ground from which the body as dynamic object (the real body of the child as well as that of the mother) becomes the body as immediate object (the subject's body-image as well as the fantasmatic breast) and *as such* enters into the process of semiosis, the world of signs, through the chain of interpretants and their significate effects. In other words, if what performs the displacement of the real body onto the fantasmatic body can be seen as the semiotic displacement of a dynamic object onto an immediate object, then the reference of this representational displacement, the ground of the representation, is the parental fantasies; and from this ground are initially constituted the subject's infantile fantasies. Subsequently, in the subject's further interaction with the external world, these fantasies will be modified through other representations and interpretants; other fantasies both private and public will provide the grounds for self-representation in sexuality and for what objects may *become assigned* to the instinct.[3]

In the terms of this study, the process by which fetish-objects become assigned to the signification of perverse desire may be recast as follows. On the ground of a fantasy of castration as dispossession of the female body, a particular but variable and typically inappropriate object (dynamic object) becomes assigned to the sexual instinct as object (immediate object) of the subject's perverse desire. The real object may be a part of the body, clothing, or other prop or element of the subjective fantasy scenario; however inappropriate it may seem to sexual ends (read: genital or reproductive ends), the fetish is "peculiarly fitted to make satisfaction possible," in Freud's words (where "peculiarly" remarks the inappropriateness, as well as the singularity, of the fetish-object), because it stands for what is absent or denied but fantasmatically wished for, and is suit-

---

3. I may reiterate here Laplanche and Pontalis's emphasis on the structuring action of fantasy, already noted in chapter 6: "the phantasy structures seek to express themselves, to find a way out into consciousness and action, and they are constantly drawing in new material" (*The Language of Psycho-Analysis* 317).

able to signify at once its absence and the subject's desire for it. Foucault's term *"reverse" discourse* actually suggests something of the process by which a representation in the external world is subjectively assumed, reworked through fantasy, in the internal world and then returned to the external world resignified, rearticulated discursively and/or performatively in the subject's self-representation—in speech, gesture, costume, body, stance, and so forth. Therefore, as I have suggested, the popularity of *visible* masculine signifiers as lesbian fetish in Western cultures is directly proportionate to the latter's enduringly hegemonic representation of lesbianism as phallic pretension or male identification.

However, the fundamental role of fantasy in sexuality as the ground from which the socio-psycho-sexual subject is constituted through the semiosic process that assigns object to instincts is certainly not limited to the subject of perverse desire; think, for one thing, of the importance that fashion and social performance have, in all cultures and cultural (self-)representations, for the normative sexual identity of their subjects; and, for another, of the popularity of the Oedipus fantasy in Western cultures before and after Freud, a popularity so deeply grounded in cultural representations and so widely perpetuated by social arrangements that it could be not only naturalized as phylogenesis but projected onto the entire world as a universal phenomenon. Obviously Freud was neither the first nor the last to know the profound effect of the Oedipus fantasy in Western subjectivities, but by placing it at the center of the psyche and of his theory of sexuality, he articulated its *structuring role* in the social construction of sexuality as the West knows it. Thus, while the Oedipus may be a dominant, even a founding, fantasy of Western representation, as I argued elsewhere (*Alice Doesn't*, chapter 5), the importance of theorizing fantasy as the semiosic ground of sexuality lies in that fantasy itself, as sociopsychic process, exceeds its historically contingent configurations, the Oedipus included. In other words, the value of Freud's theory of sexuality far exceeds the normative Oedipal fantasy that grounds it; for in analyzing how subjectivity (his own, as well as his patients') is constructed from the ground of a dominant—social *and* psychoanalytic—fiction, he intimated and opened the critical path to understanding the semiosic nature of fantasy as that which links the subject to the social through sexuality.

I began this study in chapter 1 from Freud's assertion in the *Three Essays* that the sexual instinct is *in the first instance* independent of its object (*SE* 7: 148). Now, in light of the various texts through which I have developed the notion of perverse desire, I think it is possible to conclude that *in the last instance* the sexual instinct *as* perverse desire is dependent on a fantasy scenario which the object evokes and helps to restage; conversely, it is in that scenario, in that restaging, that the object acquires its fantasmatic value as object. How objects may become attached to a desiring fantasy can be conceptualized as a semiosic process in which objects and bodies are displaced from external to psychic reality (from referent to object/sign, or from representation to fantasy) through a series of significate effects, habits and habit-changes. And as the subject is the place in which, the body in whom, the significate effects of signs take hold and are real-ized, there is always something real in psychic fantasy: real for the subject's internal world and real for the external world, from which the fantasy is mediated and to which it returns, again mediated and to a greater or lesser extent resignified through the subject's agency in the social. For in the infinite universe of signs that is social reality, each subject is in turn object and sign. To say that sexuality is an effect of semiosis is to say that public and private fantasies, or social representations and subjective representations, work as a nexus of reciprocally constitutive effects between the subject and the social.

I will end with an observation of perhaps no greater significance than that of an interesting coincidence in the universe of signs. Several times throughout this book references have been made to Foucault, and not casually. For my study of perverse desire, although concerned more with intrapsychic than with institutional mechanisms, is premised on a conception of the sexual that is actually closer to Foucault than to Freud; namely, that individual sexual structuring is both an effect and a condition of the social construction of sexuality. While the first volume of Foucault's *History of Sexuality* describes the discursive practices and institutional mechanisms that implant sexuality in the social subject, Freudian psychoanalytic theory describes the subjective mechanisms through which the implantation takes, as it were, producing the subject as a sexual subject. Although I have been working through the latter, both Freud's and Foucault's theories of sexuality delineate the conceptual horizon of my study. In this chapter, in particular, I have considered sexuality as an instance of semiosis in order to identify the process by which the social subject is produced as a sexual subject and a subjectivity. To that end I have suggested that Peirce's notions of interpretant and habit-change may serve as the juncture or point of theoretical articulation of Freud's psychosexual view of the internal world with Foucault's sociosexual view, by providing an account of the manner in which the implantation of sexuality as perversion actually occurs in one subject, one body-ego. When, reading one of Foucault's last published works, which outlines his projected study of the "Technologies of the Self," I encountered the term *self-analysis* in relation to the introspective exercises and the writing of self that, according to him, defined a new experience of the self in Greco-Roman thought of the first two centuries A.D., the coincidence of that term, *self-analysis*, with Peirce's "self-analyzing habit" could hardly fail to strike me.

As Foucault's own research in volumes 2 and 3 of his *History* shifted from the macrohistory of modern sexuality in the West to "a genealogy of desiring man" (*The Use of Pleasure* 12) and thus to the microhistory of localized practices and discourses on one type of sexuality (between men and boys), his focus, too, shifted from the social to the subjective, from the technology of sex to the "technologies of the self," the discursive practices and techniques of the individual's construction of self. As he described it retrospectively, his project was

> a history of the experience of sexuality, where experience is understood as the correlation between fields of knowledge, types of normativity, and forms of subjectivity in a particular culture. . . . But when I came to study the modes according to which individuals are given to recognize themselves as sexual subjects, the problems were much greater. . . . It seemed to me that one could not very well analyze the formation and development of the experience of sexuality from the eighteenth century onward, without doing a historical and critical study dealing with desire and the desiring subject. . . . Thus, in order to understand how the modern individual could experience himself as a subject of a "sexuality," it was essential first to determine how, for centuries, Western man had been brought to recognize himself as a subject of desire. . . . It seemed appropriate to look for the forms and modalities of the relation to self by which the individual

constitutes and recognizes himself *qua* subject. (*The Use of Pleasure* 4–6)

In the introductory volume, he had indicted psychoanalysis as complicit with the dominant power-knowledge apparati of the modern era. Here, even as he speaks of the subject of desire, Foucault pointedly sidesteps the psychoanalytic knowledge on that subject, looking instead for another approach. The whole first part of volume 3, for example, is devoted to Artemidorus's *Interpretation of Dreams* without a single reference to Freud, whose homonymous text also marked the starting point and first elaboration of his theory of desire on the basis of his *self-analysis*. It is impossible to imagine that Foucault missed these obvious analogies; indeed they must have been intended to emphasize the distance between Freud's scientific project, if based on his personal and admittedly Oedipal fantasy, and Foucault's critical genealogy of desire. But neither his pointed taking of distance from psychoanalysis nor his much greater historical distance from his materials and sources can altogether erase the effective presence of an enabling fantasy, though not an Oedipal fantasy, in Foucault's authorial subject of desire. The care with which the erotic relations between men and boys are examined, described, and pursued from Greece to Rome, through modifications in sexual ethics, to the development of "an art of existence" and the constitution of the self "as the ethical subject of one's sexual behavior" (*The Care of the Self* 238–40), more than suggests the presence of both a *self-analysis* and an enabling fantasy in Foucault's theory—the fantasy of a non-Oedipal world, beyond the Fall, perversion, repression, or Judeo-Christian self-renunciation, and sustained instead by a productively austere, openly homoerotic, virile ethics and practice of existence.

It is in the context of this genealogical project, effectively a genealogy of man-desiring man, that the coincidence in the universe of signs occurs. In describing the "new experience of self" derived from introspection, from taking care of oneself, and from the practice of writing about oneself that was prominent in the second century A.D., as exemplified in Marcus Aurelius's letter to his older lover and "sweetest of masters," Foucault highlights "Marcus's meticulous concern with daily life, with the movements of the spirit, with self-analysis" ("Technologies of the Self" 28). This latter term, *self-analy-*

sis, together with *self-exercise* (27) and other techniques "which permit individuals to effect by their own means or with the help of others a certain number of operations on their own bodies and souls, thoughts, conduct, and way of being" (18), is altogether convergent with Peirce's notion of habit, the "deliberately formed, self-analyzing habit—self-analyzing because formed by the aid of analysis of the exercises that nourished it" (5.491, cited above) as the final interpretant, the "living" effect of semiosis. The new *experience* of self Foucault describes is, in effect, a habit-change.

Finally, my understanding of sexual structuring as semiosis, as the mutual overdetermination in experience of habits, representations, fantasy, and the practice of love; or, put otherwise, my understanding of sexuality as a nexus of reciprocally constitutive effects between psychic and social realities, which entails a continuing *modification* in the subject as a body-ego, also finds a welcome coincidence in Foucault's statement that "every technique of production requires modification of individual conduct—not only skills but also attitudes" (18). But that his reference to a nowadays unpopular text, Marx's *Capital*, intersects with references to Peirce and Freud—themselves less than popular in contemporary feminist, lesbian, and gay studies—in these closing pages of a study of *perverse desire*, is perhaps not a coincidence, after all.

Works Cited

Abel, Elizabeth. *Virginia Woolf and the Fictions of Psychoanalysis.* Chicago: University of Chicago Press, 1989.

Abelove, Henry. "Freud, Male Homosexuality, and the Americans." In *The Lesbian and Gay Studies Reader,* ed. Henry Abelove, Michèle Aina Barale, and David Halperin, pp. 381–93. New York: Routledge, 1993.

Adams, Parveen. "Of Female Bondage." In Brennan, pp. 247–65.

————. "Per Os(cillation)." *Camera Obscura* 17 (1988): 7–29.

Alarcón, Norma. "Chicana's Feminist Literature: A Re-Vision through Malintzin/or Malintzin: Putting Flesh Back on the Object." In *This Bridge Called My Back: Writings by Radical Women of Color,* ed. Cherríe Moraga and Gloria Anzaldúa, pp. 182–90. New York: Kitchen Table: Women of Color Press, 1981, 1983.

Altman, Meryl. "How Not to Do Things with Metaphors We Live By." *College English* 52.5 (September 1990): 495–506.

Apter, Emily. *Feminizing the Fetish: Psychoanalysis and Narrative Obsession in Turn-of-the-Century France.* Ithaca: Cornell University Press, 1991.

Bad Object-Choices, eds. *How Do I Look? Queer Film and Video.* Seattle: Bay, 1991.

Baker, Kathryn Hinojosa. "Delinquent Desire: Race, Sex, and Ritual in Reform Schools for Girls." *Discourse* 15.1 (Fall 1992): 49–68.

Baker, Michael. *Our Three Selves: A Life of Radclyffe Hall.* London: GMP Publishers, 1985.

Balmary, Marie. *Psychoanalyzing Psychoanalysis: Freud and the Hidden Fault of the Father.* Trans. Ned Lukacher. Baltimore, Md.: Johns Hopkins University Press, 1982.

Barale, Michèle Aina. "Below the Belt: (Un)Covering *The Well of Loneliness.*" In Fuss, ed., pp. 235–57.

Bass, Alan. "Fetishism, Reality, and 'The Snow Man.'" *American Imago* 48 (Fall 1991): 295–328.

Baudrillard, Jean. *Seduction.* Trans. Brian Singer. New York: St. Martin's, 1990.

Beinstein, Krista. *Obszöne Frauen.* Vienna: Promedia, 1986.

Benjamin, Jessica. *The Bonds of Love: Psychoanalysis, Feminism, and the Problem of Domination.* New York: Pantheon, 1988.

————. "A Desire of One's Own." In de Lauretis, ed., pp. 78–101.

Bennett, Paula. "Critical Clitoridectomy: Female Sexual Imagery and Feminist Psychoanalytic Theory." *Signs: Journal of Women in Culture and Society* 18.2 (1993): 235–59.

Berg, Elizabeth. "The Third Woman." *Diacritics* 12 (1982): 11–20.

Bernheimer, Charles. "Penile Reference in Phallic Theory." *d i f f e r e n c e s: A Journal of Feminist Cultural Studies* 4.1 (1992): 116–32.

Bernheimer, Charles, and Claire Kahane, eds. *In Dora's Case: Freud—Hysteria—Feminism.* New York: Columbia University Press, 1985.

Bersani, Leo. *The Freudian Body: Psychoanalysis and Art.* New York: Columbia University Press, 1986.

———. "Is the Rectum a Grave?" In *AIDS: Cultural Analysis Cultural Activism,* ed. Douglas Crimp, pp. 197–222. Cambridge, Mass.: MIT Press, 1988.

Bersani, Leo, and Ulysse Dutoit. *The Forms of Violence: Narrative in Assyrian Art and Modern Culture.* New York: Schocken Books, 1985.

Blau, Herbert. "Disseminating Sodom." *Salmagundi* 58–59 (Fall 1982–Winter 1983): 221–52.

Borch-Jacobsen, Mikkel. *The Freudian Subject.* Trans. Catherine Porter. Stanford, Calif.: Stanford University Press, 1988.

Braidotti, Rosi. *Patterns of Dissonance: A Study of Women in Contemporary Philosophy.* Trans. Elizabeth Guild. London: Polity, 1991.

Brennan, Teresa, ed. *Between Feminism and Psychoanalysis.* London: Routledge, 1989.

Brodzki, Bella, and Celeste Schenck, eds. *Life Lines: Theorizing Women's Autobiography.* Ithaca: Cornell University Press, 1988.

Brown, Rita Mae. *Rubyfruit Jungle.* New York: Bantam, 1977.

Brownworth, Victoria. "Dyke S/M Wars Rage in London: Racism and Fascism Alleged." *Coming Up!* 10 (October 1988): 14–15.

Burgin, Victor. "Perverse Space." In *Interpreting Contemporary Art,* ed. Stephen Bann and William Allen, pp. 124–38. New York: Icon Editions [Harper Collins], 1991.

Burgin, Victor; James Donald; and Cora Kaplan, eds. *Formations of Fantasy.* London: Methuen, 1986.

Butler, Alison. " 'She Must Be Seeing Things': An Interview with Sheila McLaughlin." *Screen* 28.4 (Autumn 1987): 20–28.

Butler, Judith. "The Force of Fantasy: Feminism, Mapplethorpe, and Discursive Excess." *d i f f e r e n c e s: A Journal of Feminist Cultural Studies* 2.2 (1990): 105–25.

———. *Gender Trouble: Feminism and the Subversion of Identity.* New York: Routledge, 1990.

———. "The Lesbian Phallus and the Morphological Imaginary." *d i f f e r e n c e s: A Journal of Feminist Cultural Studies* 4.1 (1992): 133–71.

Canguilhem, Georges. *The Normal and the Pathological.* Trans. Carolyn R. Fawcett and Robert S. Cohen. New York: Zone Books, 1989.

Carotenuto, Aldo. *A Secret Symmetry: Sabina Spielrein between Freud and Jung.* Trans. Arno Pomerans, John Shepley, and Krishna Winston. New York: Pantheon, 1982.

———. *Tagebuch einer heimlichen Symmetrie. Sabina Spielrein zwischen Jung und Freud.* Freiburg: Kore, 1986.

Case, Sue-Ellen. "Towards a Butch-Femme Aesthetic." *Discourse: Journal for Theoretical Studies in Media and Culture* 11.1 (1988–89): 55–73.

———. "Tracking the Vampire." *d i f f e r e n c e s: A Journal of Feminist Cultural Studies* 3.2 (Summer 1991): 1–20.

Case, Sue-Ellen, ed. *Performing Feminisms: Feminist Critical Theory and Theatre.* Baltimore: Johns Hopkins University Press, 1990.

Cavell, Stanley. "Ugly Duckling, Funny Butterfly: Bette Davis and *Now, Voyager* Followed by Postscript (1989): To Whom It May Concern." *Critical Inquiry* 16 (1990): 213–89.

Chase, Cynthia. "Desire and Identification in Lacan and Kristeva." In Feldstein and Roof, pp. 65–83.

Chasseguet-Smirgel, Jeannine. "Reflections on Fetishism." In *Creativity and Perversion,* pp. 78–88. London: Free Association, 1985.

Chasseguet-Smirgel, Jeannine, ed. *Female Sexuality: New Psychoanalytic Views* [1964]. Ann Arbor: University of Michigan Press, 1970.

Chodorow, Nancy J. *Feminism and Psychoanalytic Theory.* New Haven: Yale University Press, 1989.

———. *The Reproduction of Mothering: Psychoanalysis and the Sociology of Gender.* Berkeley: University of California Press, 1978.

Colapietro, Vincent M. *Peirce's Approach to the Self: A Semiotic Perspective on Human Subjectivity.* Albany: State University of New York Press, 1989.

Copjec, Joan. "Cutting Up." In Brennan, pp. 227–46.

Cowie, Elizabeth. "Fantasia." *m/f* 9 (1984): 70–105.

Creet, Julia. "Daughter of the Movement: The Psychodynamics of Lesbian S/M Fantasy." *d i f f e r e n c e s: A Journal of Feminist Cultural Studies* 3.2 (Summer 1991): 135–59.

Davidson, Arnold I. "Closing Up the Corpses: Diseases of Sexuality and the Emergence of the Psychiatric Style of Reasoning." In *Meaning and Method: Essays in Honor of Hilary Putnam,* ed. George Boolos, pp. 295–325. Cambridge: Cambridge University Press, 1990.

———. "How to Do the History of Psychoanalysis: A Reading of Freud's *Three Essays on the Theory of Sexuality.*" In *The Trial(s) of Psychoanalysis,* ed. Françoise Meltzer, pp. 39–64. Chicago: University of Chicago Press, 1987, 1988.

Davis, Whitney. "HomoVision: A Reading of Freud's 'Fetishism.'" *Genders* 15 (Winter 1992): 86–118.

Dekker, Rudolf, and Lotte van de Pol. *The Tradition of Female Transvestism in Early Modern Europe.* New York: St. Martin's, 1989.

de Lauretis, Teresa. *Alice Doesn't: Feminism, Semiotics, Cinema.* Bloomington: Indiana University Press, 1984.

———. "The Female Body and Heterosexual Presumption." *Semiotica* 67.3–4 (1987): 259–79.

———. "Film and the Visible." In Bad Object-Choices, pp. 223–76.

———. "Guerrilla in the Midst: Women's Cinema in the 80s." *Screen* 31.1 (Spring 1990): 6–25.

———. "Perverse Desire: The Lure of the Mannish Lesbian." *Australian Feminist Studies* 13 (Autumn 1991): 15–26.

———. "The Practice of Sexual Difference and Feminist Thought in Italy: An Introductory Essay." In Milan Women's Bookstore Collective, pp. 1–21.

———. "Sexual Indifference and Lesbian Representation." *Theatre Journal* 40.2 (1988): 155–77. Reprinted in Case, ed., pp. 17–39.

———. *La sintassi del desiderio: struttura e forme del romanzo sveviano.* Ravenna: Longo, 1976.

de Lauretis, Teresa, ed. *Feminist Studies/Critical Studies.* Bloomington: Indiana University Press, 1986.

de Lauretis, Teresa, and Stephen Heath, eds. *The Cinematic Apparatus.* London: Macmillan, 1980.

de Man, Paul. *Allegories of Reading.* New Haven: Yale University Press, 1979.

De Quincey, Thomas. "The Spanish Military Nun" [1847]. In *The Collected Writings of Thomas De Quincey,* vol. XIII, ed. David Masson, pp. 159–250. Edinburgh: Adam and Charles Black, 1890.

Derrida, Jacques. *Spurs: Nietzsche's Styles/Eperons: Les styles de Nietzsche.* Trans. Barbara Harlow. Chicago: University of Chicago Press, 1979.

Deutsch, Felix. "A Footnote to Freud's 'Fragment of an Analysis of a Case of Hysteria.'" In Bernheimer and Kahane, pp. 35–43.

Deutsch, Helene. "On Female Homosexuality." Trans. Edith B. Jackson. *Psychoanalytic Quarterly* 1 (1932): 484–510.

———. *The Psychology of Women.* New York: Grune and Stratton, 1944.

Díaz-Diocaretz, Myriam. *The Transforming Power of Language: The Poetry of Adrienne Rich.* Utrecht: H&S, 1984.

Doane, Mary Ann. "Commentary: Post-Utopian Difference." In Weed, pp. 70–78.

———. *The Desire to Desire: The Woman's Film of the 1940s.* Bloomington: Indiana University Press, 1987.

———. *Femmes Fatales: Feminism, Film Theory, Psychoanalysis.* New York: Routledge, 1991.

———. "Responses." *Camera Obscura* 20–21 (1989): 142–47.

Doane, Mary Ann; Patricia Mellencamp; and Linda Williams, eds. *Re-vision: Essays in Feminist Film Criticism.* Frederick, Md.: University Publications of America and The American Film Institute, 1984.

Dolan, Jill. "The Dynamics of Desire: Sexuality and Gender in Pornography and Performance." *Theatre Journal* 39.2 (May 1987): 157–74.

Dollimore, Jonathan. *Sexual Dissidence: Augustine to Wilde, Freud to Foucault.* Oxford: Clarendon Press, 1991.

Donald, James, ed. *Fantasy and the Cinema.* London: British Film Institute, 1989.

Dworkin, Andrea. *Pornography: Men Possessing Women.* New York: Seal, 1981.

Echols, Alice. *Daring to Be Bad: Radical Feminism in America 1967–1975.* Minneapolis: University of Minnesota Press, 1989.

Eco, Umberto. "Peirce and the Semiotic Foundations of Openness." In *The Role of the Reader: Explorations in the Semiotics of Texts,* pp. 175–99. Bloomington: Indiana University Press, 1979.

Erauso, Catalina de. *Historia de la Monja Alférez Dona Catalina de Erauso, escrita por ella misma,* ed. Joaquin Maria de Ferrer. Paris: Julio Didot, 1829.

Erhart, Julia. "Representation and the Female Symbolic: What's Lesbianism Got to Do with It?" Ph.D. Qualifying Essay in History of Consciousness, University of California, Santa Cruz, 1992.

Evans, Martha Noel. "Hysteria and the Seduction of Theory." In Hunter, pp. 73–85.

Faderman, Lillian. *Surpassing the Love of Men: Romantic Friendship and Love between Women from the Renaissance to the Present.* New York: William Morrow, 1981.

Feldstein, Richard, and Judith Roof, eds. *Feminism and Psychoanalysis.* Ithaca, N.Y.: Cornell University Press, 1989.

Felman, Shoshana. *Jacques Lacan and the Adventure of Insight: Psychoanalysis in Contemporary Culture.* Cambridge, Mass.: Harvard University Press, 1987.

———. "To Open the Question." In *Literature and Psychoanalysis: The Question of Reading; Otherwise,* ed. Shoshana Felman, pp. 5–10. Baltimore: Johns Hopkins University Press, 1982.

Findlay, Heather. "Is There a Lesbian in This Text? Derrida, Wittig, and the Politics of the Three Women." In Weed, pp. 59–69.

Flax, Jane. *Thinking Fragments: Psychoanalysis, Feminism, and Postmodernism in the Contemporary West.* Berkeley: University of California Press, 1990.

Fletcher, John. "Freud and His Uses: Psychoanalysis and Gay Theory." In *Coming On Strong: Gay Politics and Culture,* ed. Simon Shepherd and Mick Wallis, pp. 90–118. London: Unwin Hyman, 1989.

———. "Versions of Masquerade." *Screen* 29.3 (1988): 43–70.

Forrester, John. *The Seductions of Psychoanalysis: Freud, Lacan and Derrida.* Cambridge: Cambridge University Press, 1990.

Foster, Jeannette H. *Sex Variant Women in Literature* [1956]. Tallahassee: Naiad, 1985.

Foucault, Michel. *The History of Sexuality.* Vol. 1: *An Introduction.* Trans. Robert Hurley. New York: Random House, 1980.

———. *The History of Sexuality.* Vol. 2: *The Use of Pleasure.* Trans. Robert Hurley. New York: Random House, 1985.

———. *The History of Sexuality.* Vol. 3: *The Care of the Self.* Trans. Robert Hurley. New York: Random House, 1986.

———. "Technologies of the Self." In Martin, Gutman, and Hutton, pp. 16–49.

Frank, Lawrence. "Freud and Dora: Blindness and Insight." In Hunter, pp. 110–32.

Freud, Anna. "Beating Fantasies and Daydreams" [1922]. In *Introduction to Psychoanalysis: Lectures for Child Analysts and Teachers 1922–1935,* pp. 137–57. [*The Writings of Anna Freud,* vol. I.] New York: International Universities Press, 1974.

———. *The Ego and the Mechanisms of Defense* [1937]. [*The Writings of Anna Freud,* vol. II.] Trans. Cecil Baines. New York: International Universities Press, 1966.

Freud, Sigmund. *The Standard Edition of the Complete Psychological Works of Sigmund Freud.* Trans. and ed. James Strachey. 24 vols. London: Hogarth Press, 1953–74.

———. "Zur Einführung des Narzissmus." In *Studienausgabe,* vol. III, pp. 39–68. Frankfurt am Main: Fischer, 1982.

Friday, Nancy. *My Secret Garden.* New York: Pocket Books, 1974.

Frye, Marilyn. *The Politics of Reality: Essays in Feminist Theory.* Trumansburg, N.Y.: The Crossing Press, 1983.

Fuss, Diana. "Fashion and the Homospectatorial Look." *Critical Inquiry* 18 (Summer 1992): 713–37.

Fuss, Diana, ed. *inside/out: Lesbian Theories, Gay Theories.* New York: Routledge, 1991.

Gaines, Jane. "The Queen Christina Tie-Ups: Convergence of Show Window and Screen." *Quarterly Review of Film and Video* 11.1 (1989): 35–60.

Gallop, Jane. *The Daughter's Seduction: Feminism and Psychoanalysis.* Ithaca, N.Y.: Cornell University Press, 1982.

——. "Keys to Dora." In Bernheimer and Kahane, pp. 200–20.

——. *Thinking through the Body*. New York: Columbia University Press, 1988.

Garber, Marjorie. *Vested Interests: Cross-Dressing and Cultural Anxiety*. New York: Routledge, 1992.

Garner, Shirley Nelson. "Feminism, Psychoanalysis, and the Heterosexual Imperative." In Feldstein and Roof, pp. 164–81.

Gearhart, Suzanne. "The Scene of Psychoanalysis: The Unanswered Questions of Dora." In Bernheimer and Kahane, pp. 105–27.

Gever, Martha. "Girl Crazy: Lesbian Narratives in *She Must Be Seeing Things* and *Damned If You Don't*." *The Independent* (July 1988): 14–18.

Gilbert, Sandra. "Costumes of the Mind: Transvestism as Metaphor in Modernist Literature." *Critical Inquiry* 7.2 (Winter 1980): 391–417.

Gilman, Sander L. "Black Bodies, White Bodies: Toward an Iconography of Female Sexuality in Late Nineteenth-Century Art, Medicine, and Literature." In *"Race," Writing, and Difference*, ed. Henry Louis Gates, Jr., pp. 223–61. Chicago: University of Chicago Press, 1985, 1986.

——. *Difference and Pathology: Stereotypes of Sexuality, Race, and Madness*. Ithaca, N.Y.: Cornell University Press, 1985.

Goux, Jean-Joseph. "The Phallus: Masculine Identity and the 'Exchange of Women.'" Trans. Maria Amuchastegui, Caroline Benforado, Amy Hendrix, and Eleanor Kaufman. *d i f f e r e n c e s: A Journal of Feminist Cultural Studies* 4.1 (1992): 40–75.

Green, André. *Le complexe de castration*. Paris: Presses Universitaires de France, 1990.

Greenacre, Phyllis. "Certain Relationships between Fetishism and Faulty Development of the Body Image." *Psychoanalytic Study of the Child* 8 (1953): 79–98.

——. "The Transitional Object and the Fetish with Special Reference to the Role of Illusion." *International Journal of Psycho-Analysis* 51 (1970): 447–55.

Greig, Donald. "The Sexual Differentiation of the Hitchcock Text." In Donald, pp. 175–95.

Grosz, Elizabeth A. "The Hetero and the Homo: The Sexual Ethics of Luce Irigaray." *Gay Information* [Australia] 17–18 (March 1988): 37–44.

——. "Lesbian Fetishism?" *d i f f e r e n c e s: A Journal of Feminist Cultural Studies* 3.2 (Summer 1991): 39–54.

Grunberger, Béla. "Outline for a Study of Narcissism in Female Sexuality." In Chasseguet-Smirgel, ed., pp. 68–83.

Hake, Sabine. "'Gold, Love, Adventure': The Postmodern Piracy of *Madame X*." *Discourse* 11.1 (Fall–Winter 1988–89): 88–110.

Hall, Radclyffe. *The Well of Loneliness* [1928]. New York: Avon Books, 1981.

Hamer, Diane. "Significant Others: Lesbianism and Psychoanalytic Theory." *Feminist Review* 34 (Spring 1990): 134–51.

Haraway, Donna. "A Manifesto for Cyborgs: Science, Technology, and Socialist Feminism in the 1980s." In Weed, pp. 173–204.

Hartmann, E. von. *Philosophie des Unbewussten*. Berlin, 1869. Translated by W. C. Coupland as *Philosophy of the Unconscious*. London, 1884.

Hartsock, Nancy. *Money, Sex, and Power*. Boston: Northeastern University Press, 1984.

Havelock Ellis, John. *Studies in the Psychology of Sex.* Vol. 2 [1897]. Phila-
delphia: F. A. Davis, 1928.
Heath, Stephen. "Joan Riviere and the Masquerade." In Burgin, Donald,
and Kaplan, pp. 45–61.
———. *Questions of Cinema.* Bloomington: Indiana University Press, 1981.
Henry, George W. *Sex Variants: A Study of Homosexual Patterns.* One-vol-
ume edition. New York: Hoeber, 1948.
Heresies [The Sex Issue] 12 (1981).
Hertz, Neil. "Dora's Secrets, Freud's Techniques." In Bernheimer and
Kahane, pp. 221–42.
Hirsch, Marianne. *The Mother-Daughter Plot: Narrative, Psychoanalysis,
Feminism.* Bloomington: Indiana University Press, 1989.
Hocquenghem, Guy. *Homosexual Desire.* Trans. Daniella Dangoor. London:
Allison & Busby, 1978.
Hollibaugh, Amber, and Cherríe Moraga. "What We're Rollin Around in Bed
With: Sexual Silences in Feminism." In Snitow, Stansell, and Thomp-
son, pp. 394–405.
Holmlund, Christine. "I Love Luce: The Lesbian, Mimesis, and Masquerade
in Irigaray, Freud, and Mainstream Film." *New Formations* 9 (Winter
1989): 105–23.
Hoogland, Renée. "Fallische perversie: psychoanalyse en lesbische seksual-
iteit." *Allure: Jaarschrift voor Vrouwenstudies Letteren* 1 (1993): 13–25.
Hunter, Dianne, ed. *Seduction and Theory: Readings of Gender, Representa-
tion, and Rhetoric.* Urbana and Chicago: University of Illinois Press,
1989.
Irigaray, Luce. *Speculum of the Other Woman.* Trans. Gillian C. Gill. Ithaca,
N.Y.: Cornell University Press, 1985.
———. *This Sex Which Is Not One.* Trans. Catherine Porter and Carolyn
Burke. Ithaca, N.Y.: Cornell University Press, 1985.
Isaacs, Susan. "The Nature and Function of Phantasy." *International Jour-
nal of Psycho-Analysis* 29 (1948): 73–97.
Jacobus, Mary. "Freud's Mnemonic: Women, Screen Memories, and Femi-
nist Nostalgia." *Michigan Quarterly Review* 26.1 (Winter 1987): 117–
39.
Jardine, Alice. "Notes for an Analysis." In Brennan, pp. 73–85.
Johnston, Claire. "Femininity and the Masquerade: *Anne of the Indies.*" In
Jacques Tourneur, ed. Claire Johnston and Paul Willemen. Edin-
burgh: Edinburgh Film Festival, 1975.
Jones, Ernest. "The Early Development of Female Sexuality." *International
Journal of Psycho-Analysis* 8 (1927): 459–72.
———. "Early Female Sexuality." *International Journal of Psycho-Analysis*
16 (1935): 263–73.
———. *The Life and Work of Sigmund Freud.* Edited and Abridged in One
Volume by Lionel Trilling and Steven Marcus. New York: Basic
Books, 1961.
———. "The Phallic Phase." *International Journal of Psycho-Analysis* 14
(1933): 1–33.
Kahane, Claire. "Introduction: Part Two." In Bernheimer and Kahane, pp.
19–32.
Kaufmann, Erika. *Transfert.* Milan: Feltrinelli, 1974.
Keller, Yvonne. "Tracking Lesbian Pulp Novels of the 1950s and Early

1960s." Ph.D. Qualifying Essay in History of Consciousness, University of California, Santa Cruz, 1992.

Kennedy, Elizabeth Lapovsky, and Madeline D. Davis. *Boots of Leather, Slippers of Gold: The History of a Lesbian Community.* New York: Routledge, 1993.

Khan, M. Masud R. *Alienation in Perversions.* London: Hogarth, 1979.

Klein, Melanie. *Contributions to Psycho-Analysis, 1921–1945.* New York: Hillary House, 1948.

Kofman, Sarah. " 'Ça cloche.' " Trans. Caren Kaplan. In *Derrida and Deconstruction,* ed. Hugh Silverman, pp. 108–38. New York: Routledge, 1989.

——. *The Enigma of Woman: Woman in Freud's Writings.* Trans. Catherine Porter. Ithaca, N.Y.: Cornell University Press, 1985.

Kristeva, Julia. *About Chinese Women.* Trans. Anita Barrows. New York: Urizen Books, 1977.

——. *Desire in Language: A Semiotic Approach to Literature and Art.* Ed. Leon S. Roudiez. Trans. Thomas Gora, Alice Jardine, and Leon S. Roudiez. New York: Columbia University Press, 1980.

——. "Stabat Mater." In Suleiman, pp. 99–118.

——. *Tales of Love.* Trans. Leon S. Roudiez. New York: Columbia University Press, 1987.

Lacan, Jacques. *Écrits: A Selection.* Trans. Alan Sheridan. New York: W. W. Norton, 1977.

—— [and the *école freudienne*]. *Feminine Sexuality.* Ed. Juliet Mitchell and Jacqueline Rose. Trans. Jacqueline Rose. New York: Norton, 1982.

——. *The Four Fundamental Concepts of Psycho-Analysis.* Trans. Alan Sheridan. New York: W. W. Norton, 1978.

——. "Intervention on Transference." In Bernheimer and Kahane, pp. 92–104.

——. *Le Séminaire, livre I: Les Ecrits techniques de Freud.* Paris: Seuil, 1975.

——. "Some Reflections on the Ego." *International Journal of Psycho-Analysis* 34 (1953): 11–17.

Lampl–de Groot, A. "The Evolution of the Oedipus Complex in Women." *International Journal of Psycho-Analysis* 9 (1928): 332–45.

Laplanche, Jean. *Life and Death in Psychoanalysis.* Trans. Jeffrey Mehlman. Baltimore: Johns Hopkins University Press, 1976.

——. *New Foundations for Psychoanalysis* [1987]. Trans. David Macey. Oxford: Basil Blackwell, 1989.

Laplanche, Jean, and Jean-Bertrand Pontalis. "Fantasy and the Origins of Sexuality." In Burgin, Donald, and Kaplan, pp. 5–34.

Laplanche, Jean, and J.-B. Pontalis. *The Language of Psycho-Analysis.* Trans. Donald Nicholson-Smith. New York: W. W. Norton, 1973.

Laqueur, Thomas. *Making Sex: Body and Gender from the Greeks to Freud.* Cambridge: Harvard University Press, 1990.

Lorde, Audre. *Sister Outsider: Essays and Speeches.* Trumansburg, N.Y.: Crossing Press, 1984.

——. *Zami: A New Spelling of My Name.* Trumansburg, N.Y.: Crossing Press, 1982.

Lowell, Amy. "The Weather-Cock Points South." In *The Complete Poetical Works of Amy Lowell,* p. 211. Boston: Houghton Mifflin, 1955.

Lukacher, Ned. *Primal Scenes: Literature, Philosophy, Psychoanalysis.* Ithaca, N.Y.: Cornell University Press, 1986.

Marcus, Steven. "Introduction." In Sigmund Freud, *Three Essays on the Theory of Sexuality,* trans. and revised by James Strachey, pp. xix–xli. New York: Basic Books [Harper Torchbooks], 1975.

Martin, Biddy. "Lesbian Identity and Autobiographical Difference[s]." In Brodzki and Schenck, pp. 77–103.

Martin, Luther H.; Huck Gutman; and Patrick H. Hutton, eds. *Technologies of the Self: A Seminar with Michel Foucault.* Amherst: University of Massachusetts Press, 1988.

Masson, Jeffrey Moussaieff. *The Assault on Truth: Freud's Suppression of the Seduction Theory.* New York: Farrar, Straus and Giroux, 1984.

Mayne, Judith. "Lesbian Looks: Dorothy Arzner and Female Authorship." In Bad Object-Choices, pp. 103–35.

——. *The Woman at the Keyhole: Feminism and Women's Cinema.* Bloomington: Indiana University Press, 1990.

McDougall, Joyce. "Homosexuality in Women" [1964]. In Chasseguet-Smirgel, ed., pp. 171–212.

——. *A Plea for a Measure of Abnormality.* New York: International Universities Presses, 1980.

——. "Primal Scene and Sexual Perversion." *International Journal of Psycho-Analysis* 53 (1972): 371–84.

Mellencamp, Patricia. "Responses." *Camera Obscura* 20–21 (1989): 235–41.

Merck, Mandy. " 'Lianna' and the Lesbians of Art Cinema." In *Films for Women,* ed. Charlotte Brunsdon, pp. 166–75. London: BFI, 1986.

——. "The Train of Thought in Freud's 'Case of Homosexuality in a Woman.' " *m/f* 11–12 (1986): 35–46.

Metz, Christian. *The Imaginary Signifier: Psychoanalysis and Cinema.* Trans. Celia Britton et al. Bloomington: Indiana University Press, 1975–82.

——. *Language and Cinema.* Trans. Donna Jean Umiker-Sebeok. The Hague: Mouton, 1974.

Micli, Mario. *Homosexuality and Liberation: Elements of a Gay Critique* [1977]. Trans. David Fernbach. London: Gay Men's Press, 1980.

The Milan Women's Bookstore Collective. *Sexual Difference: A Theory of Social Symbolic Practice.* Trans. Patricia Cicogna and Teresa de Lauretis. Bloomington: Indiana University Press, 1990.

Millett, Kate. *Sexual Politics* [1969]. New York: Ballantine Books, 1978.

Miriam, Kathy. "Thanks for the Memory: Revisioning Lesbian-Feminism in the Age of Post-Feminism." Ph.D. Qualifying Essay in History of Consciousness, University of California, Santa Cruz, 1992.

Mitchell, Juliet. "Introduction—I." In Lacan, *Feminine Sexuality,* pp. 1–26.

——. *Psychoanalysis and Feminism.* New York: Pantheon, 1974.

Modleski, Tania. *Feminism without Women: Culture and Criticism in a "Postfeminist" Age.* New York: Routledge, 1991.

——. *Loving with a Vengeance: Mass-Produced Fantasies for Women.* Hamden, Conn.: Shoe String Press, 1982.

Moi, Toril. "Representation of Patriarchy: Sexuality and Epistemology in Freud's Dora." In Bernheimer and Kahane, pp. 181–99.

Molfino, Francesca. "Sabina Spielrein, la paziente." In Vegetti Finzi, ed., pp. 231–82.

Moraga, Cherríe. *Giving Up the Ghost: Teatro in Two Acts.* Los Angeles: West

End Press, 1986. Reprinted with revisions in *Heroes and Saints and Other Plays*, pp. 3–35. Albuquerque: West End Press, 1994.

———. *Loving in the War Years: Lo que nunca pasó por sus labios.* Boston: South End, 1983.

Mulvey, Laura. *Visual and Other Pleasures.* Bloomington: Indiana University Press, 1989.

Muraro, Luisa. *L'ordine simbolico della madre.* Rome: Editori Riuniti, 1991.

Nestle, Joan. "The Fem Question." In Vance, pp. 232–41.

———. *A Restricted Country.* Ithaca: Firebrand Books, 1987.

Newton, Esther. *Mother Camp: Female Impersonators in America.* Englewood Cliffs: Prentice-Hall, 1972.

———. "The Mythic Mannish Lesbian: Radclyffe Hall and the New Woman." *Signs* 9.4 (Summer 1984): 557–75.

Nietzsche, Friedrich. *The Gay Science.* Trans. Walter Kaufmann. New York: Vintage, 1974.

Nunziante Cesaro, Adele. "Melanie Klein, la madre." In Vegetti Finzi, ed., pp. 95–181.

O'Higgins, James. "Sexual Choice, Sexual Act: An Interview with Michel Foucault." *Salmagundi* 58–59 (Fall 1982–Winter 1983): 10–24.

Ophuijsen, J. H. W. van. "Contributions to the Masculinity Complex in Women." *International Journal of Psycho-Analysis* 5 (1924): 39–49.

O'Rourke, Rebecca. *Reflecting on* The Well of Loneliness. London: Routledge, 1989.

Otis, Margaret. "A Perversion Not Commonly Noted." *Journal of Abnormal Psychology* 8 (1913–14): 113–16.

Pajaczkowska, Claire. "The Heterosexual Presumption: A Contribution to the Debate on Pornography." *Screen* 22.1 (1981): 79–94.

Peirce, Charles Sanders. *Collected Papers.* Vols. 1–8. Cambridge, Mass.: Harvard University Press, 1931–1958.

Penley, Constance. "Time Travel, Primal Scene, and the Critical Dystopia." In Donald, pp. 196–212.

Pérez, Emma. "Sexuality and Discourse: Notes from a Chicana Survivor." In Trujillo, pp. 159–84.

Pietz, William. "The Problem of the Fetish." *Res* 9 (1985): 5–17; 13 (1987): 23–45; and 16 (1988): 105–23.

Rainer, Yvonne. *The Films of Yvonne Rainer.* Bloomington: Indiana University Press, 1989.

Ramas, Maria. "Freud's Dora, Dora's Hysteria." In Bernheimer and Kahane, pp. 149–80.

Rich, Adrienne. "Compulsory Heterosexuality and Lesbian Existence" [1980]. In *Blood, Bread, and Poetry: Selected Prose 1979–1985*, pp. 23–75. New York: Norton, 1986.

———. *The Dream of a Common Language: Poems 1974–1977.* New York: Norton, 1978.

———. *Of Woman Born: Motherhood as Experience and Institution.* New York: Norton, 1976.

———. *On Lies, Secrets, and Silence: Selected Prose, 1966–1979.* New York: Norton, 1979.

Rich, B. Ruby. "From Repressive Tolerance to Erotic Liberation: *Maedchen in Uniform.*" In Doane, Mellencamp, and Williams, pp. 100–30.

Riviere, Joan. "Womanliness as a Masquerade." In Burgin, Donald, and

Kaplan, pp. 35–44. [*The International Journal of Psychoanalysis*, vol. X (1929).]

Robertiello, Richard C., M.D. *Voyage from Lesbos: The Psychoanalysis of a Female Homosexual.* New York: Avon Books, 1959.

Roof, Judith. *A Lure of Knowledge: Lesbian Sexuality and Theory.* New York: Columbia University Press, 1991.

———. "The Match in the Crocus: Representations of Lesbian Sexuality." In *Discontented Discourses: Feminism/Textual Intervention/Psychoanalysis,* ed. Marleen S. Barr and Richard Feldstein, pp. 100–16. Urbana: University of Illinois Press, 1989.

Rose, Jacqueline. "Dora: Fragment of an Analysis." In Bernheimer and Kahane, pp. 128–48. [Also in Rose, *Sexuality in the Field of Vision*, pp. 27–47.]

———. "Introduction—II." In Lacan, *Feminine Sexuality*, pp. 27–57.

———. *Sexuality in the Field of Vision.* London: Verso, 1986. ✗

Rosen, Philip, ed. *Narrative, Apparatus, Ideology: A Film Theory Reader.* New York: Columbia University Press, 1986.

Ruehl, Sonja. "Inverts and Experts: Radclyffe Hall and the Lesbian Identity." In *Feminism, Culture and Politics*, ed. Rosalind Brunt and Caroline Rowan, pp. 15–36. London: Lawrence and Wishart, 1982.

Rule, Jane. *This Is Not for You.* Tallahassee: Naiad, 1988.

Russo, Mary. "Female Grotesques: Carnival and Theory." In de Lauretis, ed., pp. 213–29.

Sachs, Hanns. "On the Genesis of Perversion" [1923]. *American Imago* 48 (1991): 283–93.

Schor, Naomi. "Dreaming Dissymmetry: Barthes, Foucault, and Sexual Difference." In Weed, pp. 47–58.

———. "Female Fetishism: The Case of George Sand." In Suleiman, pp. 363–72.

Scott, Carla. "The Hottentot Effect: The Crisis of Black Lesbian Representa- ✗ tion." Ph.D. Qualifying Essay in History of Consciousness, University of California, Santa Cruz, 1993.

Sedgwick, Eve Kosofsky. *Between Men: English Literature and Male Homosocial Desire.* New York: Columbia University Press, 1985.

———. *Epistemology of the Closet.* Berkeley: University of California Press, 1990.

Showalter, Elaine. "Critical Cross-Dressing: Male Feminists and the Woman of the Year." *Raritan* 3.2 (1983): 130–49.

Silverman, Kaja. *The Acoustic Mirror: The Female Voice in Psychoanalysis and Cinema.* Bloomington: Indiana University Press, 1988.

———. "Fassbinder and Lacan: A Reconsideration of Gaze, Look, and Image." *Camera Obscura* no. 19 (1989): 54–85.

———. "The Lacanian Phallus." *d i f f e r e n c e s: A Journal of Feminist Cultural Studies* 4.1 (1992): 84–115.

———. *Male Subjectivity at the Margins.* New York: Routledge, 1992.

Smith, Victoria. "Birthmarks and Blind Spots: Hortense Spillers, Luce Irigaray, and Gayl Jones." Manuscript.

Snitow, Ann; Christine Stansell; and Sharon Thompson, eds. *Powers of Desire: The Politics of Sexuality.* New York: Monthly Review Press, 1983.

Spielrein, Sabina. "Die Distruktion als Ursache des Werdens." *Jarhbuch für psychoanalytische und psychopathologische Forschungen* 4 (1912): 465–503.

Spillers, Hortense J. "Mama's Baby, Papa's Maybe: An American Grammar Book." *Diacritics* (Summer 1987): 65–81.

Sprengnether, Madelon. *The Spectral Mother: Freud, Feminism, and Psychoanalysis.* Ithaca, N.Y.: Cornell University Press, 1990.

Stacey, Jackie. "Desperately Seeking Difference." *Screen* 28.1 (Winter 1987): 48–61.

Stanton, Domna. "Difference on Trial: A Critique of the Maternal Metaphor in Cixous, Irigaray, and Kristeva." In *The Poetics of Gender*, ed. Nancy K. Miller, pp. 157–82. New York: Columbia University Press, 1986.

Stimpson, Catharine R. "Zero Degree Deviancy: The Lesbian Novel in English." In *Writing and Sexual Difference*, ed. Elizabeth Abel, pp. 243–60. Chicago: University of Chicago Press, 1982.

Suleiman, Susan Rubin, ed. *The Female Body in Western Culture: Contemporary Perspectives.* Cambridge, Mass.: Harvard University Press, 1986.

Terry, Jennifer. "Siting Homosexuality: A History of Surveillance and the Production of Deviant Subjects (1935–1950)." Doctoral dissertation in History of Consciousness, University of California, Santa Cruz, June 1992.

———. "Theorizing Deviant Historiography." *d i f f e r e n c e s: A Journal of Feminist Cultural Studies* 5.2 (Summer 1991): 55–74.

Theweleit, Klaus. *Male Fantasies.* Trans. Stephen Conway. Minneapolis: University of Minnesota Press, 1987.

———. *Male Fantasies.* Trans. Erica Carter and Chris Turner. Minneapolis: University of Minnesota Press, 1989.

Trasforini, Maria Antonietta. *La professione di psicoanalista.* Turin: Bollati Boringhieri, 1991.

Trask, Haunani-Kay. *Eros and Power: The Promise of Feminist Theory.* Philadelphia: University of Pennsylvania Press, 1986.

Traub, Valerie. "Ambiguities of 'Lesbian' Viewing Pleasure: The (Dis)articulations of *Black Widow.*" In *Body Guards: The Cultural Politics of Gender Ambiguity*, ed. Julia Epstein and Kristina Straub, pp. 305–28. New York: Routledge, 1991.

Treut, Monika. "Perverse Bilder." In Beinstein, pp. 5–19.

Trujillo, Carla, ed. *Chicana Lesbians: The Girls Our Mothers Warned Us About.* Berkeley: Third Woman Press, 1991.

Vance, Carole S., ed. *Pleasure and Danger: Exploring Female Sexuality.* Boston: Routledge and Kegan Paul, 1984.

Vegetti Finzi, Silvia. *Il bambino della notte: divenire donna divenire madre.* Milan: Mondadori, 1990.

Vegetti Finzi, Silvia, ed. *Psicoanalisi al femminile.* Bari: Laterza, 1992.

Vermeule, Blakey. "Is There a Sedgwick School for Girls?" *Qui Parle* 5.1 (1991): 53–72.

Warner, Marina. *Alone of All Her Sex: The Myth and Cult of the Virgin Mary.* New York: Knopf, 1976.

Weed, Elizabeth, ed. *Coming to Terms: Feminism, Theory, Politics.* New York: Routledge, 1989.

Westkott, Marcia C. "On the New Psychology of Women: A Cautionary View." *Feminist Issues* 10.2 (Fall 1990): 3–18.

White, Hayden. *The Content of the Form: Narrative Discourse and Historical Representation*. Baltimore: Johns Hopkins University Press, 1987.

White, Patricia. "Governing Lesbian Desire: *Nocturne*'s Oedipal Fantasy." In *Feminisms in the Cinema*, ed. Ada Testaferri and Laura Pietropaolo. Bloomington: Indiana University Press, 1994.

———. "Madame X of the China Seas." *Screen* 28.4 (Autumn 1987): 80–95.

Whitford, Margaret. "Rereading Irigaray." In Brennan, pp. 106–26.

Williams, Linda. "When the Woman Looks." In Doane, Mellencamp, and Williams, pp. 83–99.

Wittig, Monique. *Le corps lesbien*. Paris: Minuit, 1973.

———. *The Lesbian Body*. Trans. David Le Vay. Boston: Beacon, 1986.

———. *The Straight Mind and Other Essays*. Boston: Beacon, 1992.

Woolf, Virginia. *Mrs. Dalloway*. New York: Harcourt, Brace and World, 1925.

Yarbro-Bejarano, Yvonne. "Cherríe Moraga's *Giving Up the Ghost:* The Representation of Female Desire." *Third Woman* 3.1–2 (1986): 113–20.

Young-Bruehl, Elizabeth. *Anna Freud: A Biography*. London: Macmillan, 1988.

Films Cited

Adam's Rib. Dir. George Cukor, 1949.
All about Eve. Dir. Joseph Mankiewicz, 1950.
Back to the Future. Dir. Robert Zemeckis, 1985.
Black Widow. Dir. Bob Rafelson, 1987.
Bonnie and Clyde. Dir. Arthur Penn, 1967.
Born in Flames. Dir. Lizzie Borden, 1983.
Caught. Dir. Max Ophuls, 1949.
Damned If You Don't. Dir. Su Friedrich, 1987.
Desert Hearts. Dir. Donna Deitch, 1985.
Desperately Seeking Susan. Dir. Susan Seidelman, 1984.
Dial M for Murder. Dir. Alfred Hitchcock, 1954.
Die Praxis der Liebe [*The Practice of Love*]. Dir. Valie Export, 1984.
Duel in the Sun. Dir. King Vidor, 1946.
Edipo Re [*Oedipus Rex*]. Dir. Pier Paolo Pasolini, 1967.
Gilda. Dir. Charles Vidor, 1946.
The Gold Diggers. Dir. Sally Potter, 1983.
Gone with the Wind. Dir. Victor Fleming, 1939.
Invisible Adversaries [*Unsichtbare Gegner*]. Dir. Valie Export, 1976.
I've Heard the Mermaids Singing. Dir. Patricia Rozema, 1987.
Je tu il elle. Dir. Chantal Akerman, 1974.
Johanna d'Arc of Mongolia. Dir. Ulrike Ottinger, 1988.
La monja alférez. Dir. Javier Aguirre, 1987.
Lianna. Dir. John Sayles, 1983.
Madame X—Eine absolute Herrscherin. Dir. Ulrike Ottinger, 1977.
Maedchen in Uniform. Dir. Leontine Sagan, 1931.
Nocturne. Dir. Joy Chamberlain, 1991.
Now, Voyager. Dir. Irving Rapper, 1942.
Personal Best. Dir. Robert Town, 1982.
Rebecca. Dir. Alfred Hitchcock, 1940.
She Must Be Seeing Things. Dir. Sheila McLaughlin, 1987.
Sotto sotto. Dir. Lina Wertmeuller, 1984.
The Virgin Machine [*Die Jungfrau Machine*]. Dir. Monika Treut, 1988.
Thelma and Louise. Dir. Ridley Scott, 1991.
Thriller. Dir. Sally Potter, 1979.
Vera. Dir. Sergio Toledo, 1987.
Walk on the Wild Side. Dir. Edward Dmytryk, 1950.

General Index

Abel, Elizabeth, 238–39, 239n
Abelove, Henry, 19–20
Adams, Parveen, 31; on lesbian
    sadomasochism, 33, 47, 225–26; on
    bisexuality, 48n, 186, 269
Alarcón, Norma, 214
Altman, Meryl, 149, 191n
Anzaldúa, Gloria, 205
Apter, Emily, xix, 268n, 273–75
Arquette, Rosanna, 116
Artemidorus, 311
Arzner, Dorothy, 138

Baartman, Saartje, 36
Baker, Kathryn Hinojosa, 35n
Baker, Michael, 204n
Balmary, Marie, 26
Barale, Michèle Aina, 204
Barthes, Roland, 7, 157
Bass, Alan, 260
Baudrillard, Jean, 155
Baxter, Anne, 116
Beinstein, Krista, 226n
Bellini, Giovanni, 172, 173
Bellini, Vincenzo (La sonnambula), 102
Benjamin, Jessica, 184–85, 186, 188n
Bennett, Paula, 232–36, 237
Berg, Elizabeth, 252n
Bernheimer, Charles, 47, 219–20
Bersani, Leo, 13n, 27, 105n
Bersani, Leo, and Ulysse Dutoit, xiv, xviii, 3,
    8; on fetishism, 79, 203, 222–29, 231, 243,
    250, 261, 269, 272
Bisexuality: in Freud, 39–57 passim; as
    inhibition of sexuality, 57, 59, 181;
    philosophical, 252n; feminine, xvii, 32, 48,
    75, 267–69, 275
Blau, Herbert, 105
Bonaparte, Marie, 38, 270n
Borch-Jacobsen, Mikkel, 22n, 119
Braidotti, Rosi, 7
Brecht, Bertolt, 205
Brennan, Teresa, 219
Brown, Rita Mae, 200–201
Brownworth, Victoria, 102n
Burgin, Victor, 124, 273n
Burlingham, Dorothy Tiffany, 37n, 38
Butler, Alison, 102n, 111
Butler, Judith: on fantasy, 143–48; on
    Kristeva, 179–80; on the phallus, 231, 271

Cafaro, Terri, 85n
Califia, Pat, 282
Camp: lesbian, 102–103, 104–10, 114n, 289;
    gay, 105n, 135, 137n
Canguilhem, Georges, 24
Case, Sue-Ellen, xix; on the butch-femme
    subject, 86–87, 123, 276; and lesbian camp
    aesthetic, 104–109, 282
Case histories (Freud): "Dora," xv, 14, 35, 40,
    45–54, 76, 148, 152, 166, 169n, 278;
    "Psychogenesis of a Case of Homosexuality
    in a Woman," xiv, 24, 38–45, 49–54, 76,
    148, 152, 221; "A Case of Paranoia . . . ,"
    xiv, 24, 42, 76–78; "Leonardo," 24, 169n;
    "Schreber," 76, 169n. See also Deutsch,
    Helene; Jones, Ernest; Lampl–de Groot,
    Jeanne; van Ophuijsen, J. H. W.
Castration: fantasy of, xviii, 31–34, 70,
    100–101, 203–32, 239–53, 261–67, 307;
    complex, xviii, 216–20, 227n, 241, 261–63,
    274, 289
Cavell, Stanley, 132–39
Chase, Cynthia, 189–90n, 201n
Chasseguet-Smirgel, Jeannine, 27, 272–73n
Chicago, Judy, 236
Chodorow, Nancy, 62n, 155n, 159, 163, 166;
    on lesbianism, 195; and maternal fantasy,
    200–201
Cixous, Hélène, 47, 93, 107, 163
Cliff, Michelle, 167
Colapietro, Vincent, 299
Copjec, Joan, 140n
Cowie, Elizabeth, 124, 125–39, 140, 147
Creet, Julia, 226n, 282
Crimp, Douglas, 85n
Cunningham, Elizabeth, 100

Dabney, Sheila, 86n
Davidson, Arnold, 8, 15–18, 20, 23
Davis, Bette, 116, 133–35, 136n
Davis, Madeline, 228n
Davis, Whitney, 261, 266–67
de Beauvoir, Simone, 185
de Erauso, Catalina, 87
de Lauretis, Teresa, xi, 5–6, 166n, 204n,
    298–99
de Man, Paul, 113
de Quincey, Thomas, 87
Dean, James, 104
Dekker, Rudolf, and Lotte van de Pol, 103

170; psychoanalytic, 45, 63, 65, 149–56;
  maternal, 7, 121–22, 159–63
Semiosis, xix, 299, 300, 302–309, 310, 312
Sexual (in)difference, 4, 5–7, 75, 139, 142,
  279
Sexual structuring, xix, 28, 261, 303, 309, 312
Shaw, Peggy, 100, 104
Showalter, Elaine, 104
Silverman, Kaja, xvii, 27, 144n; reading
  Kristeva, 172–75, 180, 184; "the Oedipal
  mother," 180–84; on narcissism and desire,
  185, 186–87; on castration, 180, 217–18; on
  the phallus, 219–20
Smith, Victoria, 198–200
Smith-Rosenberg, Carroll, 192–93
Spectatorship, theory of, xvi, 84–142; and
  fantasy, 94–99, 124–42
Spielrein, Sabina, 156n, 167
Spillers, Hortense, 198–200
Sprengnether, Madelon, xvii, 156n; *The
  Spectral Mother*, 163–66, 182; reading of
  Rich, 167–69, 171
Stacey, Jackie, 116–20
Stanton, Domna, 165, 197–98
Stanwyck, Barbara, 112
Stimpson, Catharine R., 204n, 211
Stoller, Robert, 163
Suleiman, Susan, 176n

Terry, Jennifer, 24, 229n
Tracy, Spencer, 104, 137
Transference (and counter-transference), xvi,
  51–52, 149–54, 157
Trasforini, Maria Antonietta, 155n
Trask, Haunani-Kay, 193–96
Traub, Valerie, 120, 121–22n
Treut, Monika, 226n

van Ophuijsen, J. H. W., xv, 31n, 34–35,
  37–38
Vegetti-Finzi, Silvia, 155n, 182
Vermeule, Blakey, 116, 120, 120n

Warner, Marina, 177
Weaver, Lois, 86n, 104, 123
The Well of Loneliness. See Hall, Radclyffe
Westphal, Carl, 16
Westkott, Marcia, 159
White, Hayden, 79, 128n
White, Patricia, xi, 91n, 109
Whitford, Margaret, 181
Whitman, Walt, 134, 135
Wilde, Oscar, 25, 27
Williams, Linda, 94
Wittig, Monique, 101, 225n; *The Lesbian
  Body*, 157, 252–53
Woolf, Virginia, 204; *Mrs. Dalloway*, 236–39

Yarbro-Bejarano, Yvonne, 205n
Young-Bruehl, Elisabeth: on Freud, 19, 37,
  46, 66; on Anna Freud, 38, 257

Zschokke, Magdalena, 60n

Index of Films Cited

Adam's Rib (George Cukor, 1949), 137
All about Eve (Joseph Mankiewicz, 1950),
  117, 121, 190n
Back to the Future (Robert Zemeckis, 1985),
  90, 128, 129, 139n
Black Widow (Bob Rafelson, 1987), 88, 114,
  121, 122n
Bonnie and Clyde (Arthur Penn, 1967), 100
Born in Flames (Lizzie Borden, 1983), 88n
Caught (Max Ophuls, 1949), 112, 117
Damned If You Don't (Su Friedrich, 1987),
  88n
Desert Hearts (Donna Deitch, 1985), 68n,
  114–15, 122
Desperately Seeking Susan (Susan Seidelman,
  1984), 116–17, 119–21
Dial M for Murder (Alfred Hitchcock, 1954),
  100
Die Praxis der Liebe [*The Practice of Love*]
  (Valie Export, 1984), vii.
Duel in the Sun (King Vidor, 1946), 104
Edipo Re [*Oedipus Rex*] (Pier Paolo Pasolini,
  1967), 128, 129
Film about a Woman Who . . . (Yvonne
  Rainer, 1974), 86
Gilda (Charles Vidor, 1946), 108
The Gold Diggers (Sally Potter, 1983), 88n
Gone with the Wind (Victor Fleming, 1939),
  88
Invisible Adversaries [*Unsichtbare Gegner*]
  (Valie Export, 1976), 100
I've Heard the Mermaids Singing (Patricia
  Rozema, 1987), 115, 122
Je tu il elle (Chantal Akerman, 1974), 88n
Johanna d'Arc of Mongolia (Ulrike Ottinger,
  1988), 88n
La monja alférez (Javier Aguirre, 1987), 87
Lianna (John Sayles, 1983), 68n, 115, 122
Madame X—Eine absolute Herrscherin (Ulrike
  Ottinger, 1977), 88n, 105n, 109
Maedchen in Uniform (Leontine Sagan,
  1931), 90–91
Nocturne (Joy Chamberlain, 1991), 88n, 91n
Now, Voyager (Irving Rapper, 1942), 130–39,
  147
Personal Best (Robert Town, 1982), 114
Rebecca (Alfred Hitchcock, 1940), 88
She Must Be Seeing Things (Sheila McLaugh-
  lin, 1987), xvi, 85–103, 109–10, 112–13,
  116, 122–23, 130, 142, 251, 276
Sotto sotto (Lina Wertmueller, 1984), 114
The Virgin Machine [*Die Jungfrau Machine*]
  (Monika Treut, 1988), 88n
Thelma and Louise (Ridley Scott, 1991), 120
Thriller (Sally Potter, 1979), 88n
Vera (Sergio Toledo, 1987), 112
Walk on the Wild Side (Edward Dmytryk,
  1950), 112

Teresa de Lauretis is Professor
of the History of Consciousness at the
University of California, Santa Cruz. She
is the author of *Alice Doesn't: Feminism,
Semiotics, Cinema* and *Technologies of Gender*
and the editor of *Feminist Studies/Critical
Studies* and of *Queer Theory: Lesbian and Gay
Sexualities* (a special issue of the journal
d i f f e r e n c e s).